D1046981

DATE DUE

MAR 10 2008	APR 03 2008		
	MAR 06 2012		
GAYLORD			PRINTED IN U.S.A.

John C. Waugh

ONE MAN
GREAT
ENOUGH

Abraham Lincoln's
Road to Civil War

Harcourt, Inc.
Orlando Austin New York San Diego London

www.HarcourtBooks.com

Library of Congress Cataloging-in-Publication Data
Waugh, John C.
One man great enough : Abraham Lincoln's road to
Civil War / John C. Waugh.—1st ed.
p.   cm.
Includes bibliographical references and index.
1. Lincoln, Abraham, 1809–1865—Childhood and youth. 2. Lincoln, Abraham,
1809–1865—Political career before 1861. 3. Lincoln, Abraham, 1809–1865—
Political and social views. 4. Presidents—United States—Biography. 5. United
States—Politics and government—1837–1841. 6. United States—Politics and
government—1841–1845. 7. United States—Politics and government—1845–1861.
8. United States—History–Civil War, 1861–1865—Causes. 9. Illinois—Politics and
government—To 1865. I. Title.
E457.3.W25 2007
973.7092—dc22   2007009588
978-0-15-101071-4

Text set in Simoncini Garamond
Designed by Lydia D'moch

Printed in the United States of America
First edition
A C E G I K J H F D B

For my father,
who had a sense of humor
Lincoln would have appreciated.

CONTENTS

ONE MAN GREAT ENOUGH

The Uncoiling of the Serpent

The new two-story statehouse in Vandalia, Illinois, stood unfinished in early 1837. Workmen had slapped plaster on the walls just before the Tenth General Assembly convened in December. Its damp, displeasing essence still hung in the legislative chambers upstairs.[1]

Abraham Lincoln, a young Whig legislator from Sangamon County, was beginning his second term. He was not as new to politics as the plaster was to the walls, but the plaster was more likely to stick than what he was about to do. In a bold move, he was about to drop a resolution into the record that ran emphatically against dominant public opinion in his state—on slavery, which raised hackles as no other issue did.

The issue was uncoiling across the country like a hissing serpent. Abolition societies proliferated in the North, blanketing the Union with incendiary antislavery pamphlets. Alarmed and angry Southern legislators were passing resolutions violently condemning these "fire brands of discord and disunion."[2] The South's mightiest guns, its most articulate and powerful ideologues, were answering in kind, showering shot and shell on abolitionism in the defense of their "peculiar institution."

Southern legislatures were not only passing angry resolutions against abolitionists, they were demanding that Northern legislatures do the same. Virginia, Alabama, and Mississippi had sent memorials to Illinois, which Governor Joseph Duncan had transmitted to the General Assembly in December 1836.

In January, the Illinois legislature resoundingly passed a set of sympathizing resolutions—that "we highly disapprove of the formation of abolition societies, and of the doctrines promulgated by them"; that the right of property in slaves is "sacred to the slave-holding States by the Federal Constitution, and that they can't be deprived of that right without their consent."[3]

Lincoln quietly voted against the resolutions, one of only six of the legislature's ninety-one members who did. In early March, three days before adjournment, he wanted to quietly add something more to the record.

The issue was important to many in Illinois, but it mattered to Lincoln in a different way. For the most part, the people of Illinois were emigrants from Southern states, as was Lincoln himself—born in Kentucky and grown to manhood in southern Indiana. Most of these former Southerners were for slavery and against anything that wasn't.

Lincoln, though a Southerner, didn't see it exactly that way. Not that this gangly young lawmaker bought into the idea of Negro equality. He didn't. With most white opinion, Northern and Southern, he embraced white supremacy. He opposed black suffrage, voting in his first term for a resolution "that the elective franchise should be kept pure from contamination by the admission of colored votes."[4] He rejected outright the idea of racial intermarriage.

But in Lincoln's mind slavery was a different matter. It was immoral, crowding the outer limit of inhumanity. He was to say, "I am naturally anti-slavery. If slavery is not wrong, nothing is wrong. I can not remember when I did not so think, and feel."[5]

In March 1837, he wanted to introduce a resolution that would mirror this feeling. But he was playing with dynamite. The wording had to be hedged; it would be political suicide in Illinois to be lumped with abolitionists. And he would have to do it virtually alone. The only other House member willing to go with him was Dan Stone, a fellow Whig legislator who had brought his anti-slavery psyche with him from his native Vermont.

On March 3 they introduced their resolution, protesting the longer ones passed in January. It was entered in the record without comment or debate. It said: "Resolutions upon the subject of domestic slavery having passed both branches of the General Assembly at its present session, the undersigned hereby protest against the passage of the same. They believe that the institution of slavery is founded on both injustice and bad policy; but that the promulgation of abolition doctrines tends rather to increase than to abate its evils."[6]

That was the nub of it. Abolitionist agitation was bad enough, but the greater evil was slavery itself. The original resolutions hadn't said that. There was a moral issue here. And that was the distinction Lincoln and Stone wanted to make. They made it quietly, as they went out the door.

Softly introduced, those lines made virtually no noise in the state. But it was the first public stand that this young politician ever took on the institution of slavery. It was to be the first of many on a road that would lead him—and his country—to the very gates of disunion and civil war.

PART ONE

Who He Was
and Where
He Came From

1

The Dark and Bloody Ground

ABRAHAM LINCOLN'S ANCESTRAL LINE, like so many others in the New World, followed a southwesterly drift—from England to Massachusetts, into New Jersey and Pennsylvania to Virginia, then through the Cumberland Gap into Kentucky. In the late 1700s, Lincoln's Grandfather Abraham followed the flood of migration to the Wilderness Road through that Gap, the "great cleft" in the mountains,[1] past dark cliffs "so wild and horrid" in aspect "that it is impossible to behold them without terror."[2]

The Wilderness Road itself, that track through Kentucky beyond the Gap, was just as terrorizing—"a lonely and houseless path" into "a wild and cheerless land."[3] The road was an ancient Indian warrior path over a hunting ground still bitterly disputed by fierce, unwelcoming, massacre-minded Shawnee, Iroquois, Cherokee, and Chickasaw. Kentucky, crossed by that rough

Indian road, was faithful to its reputation and definition—"the dark and bloody ground."[4]

But these pioneers were pilgrims, drawn irresistibly over this "gash through the wilderness,"[5] to an abundant, rich, and beckoning promised land. The abiding presence of instant death by rifle, tomahawk, or arrow seemed worth the cost for such ground. Moses Austin, himself a pilgrim to Texas, said of them, "hundreds Travelling hundreds of Miles, they know not for what Nor Whither, except its to Kentuckey . . . the Promised land . . . the land of Milk and Honey."[6]

Lincoln's grandfather pushed "on the crest of the wave of Western settlement," deep into this land of milk and honey to settle on over 5,000 acres of ground near Bear Grass Fort, the site of present day Louisville. There he built a log cabin, and soon the dark and bloody ground claimed him. In an unprotected moment, as he was sowing a crop of corn with his three sons, Indians killed him.[7]

The youngest of those surviving sons was Thomas, only eight years old when his father died. But he lived to grow up and become a carpenter, and to meet a woman named Nancy Hanks. A frontier child like him, she had also mourned the early death of a parent and was a woman "of sorrows and acquainted with grief."[8] She had come to Kentucky and to her destiny, like Tom, through the Cumberland Gap over the Wilderness Road.

Tom was short, stout, and strong, raven-haired and black-eyed, a man of "uncommon Endurance." He was illiterate, but he had a knack for telling a story, and he was a good carpenter, said to have the best set of tools in Washington County. He was thought to be "good, clean, social, truthful and honest . . . a plain unpretending plodding man," who "never thought that gold was God" and "didn't drink an' cuss none."[9]

Nancy was said to be tall, slender, and delicate of frame—
"Spare made" with dark hair and hazel eyes. She struck people
as spiritually inclined, amiable, kind, charitable, affectionate,
even-tempered, tender, and intelligent, but sad by nature.[10] It
was said that she was "touched with the divine aptitudes of the
fireside," mistress of the arts of "the skillet, the Dutch oven, the
open fireplace."[11]

They were married on June 12, 1806. He was twenty-eight
years old and she was twenty-three. The wedding vows were
read by Jesse Head, an itinerant Methodist minister, one of the
best known in that part of Kentucky. The bride wore a rough
wedding dress stitched by a friend, and afterward there was the
typical frontier infare (post-vows reception). One guest remembered it for the bear meat, venison, wild turkey, duck, a barbe-
qued sheep, eggs wild and tame, coffee, syrup in big gourds, and
"a race for the whisky bottle."[12]

Thomas took his young bride to live in Elizabethtown, a new,
swiftly growing Kentucky settlement, a good fit for a good carpenter. There a little daughter, Sarah, was born. When she was
eighteen months old, Tom moved wife and daughter to Nolen
Creek, fourteen miles south of Elizabethtown and three miles
from Hodgenville, on the edge of the "barrens," a 70-mile-long,
60-mile-wide slice of mostly treeless land burned off by Indians
to make a buffalo grazing ground.[13]

There, in a rough one-room log cabin above an oak-shaded
sinking spring, young Lincoln was born. Dennis Hanks, Lincoln's older cousin, later recollected Tom "comin' over to our
house one cold mornin' in Feb'uary an' sayin' kind o' slow,
'Nancy's got a boy baby.'" Dennis remembered that "Mother
come over and washed him an' put a yaller flannen petticoat
on him."[14]

In 1811, the year the first steamboat paddled down the Mississippi, when Lincoln was two years old, they moved again—this time to 230 acres in Knob Creek valley ten miles north of Nolin Creek and six miles east of Hodgenville. Their next cabin stood on the bank of the creek that emptied into Rolling Fork, which emptied into the Salt, which emptied into the Ohio twenty-four miles below Louisville. It sat between two steep-rising knobs beside the Cumberland Road from Louisville to Nashville, the heaviest-traveled highway on the Kentucky frontier.[15]

But Tom had a hankering to drift west. The Kentucky of his childhood was gone. Clear title to land was hard to come by in the once dark and bloody ground. And it was dark for another reason: It was a slave state, and Tom was at heart an anti-slavery man. It was said that he and Nancy were "just steeped full of notions about the wrongs of slavery and the rights of men."[16]

Dennis Hanks said, "Tom got hold o' a better farm [at Knob Creek] after while but he couldn't git a clear title to it, so when Abe was eight year old, an' I was eighteen, we all lit out for Indiany. Kaintucky was gittin' stuck up, with some folks rich enough to own niggers, so it didn't seem no place fur pore folks any more.... [Nancy] piled everything they had wuth takin' on the backs o' two pack hosses."[17]

They set out for slave-free southern Indiana in late 1816 when the ground was hard with frost, arriving in mid-December, the same month and year that territory became the nineteenth state in the young Union.

2

The Hoosier Years

THERE WERE BUT THIRTEEN thinly settled counties in Indiana when it became a state, all bunched along the Ohio and the southern stem of the Wabash. The upper two-thirds of the new state was still Indian hunting ground. There was not a mile of turnpike, plank road, or canal linking the towns anywhere in Indiana, just Indian trails that could only be traveled by horseback.[1]

The Lincolns had to cut their way through a grapevine tangle, teeming with wildlife, where there was no prairie to break the wilderness. There were "woods, woods, woods, as far as the world extends," and but one family of settlers for every four square miles.[2] It was said: "When one could see the smoke of a neighbor's chimney the country was too crowded for comfort."[3]

Later in life Lincoln was to write of this wilderness:

When first my father settled here,
   'Twas then the frontier line:
The panther's scream, filled night with fear
   And bears preyed on the swine.[4]

Dennis Hanks said of life on that frontier line, "We wasn't much better off 'n Indians, except we tuk an interest in religion an' polyticks." It was, he thought, a "mighty interestin' life fur a boy, but thar was a good many chances he wouldn't live to grow up."[5]

The Lincolns settled in a little cabin in Spencer County near Gentryville on Little Pigeon Creek sixteen miles north of the Ohio River. When he was growing up and not yet nine years old, Tom put an axe in his son's hands, and many later believed the axe became an extension of his being. Dennis Hanks was to say of Lincoln as he grew to manhood, "You'd 'a' thought there was two men in the woods when he got into it with an ax."[6]

The year of the axe was also the year when a deadly, mysterious pestilence called the "milk sick" fell on Spencer County. Only after a time did men understand that it came from the milk of a cow that had fed on an evil chalk-blossomed weed called white snakeroot. It killed Nancy Lincoln.

As she lay dying, she called her little son to her bedside and said, "I am going away from you Abraham, and I shall not return. I know you will be a good boy, that you will be kind to Sarah and your father. I want you to live as I have taught you, and love your heavenly Father."[7] She was laid to rest in a rude coffin whipsawed and planed into planks by Tom and held together by wooden pegs whittled by young Lincoln. It seemed to one neighbor that in the year of the milk sick, "Tom was always making a coffin for some one."[8]

"Oh Lord, oh Lord, I'll never furget it," Dennis Hanks said, "the mizry in that cabin in the woods when Nancy died." Dennis believed Lincoln "never got over the mizable way his mother died," and that "Sairy was a little gal, only 'leven, an' she'd git so lonesome, missin' her mother, she'd set an' cry by the fire."[9]

Tom Lincoln could only stand that misery so long—he without a wife, his two children without a mother. He remembered a woman in Elizabethtown named Sarah Bush Johnston. She had married, the keeper of the Hardin County jail. But he had since died, leaving her widowed with three children. So the year after Nancy died, Tom rode back to Elizabethtown to try his luck.

He went direct to the point with Sarah Johnston: "Well, Miss Johnson [*sic*], I have no wife & you have no husband. I came a purpose to mary you[,] I *knowed* you from a gal & you *knowed* me from a boy. I have no time to lose and if you are willing, let it be done Straight off."

Sarah is said to have said, "Tommy I know you well & have no objection to marrying you, but I cannot do it straight off as I owe some debts that must first be paid." Tom paid her debts that same day, and the next day, December 2, 1819, they were married straight off.[10]

They packed all she owned—and her three children, ages nine, seven, and five—in a four-horse wagon and left for Indiana. They came, Dennis Hanks remembered, with a "wagon load o' goods; feather pillers an' homespun blankets, an' patchwork quilts an' chists o' drawers, an' a flax wheel, an' a soap kettle an' cookin' pots an' pewter dishes."[11]

But it wasn't the load that impressed Dennis the most. It was Sarah herself. "Cracky, but Aunt Sairy was some punkins!" he said.[12]

Sarah was tall, like Nancy, fair complexioned, handsome,

sprightly, talkative, kind-hearted, quick-minded, industrious, and good humored. She was also said to be proud, brave, patient, and enduring.[13] It didn't take her long to clean up the cabin, the children, and the situation. "You jist had to be somebody when Aunt Sairy was around," Dennis Hanks said.[14]

There was springtime beauty everywhere around the rough Indiana cabin, wildflowers in abundance overflown by armadas of passenger pigeons, which gave the Little Pigeon Creek its name. They swarmed in the western skies "as far as the eye could reach" and roosted in the limbs of the great trees. It was said that in the migrating months of September and October, wild pigeons swarmed in numbers so dense they blackened the sky, with a roar of wings so deafening that it drowned out speech.[15]

No less abundant, it seemed, was the number of people roosting in the cabin since Sarah and her children had come. Three Lincolns, four Johnstons, and Dennis Hanks, taken in after his folks had died of the 1818 milk sick, were crammed into the windowless cabin that measured 18 feet by 20 feet. As a saying of the time in southern Indiana had it, "There wasn't room to cuss the cat without gittin' its hairs in your teeth."[16]

From the beginning, in this crowd, Sarah and little Abraham connected. Dennis Hanks remembered, "Aunt Sairy thought a heep o' Abe, an' he did o' her, an' I reckon they'd 'a' done most anything fur one another."[17]

Lincoln was to say of Sarah that she "proved a good and kind mother."[18] She was to say of him, "His mind & mine—what little I had seemed to run together—move in the same channel." She said he never gave her a cross look or refused to do anything she asked him to do. "He never told me a lie in his life—never Evaded—Equivocated, never dodged." He "treated every body & every thing kindly.... the best boy I Ever Saw or Ever ... Expect to see." Dennis Hanks also thought him good and kind, but of a "somewhat wild nature."[19]

This good, somewhat wild boy was already marvelously spindly for his age, "a long tall dangling a[wk]ward drowl looking boy."[20] He was rapidly growing into what he would someday become a human tower, like the trees he felled to clear the land.

"He . . . cared nothing for clothes—so that they were clean & neat," Sarah said, "fashion cut no figure with him." Already there was a widening gap of bare shinbone visible between the top of his shoes and the hem of his buckskin britches. It was a gap that was to become his sartorial trademark throughout much of his life. No clothes ready-made ever would fit him.[21]

He was "notoriously good natured," one of his boyhood friends remembered—temperate in all things—too much so at times, Sarah thought. He was "witty & Sad and thoughtful by turns," his boyhood friend remembered. But he was a boy's boy, not seeming to care much for the company of girls.[22]

One of those girls, a neighbor, said Lincoln was "the learned boy among us unlearned folks." A neighbor boy said of him, he "soared above us," reading his books "whilst we played." He seemed, another said, despite his good nature, to have a "liking for solitude."[23] The Indiana of Lincoln's youth was an "unvarnished society."[24] But he seemed bent on applying some varnish to himself and the mind within his lank frame.

There wasn't anything in the way of long-term schooling in Gentryville, but Lincoln and his sister went for a time—"by littles," as he put it—to a blab school where they taught aloud "readin, writin, and cipherin, to the Rule of Three," the only disciplines the teacher was required to know. The teaching, like the schooling itself, was fundamental. "If a straggler supposed to understand latin happened to sojourn in the neighborhood,"

Lincoln later said, "he was looked upon as a wizzard." Lincoln learned to read and write and cipher to the rule of three. But the aggregate of all his schooling didn't amount to one year—part of it with two teachers at Knob Creek and the rest in the blab school in Indiana.[25]

That didn't matter. After he learned to read that is all he wanted to do—read and learn. Sarah called him "diligent for Knowledge."[26] Dennis Hanks said, "Seems to me now I never seen Abe after he was twelve 'at he didn't have a book in his hand or in his pocket . . . constant and I may say stubborn reader." To Dennis "it didn't seem natural, nohow, to see a feller read like that."[27]

Lincoln liked doing that unnatural thing lying down with his long legs shooting up against a tree—"sitting on his shoulder blades."[28] Sarah brought three books with her in the wagon from Kentucky, *Webster's Speller,* Defoe's *Robinson Crusoe,* and *The Arabian Nights.*[29] He read those and anything else he could get his hands on within fifty miles of Gentryville.[30] And it wasn't easy. Books were hard to come by in that time and place and "book larnin'" wasn't seen as a very practical virtue.[31]

But Lincoln filled his growing-up years with all the books he could: The Bible, the book in most common reach, and "more congenial books" suitable to his age—*Aesop's Fables, Pilgrim's Progress,* and Parson Weems's *Life of Washington*—one of the first and most lasting in his later memory.

And there were the books that augmented his "by littles" schooling: Thomas Dilworth's *A New Guide to the English Tongue in Five Parts,* Asa Rhodes's *An American Spelling Book,* Nicolas Pike's *A New and Complete System of Arithmetic,* Lindley Murray's *English Reader,* and Grimshaw's *History of the United States* with its antipathy for slavery and intolerance. He read William Scott's *Lessons in Elocution,* Benjamin Franklin's *Autobiography,* Bailey's *Etymological Dictionary,* the *Kentucky Preceptor,* and *Revised Statutes of Indiana* (where he probably first read the Declaration of Independence, the United States Constitution, and the Articles of 1787 outlawing slavery in the Northwest Territory). Early on he also acquired a passion for newspapers that never cooled.[32]

As young Lincoln's command of words quickened, they began to take shape in his own creations:

> Abraham Lincoln
> his hand and pen
> he will be good but
> god knows When.

And,

> Abraham Lincoln is my nam[e]
> And with my pen I wrote the same
> I wrote in both hast and speed
> and left it here for fools to read.[33]

He wrote one day in a friend's copybook something he probably very much hoped for himself:

> Good boys who to their books apply
> Will make great men by & by.[34]

When he began to write, Sarah said, it was in "boyish scrawls." He had his own copy book, she remembered—a sort of scrapbook. But not having that at hand, or any other slip of paper, he wrote what he wanted to remember on boards or slates, then studied what he wrote and repeated it, "treasuring up" in his memory what he read. He ciphered often on the boards, and when they became overcrowded he shaved them off with a knife and started over.[35]

From boyhood Lincoln had the knack for giving learning a practical turn. Dennis Hanks said, "He excelled any boy I ever saw, putting his opportunities into Conversation." He was "head & shoulders above us all—would learn us." He would tell stories and take to a stump to deliver mock political speeches or mimic sermons of itinerant preachers. His stepsister, Matilda, said Lincoln "would preach & we would do the Crying—sometimes he would join in the Chorus of Tears."[36]

So Lincoln grew up in Indiana, turning twenty-one in 1830, old enough to follow his own star. But Tom had sand in his shoes again, wanting to move the Lincoln line westward into another promised land. "I reckon we was like one o' them tribes o' Israel," Dennis Hanks said, "an' Tom was always lookin' fur the land of Canaan."[37]

The family had long since outgrown the little one-room cabin and burgeoned to a crowd of thirteen. Those grown to maturity with Lincoln—all but him—had since married and had children. His sister Sarah had grown up and wed, but died bearing a child, dying as her mother had—much too young. Mourned by her brother, she rested in the burial ground of the Pigeon Baptist Church.

The thirteen left Indiana for Illinois in March 1830 in three wagons, two drawn by oxen, Lincoln driving one. They were bound for Macon County, where a cousin of Nancy's, John Hanks, had preceded them. Dennis Hanks said, "I reckon it was

John Hanks 'at got res'less fust an' lit out fur Illinois, an' wrote fur us all to come, an' he'd git land fur us."[38]

They crossed the Wabash, high with spring rains, at Vincennes and slogged northwestward across eastern Illinois to Decatur, 225 miles from Gentryville. "It tuk us two weeks to git thar," Dennis Hanks said, "raftin' over the Wabash, cuttin' our way through the woods, fordin' rivers, pryin' wagons an' steers out o' slough with fence rails, an' makin' camp."[39]

The Lincolns did not pause long in Decatur, pushing on ten miles southwest to the north bank of the Sangamon River, where John Hanks awaited them and where forest met prairie. There Tom built another cabin, a smokehouse, and a barn on a bluff about a hundred steps from the river. Lincoln broke the prairie land with a plow, and he and John Hanks cut rails from the black oak trees to fence it in.[40]

The snow began to fall on their first Christmas Eve in Illinois in 1830, the deepest anybody had ever seen. It fell day after day into the next year, dropping four or five feet and humping it into heroic drifts. The bitter cold killed stock and wildlife wholesale. They who endured it remembered it in their lifetimes as the winter of the deep snow, dating births, deaths and weddings from it.[41]

In the spring of the year when the snows melted, Tom and Sarah backtracked a few miles to settle in Coles County near the eastern edge of Illinois. Abraham Lincoln, now twenty-two years old, separated from them and cast off on his own down the Sangamon River, riding the freshet from the thawing snow.[42]

He had been offered a job. A speculating entrepreneur named Dennis Offutt hired him, his stepbrother, and John Hanks to run a flatboat of barrel pork, corn, and live hogs from

Beardstown on the Illinois down the Mississippi River to New Orleans. It would be Lincoln's second journey down the great river; he had made it once before in a flatboat in 1828.

In Beardstown, when they were building the boat, Offutt took a liking to Lincoln and offered him another job when he returned, clerking in a store in the budding little settlement of New Salem on the Sangamon.[43]

The flatboat crew left for New Orleans in April 1831. Three months later, he was back in Illinois, "a piece of floating driftwood," two years into adulthood and bound for New Salem—and for whatever destiny held for him.[44]

PART TWO

Making His Way

3

New Salem

LIKE EVERY OTHER STATE in the Union, like every other frontier settlement, Illinois was a new world being stamped on an old.

As a state it was nearly fire-new, admitted to the Union in
1818, little more than a dozen years before Lincoln plodded into
New Salem. Its name was Gallic, the word the French gave the
Illini Indians, meaning "tribe of men." In 1818 it was a territory
of but 35,000 settlers—four of every six from Southern stock—
the least-populated state ever folded into the Union. But it made
up in size what it lacked in citizens. It was a long, wide-bodied
giant—385 miles end-to-end and 218 miles side-to-side, measured at its widest reach. It was larger than any of the original
thirteen states, except Georgia—larger than Ohio, Kentucky, Indiana, Wisconsin or Iowa, larger than all the New England states
combined, minus Maine.[1]

In the heart of the rich, mountainless Mississippi Valley, it was one of the flattest states in the Union—a geological pancake. It lacked lakes of a size to boast about but had rivers and streams in overabundance—288 of them in a grab bag of lengths and widths and size and speed of flow. The biggest of them was the Illinois River running down the state's western side and emptying into the Mississippi forty miles above St. Louis. It was the most important river in North America with its entire length rising and emptying within a single state.[2]

When Illinois became a state, its seat of government was Kaskaskia down the river below St. Louis, at the lower end of the American Bottom, a soil-rich eighty-mile-long, 450-square-mile flood plain on the Illinois side of the Mississippi. New as a state capital, Kaskaskia was nonetheless a century old, the center of the earliest French settlement. It existed before St. Louis, before New Orleans and Pittsburgh. It antedated Cincinnati by half a century, Chicago by more than a century.[3]

From statehood Illinois ceaselessly reinvented itself while its center of gravity inched relentlessly northward. By 1831 its population had ballooned to over 150,000, and like most of the west it was "boiling" with land speculation. Even so, in these beginning years there wasn't much in the way of settlement on the open prairies north of Sangamon County in the state's midriff. Most of those 150,000 still hugged the wooded banks of the rivers and their ancillary waterways in the protective shadow of the timberlands. But for narrow strips of cultivated ground at the timber's edge, the rich-soiled prairie was mostly still "an immaculate tablet, unscarred by the plow," the track across it seeming "as interminable as Paddy's rope, from which, he swore, some one had cut off the other end altogether." Crossing it was akin to a mariner "[steering] over the trackless ocean."[4]

Yet the prairie conjured eloquence, stirred aspirations and fired imaginations. "Never shall I forget the grand prairie as I first saw it," one young newcomer from Kentucky wrote, "covered with grass as high as our wheat, waving in the breeze and resembling the billows of the ocean as the shadows of the fleeting clouds passed over it. Sometimes the prairie was lit up by the burning grass, and as the flames were seen in the distance, like a ribbon of fire belting the horizon, it would almost seem that the distant clouds were on fire."[5]

The settlers, however, ventured only warily at first into that vast, rich, prodigiously endowed prairieland. And they sited their villages conservatively, no more than fifteen miles apart—only as far as a man and his horse and wagon might travel to and back in a day.[6]

The richest soil in this boundless, mostly trackless prairie—"almost proverbial" for its fertility—was Sangamon County. In 1821, this "verdant solitude" of more than a million acres in the middle of the state was created by an act of the legislature. It was the biggest county in Illinois, as big as all of Rhode Island, and a magnet for settlement. It was dominated and named, as so many counties were, by and for a river, the Sangamon, a shallow, snag-ridden, quiet-moving stream that rose in Champaign County and emptied into the Illinois at Beardstown, less than a hundred miles above that larger river's junction with the yet larger Mississippi.[7]

New Salem was second in stature only to Springfield in this largest county in Illinois. Laid out in 1829, only two years before Lincoln first saw it, this was a settlement with all the big-shouldered, jagged edges of the typical frontier village and a reputation for the rough and tumble. The surrounding country had its toughs and bullies, local boys, ever ready to wrestle or brawl, hanging out at the cockfights and gander pullings in town and the horse races down Main Street.[8]

Twenty-two-year-old Abraham Lincoln drifted into this frontier tableau in July 1831. He was something to see, a long giant— a rail-thin human tower. He was somewhat stoop-shouldered, his long legs keeping company with overlarge feet housed in outsized brogans "not over-fastidious as to their polish." To his basic frame, as unpolished as his shoes, were fixed arms that were, as one friend said, "longer than [on] any man I ever knew." He seemed made up, another said, "of head, hands, feet and length." He was wearing a blue cotton roundabout coat, a calico shirt, the coarse brogans, and a bandless straw hat. His legs were thrust into pale blue pantaloons held up by a single suspender. The quantity of cloth was, as usual, inadequate to its mission: the pantaloons failed "to make the connection with either coat or socks, coming about three inches below the former and an inch or two above the latter."[9]

Here he had come, "This long, bony, sad man," floating "like a piece of driftwood," lodging at last, "without a history, strange, penniless, and alone."[10] Lincoln was to describe himself when he came to New Salem as "a strange, friendless, uneducated, penniless boy." He spoke of "this stiff, ungovernable hair of mine," and of his "full-length 'landscape'"—six feet four inches of it "when I get the kinks all out." He was "as ruff a specimen of humanity as could be found."[11]

But these rough looks didn't fit well with what was really there. This angular, antic, unpolished, clod-hopping veneer belied his interior. He startled everybody by being articulate, book-read, studious, politically aware, strikingly acute and intelligent, having a way with words, a genius for telling a story, and a weakness for poetry.[12]

He came off as "a very simple open souled man," one friend said, "a sincere man—a man of purpous...frank—ingenuous... kind, humerous and deeply honest—never deviating from the Exact truth." He "paddled his own Canoe," another said, "With a good Supply of Good humor & affability...fun and gravity both grew on him alike."[13]

Lincoln was a rough specimen working for a fly-by-night. Most in the town seemed to agree about Dennis Offutt. A cross-section of New Salem witnesses found him "a gassy—windy—brain rattling man," a "wild—recless—careless man—a kind of wandering horse tamer," but not much of a businessman. Harum-scarum or not, Offutt thought well of his young shop-keeper and bragged about his attributes and his potential.[14]

Lincoln began clerking Offutt's little fourteen-by-sixteen-foot one-room store when it opened around the first of September 1831. The store, like Offutt's enthusiasms, was short-lived. It was the third one in a town that could only support two.[15] Within the year it had folded and Lincoln was out of a job. He would soon try his hand again as a storekeeper—the surest way to make money on the frontier, the business to be in if done right—this time as a co-owner with a partner named William F. Berry, a local minister's son. But Lincoln hadn't learned the art of successful entrepreneurship, and it is believed by some that the preacher's son was drinking away the inventory. They fell deeper and deeper in debt, and after a while, the store "winked out" and Berry died, leaving Lincoln with what he would call the "*National Debt,*" which he resolved to pay off in the coming years.[16]

The law pulled at him, but he believed that lofty calling was beyond his reach without a better education.[17] He knew enough about it, and could write well enough—"make a few rabbit tracks,"[18] he said—to let him draw up contracts, draft agreements, and witness deeds for fellow townsmen, which he did *pro bono*. He started running through a gamut of callings—a near dozen different jobs, none of them full time—hewing fence rails, running a mill, clerking in another store for one of the more successful storekeepers, harvesting crops, tending a still, and clerking at local elections. Somewhat steady employment came when John Calhoun, the county surveyor, offered him a deputyship to help with the land surveys on the burgeoning Illinois frontier. Lincoln knew nothing of surveying, but with the help of two books on the subject and Mentor Graham, New Salem's schoolmaster, he became a surveyor after only six weeks' study.

After not quite two years in New Salem, he was named postmaster of the town—a budding Whig appointed by a Democratic administration. Political alignments were somewhat blurred at that level on the frontier and the office was hardly a politically sensitive sinecure. He could take it without violating his nascent political principles. And it served a double purpose. When he had a call for a survey, he combined the two callings, stuffing his hat with mail slated for delivery in the neighborhood to be surveyed.[19]

In a benefit of this two-sided semi-employment, his assortment of odd jobs, and his volunteer legal work, Lincoln was getting to know "every man, woman, & child for miles around," building equity and goodwill in the hearts and minds of his fellow townsmen and neighbors. There was nobody who didn't like this rough specimen when they met him. They liked him for his gentle-giantness and for the hilarity he brought into their lives with his endless trove of droll stories. "He was always at home wherever he went," one townsman recalled, and "he Could Beat all of them on anictdote."[20]

At some point he had to pass muster with the toughs in New Salem—the Clary's Grove boys, the toughest of the tough in the town—and their leader Jack Armstrong. They challenged him soon enough. In his admiration of his young storekeeper, Offutt gave loud and inadvisable public praise to Lincoln's physical prowess, betting five dollars that he could throw Armstrong. So Lincoln had to wrestle this new foe. They grappled in what amounted to a standoff, and Armstrong was wise enough to see that he had met his equal. He became Lincoln's friend. The Clary's Grove Boys never again challenged Lincoln but became, with Armstrong, loyal admirers, followers, and supporters.[21]

Lincoln spent his down time—which he had plenty of— telling his stories and doing what he did best, reading and studying. Reclining on his back with his long legs propped up a tree trunk, he continued his self-education. He borrowed books he hadn't read as a youth in Indiana, digesting them, pondering them, remembering them. He read poetry—Shakespeare, Byron, Burns—books of history, and two books that tended to make for religious skepticism in a basically God-fearing time: Thomas Paine's *Age of Reason* and Constantin de Volney's *Ruins.* With Mentor Graham's help and Samuel Kirkham's *English Grammar in Familiar Essays,* he brushed up his syntax.[22]

What Lincoln really liked to read were newspapers, reading them, a friend said, "more than he did books." Another friend said he "never saw a man better pleased" than when Lincoln was appointed postmaster, because he could read the *Louisville Journal,* the *Missouri Republican,* the *Cincinnati Gazette,* the *Sangamo Journal,* the *National Intelligencer*—before delivering them to their subscribers.[23]

There was a fundamental intellectual refinement in that rough frontier town in the shape of a debating society. Lincoln joined it, and his fellow debaters noted that how he performed didn't square at all with what he looked like or what they had come to expect. One participant described this contradiction:

> As he rose to speak, his tall form towered above the little assembly. Both hands were thrust down deep into the pockets of his pantaloons. A perceptible smile at once lit up the faces of the audience, for all anticipated the relation of some humorous story, but he opened up the discussion in splendid style, to the infinite astonishment of his friends. As he warmed to his subject, his hands would forsake his pockets, and would enforce his ideas by awkward gestures.... He pursued the question with reason and argument so pithy and forcible that all were amazed. The president, at his fireside after the meeting, remarked to his wife that there was more than wit and fun in Abe's head.[24]

The weeks after Offutt's store closed, in 1832, Lincoln filled his down time by going to war.

A tribe of Sauks under a rebellious Indian chief named Black Hawk had lost its ancestral land in western Illinois to avaricious white settlers, and he and his people had been exiled across the Mississippi. When he ventured an unauthorized recrossing of the river on April 5, 1832, with 400 to 500 braves and more than 1,000 women, children, and old men, Illinois' whites were called to arms.

Illinois Governor John Reynolds summoned the militia and called for volunteers to drive Black Hawk from appropriated white soil. Some 350 men from Sangamon County answered the call, Lincoln among them. Jack Armstrong and his Clary's Grove boys went too, electing Lincoln captain of their company. Armstrong became its sergeant, and William Berry, Lincoln's store partner-to-be, its corporal. It was perhaps the most uncommandable company of men ever to take up arms, these toughs from Sangamon. "As regards Lincoln's company," it was said, "they was a whole souled hard set of men all fighting stock after the Pugalistic Stile.... Wm Miller who Belonged to another Company says the Lincoln's Company was the hardest set of men he ever saw and no man but Lincoln Could do anything with them."[25]

With zero military experience, Lincoln hardly knew what to do with them himself, so he made it up as he went along. Marching the company one morning, twenty abreast, it became necessary to pass through a narrow gate. Not knowing the order for turning troops endwise, Lincoln shouted, "Halt! This company will break ranks for two minutes and form again on the other side of the gate."[26]

Lincoln's first enlistment ended after a month. He reenlisted for another month as a private in another company, then yet a third time—again as a private—when that month was up. He served for three months in the Black Hawk War and never saw the suggestion of a battle. He would later say that while he never saw any "live, fighting Indians... I had a good many bloody struggles with the Musquetoes."[27]

At the end of the three months he was mustered out in Peoria on the Illinois River and started home to New Salem on foot. He was now a veteran of the Indian Wars. And for the same reason he had gone to war—to fill up his down time—he then went into politics.

4

Politics

POLITICS WAS A STRONG seasoning agent on the frontier. "Polytics had sort o' follered us over the Gap trail," Dennis Hanks explained, "an' roosted in the clearin's. Thar was Henry Clay in Kaintucky an' Old Hick'ry in Tennessee at it tooth an' nail, an we all tuk sides."[1]

Sometime before he was old enough to vote, when he was about twenty, Lincoln took Clay's side. He soon became "one of the most Devoted Clay whigs in all the State," a friend in Illinois said—"stiff as a man could be in his Whig doctrines," said another.[2]

It is said that he made his first political speech in Illinois at a rump political meeting in front of Renshaw's tavern on the square in Decatur, in the summer of 1830. Two candidates for the legislature were having it out. Lincoln was plowing in a nearby field when he heard the commotion on the square. Driving his oxen into a corner, he vaulted the fence and went to see what was going on. A Democratic candidate for office stood in a wagon bed pleasing his generally Democratic-leaning audience with a tirade against "old line Whigs," Lincoln's party of recent choice.

Hearing the speaker out and much offended by what he heard, Lincoln leaped up on a splintered stump and tore into him with a rousing rebuttal. Landy Harrell, the tavern landlady overlooking the event from her veranda, testified that the audience cheered him "for his earnestness and pluck."[3]

This doubtless wouldn't have surprised Lincoln's stepmother if she heard about it, for as Dennis Hanks said, "Aunt Sairy always said he'd oughter go into polytics, because when he got to argyin' the other feller'd purty soon say he had enough."[4]

Indeed, Lincoln had gone into politics just before leaving to fight Black Hawk, announcing his candidacy for the state legislature on March 9, 1832, in a public communication that was published a week later in the *Sangamo Journal,* Springfield's Whig newspaper. He was only twenty-three years old and had voted for the first time in his life just the year before. He had balked at first when friends urged him to run. He believed it impossible to be elected, being too young and virtually unknown outside of New Salem—and a Clay Whig besides, in a state where Whiggery was "at a discount."[5] But he had yielded and entered the race anyway.

"Every man," he wrote in his announcement in the *Journal,* "is said to have his peculiar ambition. Whether it be true or not, I can say for one that I have no other so great as that of being truly esteemed of my fellow-men, by rendering myself worthy of their esteem.... I am young and unknown to many of you. I was born and have ever remained in the most humble walks of life. I have no wealthy or popular relations to recommend me. My case is thrown exclusively upon the independent voters of the county, and ... if the good people in their wisdom shall see fit to keep me in the background, I have been too familiar with disappointments to be very much chagrined."[6]

Time was short. Other than publicly signaling his intent, he hadn't campaigned before leaving for the war. Now he had less than two weeks before election day to make up for three months of lost time.

Politicking for the legislature was a random pursuit, no scheduled itinerary necessary; just show up and speak at any public event that would draw a crowd. Decked out for the campaign in a claw-hammer coat, bob-tailed and too short in the sleeves, and his tow-linen pantaloons, coarse black leather brogans, and straw hat, he made his first speech of the campaign at a public sale in Pappsville, a village eleven miles west of Springfield.[7]

It was inordinately dry the summer of 1832, as dry as anybody could remember. The Sangamon River was running so low, one sufferer said, "that by laying a few rocks, one could cross it dryshod almost anywhere."[8] But the politicking wasn't so dry. A fight broke out in the crowd in Pappsville as Lincoln started to speak. Noticing that one of his friends was being mauled by toughs, Lincoln descended the rude speaker's platform, shouldered through the crowd, seized the principal offender by the scruff of the neck and seat of his trousers, and threw him, one spectator insisted, "twelve feet away." The duty done, Lincoln then returned to the speaker's stand to deliver his maiden speech.[9]

"Fellow Citizens," he began, "I presume you all know who I am. I am humble Abraham Lincoln. I have been solicited by many friends to become a candidate for the Legislature. My politics are short and sweet, like the old woman's dance. I am in

favor of a national bank. I am in favor of the internal improvement system and a high protective tariff. These are my sentiments and political principles. If elected I shall be thankful; if
not it will be all the same."[10]

It was to be all the same. In the election on August 6, he
polled 657 votes, eighth in a field of thirteen, four candidates
short of election. But he carried his own precinct, which had a
strong Whig coloring and where he was known. There he won a
nearly unanimous 277 of the 300 votes cast.[11] It was clear that
where people knew him he was a shoo-in. Outside New Salem
he was as yet little known and his vote total fell off sharply. But
this was a situation that could be remedied, if he had any thought
of trying again.

He indeed had the thought. In the spring of 1834 his name
appeared again as a candidate for the legislature in the *Sangamo
Journal*. Two summers had passed and he was as widely known
throughout the region now as he had been unknown in 1832,
and well thought of everywhere. Outsiders tended to be skeptical at first. Seeing him, one of them asked, "Can't the party raise
any better material than that?" But after hearing Lincoln talk he
changed his opinion, convinced then that he "knew more than
all of the other candidates put together."[12]

By this time Lincoln had become a pretty good "stump
speaker and corner-grocery debater."[13] Besides, he had a natural
bent for down-home, face-to-face, candidate-to-voter politicking, and for telling jokes and stories as "plenty as blackberries."[14]

A day on the hustings was often a day in the harvest field. At
Island Grove, twelve miles west of Springfield, Lincoln approached some likely voters working in a field. Looking him
over, they said they couldn't vote for a man unless he could
"make a hand."

"Well," said Lincoln, "if that is all I am sure of your votes."

He "took hold of the Cradle," his friend J. Rowan Herndon testified, "led the way all the Round with Perfect ease [and] the Boys was satisfide and i dont think he Lost a vote in the Croud."[15]

Thus Lincoln campaigned, moving among his constituency, mowing grain with them, splitting rails, putting up hay—anything they were doing—and generally doing it better and faster. His father had taught him to work, and work was the staple of his campaign strategy. He won big, with 1,376 votes, second among four successful candidates in a field of thirteen hopefuls who perhaps didn't know as much and didn't have as hot a hand with a cradle. He was only fourteen votes shy of coming in first.[16]

After he was elected he said to his friend Coleman Smoot, who had voted for him, "Well you must loan me money to buy Suitable Clothing for I want to make a decent appearance in the Legislature." Smoot loaned him $200, a not unreasonable loan to repay over time, in Lincoln's mind, considering he would be making $4 a day as a legislator—"more," he told a friend, "than I had ever earned in my life."[17]

So in late November, in his new-tailored suit, which no tailor living could form fit to such an irregular frame, and with five other members of the new Ninth General Assembly from Sangamon County, Lincoln caught the Springfield-to-Vandalia stage at six o'clock in the morning. When it rolled to a stop in Vandalia seventy-five miles down the road the following afternoon, Lincoln uncoiled his long legs and got out. His new life as perhaps the General Assembly's tallest and greenest lawmaker was about to begin.[18]

5

Vandalia

KASKASKIA HAD BEEN the first capital of Illinois by dent of location. Vandalia was its second capital by dent of still better location.

Despite a dominance during territorial times and a kinship with the Mississippi, Kaskaskia was but a temporary single-session fallback. It had no future as a permanent capital of Illinois. It was too far south and too close to the edge of a state whose center of gravity was shifting swiftly inward and northward. In 1819, a five-man commission was named to go up the Kaskaskia River to find a new site for the capital. Ninety miles northeast of Kaskaskia they found it—an uninhabited oak-forested bluff on the river's west bank.

By 1820 surveyors and men with axes in their hands and tools on their belts were hurrying to build a town before the state's second legislature convened in early December. If the new capital didn't yet have finished form, it had a name. Its founders had in mind something that mixed history and euphony—something honoring the memory of early aboriginal inhabitants and yet was pleasing to the ear. A wag, pulling from thin air, suggested that the Vandals were such a tribe. So the new capital became Vandalia. It was all based on myth, but it sounded good.

A plain, rough two-story capitol building, swiftly constructed on the west side of an emerging public square in 1820, had a swift end; it burned down in 1823. Its replacement was erected the following summer, once again on a tight deadline that discouraged quality. Ten years later, when Lincoln stepped from the Springfield-to-Vandalia coach onto this rickety political stage, the capitol structure had badly sagging floors and dangerously bulging walls.[1]

The new Ninth General Assembly convened in this architectural wreck on December 1, 1834. Lincoln was one of eighty-one members—fifty-five representatives and twenty-six senators. The legislature was the power center of the state government, peopled by the cream of the state's political talent. It was a very heady level for a twenty-five-year-old with no formal education just starting out in politics.

Illinois itself was booming—newcomers poured into it from all of the old states of the Union—"from the ever teeming East and from the bordering slave states." It was, one observer said, as if "an emigration fever seized the people of the eastern states, and the rude and rough highways which led westward were dotted thickly with hundreds of emigrant wagons headed toward Michigan, Wisconsin, Ohio, and Illinois, or anywhere towards the setting sun."[2] One of these newcomers following the westward moving sun wrote home from Illinois, "Towns are being laid out every few days." The state was afire with land speculation. Fortunes were being made.[3]

The legislators and their proposed legislation mirrored the demographic vigor. They were soon sending bills to the hopper to incorporate banks, turnpikes, insurance companies, towns, railroads, and even female academies—muscle-flexing legislation. In this tableau Lincoln did not figure large at first. He was not a major player in his first legislative session. But he was a quick study, and in the next legislature convening in 1836, it would likely be different—if he decided to return for a second term.

He intended to return. In June 1836, he said so, in another notice to the editor of the *Sangamo Journal.* His missive called for suffrage rights for all whites who paid taxes or bore arms— "by no means excluding females." There was no mention of any right of blacks to vote; that would be political suicide. He pledged to be governed in Vandalia by the will of the people "on all subjects upon which I have the means of knowing what their will is." In all other things he would do "what my own judgment teaches me will best advance their interests."[4]

One subject in which their will was clear and his best judgment seconded, was a massive program of internal improvements that was exciting imaginations statewide. This was to be *the* issue of the legislative session. In December, districts all over the state would send their representatives to the legislature, pledged heart and soul to a lavish dream of public works. Some would call this dream a "mania."[5]

But first there was the election campaign, and getting elected was going to be easier. The State Assembly alone, chasing the population boom, now called for ninety-one representatives, nearly double the number in 1834. Sangamon County's share would be seven seats. Two senate seats would bring the county's representation to nine all told.

This time, when the returns were in, Lincoln's 1,716 votes led the entire field of seventeen Sangamon County candidates for the Assembly.[6] The top seven would go to the legislature, and all seven elected were Whigs. Coupled with the two senators also elected—one Whig and one Democrat—the county contingent literally stood out. They were all inordinately tall, averaging over six feet, five stories high in aggregate—a delegation of giants. They were therefore called the Long Nine, but might just as well have been called the Heavy Nine, because their weight averaged over 200 pounds—just short of one ton in aggregate heft. Lincoln's 180 pounds didn't make him the heaviest, but he was the tallest. In political weight and height he bulked large. He would go to Vandalia this time as not just another legislator. He would go as a Whig leader in the House and the leader of this elongated heavyweight delegation. Men would take to calling him the "Sangamon Chief."[7]

Because Sangamon County was seized by the internal improvements mania, maybe more passionately than most, there was a clear mandate to ram through an internal-improvements package. Lincoln would happily follow the people's mandate for this, as he strongly believed in it. His enthusiasm for bringing this improvements bonanza to the state was at such white heat that he fancied he might "become the De Witt Clinton of Illinois"—after the New York governor who had become famous for promoting improvements for the Empire State, notably the wondrous Erie Canal.[8] It might happen. Lincoln was to be a member of the internal-improvements committee in the House.

But there was yet one other passion burning in the bosoms

of Lincoln and the Long Nine, burning with a heat more intense even than internal improvements. That passion was to get the state capital uprooted again and moved from Vandalia northward—to Sangamon County's Springfield. That, and not internal improvements, was the Long Nine's not-so-secret high-priority ambition for this Tenth General Assembly.

Vandalia from the beginning was like Kaskaskia before it—only a conditional capital, meant to serve as the seat of government for only twenty years. At the end of that time—1840—it might be moved yet again if the legislators wished. A fight over moving it started as early as 1832. In 1836 the time to make it happen had come. Several towns in the state, besides Springfield, coveted it—among them Alton, Jacksonville, Decatur, Peoria, and a town futuristically named Illiopolis. The fight to have it—or keep it—would be bitter and intense.

Vandalia desperately wanted to keep it. But Vandalia had never been quite right. It was too reminiscent of the frontier and too small, no longer up to the growing sophistication of the state. Its environment was thought of as unhealthy, its inns and boarding houses notoriously inadequate and overpriced, and the cuisine questionable.[9] "They did not feed us on anything but prairie chickens and venison," one legislator complained.[10] And there was that dilapidated capitol building from 1824 with the sagging floors, bulging walls, and the plaster now peeling away and falling down. People were loath to enter it for fear it would collapse.

In a replay of the crash building program of 1820, Vandalia was eagerly erecting yet a third capitol building for $16,000. Work had been underway since summer and the new structure was rising, in part, with material salvaged from the old. But when the legislature convened in early December, construction was not yet finished. There was that aroma of damp plaster upstairs, and the main floor was still a work in progress.

Into these new, unfinished chambers came the Long Nine, in a fever to see the internal-improvements legislation passed and the capital moved to Springfield. It is said that they vigorously rolled logs, trading votes for internal improvements with votes for Springfield when the matter of a new capital came to the floor.[11]

The management for whatever strategy they used fell on the young second-term legislator from the Sangamon, the longest of the Long Nine. It was a good fit. "Lincoln was a natural debater," colleague Robert L. Wilson said of him. "He was always ready and always got right down to the merits of his case, without any nonsense or circumlocution. He was quite as much at home in the Legislature as at New Salem; he had a quaint and peculiar way, all his own, of treating a subject, and he frequently startled us by his modes—but he was always right."

Wilson thought him a born politician. "We followed his lead, but he followed nobody's lead; he hewed the way for us to follow, and we gladly did so. He could grasp and concentrate the matters under discussion, and his clear statement of an intricate or obscure subject was better than an ordinary argument. It may almost be said that he did our thinking for us." But Wilson saw no arrogance in him, nothing dictatorial. "It seemed the right thing to do as he did. He excited no envy or jealousy."[12]

Appreciation for him was spreading beyond the damp-plastered capitol. By the end of January, Simeon Francis, editor of the *Sangamo Journal,* was saying of him, "Our friend carries the true Kentucky rifle, and when he fires seldom fails of sending the shot home."[13]

The internal-improvements legislation passed the House on

the last day of January 1837. The next day it became law. The track was now clear to take on the job of moving the state capital to Springfield. Lincoln and the Long Nine began calling in the pledges they had traded for. It wasn't easy. Throughout February the battle over a permanent site for the capital raged. When it came time to vote, Springfield led twenty other towns on the first ballot, including Vandalia, which ran second. Springfield didn't yet have the necessary majority, but three ballots later it did. The Long Nine, led by Lincoln, had won. The next session of the legislature in 1839 would convene in the new capitol in Sangamon County.

With little time remaining in the session and the two big victories won, there was still that other item on Lincoln's mind—the slavery resolution. He and Dan Stone introduced it three days before adjournment, slipping it quietly in the welter of nearly 400 bills passed in that busy legislative session. Lincoln had stated his mind, for the first time, on the issue that would dominate the rest of his political life—and the state's and the nation's.

PART THREE

The Issue's Dark Side

6

Death in Alton

POLITICS, PARTIES, AND POSITIONS in the young Union were reasonably clear-cut in 1837. The Whigs, newly-emerging in the political world, had become one of the two major parties—in the Union and in Illinois. They were the champions of rapid economic development driven by an active, centrally controlled government. Indeed the Whigs, Henry Clay's party, believed government ought to exist to support development while shaping the economy and society. They believed, as Lincoln did, in an internal-improvements system, a national bank, and a high protective tariff. Those were their basic sentiments—simple, like the old woman's dance—that had turned Lincoln into a Whig.

The Democrats—the party Andrew Jackson had long dominated—believed in none of those things. They believed in keeping the Union as it had always been, an idyllic nation of small subsistence agriculture, family farms, and small shops. They abhorred the idea of a national bank and believed the less active the government was, the better it was.[1]

In a more or less ordered political world those were the issues that mattered, the line drawn in the sand between the two parties. But it was not an ordered political world. The line in the sand was being blurred by the maverick issue that Lincoln and Dan Stone had addressed in their resolution—slavery. It was polarizing opinion and splitting the Union in ways that none of the other issues dividing the two parties were—or ever had before.

The issue had been lying there, a serpent in the grass, for a long time, from the beginning of the young country. It had nearly fatally poisoned the body politic in 1820, before a compromise was reached between North and South in the Congress. But not until the beginning of the 1830s did the serpent, with what Shakespeare had described as "indented glides,"[2] uncoil, take on a new skin, and insinuate itself into politics as a malignant new strain—virulent abolitionism.

Common wisdom credits William Lloyd Garrison, a New Englander with a sleepless, radical antipathy to slavery, with loosing this lethal new strain on the Union. On January 1, 1831, he launched a newspaper in Boston called *The Liberator,* dedicated to a relentless campaign for immediate, complete, unconditional abolition. In 1832 he founded the New England Antislavery Society in Boston. A national umbrella organization, the American Antislavery Society, followed in 1833.

In 1835 Northern abolitionists launched a campaign to flood the country with antislavery pamphlets and newspapers. In 1836 they sent antislavery petitions with more than 30,000 signatures to Congress. Driven by Southern outrage, the House passed a "gag rule" tabling the petitions without discussion. But they continued to pour in. In 1837 more than 400,000 signatures reached Congress. By 1840 more than two million would sign antislavery petitions.

Garrison became public enemy number one in the South. The Georgia legislature offered a $5,000 reward for his capture and passed a law making it a hanging offense to distribute material that would incite slave rebellions. South Carolina offered a $1,500 reward for the arrest of anyone distributing Garrison's newspaper. A mob in Charleston, South Carolina, seized bags of mail with abolitionist writings and burned them, and Jackson, then still president, urged Congress to ban abolitionist materials from the mails.[3]

Southern legislatures passed their own urgent anti-abolitionist resolutions and insisted northern states, such as Illinois, do the same. A congressional select committee sympathetic to the Southern angst, reported that it could not "conceive how any true friend of the black man can hope to benefit him through the instrumentality of abolition societies.... They have forged new fetters for the black man and added a hundred fold to the rigors of slavery. They have scattered firebrands of discord and disunion among the different States of the Confederacy. They have excited the most rancorous and embittered feelings in the same community. They have aroused the turbulent passion of the monster mob."[4]

That indeed is what it had come down to. The issue had slipped its moorings and drifted into the dark waters. Anti-abolitionist anger swept the North and the South. Mobs were disrupting abolitionist meetings and attacking abolitionist editors. Gentlemen "of property and standing," did not consider it beneath their dignity "to hunt and whip men who were even suspected of abolitionism." In October 1835, a mob dragged

Garrison through the streets of Boston at the end of a rope. By 1838, by count of the abolitionist press, there would be 160 acts of violence against abolitionism nationwide.[5]

The violence would not take long to reach Illinois. There, indeed, not nine months after, and not 100 miles from Vandalia, where Lincoln and Dan Stone entered their dissenting resolution, an act of an anti-abolitionist mob would shake the state and the nation, elevating the slavery issue to a new zenith in the body politic.

The violence would center in Alton, on the Illinois side of the Mississippi, and involve a man Lincoln did not know personally—an ordained minister-editor named Elijah Parish Lovejoy.

Lovejoy was an ardent, idealistic New Englander transplanted to the frontier West with a heedless passion for telling it like it was—or how he believed it to be—whatever the consequences. On the subject of slavery, he would indeed say what he believed, and the consequences would be deep and far reaching.

He was born in Albion, Maine, on November 9, 1802, the son of a Congregational minister. His parents and three brothers and two sisters called him Parish. He was of medium stature—about five feet nine inches tall, muscular and thickset, dark complexioned with piercing black eyes. The eyes, however, were softly lit by "a certain twinkle," suggesting a working sense of humor. His demeanor bespoke an inner kindness and sympathy.[6]

Parish was pulled westward in May 1827, less than a year out of Maine's Waterbury Academy. He headed for St. Louis and there soon found himself the editor of the *St. Louis Times,* a Whig newspaper pushing Henry Clay for president. But he craved a less secular life. Long a seeker of a religious epiphany, he found one in January 1832 at a series of religious revival meetings that shed "a flood of new light into his soul."[7]

Driven by this new light, he sold his share in the *Times,* returned East, intent on working "in the vineyard of the Lord." He enrolled in the Princeton Theological Seminary in New Jersey, and within thirteen months he was an ordained minister. Very soon he turned his face again to the heathen West, believing that was where Christian preaching was most desperately needed. A circle of Presbyterians and Congregationalists in Missouri and Illinois called him back to edit the *St. Louis Observer,* a new religious weekly, the first Protestant sheet west of the Mississippi.[8]

Congregationalists and Presbyterians were pouring into Missouri and Illinois, founding colleges and other institutions— Lovejoy's newspaper among them—to "mould society according to the principles of the gospel." Riding this fervent wave of evangelistic migration, Lovejoy felt it his duty "boldly to attack sin, irrespective of how strongly or how respectably it was intrenched."[9]

At first Lovejoy did not pay much notice to slavery in his editorial columns. When he did, his opinions were moderate, calling for a gradual end to the peculiar institution. He was willing to give recolonization a chance, a scheme advanced by Henry Clay, and favored by Lincoln himself, to purchase freedom for Negro slaves and resettle them in Liberia.

But even moderation was unacceptable to anti-abolitionists in ardently anti-abolitionist St. Louis. In the summer of 1835, abolition excitement was rising to a crescendo in the city. Slaveholders didn't want to hear anyone address "cool and temperate arguments," or arguments of any kind, on the subject of slavery. Lovejoy's editorials, though conciliatory, were considered offensive. While he argued for free speech, they argued for not a word on the subject—only "the silence of death alone would satisfy them." There was no middle meeting ground between the two.

The anti-abolitionists heaped their hatred on him, called him an amalgamationist—about the most damning pejorative a slave-holder could hurl at an abolitionist—and threatened to destroy his office and tar and feather him. There were few in St. Louis with the courage to take his side.[10]

Two events in St. Louis turned Lovejoy from a moderate anti-slavery man into an out-and-out abolitionist. Several of "the most respectable citizens" of St. Louis caught two white men suspected of having decoyed slaves from their owners. The two were dragged two miles from the city to be whipped or hanged. They were not hanged, but each took a hundred to two hundred lashes, every respectable citizen taking his turn with the whip.[11]

In the second galvanizing event, Frank McIntosh, a young free Negro hand on the steamboat *Flora,* docked in St. Louis, went calling on a young Negro girl he knew, and was immediately arrested. Seizing free Negroes in the street and sending them back to slavery was a commonplace occurrence in St. Louis. McIntosh was having none of it. He pulled a knife, killing one officer and wounding another. It was his death warrant. He was quickly recaptured and jailed. An enraged mob stormed the jail, dragged him to a large locust tree, chained him there, and incinerated him.[12]

Lovejoy began writing with enraged venom. He was soon just another editorial away from being mobbed himself. And he knew it. He wrote to his brother in November, "And now that I am here, it is at the daily peril of my life. I am accused of being an Abolitionist, and threatened . . . with violence. *I expect it.* I expect that I shall be *Lynched* or tarred and feathered, or it may be, *hung up.* All are threatened."[13]

By the summer of 1836, he had not yet been lynched, tarred and feathered, or hung up, but he had had enough of St. Louis.

Alton, across the river in Illinois, looked to him to be a more congenial venue for his views and his newspaper. He decided to move there.[14] But its citizens were also, like most in southern Illinois, predominately of Southern origin, with a rabid pro-slavery, anti-abolitionist point of view. Before Lovejoy could move his press from St. Louis, the mob struck. It broke into his office, destroyed furniture and part of the press, and cast it into the river. What was left of it was shipped to Alton, followed by Lovejoy.[15]

He wouldn't temper his abolitionist editorials any more in Alton than he had in St. Louis. Anger against him for this apostasy was soon as heated as it had been in the city across the river. "Men's brains," one writer wrote, "were at fever heat" on the subject of slavery. Many pro-slavery, anti-abolition men considered capital punishment a reasonable antidote for Lovejoy's odious ideas.[16]

The *Missouri Republican* in St. Louis, caught up in the fever heat, wrote that Lovejoy "has, by his adhesion to the odious doctrine of Abolitionism . . . and by his continued efforts to disseminate those odious doctrines, forfeited all claims to the protection of that or any other community." The *Republican* wrote: "We perceive that an Anti-Slavery Society has been formed at Upper-Alton, and many others, doubtless will shortly spring up in different parts of the State. We had hoped that our neighbors would have ejected from amongst them that minister of mischief, the *Observer,* or at least corrected its course. Something must be done in this matter, and that speedily!"[17]

Something was done speedily. On August 21 a mob entered the *Observer*'s upstairs offices on Second Street and destroyed the second press, its type, and other materials. Lovejoy wrote to his mother in New England, "My press has again been mobbed down."[18]

A third press was ordered, arriving in Alton a month later, while Lovejoy was away at a meeting of the Presbytery. Several of Lovejoy's Alton friends escorted it to the Gerry & Weller warehouse, with no interference, despite calls along the route, "there goes the Abolition press, stop it, stop it." A constable was posted for a time at the door of the warehouse by Alton's mayor, twenty-eight-year-old John M. Krum. But when the constable left between ten o'clock and midnight, ruffians with handkerchiefs covering their faces rolled this third press out, broke it up, and threw it in the river.[19]

What the mob really wanted was to get rid of Lovejoy—by any means. And he was under no delusions. "I am to receive no protection here," he wrote a brother, "the way is open for them to do with me what they please." He wrote that four-fifths of the citizens of Alton were glad the press had been destroyed again. "They hate mobs, it is true," Lovejoy wrote, "but they hate Abolitionism a great deal more." But if he was not deluded, neither was he panicked. He wrote, "my own feelings at a time like this [are] perfectly calm, perfectly resigned." If he was to die, he said, "it cannot be in a better cause."[20]

When the mob destroyed Lovejoy's third press, his sympathizers in Ohio ordered a fourth one, and as the town waited for it, excitement rose "to a perfect tornado." The new press arrived at three o'clock in the morning on Tuesday, November 7, to "furious excitement."[21] A band of fifty to sixty sympathetic citizens, armed with rifles and muskets loaded with buckshot or small balls, met the shipment and escorted it without interference to the third floor of the Godfrey, Gilman & Company warehouse, a block-long three-story stone building hard on the river. It was not that these sympathizers loved abolitionism. Lovejoy and one other were the only abolitionists in the company. The rest of them were acting "in defense of the law" and against mobism.[22]

The mob was not long following. At about ten o'clock that evening, they arrived armed with stones and guns and demanded the press. They began throwing stones at the building and then fired shots, answered in kind by the defenders. After one in the mob was killed, it brought up a ladder and a lit torch, intending to set fire to the warehouse roof.[23]

A sortie of volunteers, including Lovejoy himself, rushed out of the warehouse to stop the torching. As they emerged from the building into a brilliant moonlit night—it was now near midnight—they met a volley of fire from a two-barreled shotgun. Five balls struck Lovejoy, three in the chest, one in the abdomen, and one in his left arm. He staggered back up the stairs, crying, "I am shot! I am shot! I am dead!" In the counting room of the warehouse he fell into the arms of a defender and was laid on the floor. He died without a struggle and without another word.[24]

As the tumult at the warehouse mounted to its tragic crescendo, a church bell had been ringing in the town, summoning help. At the bell-rope's end was Mrs. Frederick Graves, the wife of the Presbyterian minister, a frail slip of a thing, hauling at it with all her slender strength. But no help came.[25]

As Lovejoy died and the ringing stopped, life also went out of the resistance. The defenders agreed to give up the press if the mob agreed not to enter the warehouse until they left, unmolested. The agreement was struck, the fire was extinguished, and the defenders fled. The exultant mob rushed into the building, threw the press out the window onto the shore, broke it up, and threw it into the river. By 2 o'clock in the morning it was all over.[26]

On his thirty-fifth birthday Lovejoy was buried in the rain and the mud and the cold in a simple ceremony with prayers, but with no speeches and "no inquest over his body, no flowers... strewn upon his coffin." Throughout the short service the bell of the Presbyterian church tolled again. [27]

As the news of Lovejoy's killing spread through the country it raised a peal of outrage that seemed to echo the urgency of Mrs. Graves's frantic ringing. Lovejoy was hailed as "the first martyr in the cause of Abolition." Garrison's newspaper was "draped in mourning," and he wrote, "May his fall agitate all heaven and earth."[28]

In Illinois, however, the violence was largely ignored. Few spoke out against it, except Governor Duncan, who was blunt about it. "The outrage at Alton," he said, "must be disapproved and regretted by all good citizens, and nothing has happened within our peaceful State that has filled me with so much regret as this event." He cited it as "evidence that all is not right with us."[29]

In Springfield, Abraham Lincoln, looking at what had happened in Alton, also deplored it and agreed all was not right. But he was much less blunt. In a January 1838 address before the Young Men's Lyceum, a forum for Springfield's young intellectuals, he did not strike out against the anti-abolitionism that had fueled the mob, nor did he mention Lovejoy by name. But he vilified the mob violence, which he saw as a lethal threat to the perpetuation of the Union—"the increasing disregard for law which pervades the country; the growing disposition to substitute the wild and furious passions, in lieu of the sober judgement of Courts; and the worse than savage mobs."

He spoke of the "accounts of outrages committed by mobs," now "common to the whole country." If he did not mention

Lovejoy, he did decry the immolation of McIntosh in St. Louis, that "horror-striking scene...perhaps, the most highly tragic, of any thing of its length, that has ever been witnessed in real life." Such, he said, "are the effects of mob law," of "this mobocratic spirit...now abroad in the land." He said, "whenever the vicious portion of the population shall be permitted to gather in bands of hundreds and thousands, and burn churches, ravage and rob provision stores, throw printing presses into rivers, shoot editors, and hang and burn obnoxious persons at pleasure, and with impunity; depend on it, this Government cannot last."

Lincoln pleaded for the end of mob rule. "Let reverence for the laws, be breathed by every American mother, to the lisping babe, that prattles on her lap," he said. "Let it be taught in schools, in seminaries, and in colleges...let it be preached from the pulpit, proclaimed in legislative halls, and enforced in courts of justice. And, in short, let it become the *political religion* of the nation; and let the old and the young, the rich and the poor, the grave and the gay, of all sexes and tongues, and colors and conditions, sacrifice unceasingly upon its altars."[30]

As in the March resolution he had introduced with Dan Stone, Lincoln stood virtually alone. No other legislator in either Missouri or Illinois was talking that way, no other condemned the mob violence in Alton.[31] Neither, apparently, did Springfield in general. It appeared antipathetic to abolitionism—not to slavery or mobism. On October 23, the month before Lovejoy died, a public protest meeting in the town resolved that "the efforts of abolitionists in this community, are neither necessary nor useful," and that immediate emancipation was at variance with Christianity.[32]

The issue had gone to the dark side.

PART FOUR

Political Enemies
and Female Enigmas

7

Springfield

WHEN "THE LONG NINE of old Sangamon, " the "nine intellectual and physical giants" rammed through the bill moving the
state capital to Springfield in the dying days of the legislative session in 1837, the city celebrated. A huge bonfire lit the night
around the whipping post on the east side of the town square.[1]
The grateful citizenry threw a big public dinner of appreciation
in Athens just north of Springfield on August 3. There Lincoln
was said to have "fulfilled the expectations of his friends and dis-
appointed the hopes of his enemies." He was, they said, "one of
nature's nobility."[2]

Lincoln was now attempting to fulfill his own loftier expectations. After he was elected to the legislature he had taken a
careful second look at lawyering. Perhaps it was within his intellectual reach after all. He had come to look on the profession as
perhaps "the grandest science of man," the best profession for

schooling the mind, and the highest platform on which to "ex-hibit his powers in a well-trained manhood"—and probably, the obvious launch pad onto yet a higher plateau in politics.[3]

Marching in the Black Hawk War, Lincoln had met John Todd Stuart, a Springfield lawyer. They became friends and fel-low candidates for the legislature in 1834. Stuart, an old hand at legislative politics, took the rough specimen from New Salem under his mentorship, rooming with him in Vandalia and show-ing him the way in his early days in the Ninth Legislature.

Stuart was one of the Long Nine in the Tenth Legislature, courtly, dignified, and affable, perhaps the best jury lawyer in Illinois. He was also thought to be "one of the handsomest men in Illinois," with "as fine and gallant a bow for his laundress as for a duchess." He was a year and a half older than Lincoln, and like him, an early Clay man in politics, a leader in organizing the Whig party in central Illinois.[4]

Stuart reinforced his young political protégé's leanings to-ward the law. After the 1834 election Lincoln borrowed law books from Stuart and studied them between his stints in the legislature, his postmastering, and his surveying. It was said by a friend that Lincoln went day after day for weeks sitting under an oak tree on a hill in New Salem reading *Blackstone's Commen-taries,* the bible of the profession, moving around the tree to stay in the migrating shade. It was said he became so absorbed that he sometimes failed to notice people when he met them. Some thought he might be crazy.[5]

Lincoln considered this leap into a legal career an "experi-ment."[6] But in the autumn of 1836 he earned his license to prac-tice law in Illinois, and Stuart invited him to become a partner in his law practice in Springfield. In the middle of April the *San-gamo Journal* announced the partnership, and Lincoln was ready to make another major experimental leap. He packed his "entire estate, real and personal, in a carpetbag," and left New Salem to follow the state capitol to Springfield.[7]

Springfield had been staked out on Spring Creek, on the edge of the flat empty prairie, in 1821—the same year Sangamon County was created. A year later the nascent settlement consisted of a store, a hotel, a blacksmith shop, a courthouse, and a jail—all built of logs. It was a settlement not only clinging to the edge of the prairie in "verdant solitude," but on "the dividing line between the white settlers and the Indians."[8] It also was on the same latitude as Philadelphia. It was on a planetary parallel just south of Madrid, Venice, Constantinople, and Rome, and 600 miles south of Paris. It was 800 miles nearer the equator than London.[9]

Lincoln first saw Springfield in the spring of 1831, after the thawing of the Deep Snow when he rode the melt-off down the Sangamon. It was a village of only 692 settlers. In 1832 it was incorporated as a town, and by 1834 its population had doubled to around 1,200. Three years later, in the spring of 1837, when Lincoln came carrying his belongings, the number was pushing 2,000. Now it was to be the state capital, and 450 new residents were pouring in every year. A building and business boom following the burgeoning growth had created 174 retail establishments, a third of them devoted to the construction tasks necessary to keep pace with the boom—especially carpentry and painting. The town now had eleven lawyers, a number Lincoln was about to augment, with a bar considered by many to be "the best in the state, and perhaps as good as any in the West." The town had eighteen doctors, four druggists, and six grocery stores. And besides being the capital-to-be, it was the Sangamon County seat.[10]

But it was still an unpaved, rough frontier town. It had streets of dirt, which rose in choking clouds of dust in the dry season and turned into hub-deep mud in the wet season. Rivaling the mud as a public nuisance were the hogs that wallowed in it, roaming at will through the town, contesting the passersby on sidewalks and rooting up the boardwalks that offered safe passage over the mud. The stench from manure (piled up around the stables) and from the often-neglected privies further defiled the civic air. Discarded clothing and garbage clogged the gutters. In the summer, flies rising from the open filth challenged the hogs, dust, and mud as pest number one.[11]

Such was Springfield's unlovely side. After the new state capitol was built, Lincoln often told the story of the supplicant who applied to the secretary of state (custodian of the statehouse) for permission to deliver a series of lectures in the Hall of the House of Representatives.

"May I ask what is to be the subject of your lectures?" the secretary of state inquired.

"They are on the second coming of our Lord," the petitioner said.

"It's no use," the secretary of state said. "If you will take my advice you will not waste your time in this city. It is my private opinion that if the Lord has been in Springfield *once*, he will not come the *second* time."[12]

Sweetening this seamier, no-second-coming side of Springfield was a lively, active upper-crust social life, which was appropriate for a state capital and which centered on the mansion of Ninian Edwards, son of the first governor of the state. Sited on what was known as "aristocrat hill," on the south side of town, the Edwards home was the house that mattered in Springfield society. Edwards and his wife, Elizabeth, threw compelling parties and Saturday soirees, and a connection with it meant entrée into what rarified social air there was in the town.[13]

Into this Springfield of high stench and high society Lincoln rode on a borrowed horse in the spring of 1837.

On his first day in town he trooped into the Bell & Co. general store on the courthouse square, with a mind to fitting up a small sleeping room adjoining the law office. He had already contracted with a local carpenter to build him a bedstead.

Behind the counter, tending store, was Joshua Speed. Lincoln and Speed had never met, but Speed knew who this lanky legislator-cum-attorney was. Speed was also an ardent anti-Jackson, pro-Clay Whig and he knew who the leading Whigs were in the state. There were few enough of them. And this one—a two-term state legislator—had a way of standing out.

Speed was five years younger than Lincoln, but the two had much in common besides their political preferences. Speed was also an émigré from "the dark and bloody ground," the son of a wealthy Kentucky planter. Though shorter than Lincoln, he had a long leg up on him in formal education. Speed had been sent to the best private schools in the West and St. Joseph's College in Bardstown, before setting out to make his way in the world. For about two years after college he had clerked in a large store in Louisville before migrating to Springfield, where he bought a part interest in Bell & Co. Like Lincoln, Speed had driving ambition. If Lincoln's was for fame and prestige, Speed's was for money and fortune.[14]

Lincoln explained to Speed that he had recently been admitted to the bar and had come to Springfield to be John Stuart's law partner. He hoped to buy furnishings for a single bed—mattress, sheets, blankets, a pillow. He walked about the store with Speed, who listed what he would need, tallied it up, and told Lincoln it would come to $17.

It was perhaps cheap enough, but Lincoln told Speed he was unable to pay it. Lincoln told him that if he would extend him credit and his experiment as a lawyer was a success, he would pay Speed at Christmas. "If I fail in this," Lincoln said, "I don't know that I can ever pay you."

Liking this tall, frank talker from the start and thinking he "never saw a sadder face," Speed pointed to a winding stair leading from the store to the second floor. "I have a large room with a double bed up-stairs," he said, "which you are very welcome to share with me."

Lincoln picked up his saddlebags—Speed later testified they were saddlebags, not a carpetbag—and climbed to the room. He set them on the floor, returned downstairs with a face beaming as the melancholy lifted, and said, "Well, Speed, I am moved."[15]

The two hit it off from the start. Like Lincoln, Speed had a keen and poetic mind and was given to melancholy—a tendency to hypochondria, anxiety attacks, and fits of depression. Springfield, however, likely came to believe that Lincoln probably outdid Speed in that department. Lincoln's edge in hypochondria, anxiety, and depression, seeping out at times from under his talent for laughter and for telling a story, was driven by worry over his debts, his uncertain prospects, and his unsteady social graces.[16]

Speed was not the only one who noticed Lincoln's melancholy. William H. Herndon, who was for a time a clerk in Speed's store, saw him as "a sad-looking man; his melancholy dripped from him as he walked." Speed doubtless subscribed to the other thing Billy Herndon believed about Lincoln—that "there was something in his tall and angular frame, his ill-fitting garments, honest face, and lively humor that imprinted his individuality on my affection and regard."[17]

Speed noted that Lincoln's eating, sleeping, reading, conversation, and study habits were "regularly irregular." He had "no stated time for eating, no fixed time for going to bed or getting up—No course of reading ever was chalked out." Lincoln told him, "I am slow to learn and slow to forget that which I have learned—My mind is like a piece of steel, very hard to scratch any thing on it and almost impossible after you get it there to rub it out." It was evident to Speed that "intense thought with him was the rule and not as with most of us the exception. He often said that he could think better immediately after Breakfast—and better walking, than sitting, lying or standing." And Speed found that when it came to translating thought to paper, Lincoln was a great admirer of the writing style of South Carolina's John C. Calhoun.[18]

Springfield didn't immediately sweep Lincoln off his feet. "We have generally in this country, peace, health, and plenty, and no news," he wrote Levi Davis, a Vandalia lawyer. Nor did Springfield immediately sweep him up in its embrace. He wrote Mary Owens, a female acquaintance whom he was irregularly courting, "This thing of living in Springfield is rather a dull business after all....I am quite as lonesome here as [I] ever was anywhere in my life. I have been spoken to by but one woman since I've been here, and should not have been by her, if she could have avoided it."[19]

So Lincoln read. He read Milton, Shakespeare, Burns, and Byron and discovered for the first time a mournful work of verse by the Scotch poet William Knox called "Mortality," which he greatly admired for its somber view of life and death. He continued his avid communion with newspapers, particularly the

Sangamo Journal and articles it reprinted from other papers around the state as well as the speeches of Clay, Calhoun, Daniel Webster, Thomas Hart Benton, and other congressional leaders. He regularly contributed anonymous writings and opinion to the editorial columns of the *Journal.*[20]

The *Journal* was as avidly Whig as he was. Founded in late 1831 by Simeon Francis, it was the first newspaper established in Springfield that had managed to last.[21] It was joined by its avidly Democratic counterpart, the *Illinois Republican,* which was to merge in 1839 with the *Illinois State Register and People's Advocate* of Vandalia, also following the seat of government to Springfield. After the merger it would be called the *Illinois State Register* and become the state's leading Democratic newspaper, with its habit of seeing things in exactly the opposite political light as the *Journal.*[22]

By the spring of 1837, when Lincoln moved to Springfield, the political lines in the town were clearly drawn between Whigs and Democrats. A small central group was in control in both parties, and often in the evenings many of the young, unattached men in Springfield, mainly lawyers, clerks, politicians, and aspiring politicians of both persuasions flocked to the big wood fireplace in the rear of Joshua Speed's store to laugh at Lincoln's stories, share poetry they had written, but not generally to talk politics—a divisive subject. Speed called it "a sort of social club without organization."[23]

Often on those evenings the dominant Democratic presence was an ardent young attorney and brash political comer, Stephen A. Douglass,* who had served with Lincoln in the Tenth Legis-

---

*It was not until 1846 that Douglass would drop one "s" from his name and become Douglas. Henceforth I will call him Douglas, the name he has carried down into history.

lature. Douglas, in his way, was as unique as Lincoln. He was as squat and stumpy as Lincoln was tall and elongated—and fully as articulate and partisan. Since they were the leaders of their respective parties in the town and in the room, the fireplace, if their conversation did degenerate into politics, would not be the only thing that was blazing.

Looking at these two men, so different in frame, so different in political persuasion, so different in demeanor, so different from what anybody was accustomed to, it was not difficult to wonder what force on earth had spit them out to meet in that room. But there they were.

8

Young Hickory

LINCOLN SAW DOUGLAS for the first time in his first month as a legislator in Vandalia—in December 1834. The young Democrat was there not as a fellow legislator, but as a lobbyist.

Viewing Douglas's low-slung physical aspect from his own towering elevation a full foot higher, Lincoln judged him to be the "least man he had ever seen."[1] Almost everything about Douglas physically—his short legs, his diminutive hands and feet—suggested "least." His one physical aspect that belied the description was a head strikingly out of proportion to the rest of him. Douglas may have inherited this configuration from a grandfather back in his native Vermont; the elder was of medium height with a similarly short neck, short limbs, and disproportionately large head.[2]

But anyone could tell that the young lobbyist, only in the first year of his majority—hardly twenty-one years old—was extraordinary in more than just physical proportion. He was smart, outgoing, intensely partisan, companionable, and talkative—indeed, a talker of remarkable "conversational power." He was a truncated charmer, graced with eyes that one friend said were "large, steady, and with a peculiar quality that impressed one as depth." The voice that rolled out of this budget-sized young phenomenon, who had more than his fair share of "animal spirits," was "broad, deep [and] vibrant."[3]

Most of those animal spirits were political. In 1834 he was in Vandalia at the opening of the Ninth General Assembly attempting to supplant the incumbent Whig state's attorney from Morgan County. Douglas's and Lincoln's paths crossed often from then on, both in politics and in law. When Douglas was himself elected to the legislature in 1836, they served together. They had often lawyered in the same courtrooms, both against one another and as co-counsels. Both had been admitted to practice in the supreme court of Illinois on the same day in 1839. They had debated one another on the same stumps and in the same legislative hall and would do so again, heatedly, in front of the fireplace in Joshua Speed's store in Springfield.

The planet welcomed Douglas to this life in Brandon, Vermont, on April 23, 1813, while Lincoln was a four-year-old playing on the banks of Knob Creek in Kentucky. The infant Douglas weighed a supersized thirteen pounds at birth, promising proportions never realized in adulthood. He was never to know his father, a rising young physician in Brandon. Holding his little two-month-old son in his arms before the fire in their living room, Douglas's father had died suddenly of a stroke.[4]

Until he was in his teens, his little valley in Vermont was "the very centre of civilization" for young Douglas. All beyond the mountains that bounded his horizon he believed "was nothing, but barbarism and filibustering."[5] Nonetheless, he left in the spring of 1828 at age fifteen and ventured out into that seemingly treacherous pit to "see what I could do for myself in the wide world among strangers."[6]

He ventured but fourteen miles, as far as Middlebury, a nearby industrial and agricultural center twice the size of Brandon. Being good with wood, with a special aptitude for crafting "bureaus, cabinets, and secretaries,"[7] he apprenticed to a cabinetmaker. He also apprenticed in politics. Democrat Andrew Jackson—Old Hickory, the hero of New Orleans in the War of 1812—was running for president against John Quincy Adams, and Douglas was dazzled.

From that moment and that campaign, he later wrote, "my politics became fixed, and all subsequent reading, reflection and observation have but confirmed my early attachment to the cause of Democracy"—the Democratic Party's name in those days.[8]

The "Young Hickory" dove into the campaign, arguing the cause of Old Hickory with other young men interested in politics. He organized a band of "Jackson boys" to patrol Middlebury and rip down anti-Jackson handbills from walls and fences as fast as they were slapped up.[9]

His apprenticeship in Middlebury lasted only eight months, in part because his employer was an avid Adams man. Returning to Brandon highly politicized, but still aspiring to "the life of a mechanic," Douglas found a place in a woodworking shop. But he fell ill in the winter of 1829–30, and when he recovered, he believed himself "too feeble" to continue that career. He began looking instead to a college education and a profession.[10]

He was still a minor, only seventeen, when his older sister married a New Yorker and then his mother married the New

Yorker's father. In 1830, they both moved with their new husbands to the Finger Lakes region and settled near the upstate town of Canandaigua. Douglas moved with them and entered the Canandaigua Academy, said to be the best classical school west of Albany. For the next three years he "zealously" studied Greek, Latin, mathematics, rhetoric, and logic. But he more than minored in politics, being active in the debating club, often in defense of Andrew Jackson, his "political pole star" and "saint."[11]

Since Canandaigua was also a hotbed of legal and political talent, Douglas was soon drawn to the study of law. Legal practice in New York required four years of classical education, which Douglas largely already had, but also three additional years of study, which he didn't have the patience to acquire. He was "a young man in a hurry."[12]

Young men in a hurry were hurrying west, in seeming testimony that "Man moves with the Sun"—as New England's iconoclastic Henry David Thoreau, put it.[13] So Douglas turned his gaze westward.

In June 1833, with $300 in his pocket—the last of his patrimony—letters of introduction, and with no particular destination in mind, he set out. If he had no geographical end in mind, he did have a political one in his sights. When his mother asked when they might see him again, he said, "On my way to Congress."[14]

He stopped first in Cleveland, a small but flourishing village in Ohio hugging Lake Erie. There, with his letters of introduction, he quickly made contacts and friends, decided to stay, and then fell ill with bilious fever—malarial typhoid—and for four months hovered "on the dividing line between this world and the next."[15]

Finally recovered but with only $40 of his inheritance left, he pushed on to St. Louis, arriving with his "small pittance of money...about exhausted" and where he knew nobody and had no letters of introduction. In this predicament, he looked across the river toward Illinois.[16]

On his journey west he had heard Illinois talked about as the coming place, and he had read a new book on western travel by Englishman John Stuart, who penned panegyrics to "the beautiful valley of Illinois," the "cultivated land," and "the beautiful forest trees" on the banks of the great river. Stuart saw the state, "extending from the Mississippi to Lake Michigan" as "one vast prairie of admirable soil...*the richest country in point of soil in the world.*" And he saw the neighborhood around Jacksonville, between the Illinois River and Springfield in the Sangamon Valley, as "the most inviting part" of that inviting state.[17]

Illinois had the added allure for Douglas of being strongly Democratic. It had voted emphatically for Old Hickory in the last election. Jacksonville itself was named for Douglas's political polestar. And it looked affordable. The beautiful, black, loamy, and Democratic land around the town could be had for $1.25 an acre, exactly the amount of money Douglas had left in his pocket when he arrived there in November 1833, five months after leaving New York.[18]

When a new acquaintance mentioned that a schoolteacher was needed in the nearby village of Winchester, he immediately went there, and within a month, "this *petite* stranger, this little man," had rounded up about forty students for three months at $3 a head. So he pitched up for the winter in Winchester and wrote home proudly on December 15, "I have become a *Western* man."[19]

In Winchester he continued his study of the law, with an eye to returning to Jacksonville, the Morgan County seat of a thousand residents and some eleven lawyers, to "stick up his shingle."[20] On March 4, his pedagoguing done, he returned to Jacksonville, and not yet twenty-one years old, he was licensed to practice law in Illinois.

He was not yet, by any stretch, well schooled in the law. But it hardly mattered. The law was not his real passion. Just as his head was disproportionate to his body, politics was disproportionate to everything else in his psyche. Being a lawyer was a distant second in his agenda of priorities, merely a means to a political end. A fellow lawyer in Jacksonville said, "Clients were rare visitants to his office, nor was he a close keeper of his office for either business or study; but he was out among the 'boys,' assuming the part of a politician from the start."[21]

In Winchester he had read newspapers, as Lincoln so avidly did, talking politics with the locals and building a budding reputation as a debater. He stepped all this up in Jacksonville. He was armed and ready, inserting himself into the political mix and debate in the county seat, always ardently in defense of its namesake. He was soon exciting the "bitter hostility" of some and the "warm support" of others.[22] He was so ardent, so intent, and so skillful that he was being called "the little fighting orator," and, for the first time—"Little Giant," nomenclature that would stick to him the rest of his life.[23]

Just as there were still large gaps of available, untilled land in this frontier state, there was a large gap in the available leadership of the Democracy in Morgan County, a vacuum Douglas quickly moved to fill.[24]

Through the summer of 1834 he divided his time equally between the law and politics, "reading and practicing the one and preaching the other."[25] In December he had gone to Vandalia for the opening of the Ninth General Assembly, where he first looked upward at Lincoln, whom he very likely considered one of the "most" men he had ever seen. He was in Vandalia as a co-conspirator in a plan to push legislation to write John J. Hardin, the Whig state's attorney in the First Judicial District, out of his job. His strategy was to take the appointment of that office out of the governor's hands and put it in the legislature's. It worked, and though Douglas vigorously denied that he had foreseen it, the legislature then picked him for the position over its incumbent. It was Douglas's first political office. Overnight he was the prosecuting attorney of a circuit covering eight counties, and he was still only twenty-one years old.[26]

A lawyer watching him ride out to assume his duties as state's attorney said, "His short legs allowed his feet to reach scarcely below the saddle skirts. He had stowed in his saddle bags a book on criminal law, which I had lent him; it was his whole library."[27]

In the spring of 1836, Douglas was drafted to run as a Democratic candidate for the legislature, against his inclination; he was well fixed in a good and lucrative job. But resigning as state's attorney and running against, among others, John J. Hardin again, he was elected—and so was Hardin—and in December he joined both Hardin and Lincoln in the Tenth General Assembly.

At age twenty-three, he was the state's youngest legislator. But he acted from the start as if he were the oldest and longest serving, brashly introducing bills and resolutions and plunging into debates.[28] He differed with Sangamon's Long Nine "on almost every important question that came before the Assembly, and more especially on the new location of the seat of government."

That measure, he wrote in a letter to the editor of the *Illinois Patriot,* he "opposed in every form and shape it assumed, from its first appearance in the House up to its final passage," a position that "arrayed the Sangamon delegation *en masse* against me."[29]

The internal-improvements legislation, which dominated the session, was a more complex matter, and Douglas's position more equivocal. He supported internal improvements—he could hardly do otherwise given the mania for it throughout the state and in his own district. But he did not favor "such a wild and extravagant scheme" that finally passed, and he had unsuccessfully introduced legislation to "cripple it." In the end he voted for it, because it was politically lethal not to.[30]

In January 1837, when the resolutions condemning abolitionism came before the legislature, Douglas was one of the many voting for it. Lincoln was one of the few voting against it.

Douglas resigned his seat in the legislature immediately after the session ended, in March 1837, when the newly inaugurated Democratic President Martin Van Buren appointed him Register of the Springfield Land Office. He had ardently opposed the Sangamon Whigs in relocating the capital to Springfield. But now he joined them there, and he was a canker in their midst.

Since getting into politics in Illinois he had been busy doing yet another political thing they didn't like—installing an open convention system for nominating and electing Democrats to office. Although there were political parties on the frontier, like anywhere else, they had not yet crystallized into cohesive vehicles. It was every man for himself, and the premium was on personal popularity. There was no system of calling an open convention and naming a ticket—one man for each office. Whoever wanted to run for a state office simply announced he was running, as

Lincoln had, and ran, very likely against other members of his party.

That system made no sense to Douglas. He was schooled in the politics of the East, where the parties held conventions and named only one candidate for each office. He knew it to be the only way to manage elections successfully and get Democrats elected.[31]

It was the system he wanted installed in the Democracy in Illinois, and he had been working at it—first in Morgan County, and then statewide. He had helped set up the system for Democrats in Morgan County in 1836, and the convention that met had nominated him to run for the legislature. In 1837 the Democrats, led by Douglas, convened the first ever such open statewide convention in Illinois to nominate candidates for governor and lieutenant governor.

At first Whigs decried this open convention system as "new fangled," and odious.[32] The *Sangamo Journal* in the spring of 1835 printed articles and letters describing the Democratic National Convention as alien to the ways of popular government, an evil unconstitutional device "of the *few* to govern the *many*," violating "every principle" of democracy.[33] The same, it held, could be said of state conventions. But they were working so well for the Democrats that the Whigs were soon imitating them in self-defense.

In November 1837 the Democrats in the Third Congressional District, the largest and northernmost of the state's three districts, also met in convention in Peoria and nominated the main instigator of the system, Stephen Douglas, as their candidate for that office, even though at twenty-four he was not yet legally old enough. Douglas threw himself into the campaign heart and soul. Here he was with a chance to fulfill his promise to his mother.

To run against this callow upstart, the Whigs picked John Stuart, Lincoln's law partner, who had run unsuccessfully for the office two years before. On January 27, 1838, the *Sangamo Journal* published a letter by "The Conservative," who was believed to be Lincoln, and an addendum on February 3, that questioned the wisdom of running "that thing," Douglas for Congress "in these trying times, instead of some man of talent and acquaintance with the people, and possessing other suitable qualifications."[34]

But that thing was running, and Stuart had to run against it. The two men began stumping extensively across the district, frequently traveling together, often eating at the same table and sleeping in the same bed—a not unique campaign arrangement on the frontier. Following the panic of 1837, the campaign was fought on national issues. In dispute was the bank question and how to handle the nation's money. The Democrats and Douglas were solid for President Martin Van Buren's "Divorce Bill," a so-called hard money, or sub-treasury, system in which all relationships between the banks and the national finances were divorced and kept separate. Instead of in banks, government money was to be stored in an independent treasury system of strong government vaults—sub-treasuries—scattered about the country. The Whigs vigorously opposed the bill, favoring a strong national bank system instead. That was the central issue of the day nationwide and in the campaign for Congress in Illinois in 1838.[35]

The Illinois Third District sprawled from Morgan and Sangamon counties north to Lake Michigan and the Wisconsin line. The two candidates traveled across it for five months speaking six days a week, every day except Sunday, from any slightly raised dais—platforms, tree stumps, ox carts, wagons, stacks of rails, barrels—anything that gave them a little elevation above their audiences.[36]

Through all of this, Lincoln kept legal shop in Springfield, except for a week in May when Stuart fell ill and he filled in, debating the issues with Douglas in Stuart's stead, lending added elevation to whatever platform, stump, ox cart, wagon, stack of rails, or barrel they were speaking from.[37]

Generally speaking, Stuart and Douglas got along well together in the canvass, except near the end when nerves began to fray. On August 3—only days before the election—Douglas used language Stuart found offensive. A strapping six-footer, a Long Niner, Stuart tucked the Little Giant under his arm and toted him about the marketplace in Springfield. Fighting back in one of the only ways he could, Douglas caught Stuart's right thumb between his teeth and bit down hard, opening a wound and leaving a scar for life.[38]

Stuart barely won the election—with bandaged thumb—by a cliff-hanging thirty-six votes, of 36,495 cast.[39] It could hardly have been closer. When the winner was finally announced, Douglas sought to have the votes recanvassed. But Stuart refused and took his seat in Washington in December 1839. Douglas's promise to his mother would have to wait. But he had made a shockingly strong showing, surprising everybody and leaving the impression in both parties that he would be heard from again, probably sooner rather than later.

In early March 1839, after the campaign, Douglas resigned as register in the Springfield Land Office to practice law and organize the Democratic Party for the coming presidential campaign in 1840. He was now the Illinois Democracy's acknowledged champion and ablest debater. In December, Lincoln wrote Stuart that Douglas, "The Democratic Giant," was in town, "but he is not now worth talking about."[40]

But he could hardly avoid being talked with, and they were talking regularly in the evenings around the fireplace in Speed's store.

9

The Ballyhoo Campaign

THE HOT SUBJECT in the store in late 1839 was the coming presidential canvass. The subject had been simmering for four years—since the last national election in 1836.

Two sea changes in politics coincided in 1836. Andrew Jackson ended his two terms in the presidency and was stepping down. The new party—the Whigs—with no common ideology except its hatred of him, had been cobbled together to try to keep his hand-picked successor, Martin Van Buren, from succeeding him. Democrats described this new party opposing them as an odd assortment of "Federalists, nullifiers, and bank men" and believed they had little to fear from such "combined fragments."[1]

For two terms, most of a decade, Jackson had dominated American politics and frustrated the ambitions of such potent political enemies as Henry Clay and Daniel Webster, both power players now in the new Whig party. The goal of these Jackson haters in 1836 was to defeat Old Hickory's anointed successor and end forever the old man's mesmeric hold on American politics.

The Whigs had three major mountains to climb. One was the political heft of Jackson, still potent in the country. The second was Van Buren himself, Jackson's vice president, the successor-designate, a canny political operator in his own right. The third was the loose ideological makeup of the new Whig party itself, which defied shaping into a seamless whole. It was impossible to write a platform all could agree on.

The Whigs couldn't even agree on a single candidate. They didn't bother holding a national convention but fell back on leg-islative caucuses, local meetings, and state conventions, which produced a battery of candidates—four in all, a quartet of fa-vorite sons, who together, hopefully, would siphon enough votes from Van Buren to deny him a majority in the electoral college and throw the election into the House of Representatives. There they might have the combined muscle to see one of their own elected, not necessarily one of the four, but a mightier Whig who was not a candidate—Clay perhaps.[2]

Comprising this armada of hopefuls was General William Henry Harrison, the favorite of the West; Hugh Lawson White of Tennessee, the choice also of Virginia and Illinois, and favored by young Abraham Lincoln; Daniel Webster of Massachusetts, backed by Pennsylvania and New York; and Willie P. Mangum of North Carolina, who could only count on the support of his own state. Supreme Court Justice John McLean of Ohio was also in the mix, but hardly able to count on any state, even his own.[3] Conspicuously absent from this lineup was Clay himself, who ardently wished to be in it, but whose stars were not yet properly aligned in the presidential firmament.

It didn't work. This broadside of candidates from that cobbled-together new party misfired. Van Buren won easily, outpolling all four Whigs combined in the Electoral College, 170 to 124.

But if the Whigs couldn't swing it in 1836, by 1840 there were good omens. Van Buren was tainted and vulnerable. The panic of 1837, which broke three months after he was inaugurated, had been followed by a debilitating economic depression still ravaging the country. This persistent downturn had made him a juicy target.

The Whigs thought they had just the right weapon to hurl at that bullseye. William Henry Harrison had made a solid showing in 1836—the strongest among the party's battery of candidates. He had collected seventy-three electoral votes, carried seven states, and fallen only 4,300 votes short of winning Pennsylvania. That had been impressive. He also had other tantalizing assets. He was, like Jackson, a military hero, and unlike Jackson, he had no strong track record on issues that would rivet political hatred. They couldn't agree on issues, but the Whigs seemed to agree on him. His sole drawback was his age. If elected, he would be sixty-eight when inaugurated, an antique for that era. He would be the oldest president in the young republic's history.

Like so many others on the frontier, Harrison was a western man with eastern antecedents. He was born in 1773 on a plantation in Virginia, still a British colony. He was a child of the gentry born to a famous father, Benjamin Harrison, who had been a signer of the Declaration of Independence and an early governor of Virginia.

Raised to privilege on his father's Berkeley plantation on the James River south of Richmond, William Henry had wanted to be a doctor. He studied briefly under the eminent Benjamin Rush in Philadelphia before deciding that medicine didn't really suit him. He became a soldier instead, entering the regular army in 1791 as a lieutenant and posted to the Northwest Territory.

There he had transmogrified from a soldier into a sometime politician. In 1789 he resigned from the army to become the secretary of the territory, and in 1799, its first delegate to Congress. There he helped engineer legislation that separated the Indiana Territory from the Northwest Territory, and at the age of twenty-eight he became that breakaway territory's governor, a job he would hold for the next dozen years.

In 1811, near the end of those twelve years, the Shawnees under a couple of troublesome leaders, Tecumseh and his brother, The Prophet, were restless, wanting back the land wrenched from them by white settlers. Reassuming his military persona, Harrison marched a force of more than a thousand men to a camp a mile northwest of the Prophet's bailiwick on Tippecanoe Creek, a tributary of the Wabash, burned their village, and put the Shawnees to flight, losing 180 men of his own in the attack.

It was a quasi-victory at a whopping price, but it captured the American imagination, brought Harrison national notice, made him a brigadier general, and gave him a *nom de guerre* with a ring to it, "Old Tippecanoe." In the War of 1812, in early October 1813, he further distinguished himself with a victory over the British and their Indian allies on the Thames River north of Lake Erie, killing his old enemy, Tecumseh. This was his greatest military victory, greater than Tippecanoe. However, "Old Thames," did not have the ring of "Old Tippecanoe." So the name he won on the Wabash had by 1840 become a campaign code word and possible Open Sesame to the presidency. Although he had been a U.S. senator for a short time, he had never held a national office long enough or dealt with national issues long enough to embarrass himself or cripple his candidacy. This looked to be an advantage in any attempt to unhorse the outrider of Jacksonism in the White House.

That outrider was no mean political horseman. Martin Van Buren was president because Andrew Jackson had willed it. But Jackson, a Tennessean, had become president in 1828 in large part because of an enthusiastic and politically muscular hand up from Van Buren, who was the Democratic power in New York and Jackson's predominant supporter in the North. He became Old Hickory's secretary of state, his vice president in his second term, and through his entire presidency was his most trusted advisor.

Unlike Harrison, Van Buren was not to the manor born—but he acted like it. His father had been a Dutch tavern keeper and farmer around Kinderhook in the Hudson River Valley in upstate New York. But when he went out into the world on his own and began his impressive climb to the summit of politics in the Empire State, Van Buren always carried himself with Victorian manners and dressed with fastidious elegance.

Some thought him somewhat dandified. He was a bald and pudgy five feet six inches tall, with a pleasant face ringed in muttonchop whiskers, which had been reddish but were now graying. He traveled with a brown leather hat case among his luggage. It was rumored by his political opponents that he sprayed himself with Cologne water and cinched himself up in corsets.

He was called the "Red Fox of Kinderhook," for his red hair

and political cunning, and the "Little Magician," for his size and sagacity. He had been a U.S. senator, and in 1828 he was elected governor of New York, an office he resigned within three months of his election to become Jackson's secretary of state and finally his vice president and then president.[4]

So those were the two men from the two parties—Van Buren the political sage and Harrison the military hero—who on the eve of the canvass in late 1839, looked to be the two certain contenders.

Lincoln was playing a lead role in organizing the Whig campaign in Illinois. He was a rising star in the state, more and more frequently called on as a party spokesman. He was part of the so-called Springfield Junto, an inner circle of Whigs in the new capital who were dictating party strategy and waging war against the Democrats in the newspapers.[5]

Lincoln had been denouncing Democrats in Whig newspapers—particularly in the *Sangamo Journal*—since as early as 1834–35, his first term in the legislature—under pseudonyms. Reasonable, fair, and honorable in his public persona, he could dish out anonymous partisan, abusive, and reckless ridicule in the newspapers with the best of them.[6]

As Lincoln was rallying the Whigs for the campaign and hurling his anonymous invectives, Stephen Douglas was dedicating himself to rallying the state's Democrats behind Van Buren. In early October the first Whig convention in the state met. Lincoln was not a delegate, but he was one of its instigators and leaders. Committees were elected and enthusiasm kindled for Harrison as the party's choice for president. The next day the convention chose Lincoln as one of the party's five presidential electors. With four others, he was also named to the state central committee. The *Illinois State Register* reported sardonically that these five were appointed exclusively for "their supposed *stumping* abilities."[7]

That was the situation one evening in November 1839, when the usual habitués were gathered around Speed's fireplace. The discussion between Lincoln and Douglas veered off into politics and waxed unusually warm—hot and angry, according to Speed. Douglas sprang to his feet—not a long jump given his stature— and threw down the gauntlet. "Gentlemen," he said, "this is no place to talk politics; we will discuss the questions publicly with you."[8] The Whigs, led by Lincoln, snatched up the challenge.

This public political "tournament"[9] opened on November 19 in the Second Presbyterian Church, where the House of Representatives was to meet when the legislature convened in early December; the new capitol was still under construction. Whig and Democratic speakers alternated. On the first day of the debate Douglas was sandwiched between two Whigs: Cyrus Walker, who opened the debate, and Lincoln, who closed it in the evening.[10]

Lincoln was in top form that first night. The *Illinois State Register,* which rarely had anything good to say about him, called his argument "truly ingenious." However, the paper detected "a sort of assumed *clownishness* in his manner," which is "assumed for effect" and "does not truly belong to him." The next night Douglas discussed the national bank and Lincoln replied, but with less ingenuity and to sharply less effect. The *Register* wrote, "The Mr. Lincoln of Wednesday night, was not the Mr. Lincoln of Tuesday. He could only meet the arguments of Mr. Douglass by relating stale anecdotes and old stories, and left the stump literally whipped off of it, even in the estimation of his own friends." He "got *used up* on the occasion," the paper said.[11]

Lincoln also knew he had got used up. His friend Joseph

Gillespie later recalled that Lincoln "was conscious of his failure and I never saw any man so much distressed."[12]

On November 23 two other powerful speakers took the platform—Edward Baker for the Whigs and John Calhoun, Lincoln's surveyor boss in New Salem, for the Democrats. Baker, one of Lincoln's closest political and personal friends, was considered one of the best stump speakers in the state. Lincoln viewed him as "a good man to raise a breeze."[13] Calhoun was hardly less of a breeze raiser. He was a polite, straightforward, intellectual, self-possessed, cultivated, speaker—"a strong, very strong, and clear-headed man." Educated for the law, Calhoun preferred to teach school. He was a hard hand in debate, and Lincoln respected him, believing he gave him more trouble than Douglas did, because Calhoun was "more captivating in his manner" and "more learned."[14]

On December 10, Democrats meeting in a statewide convention passed various resolutions denouncing Whig individuals, their policy, and their party in general. The Whigs met immediately the next day in Springfield and this time they threw down the gauntlet. In a set of resolutions written by Lincoln they challenged the Democrats to another round of debates, "man for man, and speech for speech, in order that the public may see with whom are the facts, and with whom the arguments."[15]

This new contest opened on December 18 and centered on fiscal policy. Lincoln opened with a speech lambasting the Van Buren administration. Douglas replied for the Democrats. Lincoln then closed this series of debates on December 26 with a slashing attack on Van Buren's sub-treasury scheme. Being the day after Christmas it played to a meager turnout, which embarrassed Lincoln and cast "a damp upon my spirits." But the speech he then delivered lacked nothing in spirit. He intended it as a vindication of his poor showing in his second speech in the debates in November. In arguments tightly reasoned and hard-hitting this time, he excoriated the sub-treasury.

In the first of these speeches, he had called it "a scheme of fraud and corruption." He hit it in this second delivery in detail. He described it as a scheme to remove federal government money from banks, lock it "up in idleness," and leave it "rusting in iron boxes" until needed. He decried it as the worst possible thing to do with the government's money—hurtful to the people, more expensive, and less secure.[16]

Lincoln ended his long oration with a fierce jab at the Van Buren administration, calling it "the great volcano at Washington, aroused and directed by the evil spirit that reigns there," a volcano "belching forth the lava of political corruption, in a current broad and deep, which is sweeping with frightful velocity over the whole length and breadth of the land, bidding fair to leave unscathed no green spot or living thing, while on its bosom are riding like demons on the waves of Hell, the imps of that evil spirit."[17]

Joseph Gillespie, one of the relatively few who showed up and who had seen Lincoln's distress over the November failure, said of this recovery, "He transcended our highest expectations. I never heard & never expect to hear such a triumphant vindication as he gave of Whig measures or policy."[18]

When the old year ended and the new election year dawned, the Whigs nationally had their candidate, William Henry Harrison, locked in place. Whig leaders had met in Harrisburg, Pennsylvania, on December 10, passed over Henry Clay, who yearned for the nomination, and picked Harrison—and for his vice-presidential running mate picked Clay's friend John Tyler of Virginia, to mollify those who had wanted their man nominated. So it was to be "Tippecanoe and Tyler, too," or for brevity's sake, "Tip and Ty," against the "Little Magician" and his vice president, Richard M. Johnson of Kentucky. However, as unable in 1839 as they had been in 1836 to hit on a common political ideology, no platform was even proposed.[19] It was going to be a campaign short on issues and long on ballyhoo, gimmicks, slogans, songs, and noise.

The Whigs were desperate to win. They saw the twelve-year rule of Jackson and Van Buren as stifling and oppressive, intolerable in the extreme. They had not yet elected a president in their party's young lifetime, and this was their chance. It was to be a frenzied drive to win at all costs. And as desperation often births innovation, that too would come.

The most compelling slogan for the campaign fell into their lap, an inadvertent gift from the enemy. A Democratic newspaper in Baltimore sardonically suggested that Harrison be given "a barrel of hard cider and a pension of two thousand a year, and, our word for it, he will sit the remainder of his days in a log cabin by the side of a 'sea coal' fire and study moral philosophy." A Whig in Harrisburg knew the makings of a campaign slogan when he heard one. He pulled together the phrases "log cabin" and "hard cider"—two of America's iconic frontier staples—and shaped a campaign slogan for the ages.[20]

Their man Harrison would become "the log cabin, hard cider" candidate, the frontier everyman, the man of the people—like Jackson had been—against the aristocratic, corseted, champagne-sipping, foppish president living in splendor in the sumptuously bedecked White House. That was the contrasting picture the Whigs began to paint with an enthusiasm unmatched by anything anybody had ever seen in the past—and which the Democrats denounced as an "Omnibus of Lies."[21]

One Whig, Albert Bledsoe, later described the political pandemonium. "One who witnessed the Presidential campaign of that ever memorable year," he said, "would have supposed that the whole world had run mad, and rushed into the wild contest on the sublime issues, that log cabins are the best of all buildings, hard-cider the most delicious of all drinks, and coon-skins the finest of all furs. In no age or country, perhaps, since the dawn of civilization was humbuggery exhibited in more gigantic and grotesque forms.... Reason was everywhere reeling in the storm, and madness ruled the masses."[22]

There were everywhere across the country all the madcap political fixings to go with the campaign slogan—log cabin headquarters with barrels of hard cider on tap, rallies so massive they were measured not by the numbers in attendance but by the acres those numbers filled. There were parades and processions, Whigs marching, banners snapping, and floats rolling. There were hard-cider barbeques, balloon rides, coonskin caps, log cabin speeches, log cabin newspapers, log cabin songbooks to sing along with, and log cabin quadrilles to dance to. There were Tippecanoe handkerchiefs, badges, and placards. Unlike the Democrats, the Whigs invited women into the campaign in great numbers—apt partners for the log cabin quadrilles—and they were pitching in with enthusiasm. Whig ladies were ever-present, riding on floats, decorating rallies, and adding a bird-like soprano to the deeper Whig baritone being raised in song—adding an entirely new dimension to the political canvass.[23]

There were many other gimmicks new to campaigning—great tin balls being rolled from city to city, metaphors for keeping the ball "a-rolling on for Tippecanoe and Tyler too." There were new campaign catch-phrases never before heard that would enter forever into the American vocabulary: "Keep the ball rolling"; "booz," for liquor, after E. G. Booz, the distiller in Philadelphia who supplied hard-cider for the Whig campaign— in log cabin-shaped bottles; and "O.K.," an abbreviation for Old Kinderhook, Van Buren's nickname.[24]

"Never," Hezakiah Wead, an Illinois Democrat, confessed, "had there been excited, such active exertions and endless plans devised.... Poetry was forced to lend its aid... and many songs whose spirit and pathos were worthy a better cause were composed and sung by the multitude."[25]

They sang:

Farewell, dear Van,
You're not our man:
To guide the ship,
We'll try old Tip.[26]

The most telling innovation of this innovative madcap campaign was the emergence of an entirely new breed of political bosses—spin doctors in today's political lexicon—who would invent a packaged candidate whom they could promote with a catchy slogan and a campaign unencumbered by issues. Harrison was the perfect vehicle for this never-before-seen kind of politics. He had a scant national political past to attack, and best of all he could be pictured as a simple backwoods soldier-farmer living in his little log cabin (it was actually a mansion with sixteen rooms on 2,000 acres of land), sipping hard cider (Harrison was not a heavy drinker), rough-edged and uncultured (Harrison was an avid student of the classics and history), un-aristocratic (Harrison had a far more aristocratic genealogy than Van Buren), a hero-general, and a man of the people.[27]

Harrison's managers, chief among them the canny New York editor and backroom operator Thurlow Weed, painted Van Buren in equally fictitious colors. They portrayed him as a lavish-living, splendor-loving dandy in a palatial White House, who perfumed his whiskers, dined at tables set with golden spoons, drank champagne—not hard-cider—from crystal goblets, admired his corseted figure daily in nine-foot-tall mirrors, and rode about Washington in his olive-green carriage attended by liveried footmen and drawn by spirited horses in silver-mounted harness.[28]

Some of the very weapons Democrats wielded for Jackson when he was elected for the first time in 1828 were being turned against the Democrats by the Whigs for Harrison in 1840—two hero-generals, men of the frontier, matched against aristocratic, embedded Eastern privilege.

The campaign thrilled Lincoln. "Mr. Lincoln," Albert Bledsoe testified, "was merry. He entered into the very soul of the contest with a glee which seemed perfectly assured of 'the glad success.' Hence, when we ventured to express our intense mortification that the Whig Party, which had claimed a monopoly of all the intelligence and decency of the country, should descend to the use of such means, Mr. Lincoln replied: 'It is all right; *we must fight the devil with fire; we must beat the Democrats, or the country will be ruined.*'"[29]

Lincoln's speechmaking matched his glee. He was on a roll, stumping with enthusiasm in January without manuscript or notes. Joshua Speed said of him, "He could grasp, exhaust, and quit any subject with more facility than any man I have ever seen or heard of," with "a wonderful faculty" of picking up after an interruption exactly where he left off.[30] Elizabeth Allen Bradner remembered her father, James Allen, who had served with Lincoln in the legislature, saying that Lincoln "could see through a question quicker than any one with whom he had previously had dealings."[31]

Lincoln was arming himself with all the ammunition he could scare up. On January 20 he wrote Stuart in Washington: "Be sure to send me as many copies of the life of Harrison, as you can spare.... And, in general, send me every thing you think will be a good '*war club*.'" Generally "never sanguine" about political outcomes, he was sanguine about this one. He told Stuart he believed they could carry the state for Harrison.[32]

His intention, he wrote later in a campaign circular, was "to organize the whole State, so that every Whig can be brought to the polls" on election day. The circular, to leading Whigs in the state, was intended to rally support for Harrison and marshal the party for the race. It was decried immediately by the *Illinois State Register* as a "secret circular." "They [the Whigs] prefer darkness to light," sniped the *Register,* "because their deeds are evil."[33]

By early March, Lincoln's optimism was soaring. He wrote Stuart on March 1, "I have never seen the prospects of our party so bright in these parts as they are now." He predicted a huge success in the county. But tempers were fraying. The day before, Lincoln told Stuart, Douglas tried to cane *Sangamo Journal* editor Simeon Francis on the street in Springfield. Francis, a strapping six-footer—caught Douglas by the hair and jammed him against a market cart.[34]

In early April the *Register* was calling Lincoln "the lion of the tribe of Sangamon ... and judging from outward appearance, originally from Liberia."[35] As often as not the lion of the tribe of Sangamon was going head-to-head on the stump with the lion of the Democracy. Lincoln and Douglas, being lawyers as well as politicians and having to make a living, were traveling the spring judicial circuit together, sometimes opposing, sometimes on the same side of court cases, but always on opposing sides in politics. They were hybrid specimens, lawyers who were "half legal, half political"—and unrelentingly partisan.[36]

By the end of May the *Quincy Whig* was writing, "Mr. Lincoln, one of the presidential electors for the state, is 'going it with a perfect rush' in some of the interior counties. Thus far the Locofocos have not been able to start a man that can hold a candle to him in political debate. All their crack nags . . . have come off the field crippled or broken down. He is wending his way north."[37]

When Whigs wanted to insult Democrats, which was most of the time, they called them "Locofocos." Like the Harrison slogan, "log cabin and hard-cider," this epithet was donated to the Whigs by the Democrats themselves. It stemmed from a contentious meeting of Democrats in Tammany Hall in New York City in 1836. An insurgent radical offshoot of the Democracy calling itself the Equal Rights Party, fighting against monopoly and vested interest, had seized control of the meeting. To end the discussion, the party regulars turned off the gaslights in the hall. The dissidents struck up odorous sulfur friction matches called "loco focos," lit candles with them, and continued the meeting. Whigs ever since had called all Democrats—radical or regular—Locofocos, as uniformly odious as the matches the radicals among them had lit.[38]

On June 3, a Young Men's Whig convention drew multitudes of clamorous partisans to Springfield from all over Illinois. It was thought that a spectator viewing it "might well have supposed that the whole sucker state had broken loose." They swarmed into town in long lines of carriages and wagons, on horseback, on foot, in canoes, pulling log cabins on wheels with carts drawn by oxen, waving banners, gyrating to music, and belting campaign songs, all of it lubricated by hard cider. This monumental host—an estimated forty to fifty thousand strong—covered multiple acres. The crowd was treated to a gigantic parade, barbeque, and an afternoon and evening of speechmaking. Lincoln was there, standing in a wagon making the principal speech. It was like so many Whig rallies going on all over the country—as fervent, emotional, and raucous as a religious camp meeting, but praising Harrison instead of God.[39]

They sang:

Let Frenchmen drink claret and sweet muscadine,
And Germans drink hock on the banks of the Rhine;
But give me to quaff, with friends warm and true,
A gourd of hard cider to old Tippecanoe.

In the White House Van Buren may drink his champagne
And have himself toasted from Georgia to Maine—
But we in log-cabins, with hearts warm and true
Drink a gourd of hard cider to old Tippecanoe.[40]

In something of an afterthought to this raucous campaign, Lincoln was also running for reelection to the legislature. He was campaigning for the office on the side in his regular style, winning votes with arm strength. "See here Lincoln," said the boys at a store in the county west of Springfield, old acquaintances, but all Democrats, "if you can throw this Cannonball further than we Can, We'll vote for you." Lincoln picked up the cannonball, felt it, hefted it, swung it around and around, and said, "Well, boys if that's all I have to do I'll get your votes." He swung it again and let fly—some four to six feet farther than any of the boys could.[41]

He was also winning votes with jokes. One friend remembers him sitting up all night at Bennett's Tavern in Menard County vying with some of the boys in telling stories.[42] He generally threw those farther as well, for on election day for state offices on August 3 he was comfortably reelected. Notwithstanding his individual victory, the Democrats carried both houses of the legislature—not a good omen for the general election to come.

In mid-August Lincoln headed into the southern end of the state with several other Whigs, into heavily Democratic Little Egypt—" missionaries" to "that benighted region," as the *Register* described them and it."[43]

Whether Harrison carried Illinois or not, Lincoln was making a name for himself. Even his enemies thought so. A Democratic reporter covering his speech in Mount Vernon assessed Lincoln in the *Illinois State Register.* He wrote that Lincoln was "listened to with attention; possessing *much* urbanity and suavity of manner, he is well calculated for a public debater; as he seldom loses his temper, and always replies jocosely and in good humor—the evident marks of disapprobation which greet many of his assertions, do not discompose him, and he is therefore hard to foil."[44]

By general election day, November 2, Lincoln had devoted three months of time to the seven-month-long campaign. As an elector, he had been responsible for campaigning not only in central Illinois, but throughout the state, including the long trip into the "benighted region" of southern Illinois, and across the Wabash. Often he had traveled with Democratic opponents, particularly Douglas, who had devoted even more time and energy to it. Douglas had stumped for seven tireless months and addressed more than 200 different political meetings. People were now generally calling him "The Little Giant" and meaning it.[45]

There were no railroads and few stage lines where they stumped. So they had traveled from town to town by horseback, often together, over long distances, across prairies and swamps, "carrying their saddle-bags filled wih 'hickory' shirts and woolen socks"—and sleeping in generally wretched accommodations. It had been, the Illinois Whig Elihu B. Washburne said, "by far the most exciting election the country has ever seen, and which, in my judgment will never have a parallel, should the country have an existence for a thousand years."[46]

It was looking good for the Whigs. The economy, already deep into its fifth locust year, took another downward turn as election day approached. It didn't appear that the Little Magician had tricks enough to pull this one out of the hat, or the hatbox he carried it in.

Lincoln was still on the road campaigning on election day, unable to vote for Harrison, whom he had tirelessly stumped for all year. Harrison was elected president without his vote, edging Van Buren in the popular count nationwide, 1,275,016 to 1,129,102, and winning in the electoral college by a landslide, losing only 60 of the 294 electoral votes. "The Goths have taken Rome," moaned the editor of the Democratic *Richmond Enquirer.*[47]

But it was a bittersweet outcome for Lincoln, for Harrison lost Illinois, one of only seven states that he failed to carry. The Little Magician, while losing his own state of New York, carried Illinois, and Douglas "was recognized and applauded as the most conspicuous of the many heroes of that contest."[48] After all the challenging, all the debating, all of the hard traveling and stumping together, he had trumped Lincoln.

The voter turnout in the country had been massive, the heaviest for a presidential election in the country's history. More than eight of every ten eligible voters cast ballots—drawn to the polls by the general hullabaloo of the campaign. In the end Van Buren had almost literally been "sung and drunk" out of the White House while Harrison was sung and drunk into it. "Old Kinderhook," just didn't have the same vote-raising ring to it as "Old Tippecanoe."[49]

Early in February 1841, Old Tippecanoe entered Washington on a train, the first president-elect ever to arrive that way—and in a snowstorm. In early March he rode to his inauguration to become the young republic's ninth president in a bitter north wind on a white charger. He wore no overcoat or gloves and carried his hat in his hand, in part to show his 68-year-old frontier vigor, warmed by the acclaim of several acres of cheering spectators— a throng estimated at 50,000. It was the biggest turnout to witness a presidential inauguration since George Washington's half a century before. Harrison repaid them with an interminable inaugural address of 8,445 words, nearly a tenth as many words as there were spectators—one hour and forty minutes of words— the longest inaugural speech yet in the young republic's short half century.[50]

Washington, far shorter on words, was far longer in office. The Father of the Country spent eight years in the presidency. Harrison would spend one month, eight days of it in bed dying, having fallen ill only days after his inauguration. He had been the oldest president elected to the office, the last born as a British subject, the first Whig to hold it, and the first man to die in it. He served only from March 4 to April 4. And then Tyler, too, became president—the nation's tenth.[51]

The ballyhoo had ended on a down note.

10

Lincoln in Love

WHEN HARRISON DIED in April 1841, Lincoln had just turned thirty-three. Seasoned now in politics and the law, he was still highly unseasoned in a discipline most men of his age and station had either chosen or succumbed to—marriage.

So handy on the stump with a line of political reasoning or invective, or with the boys around the fireplace with a joke or a story, or in a field winning votes with his strong arm, axe, and harvesting skills, or in a court of law before a jury, he was not that handy with women.

He had never been particularly drawn to those creatures in their hoop gowns and their tight lacing. ("How many of the female race," one of its long-suffering members moaned, "have been sent to their eternal homes...on the account of lacing.")[1] His cousin John Hanks had early noticed Lincoln's evasion of females. "I never could get him in company with women," Hanks confessed. It didn't seem to Hanks that Lincoln was timid, just that he lacked interest.[2]

"He didn't go to see the girls much," a friend, James Short, said of him. "He didn't appear bashful, but it seemed as if he cared but little for them. Wasn't apt to take liberties with them." At social events he "would just as lieve [leave] the company were all men as to have it a mixture of the sexes." In his storekeeping days in New Salem, another friend, Abner Y. Ellis, noticed that he "allways disliked to wait on the Ladies[;] he preferred trading with the Men & Boys.... a Verry shy Man of Ladies."[3]

Mrs. Ninian Edwards, doyenne of Springfield society on aristocrat hill, had her own theory about Lincoln and love. Lincoln, she believed, "was a cold Man—had no affection—was not Social—was abstracted—thoughtful.... Could not hold a lengthy Conversation with a lady—was not sufficiently Educated & intelligent in the female line to do so."[4]

But then he hadn't had much practice, and what practice he did have had generally backfired. Nor did he enter into the gender chase with confidence. After moving to Springfield, acclaimed as one of the Long Nine, he said, "If any woman, old or young, ever thought there was any peculiar charm in this distinguished specimen of number 9, I have, as yet, been so unfortunate as not to have discovered it."[5] One writer, in a fit of hyperbole, suggested that Lincoln was simply "too ugly to suit the Girls... homely enough to stop an eight-day wooden-wheel clock, and cows refused to give down their milk when he was around."[6]

It is said, however, that he fell in love in New Salem with Ann Rutledge, the daughter of one of the founders of the town and its tavern-keeper, where Lincoln came to board in 1833 after the Black Hawk War.

One who had seen Ann "a thousand times" said she was not hard to look at, blue-eyed, fair-skinned, and sandy-haired. She was slender, quick—somewhat nervous—kind, social, and good-hearted. A younger sister remembered that "every one said she was pretty." She was of ordinary height, straight-standing, and weighed about 120 pounds. She was the third of James Rutledge's nine children, but the oldest girl and, like Lincoln, was born in Kentucky, in 1813—the same year as Stephen A. Douglas.[7]

Lincoln wasn't Ann's first love. John McNamar, a New York emigrant to New Salem, had earlier won her heart and hand. But when he returned east to visit his parents and she didn't hear from him for three years, Lincoln paid his addresses to her and they became conditionally engaged. Their developing courtship in 1835 was accompanied by an unprecedented blast of heat. That spring and summer were believed to be "the hottest ever known in Illinois." Through March to the middle of July, it rained nearly every day, covering the state with water. Searing heat followed the rain and lasted until sometime in August, and on about the 10th of that month people began getting sick and dying. They called it "brain fever." It was probably typhoid.[8] Ann came down with it.

In late August she was ill and singing her favorite hymn to Lincoln: "Vain, man, the fond pursuits forebear." It was perhaps the last thing she ever sang before she died on August 25.[9]

Lincoln was reportedly devastated. But by 1836, he was trying to raise a phoenix from the ashes of that tragic first love. This time it was with Mary Owens, a visitor to New Salem from Kentucky. She was ten years older than Ann. New Salem's schoolmaster, Mentor Graham, her cousin, described her as black-haired, roundish in both features and figure—far shorter than Lincoln but as heavy (Lincoln later described her as a fair

match for Falstaff). She was good-natured, intellectual, well educated, well-raised, well-off, jovial, and lively. One of Lincoln's
friends testified that she had "large blue eyes with the finest
trimings I ever saw." One who had known both Ann and Mary
believed Ann to be beautiful and Mary handsome.[10]

It was a mismatch from the start. Mary believed Lincoln had
"a heart full of human kindness and a head full of Common
sense" and a "fine intellect." He was "energetic and aspiring,"
and she believed he would likely rise far above his then humble
and modest position in the world. But his training had been different from hers, hence she believed "there was not that conge-
niality which would have otherwise existed." She found him
"deficient in those little links which make up the great chain of
womans happiness, at least it was so in my case." She believed,
from his own showing, that "his heart and hand were at my dis-
posal," but her feelings were "not sufficiently enlisted to have
the matter consumated."[11]

So by the end of summer 1837, the courtship had foundered.
Lincoln figured he was probably well "out of the 'scrape.'" "I
can never be satisfied," he wrote a friend, "with any one who
would be block-head enough to have me."[12]

By 1840 he was in yet another scrape—with yet another
Mary.

The story of this new one began, like everything else with
Lincoln, in Kentucky. However, it began on a much higher social
level, with the merger of two of the bluegrass state's distinguished aristocratic lines—the Todds and the Edwardses.

Ninian Edwards was a prominent attorney and chief justice
of the Court of Appeals in Kentucky when he was called to the
new territory of Illinois as its first governor. Some years later Ed-

wards, who was still governor, died of cholera. The new governor called Ninian's son, also named Ninian, to be his attorney general. The young Ninian and his new bride, Elizabeth, the eldest of several daughters of the prominent Lexington Todds, moved to Vandalia, the new state capital.

Two other Todds—John Todd Stuart, a lawyer and Elizabeth's cousin, and John Todd, a physician, her uncle—had earlier moved from Kentucky to Springfield, where they had set up the Todd line as the aristocracy of the town. Ninian soon resigned his office in Vandalia and followed them to Springfield, where he became, like Stuart, one of the town's leading lawyers.

Ninian and Elizabeth settled into their celebrated home on aristocrat hill, where anybody who was anybody gravitated. Among them was a round of Elizabeth's sisters from Lexington, sent by their parents, one by one, to board with the Edwardses with the idea of fitting into Illinois society and being fitted out in good marriages.

The first sister to come was Frances, who boarded with the Edwardses for a time and was introduced to Springfield society, where she met and married William Wallace, a young physician from Pennsylvania. The newly married couple moved into the Globe Tavern, a Springfield boarding house, which opened up the bedroom in the Edwards home for the next Todd daughter in line, the one named Mary. She came to Springfield for an extended visit first, to get the lay of the land, and then in 1839 moved in with the Edwardses.[13]

By then Lincoln had been two years in Springfield, living above Speed's store and boarding at the home of William Butler. There was an unbalanced man-to-woman ratio in frontier society. In Springfield there were two to three prospective grooms for every woman about Lincoln's age. This made for limited opportunities for courtship and marriage, and for intense competition among eligible bachelors. But it was ideal for young women looking to snag husbands.[14]

As John Todd Stuart's law partner, Lincoln was welcome on aristocrat hill, and he and Speed went often to the fashionable Saturday soirees in the Edwards home, where young men who qualified socially went to meet young women equally blessed. There Lincoln met Mary.[15]

Her nickname was "Molly." She had soft brown hair and alluring, clear blue eyes. She was charming—a flirt—and Lincoln was fascinated by her wit and her quick sagacity, her culture— she spoke fluent French—and her frank, spirited, candid nature. But they were otherwise polar opposites—so basically polar that Elizabeth did not remotely believe them suitable for one another, and said so to Mary.

Mary was lively and gay—shading toward the frivolous, very social, loving glitter, show, partying, and pomp. She was a skilled seamstress. Her sister Frances thought her "one of the best... I ever knew." She picked the fabric and colors herself—usually eye-smashingly rich and bright—and stitched all of her clothes by hand, all with a sense of high style. She accented what she wore with flowers in her hair. It has been said that she lived "in a cloud of beautiful colors."[16]

"She was exceedingly sensitive," one acquaintance wrote. "Her impulsiveness of thought and speech had no need of restraint, because her face was always an unerring index of her passing emotions, even if she had not expressed them in words." She thought quickly and uttered what she thought at a machine-gun rate. She was extremely ambitious, a trait which, unlike most of her other traits, she shared with Lincoln. It was said that in Kentucky she had often contended that she was destined to marry some future president—"Said it in my presence in Springfield," Elizabeth said, "and Said it in Earnest."[17]

Other ties that might have bound the two were a shared love of poetry, and of politics, power, and party affiliation—Mary at the age of fourteen was seen as "a violent little Whig," whose "dear friend" was Lexington's great Whig of Whigs, Henry Clay.[18]

Elizabeth wasn't the only friend of Lincoln's who believed the two were wholly unsuited to one another. William Herndon, who first met her at a dance, believed that in her physical proportions and figure—short and plump while Lincoln was tall and angular—in education, bearing, temperament, and background she was Lincoln's exact opposite.

So what did Mary see in Lincoln? She apparently saw much, for she was interested, even though she probably believed, as Mary Owens did, that he was deficient in some of the little links important to a woman. Dancing was one—Mary was a stepper. ("What Lincoln dance?" Herndon exclaimed when it was suggested Lincoln might have tried it. "Could a sparrow imitate an eagle?" Mary testified that he had tried it—on her. "Miss Todd," he said to her, "I want to dance with you the worst way." And, she later said, "He certainly did.") Not enamored with Mary and a cynic in the matter, Herndon believed she saw in Lincoln "position in society, prominence in the world, and the grandest social distinction," perhaps even the future president she had predicted she would marry.[19]

Despite their reputation of unsuitability for one another, Lincoln took a matrimonial interest in Mary. He wasn't, of course, the only one. His rival in politics, Stephen A. Douglas, was said to be captivated by her as well. Though on the other end of the political spectrum from the Whiggish Edwardses, the affable Douglas was a welcome and frequent visitor to their home and social set. He and Mary were often seen together walking in the town or visiting in the Edwards home. Mary later was to say, "I liked him well enough, but that was all."[20]

Lincoln's courtship of Mary coincided with the heavy presidential campaigning in 1840. He opened the courtship seriously by correspondence from the stump, writing to her during his swing into southern Illinois beginning in late August. Mary was more than willing and responsive. When he returned to Springfield in late September they had an understanding. Within a few days, Lincoln left again, this time not just for political stumping, but for the court circuit, and was gone until several days after the election. Soon after returning this second time, Lincoln was having agonizing second thoughts.[21]

A few things had changed. Mary seemed somewhat different to him than she had earlier in the year—less attractive. She had put on weight. Moreover, a striking new face and form had presented itself in Ninian Edwards's eighteen-year-old niece, Matilda, who had arrived in mid-November, only a few days after Lincoln's return to Springfield. Matilda had joined Mary at the Edwards home for the coming legislative and social season.[22]

Lincoln began to believe his commitment to Mary was a serious mistake. He told Joshua Speed that he was not "entirely satisfied that his *heart* was going with his hand," and that he intended to write her and break it off. It had all begun by correspondence. He would end it that way.[23]

Speed told Lincoln ending it with a letter would be bad practice and cowardly. In late November or early December, Lincoln confronted Mary with his feelings. She reproached herself and wept, at which point the tender-hearted and nonplussed Lincoln comforted and kissed her, a gesture Speed considered a "bad lick." Mary soon suspected that Lincoln had eyes for Matilda— a feeling not necessarily requited by Matilda herself—so she wrote Lincoln that she knew how things stood and released him from his commitment to her. However, the Edwardses believed that she left the matter open-ended, "leaving Lincoln the privilege of renewing it... if he wished," since "she had not Changed her mind, but felt as always."[24]

The Edwardses tried to convince Mary and Lincoln that it was all for the best, "that they had better not Ever marry—that their natures, mind—Education—raising"—all of it—"were So different they Could not live happy as husband & wife" and "had better never think of the Subject again."[25]

Not to think of it proved impossible for Lincoln. And the thinking was making him miserable. He went into a deep funk, which Speed described as a "crazy spell." Others agreed with that assessment. Ninian Edwards thought Lincoln "went as Crazy as a *Loon.*" Martinette Hardin, a friend about to be married herself, called Lincoln's spell "two Cat fits, and a Duck fit." Some feared he might be contemplating suicide.[26]

Lincoln wrote a letter to Stuart in Washington in late January 1841. "I have, within the last few days, been making a most discreditable exhibition of myself in the way of hypochondriaism," he wrote. Three days later he wrote him again about "the deplorable state of my mind at this time." It was a letter oozing the deepest melancholy. "I am now the most miserable man living," he wrote. "If what I feel were equally distributed to the whole human family, there would not be one cheerful face on the earth.... To remain as I am is impossible; I must die or be better, it appears to me."[27]

His friend Orville Browning explained it this way: "I think that Mr. Lincoln's aberration of mind resulted entirely from the situation he thus got himself into—he was engaged to Miss Todd, and in love with Miss Edwards, and his conscience troubled him dreadfully for the supposed injustice he had done, and the supposed violation of his word which he had committed."[28]

More than a year later, Lincoln's conscience still bothered him. In late March 1842 he wrote Speed, who had sold his store in Springfield and returned to Kentucky in January 1841, that he was haunted still by "the never-absent idea, that there is *one* still unhappy whom I have contributed to make so. That still kills my soul."[29]

With Lincoln it was a matter of personal honor and integrity. They were tainted by the Mary affair and they had to be cleansed. "Before I resolve to do the one thing or the other," he wrote Speed in early July, "I must regain my confidence in my own ability to keep my resolves when they are made. In that ability, you know, I once prided myself as the only, or at least the chief, gem of my character; that gem I lost—how and when, you too well know. I have not yet regained it; and until I do, I can not trust myself in any matter of much importance."[30] He believed that if he was to restore his self-respect and continue rising in politics he had to do something.[31]

At this point Mrs. Simeon Francis, wife of the editor of the *Sangamo Journal,* intervened. Mrs. Francis was seen as "a very shrewd and sagacious lady—one who was capable of achieving success anywhere in the ranks of diplomacy." She was a leader in

Springfield society and a warm friend of Mary Todd. She didn't necessarily agree with the Edwardses that Mary and Lincoln were unsuited for one another. She arranged a gathering at her house in the fall of 1842 for the precise purpose of getting the two back together. Both were invited, neither suspecting the other's presence. At the affair Mrs. Francis, using her gift of diplomacy, brought them together and told them, "Be friends again." Not only that, she lent her home as a haven for successive meetings.[32]

By November Lincoln was feeling honor bound to commit himself again to Mary, the sooner the better. "Jim," he told his friend, James H. Matheny, on November 4, "I shall have to marry that girl."[33]

On that same day a license was had, the Episcopalian minister, Charles N. Dresser, was summoned, and the couple was married. The ceremony took place in the Edwards home at seven in the evening, before the old fireplace by the light of astral lamps lit by sperm-whale oil. Only a handful of hastily summoned friends were present, including Matheny, Lincoln's best man, and Julia Jayne, Mary's bridesmaid. So telescoped in time was all of this—only hours after it was announced—that the wedding cake Mrs. Edwards had baked was still warm when it was cut.[34]

Mary moved out of the Edwards house, Lincoln out of his room at William Butler's, and the newlyweds took up residence in an eight-by-fourteen-foot room in the Globe Tavern. The plain two-story wooden frame structure had an ell extension, which also served as the office for several of the stage lines running through Springfield. Situated just a few rods from the new statehouse, it was a Whig hangout in the legislative session and a polling place on election days. It was run by Sarah Beck, a widow, and cost the Lincolns $8 a week for room and board, with the washing thrown in.[35]

Lincoln had redeemed his honor, but even he could hardly believe what he had done. On November 11, he wrote a lawyer friend, Samuel D. Marshall in Shawneetown: "Nothing new here, except my marrying, which to me is a matter of profound wonder."[36]

PART FIVE

On the National Stage

11

The Steam Engine
in Breeches and the Engine
that Knew No Rest

IN AUGUST 1841 when the summer term of the Sangamon Circuit Court wrapped up, Lincoln left Springfield to visit Joshua Speed in Kentucky. It had been a half-year or so of personal and professional change. Not only had Lincoln's courtship with Mary Todd taken off and crashed, but in April he had ended his partnership with John Stuart to become the junior partner of another eminent Springfield attorney, Stephen T. Logan. Lincoln was still wrestling with his conscience over the Mary "embrigglement,"[1] and the month he spent on the Speed family plantation near Louisville was a happy respite.

On September 7, with "savoury remembrances" of peaches and cream served up by Speed's half-sister, Mary,[2] he and Speed caught the steamboat *Lebanon* in Louisville, bound for St. Louis. Speed was returning to Illinois with Lincoln to be in Springfield until the year's end.

On the *Lebanon* Lincoln came into abrupt face-to-face contact with slavery, which served up far less savory remembrances for him. A fellow passenger had purchased twelve slaves in Kentucky and was taking them to a farm in the South. The blacks were linked six and six by small iron clevises on their left wrists fastened to a main chain—"strung together," Lincoln thought, "precisely like so many fish upon a trot-line." In a letter to Mary Speed from Springfield, Lincoln wrote: "In this condition they were being separated forever from the scenes of their childhood, their friends, their fathers and mothers, and brothers and sisters, and many of them from their wives and children, and going into perpetual slavery where the lash of the master is proverbially more ruthless and unrelenting than any other where."

Yet, Lincoln wrote Mary, "amid all these distressing circumstances, as we would think them, they were the most cheerful and apparently happy creatures on board." He wrote of one, "whose offence for which he had been sold was an over-fondness for his wife, played the fiddle almost continually; and the others danced, sung, cracked jokes, and played various games with cards from day to day." How true it is, Lincoln wrote, "that 'God tempers the wind to the shorn lamb,' so in other words, that He renders the worst of human conditions tolerable, while He permits the best, to be nothing better than tolerable."[3]

A few months later, on February 12, 1842, on his thirty-third birthday, Lincoln delivered a speech in Springfield on temperance—a movement, like abolition, that was agitating the public mind. He was perhaps thinking of that trotline of slaves, so strung together and so unstrung from everything they treasured. "Happy day," Lincoln said in his speech, "when, all appetites controled, all passions subdued, all matters subjected, *mind,* all conquering *mind,* shall live and move the monarch of the world. . . . when there shall be neither a slave nor a drunkard on the earth."[4]

In June, practicing law again but bedeviled still by his aborted love, and thinking of men in chains and men in thrall to drink, Lincoln encountered a brief diversion, from an entirely unexpected and unlikely political source. Former President Martin Van Buren, the Red Fox of Kinderhook, the Little Magician, the despised and ridiculed target of all the Whig campaigning of 1840, visited Springfield.

En route, on June 16, Van Buren reached Rochester, half a dozen miles southeast of the capital. The roads were muddy and it was evening, so he decided to stop there for the night. Word was sent ahead to Springfield, and the leading Democrats in the capital hurried down to meet him. Not prizing Lincoln for his politics, but highly prizing him for his wit and his exhaustless store of anecdotes, the Democrats took him along in the reception committee to entertain the touring ex-president. Lincoln spent the evening swapping stories with Van Buren until after midnight, when the ex-president called a halt, it is said, because his sides ached from laughter.[5]

The next day, Lincoln accompanied the Little Magician to Springfield. The Sangamon Guards, joined by the Springfield band and commanded by Lincoln's Whig friend, Edward Baker, met the party east of town. The Springfield artillery fired a salute of thirteen guns and the mayor delivered a gracious nonpartisan word of welcome at the statehouse. Van Buren delivered a gracious nonpartisan reply, and a reception followed. That evening his hosts threw a party in his honor at American House. The next day before winding up his visit, Van Buren toured the new capitol building—the house, it might be said figuratively, that Lincoln built.[6]

Partisanship was not long recovering from this nonpartisan attack. On July 13, Whigs met in Springfield to organize a "Clay Club." Henry Clay was expected to run again for president in 1844, and this time the likelihood of his nomination and election looked foregone.

Stephen Douglas, the squatty Little Giant, was flexing his outsized ambition again, running this time for the U.S. Senate. After 1840 Douglas had continued his rocketing rise in Illinois politics when he was elected to a seat on the Illinois Supreme Court in early 1841 and assigned to the Fifth Judicial Circuit. He was only twenty-seven years old when he was elevated to that high bench and only seven years removed from the year he had arrived in the state friendless, penniless, and without prospects.[7]

Watching Douglas perform on the high bench, Hezakiah Wead concluded that although he "had not then much idea of what the law was, yet he had a decided disposition to decide what he thought the law ought to be." He had then "not much of a reputation for anything," Wead believed. "He was not studious or industrious. He did not examine the cases submitted to him, with much care, he did not read law books to any extent." But he was, Wead said, "endowed with a strong mind" and "he decided all questions upon his own idea of what was just and fair.... If he did not know the law he could... 'guess' as well as anyone, and he did guess." He often "went astray wildly," Wead said, "but when convinced of his error would readily retract or change."[8]

Douglas sat on the bench in a hail-fellow, down-home, often less than dignified style. He had a habit of leaning back in his chair and elevating his feet, showing his soles to the courtroom. This so aggravated one lawyer that he said, "Your honor, I much prefer to address my argument to that end of the court in which intelligence is presumed to reside."[9]

Wead said, "After the evidence in a case had been heard & while the council were arguing to the jury," Douglas "would leave the bench, go round among the listeners & spectators, sit upon their knees and chat and laugh and joke with them."[10] Such lap sitting was not an uncommon way to conduct a conversation on the frontier,[11] but Douglas, given his size, could do it better than most. He was a consummate mixer; he couldn't help visiting. Besides, lap sitting was good politics. He "took great pains," Wead said, "to cultivate the acquaintance of every one, to shake them by the hand, to talk with them and to please them." In this way, Wead believed, "he soon became acquainted with nearly every one and secured their good opinion."[12] Lincoln often practiced in Douglas's court. It is doubtful, however, that the judge ever sat on Lincoln's tall knee or wrapped his arm around his gaunt shoulder.

There was political method in Douglas's mixing. He never intended the bench to be the final seat of his ambition. He had a political eye that wandered. And it wandered ever upward. The editor of the *Peoria Register* had him pegged when he wrote that Douglas was a man of no "ordinary ambition." A proper ambition, the editor believed, should be satisfied with present good and "not always hankering after things that be beyond." Instead, Douglas "is possessed of those reaching aspirations that are not quieted by an office which should suit a man of ordinary ambition." Another writer called him "a perfect 'steam engine in breeches.'"[13]

In 1842, while sitting on the supreme court, courting popularity on various laps, Douglas reached quite high above himself, for the United States Senate seat, even though he would still be too young when appointed to fill it. A new senator had to be named to the office by the legislature, and Douglas and a fellow colleague on the bench, Sidney Breese, were the leading candidates. Surprisingly it was a near miss for Douglas. The legislators picked Breese, but only narrowly, by just five votes—56 to 51.

Meanwhile, Illinois, still in population overdrive, had added four new congressional seats following the 1840 census, giving it seven. One of these seats, up for grabs in 1843, would be the Fifth District, where Douglas lived—in Quincy now—which roughly corresponded to his Fifth Judicial Circuit. It appeared at first that Douglas wasn't coveting the seat. He perhaps still had his eye on the Senate. Another chance at it was but three years away, and he could think of himself now as the front-runner to fill it. He never announced he was running for Congress, but that didn't seem to matter.

The Whigs had nominated Lincoln's friend Orville Browning to make the race in the Fifth District. Browning was a Quincy attorney, who also often practiced in Douglas's court. Like Lincoln, he was a transplanted Kentuckian, a formidable speaker, but given, unlike Lincoln, to sartorial elegance. Wead believed him to be a man of knowledge and learning, "a worker," who as a lawyer "examined his case closely, understood every point, and bestowed much thought and examined many authorities in every case," as Douglas didn't. But he was also "cold, distant, calm, eloquent, dignified," which Douglas wasn't.[14]

Believing Douglas was the only candidate likely to beat Browning, the Democrats nominated him, whether he wanted it or not. Douglas wanted it. He was holding court in Knoxville when he heard about his nomination and accepted instantly. When the court term ended on June 28 he resigned from the bench, after serving a little over two years, and hit the stump.

It was a hot, dry summer in a season of hot political rancor. But Douglas and Browning struck a gentleman's agreement, despite the political heat likely to be generated between them, "not to violate with each other the courtesies and proprieties of life; and not to permit any ardor or excitement of debate to betray us into coarse and unmanly personalities." This meant Douglas couldn't attempt to cane Browning, as he had Simeon Francis, or bite his thumb, as he had John Stuart's. Browning—another strapping six-footer—couldn't tote Douglas around the market place as Stuart had, or pin him against a market cart as Francis had. Agreeing to be civil, the two launched a two-month campaign, traveling together over one of the largest congressional districts in the U.S. They spoke from the same platform day after day except on Sundays, Douglas arguing against a national bank, Browning for it, Douglas against the tariff, Browning for it—all the regular Democrat-versus-Whig issues.[15]

Lincoln also coveted a seat in Congress in 1843—in the Seventh District, embracing eleven counties in central Illinois, including Sangamon. He was now married to Mary Todd. The chief gem of his character had been restored, and he was looking to continue his upward mobility in politics. William Herndon would later describe Lincoln's ambition as "a little engine that knew no rest—at least as fierce as Douglas's."[16]

By February Lincoln was writing fellow Whigs, planting the seed in whatever willing soil he could find. On February 14 he wrote Alden Hull, a legislator from Tazewell County, saying he wished to be elected to Congress and requesting his help if

Tazewell and Sangamon were put into the same congressional district—which seemed certain. That same day he wrote Richard S. Thomas, a Whig from Virginia, Illinois: "Now if you should hear any one say that Lincoln don't want to go to Congress, I wish you as a personal friend of mine, would tell him you have reason to believe he is mistaken. The truth is, I would like to go very much." He conceded that circumstances might occur to prevent his being a candidate, but "If there are any who be my friends in such an enterprise, what I now want is that they shall not throw me away just yet."[17]

Lincoln's first obstacle was a meeting of Sangamon County Whigs in the statehouse in Springfield on March 20, to name the candidate they would support at the district convention in Pekin on May 1. Lincoln couldn't clear this first hurdle. His friend Edward Baker was named instead, and Lincoln was picked as one of the eight Sangamon delegates to the district convention.

Lincoln said he felt "'fixed' a good deal like a fellow who is made groomsman to the man what has cut him out, and is marrying his own dear 'gal.'" But he dutifully fell in line. When Baker was derailed in favor of John J. Hardin at Pekin, Lincoln backed a resolution stating that the next convention would recommend Baker as its candidate.[18] He was hoping for a pattern of succession that would eventually get him into the seat. Lincoln gamely hit the stump for John Hardin, who was elected easily on election day, August 7.

Douglas was not so easily elected from the Fifth District. Both Douglas and Browning ended the campaign exhausted but still civil. It was another squeaker. Douglas won this time, but by only 461 votes of 17,069 cast.[19] However, he could now anticipate stopping in to see his mother in Canandaigua on his way to Congress in the fall—as he had promised ten years before.

Though his own hopes for high political office were dashed, at least for then, Lincoln was looming larger and larger in the politics of the state, wielding ever more clout both in politics and on the legal circuit. A political and legal aficionado who had listened to the best speakers in the state—Josiah Lamborn, Stephen T. Logan, Douglas, Stuart, and others—told his own son, "I wish I could raise a Son as big as Lincoln is bound to be if he lives[.] I have heard all [of them] speak at the bar and on the stump for some years and Lincoln is the greatest of them all. I say this to you, my son, though I am a democrat."[20]

12

"Who Is James K. Polk?"

JOHN TYLER, the "Too" who had been tacked on to "Old Tippecanoe" in the hell-for-leather campaign of 1840, and then succeeded him a month after his inaugural, had turned out wormwood and ashes for the Whigs.

They, particularly his friend Henry Clay, had expected President Tyler to be a pliant conduit for injecting Whig policies into the body politic. But Tyler began bucking the Whigs and thwarting their aspirations immediately. They did not agree on what Tyler could or couldn't do as the first vice president to succeed a dead president, and the constitution was unclear on the matter.

The Whig leadership believed that Tyler should be only an acting president, a go-between before a better Whig was elected. But Tyler believed he had succeeded to the presidency, and was therefore president, lock, stock and barrel—with all of its powers and prerogatives. Tyler was resolved that he would set a precedent that the vice president succeeding any dead, resigned, deposed, or disabled president would become president de facto as well as de jure—the whole package.

He acted on that interpretation from the moment he was told Harrison was dead. The Whigs were somewhat taken aback by this boldness and began calling him "His Accidency."[1]

Whatever Tyler thought himself to be, Clay saw him as the puppet with himself as the puppeteer. In the Senate, Clay cobbled together a Whig program for the country, which he expected Tyler to rubberstamp. The centerpiece of Clay's program was a central bank to replace Van Buren's sub-treasury system. But when his bill came to the White House to sign, Tyler vetoed it. When a revised bill was sent over, he vetoed that, too, on grounds it was unconstitutional and did not safeguard the rights of the states. A year later, when he also vetoed a tariff bill, this was too much. He was expelled from the party and Whigs in the House introduced an impeachment resolution, the first ever against a president.[2]

The heart of the problem was that Tyler really wasn't a true Whig. They knew he had been a Democrat in his prior political lifetime. Before being nominated and becoming "Tyler, too," he had bitterly opposed Jackson, then left his party, joined theirs, and pronounced himself "a firm and decided Whig."[3]

But he really wasn't. His party designation had changed, but not his basic beliefs. Whigs believed in a strong central bank; Tyler didn't. Whigs believed in a high protective tariff; he didn't. They believed in a strong federally financed internal-improvements system; he didn't. He had become a Whig not because he embraced their principles, but primarily because, like them, he detested Jackson.

Like Harrison, Tyler was of the Virginia gentry, born into

wealth and privilege. Tyler was raised on a 12,000-acre plantation on the James River only a few miles from the plantation
where Harrison grew up. Tyler's father, like Harrison's, had
moved in the upper strata of the state's and the nation's political
hierarchy. Young Tyler had entered politics early and risen
steadily. He had been a Virginia state legislator, then a member
of Congress, then, like his father, and Harrison's, a governor of
his state—and finally by 1828 a United States Senator, an office
he resigned in 1836 rather than vote to expunge a resolution of
censure against Jackson. But in or out of office, he was well connected in Washington, an entrenched insider. After he left the
Senate, his specialty became running as a vice-presidential nominee. He was on two of the four regional anti-Van Buren tickets
in 1836, and then on the ticket with Harrison in 1840. But when
he graduated to the presidential level, he quickly became a rank
outsider.[4]

John Quincy Adams, a former president himself, now in the
U.S. House of Representatives from Massachusetts, thought
Tyler was a slave-mongering mediocrity but good enough to be
vice president on a ticket. But "no one," Adams raged, "ever
thought of his being placed in the executive chair."[5] Yet that,
very unexpectedly, very suddenly, was where he now sat.

Tyler held strong beliefs. He was pro-slavery and a rigorous
believer in states' rights. He was as strong against the tariff as
most other Southerners were. He believed that a national bank,
the most revered of Whig causes, violated the Constitution.

Within six months of becoming president, his entire Whig
cabinet, but for his secretary of state, Daniel Webster, had resigned in protest against this apostasy. Webster stayed on only to
complete negotiations on an important treaty with Great Britain,
and after that he also left. Most Whigs agreed with Philip Hone,

a major financial backer of the party, that there had been "rhyme" in "Tyler too," but "no reason in it."[6]

What the Whigs had for the next entire presidential term was this "mongrel administration"[7] run by this loose political cannon who refused to do their bidding, who marched to his own drum, a maverick and a renegade, a president literally without a party. He himself was to admit, "my ship [was] tempest-tossed."[8] Charles Dickens, traveling in America in 1842, saw Tyler in Washington. "He looked somewhat worn and anxious," the novelist thought, "and well he might; being at war with everybody."[9]

Tyler would continue to be at war with everybody and to defy the will of the Whig congress throughout his term, which mercifully, the Whigs assured themselves, would end following the coming presidential election canvass of 1844.

The choice of a Whig candidate was obvious. It was going to be Henry Clay, a true Whig, who had been vigorously getting his ducks in a row. He had retired from the Senate in 1842 to gird himself. His prospects for the brass ring had never been brighter. He had already been nominated by state after state long before the Whig convention met in Baltimore on May 1, 1844—for one day and one session only—to make his nomination unanimous and official.

The Democrats had been left in 1840 "leaderless and mutinous."[10] But the Little Magician, Martin Van Buren, still practicing his magic, was in a comeback mode and was the frontrunner for the nomination. When the party convened its national convention, also in Baltimore, on May 27, the majority of the delegates were already pledged to him.

However, Tyler, who had been derailing Whig plans for four

years, was now bollixing Democratic plans—or at least Van Buren's. The cudgel he was using this time was Texas. It was an incendiary issue. After Texas won its independence from Mexico in 1836, there was the hope and expectation, widely held, that it would soon be annexed to the Union. Jackson had been highly sympathetic to this hope, but his presidency ended before he could see it done, having time only to recognize Texas independence. Van Buren, succeeding him, believed annexation would constitute aggression against Mexico. He was also sensitive to vigorous Northern opposition against adding a huge slave state to the Union. So he shied from bringing Texas in.

Not so Tyler, who recognized a political dinger when he saw one. Aspiring to perform a riveting act in his final presidential year, he crafted a treaty for Texas statehood and sent it to the Senate on April 22, 1844. This immediately threw the hot-potato issue onto the canvass. Senator Thomas Benton of Missouri called it the "Texas bombshell."[11] Van Buren knew he had to make a stand one way or the other. And he took his stand against admission, for the same reasons he had rejected it in his presidency.

This immediately alienated his Southern supporters, including his old mentor, Jackson, seventy-seven years old and nearing the end of his days in the Hermitage in Tennessee. The unhappy Jackson began to look for somebody else to support with his still considerable political weight. It was not a long jump for him to his fellow Tennessean, another protégé, former speaker of the House James K. Polk, already a strong contender for second place on the ticket.

The first thing the delegates did in Baltimore was to adopt a two-thirds rule for nomination rather than a majority. This was more than Van Buren could get, and it had a stirring impact on

the first ballot, in which Van Buren polled 146 of the 266 delegate votes, a clear majority, but not enough. By the seventh ballot, he had faded to 99 votes, and Lewis Cass of Michigan, his
chief rival, had moved up from 82 votes to 123. Hopelessly deadlocked, the convention adjourned for the night. On the eighth
ballot the next day, the decidedly dark horse Polk suddenly
emerged with 44 votes. A stampede followed on the ninth ballot,
and Polk was nominated unanimously. A congenial expansionist
platform was crafted for him, calling outright for both "the re-
occupation of Oregon and the re-annexation of Texas at the earliest practicable period," together with the usual anti-Whig
positions.[12]

Tyler's injection of this odious issue into the canvass also
played havoc with Clay's aspirations, for he too was publicly on
record against the annexation of Texas. In a letter to the *National
Intelligencer,* Clay had come out flatly against it on the grounds
that it would certainly involve the country "in war with Mexico
and probably with other foreign powers, dangerous to the integrity of the Union, inexpedient in the present financial condition of the country, and not called for by any general expression
of public opinion."[13]

He would soon fishtail, however, trying to reassure the South
that he had no objection to annexation if it was accomplished
without dishonor or war, with the common consent of the
Union, and on just and fair terms. As president, he said, he
would be guided "by the state of facts, and the state of public
opinion existing at the time I might be called upon to act." This
nod to the South would draw outrage in the North. It might be
that Clay would fall between the two stools of dissension in the
country, and get beat again.[14]

If that happened, James K. Polk, the first unanticipated

nomination in U.S. history, would be a highly unlikely and (in the Whig view) unsavory instrument.

Polk was the eldest of ten children, the son of a farmer and grandson of a blacksmith. He was born in a log cabin farmhouse near Charlotte, North Carolina, in 1795. When he was eleven his family moved to Tennessee. He was frail and sickly growing up, and studious. But he had little formal education when he matriculated to the new University of North Carolina, where he graduated in 1818 with honors. He was admitted to the bar in Tennessee two years later, and in 1823, began his upward climb in politics, first winning a seat in the state legislature, then graduating to Congress, where he was recognized from the start as an ardent Democratic partisan and a stalwart backer of his fellow Tennessean and mentor, Andrew Jackson—two traits alone that would fiercely alienate Clay. For eight years he politicked for Jackson in the House, four of them—1835 to 1839—as Speaker.

Sitting at the knee of Jackson all those years, Polk had become, like his mentor, an ardent expansionist. He had no trouble at all supporting that key plank in his party's platform, coveting Texas. He emphatically wrote, "The Texas question is the all absorbing one. I have no hesitation in declaring that I am in favour of . . . immediate . . . annexation."[15] In the nominating process, this set him clearly apart from Van Buren and would do the same against Clay in the canvass itself.

This time around the Whigs had managed, as they hadn't before in two previous runs for the presidency, to cobble together a platform of sorts. It came in the shape of a generic set of resolutions recapping basic Whig doctrine—a call for "a well-regulated currency," a tariff, distribution of proceeds of the land sales to the states, a one-term presidency, an end to executive usurpation of the Jackson-Tyler stripe, and an efficient and economical

administration. There was no specific mention of a U.S. Bank or
of the hot-button issue of Texas—and certainly nothing about
the re-occupation of Oregon.[16]

That couldn't be said of the Democratic platform, which was
unequivocal about both Texas and a desired second acquisition,
Oregon. The Oregon matter was even more expansionist-driven
than Texas. Americans in Oregon territory were all generally
settled south of the Columbia River. But the Democratic platform claimed the entire Oregon corridor, stretching from the
California line northward beyond the Columbia to latitude
54°40′, the southern boundary of Russian territory—which
would one day become the state of Alaska, bounded on the east
by the continental divide and on the south by the 42nd parallel.
The fighting slogan the Democrats trotted out in the campaign
was "54-40 or fight." Whether they meant it or not, it was symp-
tomatic of the aggressive expansionism driving the Democratic
campaign.[17]

The Whig campaign anchored itself on the widespread fame
of Henry Clay, without doubt the best-known politician in America. The Whigs contrasted their distinguished man's monstrous
name recognition with Polk's nearly total lack of both name and
distinction. "Who is James K. Polk?" was their call to arms. It
was a legitimate question. Polk was not well known in the country. Few outside of Tennessee who were not politicians had ever
heard of him. He could not match the fame or eloquence of Clay.
So the Democrats tried to counter it, depicting Clay as a heavy-
duty drinker and poker player, a duelist, a rake, a derelict, a
swearer, a corrupt bargainer, and a Sabbath-breaker.[18]

Clay and Polk were not the only two men wanting the office,
nor the Whigs and Democrats the only two parties in the field.
Tyler briefly mounted a campaign as a third party candidate

without a party. But he withdrew so that Polk could beat the Whigs.[19] Another man with a sliver of a party was also in the canvass—James G. Birney, executive secretary of the American Anti-Slavery Society in New York, the candidate of the abolitionist Liberty Party. He had been nominated by 148 delegates representing twelve states at his party's national convention in Buffalo in August 1843. Its leaders were mainly fanatics caught up in the anti-slavery fervor who didn't have much muscle in any of the twelve states except New York. Its single-minded platform was "the absolute and unqualified divorce of the general government from slavery, and also the restoration of equality of rights among men."[20]

The campaign got down and dirty. Tricks were pulled from political hats. Democratic bosses stepped up mass naturalizations of aliens before election day and herded them to the polls. In the three weeks before the election, New York turned thousands of them into overnight citizens. In New Orleans, Democrats sent a boatload of voters up the Mississippi, putting in at three different stops so the men could vote at each place.[21]

In Illinois, Abraham Lincoln, whose political beau ideal was Henry Clay, was into the campaign early and with his whole heart. Whig leaders in the state met in Springfield on June 10, 1843, to begin planning for it. Sangamon's Whigs met in Springfield in mid-August to open the campaign. They made ambitious plans, resolving to fight until they got a Whig legislature, a Whig U.S. senator, a majority of Whig congressmen—and a majority of 850 votes for Henry Clay in 1844. Lincoln addressed the meeting.[22]

Nearly six months before, Lincoln had rung an alarm. "In almost all the States," he had written in the Whig address to the people of Illinois on March 4, "we [the Whig Party] have fallen into the minority." In the address, signed by himself and two others, he worried that "tens of thousands, in the late elections, have not voted at all." Yet "they *can* come forward and give us victory again." He wrote, "Let us then again come forth in our might" in "our solemn conviction" that "the whigs are always a majority of this Nation; and to make them always successful, needs but to get them all to the polls and [to] vote unitedly."[23] On December 11, the statewide Whig convention met in Springfield and chose Lincoln as one of the state party's nine presidential electors.

It had been over a year since Lincoln and Mary's marriage. She had delivered a son, Robert, and they had moved out of the Globe Tavern into a rented cottage with four rooms on Fourth Street. Then early in the election year, for $1,500, they bought a house—from the Reverend Charles Dresser, the Episcopalian rector at St. Paul's Church, who had married them. Built in 1839, the house was a modest five-room, one-and-a-half-story cottage at Eighth and Jackson Streets, six blocks from the statehouse.[24]

His domestic life now securely anchored, Lincoln plunged into a busy political speaking schedule, hitting the main Whig issues. By mid-February, the *Illinois State Register* was taking sardonic note of Lincoln's activities, describing him as "another member of the Junto...our jester and mountebank." The *Register* wrote, "We have had him appointed a candidate for Clay elector. This we hope will buy him off from being a candidate for Congress.... [He] is a long-legged varmint.... [who] can make a speech which is all length and height like himself, and no breadth or thickness."[25]

By late February, Lincoln was taking all of his length, height, and breadth out of town on the stump, making speeches every night at some precinct in the county to packed houses. "We confidently expect," one Whig wrote, buoyed by the prospects, "to give 1000 majority in Sangamon County for Clay."[26]

In a speech in Virginia, Illinois, on February 23, Lincoln, as the *Sangamo Journal* put it, blasted "the absurdities of loco focoism," and praised "the soundness of whig principles, with great success."[27] By early April, David Davis, a Bloomington lawyer and friend of Lincoln's, traveling the spring court circuit with him, wrote from Tremont: "Politics rage now hereabouts.... The first day of every court is occupied with political speaking, usually by an Elector on each side of politics, each person generally taking some three or four hours.... Lincoln is the best stump speaker in the State."[28]

By mid-campaign the issue of immediate Texas annexation was clouding the canvass. Lincoln sided against it with Clay, calling it "altogether inexpedient." As Clay later waffled on the issue, so did Lincoln. In a letter to a supporter in Putnam County before the election he wrote, "I never could see much good to come from annexation; inasmuch, as they were already a free republican people on our own model." On the other hand, he said he could never see clearly "how the annexation would augment the evil of slavery." Slaves, he believed, "would be taken there in about equal numbers, with or without annexation."[29]

Just before the election—from October 24 through election day on November 4—Lincoln was back in Indiana, where he had grown to manhood, in last-hour campaigning for Clay. It was an appropriate place to praise the man he believed represented the best in political manhood.

In Indiana Lincoln was home again. Even as he stumped politically, he was thinking poetically. "That part of the country," he later wrote a friend, "is, within itself, as unpoetical as any spot of the earth; but still, seeing it and its objects and inhabitants aroused feelings in me which were certainly poetry."[30]

Those aroused poetic feelings indeed later took shape in nostalgic verse, when he wrote:

My childhood-home I see again,
    And gladden with the view;
And still as mem'ries crowd my brain,
    There's sadness in it too....

Now twenty years have passed away,
    Since here I bid farewell
To woods, and fields, and scenes of play
    And school-mates loved so well.

Where many were, how few remain
    Of old familiar things!
But seeing these to mind again
    The lost and absent brings....

The very spot where grew the bread
    That formed my bones, I see.
How strange, old field, on thee to tread
    And feel I'm part of thee![31]

But neither Lincoln's politics nor his poetry could get Clay elected. Polk, the virtual unknown, riding the issue of Texas annexation, 54-40 or fight, and vigorous American expansionism, upset the political icon of America. To deep-dyed pro-Clay Whigs like Lincoln it was a shattering blow, a virtually unthinkable outcome for all their tireless work for their idol. Polk swept in with 1,337,243 popular votes to Clay's 1,299,062, and an electoral edge of 170 to 105. Clay lost Illinois, carrying only Ohio in the Northwest. But he carried the upper tier of slave states— North Carolina, Tennessee, Kentucky, Maryland, and Delaware— and in the East, Massachusetts, Rhode Island, Connecticut, Vermont, and New Jersey.

Texas, Oregon, expansionism, and Polk carried all of the Deep South and the rest of the West. But the key had been the big swing states of Pennsylvania and New York. Polk carried both by narrow margins. Clay had desperately needed to win New York in particular, which he lost by only 4,000 votes. There the renegade abolitionist Liberty Party ruined everything. Birney won 15,812 votes in New York. If only one-third of those had gone to the Whigs, Clay would have won the election. Had he not waffled on the Texas issue he might have saved New York.[32]

In Illinois Lincoln sadly said, "If the Whig abolitionists of New York had voted with us...Mr. Clay would now be President, Whig principles in the ascendant and Texas not annexed; whereas, by the division, all that either had a stake in the contest was lost."[33]

The irrepressible John Tyler couldn't resist giving the Whigs one last lick before leaving the White House. Seeing the election returns as a mandate, he exhumed the Texas annexation treaty, dressed it up in the new garb of a joint resolution—which needed only a simple majority in the Congress, rather than the two thirds required for a treaty. This end-around strategy worked. The Congress adopted the resolution four days before Polk was inaugurated. The road was now cleared for Texas to become the twenty-eighth state.[34]

Tyler also threw a gala goodbye party in the White House. He sent out 2,000 invitations and lit the East Room with a thousand candles. As the mob surged in, he said, "They cannot say now that I am a president without a party." It was believed to have been one of the only jokes he had ever cracked in his entire tempest-torn presidency.[35]

To Lincoln and the Whigs in Springfield there was nothing to laugh about. As the disastrous year was ending, they met on December 19 to contemplate the future of their party in the wreck of their most cherished hopes. Three months later, they mourned again as Polk was inaugurated as the eleventh president. At age forty-nine, he was also the youngest to assume the office, trumping Tyler's fifty-one. As the country was growing older, its presidents were growing younger.

13

Laying Congressional Pipe

IN THE THREE YEARS since he had been denied the seat in the Illinois Seventh Congressional District, deferring first to John Hardin, then to Edward Baker, who now held it, Lincoln had not lost his lust for it. It was the only safe Whig seat in the state, and he wanted it. He believed he had a right to it by a prior agreement among the three of them, and he was laying pipe in 1846 to claim that seat when Baker's term ended in 1847.

His arch Democratic rival, the pesky Little Giant, was now looming a very big giant in national politics. He had been re-elected, decisively, to his house seat in the Fifth District in 1844 and looked now to a likely promotion to the U.S. Senate when the legislature voted to fill that seat in 1846. Douglas was a political comet rocketing into the national firmament, far outstripping his tall Whig adversary, who had not yet had liftoff.

Liftoff was what Lincoln was seeking even before the year of the election rolled around. In his seeking he was oiling the main Whig machinery that drove the district, courting political friends and party leaders, the men who controlled politics in the district and could turn out votes for him. The Whig nomination didn't seem automatically his, despite his perceived agreement with Hardin and Baker. So, traveling the judicial circuit in the fall of 1845, he began to collect pledges of support.[1]

Oiling the Whig machinery was not all he was doing. There were issues. And he was tuning the one that was growing more prominent year by year—slavery. On October 3, 1845, he wrote Williamson Durley, a Whig supporter in Putnam County: "I hold it to be a paramount duty of us in the free states, due to the Union of the states, and perhaps to liberty itself (paradox though it may seem) to let the slavery of the other states alone; while, on the other hand, I hold it to be equally clear, that we should never knowingly lend ourselves directly or indirectly, to prevent that slavery from dying a natural death—to find new places for it to live it in, when it can no longer exist in the old."[2]

That belief would indeed be his mantra for the next fifteen years as the issue continued to rise to a crescendo: let slavery alone in the states where it now exists, but under no circumstances let it spread to the territories. To make this happen he wanted to go to Congress and he was carefully positioning himself. "I wish you would let nothing appear in your paper which may operate against me," he wrote Benjamin F. James, the editor of the *Tazewell Whig,* on November 17, 1845.[3]

Hardin was worrying Lincoln. Despite any prior agreement, he seemed to be making motions to reclaim the seat for himself. Lincoln attempted to head him off with the argument that fair is fair. He wrote Henry E. Drummer, a Beardstown lawyer and fellow Whig, urging him to "set a few stakes for me"—"if it be consistent with your feelings"—on the grounds that "turn about is fair play." In early January he wrote Robert S. Boal of Lacon: "That Hardin is talented, energetic, usually generous and magnanimous, I have, before this affirmed...and do not now deny....My only argument is that 'turn about is fair play.' This he, practically at least, denies."[4]

Hardin was attempting to change the rules of the game. His plan was to abandon the system Lincoln had fought vigorously to install—a nominating convention—and institute a direct vote of Whigs in the district instead. It called for all candidates to stay out of counties other than their own and restrain friends from going out of their counties to electioneer—ostensibly to reduce excitement and leave counties with an unbiased choice.[5]

This ploy did not deceive Lincoln. "A plan is on foot to change the mode of selecting the candidate for this district," he wrote James on January 16. Warning him that it was a movement "intended to injure me," he urged the editor "to let nothing prevent your getting an article in your paper...of *this week* taking strong ground for the old system, under which Hardin & Baker were nominated."[6]

He followed that up with a letter to Hardin himself. "I do not wish to join in your proposal of a new plan," he wrote. "I am entirely satisfied with the old system under which you and Baker were successively nominated and elected to congress." His plan would not wash, Lincoln told Hardin, because "the fact of your having been in congress, has, in various ways, so spread your name in the district, as to give you a decided advantage."[7]

Even as he was writing this, Lincoln was planning, when the Supreme Court adjourned in the middle of February, "to take a quiet trip through the towns and neighbourhoods of Logan

County, Delevan, Tremont, and on to & through the upper counties"—contrary to the Hardin plan.[8]

Despite Hardin's undercutting strategy, Lincoln's ground-work was paying off. On the last day of January the Whigs in Athens chose delegates to the county convention, strongly suggesting that they stand fast for Lincoln. By early February Hardin was being told by one of his backers that Lincoln would probably get all the votes of Tazewell County even if Hardin were a candidate. "The *regular succession* principle has been accepted," Hardin's friend wrote. "It is Abrahams turn now." On February 16, Hardin pulled out, writing a public letter declining to be a candidate.[9]

The coast was now clear for Lincoln. On March 2, the Sangamon County Whig convention met to pick its delegates to the district congressional convention in May, instructing them emphatically for Lincoln. It had become a *fait accompli*. When the district convention met in Petersburg on May 2, it nominated Lincoln unanimously.[10]

Now all he had to worry about was defeating the candidate the Democrats had ponied up to run against him, and talk his way to victory on the stump. Lincoln's opponent was one who might complicate matters, despite the heavy Whig advantage in the district.

The Democrat standing in his way was Peter Cartwright, at least as well known in the district as Lincoln, a legend of sorts. He was a Methodist preacher and circuit rider, who had for years been plowing furrows for the Lord among the believers and disbelievers in Illinois from Kaskaskia to Galena. It was said that "sinners fell before him like men slain in battle." He had preached to every Methodist congregation from Springfield to Cairo—multiple times in most cases—and traveled enough preaching miles, converting "sinners in the backwoods," to circle the globe several times. It was said that the Hallelujah shouting from his camp meetings could be heard for miles.

Frontier worship in those times was in itself peculiar, visually as well as spiritually. Whole congregations were often brought to the "jerks"—also called the "shakes"—a holy hysteria whipped to frenzy by silver-tongued preachers. Cartwright was known to get more than 500 worshippers jerking at once.[11]

He was "constitutionally an eccentric minister," unconventional, candid, brusque, emotional, picturesque, and rugged. He was a very dangerous antagonist with a strong Jacksonian bias. He had been a chaplain in Jackson's army in 1814–1815 in New Orleans. He had a secular weakness for politics but not a gift for it. One of his bitterest critics said of him that he was "a most abandoned hypocrite... in politics." "None," this critic said, "has a greater thirst for political distinction than Peter Cartwright." A lifelong Democrat, he had been twice elected to the Illinois state legislature, but had then served without distinction. He did not cut as vivid a figure there as he did in a revival tent.[12]

Speaking of himself, Cartwright said, "I was born in a cane brake...to escape the tomahawks of savage Indians; I was rocked in a bee-gum for my cradle; and my graduation degrees were taken from, and in, life's thunderstorms."[13] He was a contemporary not of Lincoln, but of Lincoln's father, born about the same time, carried as a boy from Virginia through the Cumberland Gap into Kentucky, just as Tom Lincoln had been.[14] He was built to survive all that and more, about five feet ten inches tall and nearly 200 pounds, burly, massive, and powerfully constructed. He was topped by a "crowning foliage of luxuriant, coal black hair wreathed into long, but rough and curling ringlets," on "a head that looked as large as a half-bushel." He was swarthy, with "rich, rosy lips always slightly parted, as if wearing a perpetual happy smile."[15]

Risen from the laity, Cartwright was un-cultivated in a book-learning way, like most of the Methodist circuit riding preachers of the time. He said, "We could not, many of us, conjugate a verb or parse a sentence, and murdered the king's English almost every lick."[16] But like most of the good ones, he could "mount a stump, a block, or old log, or stand in the bed of a wagon, and without note or manuscript, quote, expound, and apply the word of God to the hearts and consciences of the people."[17]

He was a constant defender of the faith, often with more than spiritual weaponry. It was said he was "a Peter who had an arm of flesh as well as a word of power, and who, at times, believed in a dispensation of muscular Christianity as well as a dispensation of the Holy Ghost." As a Baptist preacher of the time said, "the Gospel cannot be carried on silver wheels."[18]

"The roughs and bruisers at camp-meetings and elsewhere," one observer noted, "stood in awe of [Cartwright's] brawny arm, and many anecdotes are told of his courage and daring that sent terror to their ranks. He felt that he was one of the Lord's breaking plows, and that he had to drive his way through all kinds of roots and stubborn soil.... His gesticulation, his manner of listening, his walk, and his laugh were peculiar, and would command attention in a crowd of a thousand."[19]

Cartwright strongly suspected Lincoln of being an infidel. He whispered this suspicion around the district, and the charge grated on Lincoln, who felt it was believed by "some honest men" in the northern counties.[20]

So he issued a handbill at the end of July, just before the election, refuting the charges. He denied being "an open scoffer at Christianity," as Cartwright was insinuating. "That I am not a member of any Christian Church, is true; but I have never denied the truth of the Scriptures; and I have never spoken with intentional disrespect of religion in general, or of any denomination of Christians in particular.... I do not think I could myself, be brought to support a man for office, whom I knew to be an open enemy of, and scoffer at, religion."[21]

While not an enemy or a scoffer, it was true Lincoln was not a churchgoer. He hewed to no organized religion and was the member of no church. Indeed, what religion he professed, was highly unorganized. Quoting "an old man named Glenn, in Indiana," he said, "When I do good I feel good, when I do bad I feel bad, and that's my religion"—not an entirely acceptable canon in an organized sect.[22]

During the campaign Cartwright held one of his camp meetings in Springfield, and Lincoln dropped in to listen. As sinners filed to the mourner's bench, Cartwright, seeing Lincoln, urged him forward, bellowing, "If you are not going to repent and go to Heaven, Mr. Lincoln, where are you going?"

Lincoln, it is said, slowly rose to his feet, and said, "I am going to Congress, Brother Cartwright."[23]

And so he was. When the vote was counted on election day, August 3, Lincoln carried the district with 56 percent of the vote—6,340 to 4,829—a virtual landslide.[24] Now that he had what he had so ardently wanted, a reverse reaction set in. Two months after the election Lincoln wrote Speed: "Being elected to Congress, though I am very grateful to our friends, for having done it, has not pleased me as much as I expected."[25]

Stephen Douglas, reelected as well—to his third term in the House—had every reason to be as pleased as he expected. Bigger things were ahead. Reelection to his House seat had only been a precautionary measure in the event he wasn't elevated to the Senate when the legislature acted to fill that seat in December. It was a little-needed precaution. Nobody was giving even long-shot odds against his elevation. He had been laying the groundwork since his first term in the Twenty-eighth Congress, and by 1846 no Democrat dared covet what he coveted. The legislature rammed him into place in the Senate by a resoundingly lopsided margin—100 votes to only 45 for his Whig opponent, Cyrus Edwards.

As custom demanded of a newly elected senator, Douglas threw a public celebratory ball in the statehouse immediately afterward, a collation and cotillion crammed into what little space could be cleared out in the mob. The hall was so crowded, one celebrant said, "that not a midget could get in." It cost Douglas $1,500. But it was only money, a small price to pay for so auspicious and promising a launching into the political stratosphere.[26]

His vacated House seat would be filled in a special election later, in the spring of 1847, by his handpicked successor, William A. Richardson. Douglas was rapidly building a budding political empire. When Lincoln was sworn into his seat in the House, Douglas would be sworn into the Senate, still a seven-league-boot-sized step ahead of his tall rival in the race for political distinction.

Neither Lincoln nor Douglas would be sworn in for more than a year, when the Thirtieth Congress convened in early December 1847. As the time approached in early July that year, Lincoln attended a big Whig harbor and river convention in Chicago. Horace Greeley, the editor of the *New York Tribune* was there, and he rather marveled not only at Lincoln's lofty physical elevation, but at his unique political status as well, describing him as "a tall specimen of an Illinoisan, just elected to Congress from the only Whig district in the State."[27]

The *Chicago Daily Journal* looked on this homegrown specimen with local-boy pride: "We expect much from him as a representative in Congress," the *Journal* wrote, "and we have no doubt our expectations will be more than realized."[28]

In October, the Lincolns leased their home for a year beginning on November 1 for $90, storing their furniture in one upstairs room. On October 28 the *Illinois Journal,* the former *Sangamo Journal,* reported that he had just set out on his way to Washington. "His family is with him," the *Journal* wrote; "they intend to visit their friends and relatives in Kentucky before they take up the line of march for the seat of government. Success to our talented member of Congress. He will find many men in Congress who possess twice the good looks, and not half the good sense, of our own representative."

In St. Louis the Lincolns caught a boat for Frankfort, Kentucky, and from there the passenger cars of the Ohio Railroad to Lexington. After nearly a month's visit in Kentucky, they started for Washington on November 25, by stage to Winchester, Virginia, where they caught the cars of the Potomac Railroad to Harpers Ferry and there the cars of the Baltimore and Ohio to Relay Station, Maryland, and the branch line into Washington. They arrived in the capital late in the night on December 2 and took lodgings in Brown's Hotel.[29]

The Thirtieth Congress convened at noon four days later. Lincoln stepped onto the national stage and took his seat.

14

Seeing Spots

ILLINOISANS LIKED TO think of themselves as "suckers," after the suckerfish that yearly ascended the streams of the state to spawn. It went back to the 1820s and early 1830s when human "suckers" ascended the Mississippi by the thousands in the spring to work the lead mines in Galena, returning downriver again in the fall.[1] This mass work migration resembled a gold rush. "It seemed the people were literally crazy," a former governor, John Reynolds, wrote. They "rushed to the mines with the same blind energy and speed, that a people would in a panic flee from death."[2]

Lincoln and Mary, two suckers from "Suckerdom" gone to Washington, took up permanent quarters in a boarding house on Carroll Row between A Street and East Capitol, run by Ann G. Spears, a Virginia widow with Whig leanings. All in her mess were Whig congressmen.[3]

When the Thirtieth Congress convened at noon on December 6, Horace Greeley was hoping for the best. "That there are rowdies among its members is quite likely," he wrote in the *Tribune,* "but I hope no determined brawlers nor confirmed drunkards, such as have made themselves disgustingly conspicuous on its floor in former years."[4]

In the drawing for seats Lincoln's name was one of the last called, and he found himself situated in the outer row, between Harmon S. Conger of New York and John Gayle of Alabama, rather like a long compromise line between the North and South.[5]

From this seat the sole Whig congressman from Illinois was feeling his way. In early January he ventured to the floor for a little speech "on a post-office question of no general interest"— "by way of getting the hang of the House." In a letter to William Herndon he wrote: "I find speaking here and elsewhere about the same thing. I was about as badly scared, and no worse, as I am when I speak in court." He assured Herndon that this early venture was but a shakedown cruise of sorts. "As you are all so anxious for me to distinguish myself, I have concluded to do so, before long." He promised in a week or two to deliver something with more heft that would make some waves.[6]

The speech with more heft, which came on January 12, following a set of resolutions he introduced in late December, would launch him into heavy seas. He had decided to take on the president, no less, over the U.S.-Mexican War.

Northern Whigs, in particular, were never enthusiastic about the war. They suspected it to be mainly a conjured-up affair designed to give the South more slave territory to expand into. In his campaign for Congress Lincoln had urged prompt and united action to support the war, the proper and usual response when your country is suddenly in one. But in late 1847, in a meeting in Lexington on November 13, Henry Clay denounced it as a war of "unnecessary and...offensive aggression." Lincoln, who was visiting in Lexington with Mary, on their way through to Washington, was doubtless in the audience. The meeting, stirred by Clay's eloquence "almost unanimously" adopted resolutions condemning the war.[7]

In the House on December 22, Lincoln, a very loyal Whig, introduced eight anti-war resolutions of his own, which were read into the record, then laid on the table. He declared that President Polk's excuse for going to war was that Mexico had "invaded *our territory,* and shed the blood of our fellow *citizens* on *our own soil.*" Lincoln's resolutions doubted the truth of that claim. Was the spot of invaded soil really ours, his resolutions demanded. Give us proof.[8]

It is doubtful Polk was paying much attention to this freshman congressman's critical maiden speech. However, in early January there was a vote in the House declaring the war with Mexico to have been unnecessarily and unconstitutionally commenced by the president. Lincoln voted for it, and in a speech on January 12 he explained why, making much of where the invaded "spot" actually was.

"Now I propose to try to show," Lincoln said, "that the whole of this—issue and evidence—is, from beginning to end, the sheerest deception." He called the claim to the spot a "naked *claim.*" If the president, Lincoln said, "can show that the soil was ours, where the first blood of the war was shed....In that case I, shall be most happy to reverse the vote I gave the other day." But, Lincoln said, "if he *can* not, or *will* not do this...I shall be fully convinced, of what I more than suspect already, that he is deeply conscious of being in the wrong," and "that he ordered

General [Zachary] Taylor into the midst of a peaceful Mexican settlement, purposely to bring on a war."[9]

Reaction from back home to the speech was mixed. Pro-Lincoln newspapers praised it. The *Missouri Republican* said the speech "was one of great power...replete with the strongest and most conclusive arguments." The *Rockford Forum* said his resolutions "stick to the spot in Mexico....Evidently there is music in that very tall, Mr. Lincoln." However, the opposition press found the Lincoln music anything but toe-tapping. The *Illinois State Register,* his old enemy, vilified him. The Peoria *Democratic Press* would soon be calling him "the miserable man of 'Spots.'"[10]

Lincoln's friends had their misgivings. Herndon, for one, believing it was not going down well with the people in general, questioned his vote and his speech. "That vote," Lincoln wrote Herndon in his own defense, "affirms that the war was unnecessarily and unconstitutionally commenced by the President; and I will stake my life, that if you had been in my place, you would have voted just as I did." It had nothing to do, Lincoln said, with the question of supplying the army and the men fighting the war. He was for that and had always voted for it. "I have always intended, and still intend, to vote supplies."

The "locos," Lincoln complained to Herndon, "are untiring in their effort to make the impression that all who vote supplies or take part in the war, do, of necessity, approve the Presidents conduct in the beginning of it; but the whigs have, from the beginning, made and kept the distinction between the two."[11]

Douglas's position in the Senate was precisely the opposite of Lincoln's in the House. From the start of the war, when he was in the House himself, Douglas was very Polk-supporting, the loyal Democrat vigorously and vocally backing every war move the president made. He still was. The line on the war clearly divided the two parties.

This was but prelude to the presidential canvass of 1848 shaping up inside and outside the congressional halls. Lincoln leaped into the campaign early. An ardent partisan who desperately longed for a Whig president, he joined a cabal of fellow Whigs in the House called the "Young Indians," organized to push the candidacy of the Mexican War hero, General Zachary Taylor. This meant supporting a principal actor in the war they abhorred and abandoning Lincoln's political beau ideal, Henry Clay, who again coveted the nomination. But Lincoln wanted victory. He believed Taylor to be "*a winning card*" and that Clay's chance of being elected was "just no chance at all." He was writing fellow Whigs that Taylor's nomination "takes the locos on the blind side. It turns the war thunder against them." Therefore, he said, "I am in favor of Gen: Taylor as the Whig candidate for the Presidency because I am satisfied we can elect him, that he would give us a whig administration, and that we can not elect any other whig."[12]

There was some question about the purity of Taylor's Whigness. The old soldier was just that, a soldier. He had never voted in his life and was appalled at first to be mentioned for the office at all. When a visitor toasted him as the next president in his tent in Mexico during the war, Taylor is said to have replied, "Stop your nonsense and drink your whisky."[13] "Such an idea," he protested to his brother, "never entered my head, nor is it likely to enter the head of any sane person."[14] He insisted to his son-in-law that he would never "be a candidate for the presidency," and said categorically he would not be a candidate for the office "if certain of reaching it."[15]

Aside from his astonishment at the very idea of it, Taylor had a non-politician's non-partisan mindset, wanting, if he was to be a candidate—as public acclaim soon forced him into being—he wanted to be elected as president of the whole nation, not of a party. But there was the nagging necessity for party affiliation of some sort. In a letter written in early 1848 he finally confessed tepidly, "I'm a Whig, but not an ultra Whig. If elected I would not be the mere President of a party. I would endeavor to act independent of party domination. I should feel bound to administer the government untrammeled by party schemes."[16]

The man was also a smashing military hero, and as Lincoln and Whigs of his stripe believed, he was a winning ticket. They desperately wanted him for their candidate—more desperately than the Democrats did.

On June 10, Lincoln attended the Whig national convention in Philadelphia and saw Taylor nominated on the fourth ballot, and Millard Fillmore of New York, picked as his vice-presidential running mate. It was called the "slaughter-house convention" because it killed so many hopes of so many other great Whig aspirants—notably Clay, Daniel Webster, and General Winfield Scott, the other towering Mexican War hero.[17] The Democrats had met the month before in Baltimore and nominated Senator Lewis Cass of Michigan.

Democrats in Congress accused the Whigs of having forsaken their financial and tariff principles and "taken shelter," one of them said, "under the military coat-tails of General Taylor." Lincoln rose on the floor and replied, taking for his text, "Military coat-tails." Benjamin Perley Poore, a Washington journalist, described it: "He had written the heads of what he had intended to say on a few pages of foolscap paper, which he placed on a friend's desk, bordering an alley-way, which he had obtained permission to speak from. At first he followed his notes, but, as he warmed up, he left his desk and his notes, to stride down the alley toward the Speaker's chair, holding his left hand behind him so that he could now and then shake the tails of his own rusty, black broadcloth dress-coat, while he earnestly gesticulated with his long right arm, shaking the bony index finger at the Democrats on the other side of the chamber. Occasionally, as he would complete a sentence amid shouts of laughter, he would return up the alley to his desk, consult his notes, take a sip of water, and start off again."

Ohio Congressman William Sawyer, a Democrat nicknamed "Sausage," for having once been pictured lunching behind the Speaker's chair on bologna sausage, was later asked, "How did you like the lanky Illinoisan's speech? Very able, wasn't it?"

"Well," replied Sausage, "the speech was pretty good, but I hope he won't charge mileage on his travels while delivering it."[18]

After Congress adjourned in August, the "Lone Star of Illinois," as one eastern newspaper described him,[19] hit the stump hard for Taylor, first in a trio of speeches around Washington before setting off in early September to sink his political blade into ground he had never plowed before—New England. He delivered the first of ten speeches for Taylor in Massachusetts at an evening speech in Mechanics Hall in Worcester on September 11, preceding a Whig state convention the following day.

He spoke for an hour and a half, ringing themes he would repeat throughout Massachusetts, attacking "locofoco" charges that Whigs had abandoned their principles when they nominated Taylor. Lincoln ranged over the familiar Whig issues—the bank, the tariff, internal improvements—and praised Taylor as the man "to whom the interests, principles, and prosperity of the country might be safely intrusted." He appealed to Whigs to do their duty and support him.

Lincoln also spoke of slavery, saying the people of Illinois agreed with the people of Massachusetts that it was "an evil, but that we were not responsible for it and cannot affect it in the States of this Union where we do not live." However, the question of extending slavery to new territories was something altogether different. Lewis Cass was an apostle of "popular sovereignty," the doctrine that would permit any territory to enter the Union either as a slave or free state—as its people willed. In Lincoln's mind it was an odious doctrine to perpetuate the spread of slavery and must be opposed.[20]

Lincoln had been troubled enough by the problem of slavery in the territories in March, to have written down what he thought Taylor ought to say of expropriating Mexican territory. "It is my desire," he wrote, "that we shall not acquire any extending so far South, as to enlarge and agrivate the distracting question of slavery."[21]

The Boston *Daily Advertiser,* which reported his Worcester speech in detail, described Lincoln as "a very tall and thin figure, with an intellectual face, showing a searching mind, and a cool judgment." It praised the speech as "truly masterly and convincing."[22] Henry J. Gardner, a New Englander in the audience, said, "No one there had ever heard him on the stump, and in fact knew anything about him. When he was announced, his tall, angular, bent form, and his manifest awkwardness and low tone of voice, promised nothing interesting. But he soon warmed to his work. His style and manner of speaking were novelties in the East. He repeated anecdotes, told stories admirable in humor and in point, interspersed with bursts of true eloquence."[23]

The next morning Lincoln was one of several impromptu speakers at the railroad station to meet incoming delegations to the Whig convention. On September 14 he spoke at Liberty Hall in New Bedford and the next day for an hour and a half at the Boston Whig Club in Washingtonian Hall on Bromfield Street. The Boston *Atlas* praised the speech "for sound reasoning, cogent argument and keen satire," such as "we have seldom heard equalled."[24]

In a speech in Lowell, Massachusetts, on September 16, speaking at what the *Atlas* described as "one of the tallest meetings...that they have yet held," he packed the large city hall "in every part."[25] There he attempted again to disabuse the public of the wrong-headed notion that Taylor was not a Whig. He blasted the candidacy of that old Whig nemesis, Martin Van Buren— running yet again, this time as a third-party free-soil candidate. Lincoln decried the folly of voting for Van Buren and siphoning away votes that ought to go instead for Taylor against Cass.[26]

Following speeches in Dorchester, Chelsea, Dedham, and Cambridge, Lincoln was in Taunton on September 21, winding up his New England stumping tour, hitting again the same themes. The unsympathetic *Bristol County Democrat* described "his awkward gesticulations, the ludicrous management of his voice and the comical expression of his countenance," all conspiring "to make his hearers laugh at the mere anticipation of the joke before it appeared."[27]

At a final Whig mass meeting in Tremont Temple in Boston on September 22, Lincoln shared the platform with New York Governor William H. Seward, and the next day he and Mary turned toward home.

Edward L. Pierce, a New Englander monitoring Lincoln's ten-speech odyssey through Massachusetts, concluded that he had made "a marked impression" with "his striking figure...his quaintness and humor—his logical power and his novel way of putting things." However, Pierce did not see him at any point rising above partisanship as he labored, like other Whig speakers, to prove Taylor a credible Whig. Lincoln's own take on his swing was, "With hayseed in my hair I went to Massachusetts, the most cultured State in the Union, to take a few lessons in deportment."[28]

Stopping off for a short visit to Niagara Falls on the way home, he and Mary arrived in Chicago on October 5, where the next evening he spoke for two hours at a Whig rally in the courthouse. He told his fellow Illinoisans that a Taylor defeat in November would be a verdict of the people "against any restriction or restraint to the extension and perpetuation of slavery in newly acquired territory."[29] He continued campaigning, stumping, and debating in Illinois—for Taylor and against that verdict—up to election day, November 7. The outcome was bittersweet. Taylor lost the state by some 3,000 votes, but he won the presidency. Lincoln had done more than his part.

In December, when he returned to Washington to serve out his term in the second session of the Thirtieth Congress, Mary remained in Lexington. Alone in Washington, Lincoln had slavery on his mind yet again, with the idea of doing something about it. Slavery was the main subject on the floor, and the proposed end of it and the slave trade in the District of Columbia were being earnestly pushed.[30]

When the capital was moved to the District in the formative years of the young republic, it was situated on land ceded by two slave states, Maryland and Virginia. Ceded with it, therefore, were both slavery and the slave trade. It was now the only place where slavery existed within reach of federal power. Lincoln and all but rank abolitionists considered slavery and its trade in the slave states untouchable.

That didn't mean that something responsible—and gradual—might not be done about it in the District. Lincoln had in mind putting something in the hopper himself. On January 13, he gave notice of his intention to introduce a bill to abolish slavery in the District—but only by consent of the free white people in the District and with compensation to the slave owners. He believed that to be a responsible approach to the matter.[31]

Before giving notice, he visited the mayor of the District, senators, and others whom he thought best acquainted with sentiment in the District, to see if they would endorse such a proposal. His Whig messmates at the Widow Spears's lodgings across from the capitol discussed it and heartily approved. However, Lincoln soon learned that Southern leaders in the House, who opposed the bill, had been to see the mayor and others who had endorsed it and had changed their minds. "Abandoned by my former backers and having little personal influence," Lincoln later confessed, "I *dropped* the matter knowing that it was useless to prosecute the business at that time." He never introduced his bill, but his intent to do so had been a notable antislavery statement.[32]

After the Thirtieth Congress adjourned *sine die* in the early morning March 4, Lincoln attended Taylor's inauguration the next day and the inaugural ball that evening. On March 20, his term in the House at an end, he started home to Springfield, where the Sangamon Circuit Court had just convened for its spring session. He had not run for reelection. Indeed, he had announced in early 1848 that he would not be a candidate for renomination or reelection. It wasn't that he might have liked to run, but he believed it would be "quite as well for me to return to the law at the end of a single term." He wrote Herndon then: "I made the declaration that I would not be a candidate again, more from a wish to deal fairly with others, to keep peace among our friends, and to keep the district from going to the enemy, than for any cause personal to myself. . . . to enter myself as a competitor of others, or to authorize any one so to enter me, is what my word and honor forbid."[33]

Besides, there was that "spot" speech, which had not, as Herndon feared, gone down well in Illinois. When Lincoln's former law partner, Stephen Logan, ran for the office as a Whig to replace him, he lost to a Mexican War veteran, Democrat Thomas L. Harris, a captain in the Fourth Illinois Regiment. The district had gone to the enemy after all.

So Lincoln was done in Washington. He had hoped, however, as a Whig congressman and an untiring soldier in the Taylor campaign, to have a say in the patronage that might rightly come to Illinois. But it wasn't working out that way. In early 1849 Lincoln knew nothing of the new administration's patronage plans.[34]

He was particularly frustrated in an effort to get a faithful pro-Taylor Whig—and finally himself—into the powerful post of Commissioner of the General Land Office, which was ticketed for an Illinoisan. The prize went instead to a lawyer from Chicago, Justin Butterfield, whom Lincoln considered an inconstant Whig—he had supported Clay, not Taylor, in the election. Rebuffed in the patronage wars, saddened and frustrated in politics, no longer in office, Lincoln could only return to Springfield—and to his law practice. At least there was still that.

PART SIX

Eclipse

15

Lincoln's Other Life

WHEN THEY STOPPED at Niagara Falls on their way home from campaigning for Taylor in Massachusetts, Lincoln found philosophy in the water.

Meditating on the boat leaving Buffalo for Chicago, he marveled at the "mysterious power" of that mighty, roaring tumult. It called to his mind "the indefinite past." "When Columbus first sought this continent," Lincoln mused, "—when Christ suffered on the cross—when Moses led Israel through the Red-Sea—nay, even, when Adam first came from the hand of his Maker—then as now, Niagara was roaring here." In all that long, long time, the great falls were "never still for a single moment. Never dried, never froze, never slept, never rested."[1]

Unlike those sleepless falls, Lincoln was about to rest—politically. The Niagara of his ambition had run dry. His future in politics was indefinite at best, dead at worst. Indeed, his law partner, Billy Herndon, believed "he despaired of ever rising again in the political world."[2] He was out of Congress, and he had failed to wrest patronage, or a job, from the new Whig administration he had worked so hard to help install in Washington. He had no options but to return to Illinois and to that other calling that defined him—the law.

That wasn't necessarily a bad thing. He looked to be a success there. And there were aspects to it—riding the judicial circuit in particular—that strongly appealed to him. He was about to put politics aside and throw himself into that other side of his life "more assiduously than ever before."[3]

Lincoln's career in the law had started under the mentorship of John T. Stuart. When he moved from New Salem to Springfield in 1837, a newly minted lawyer, he came as Stuart's partner. That partnership had lasted four years, from April 1837 to April 1841. Lincoln then became a partner to Stephen T. Logan, which lasted three more years.

Logan was, like Stuart, one of the luminaries of the Illinois bar, widely considered the best trial lawyer in the state. He was a former judge of the circuit court, and to keep his mind, judgments, and practice sharp, he reread Blackstone's *Commentaries* every year. He was a small splinter of a man, wrinkled and withered, but with a keen, shrewd face topped by an immense shock of "frowzy" yellow-white hair. He wore a flowing cape, and under it linsey-woolsey suits, shirts of unbleached and unstarched cotton unencumbered by a cravat or other neckwear. His feet, protruding from below his long cape, were clad in a pair of heavy work shoes. From this caped apparition came a high, shrill, sharp, rather jarring voice virtually bereft of oratorical grace. Yet when Logan spoke in a court of law, everybody listened, because under that antic exterior lurked "a gigantic intellect." Indeed, Elihu B. Washburne, a fellow lawyer and Whig congressman from Illinois, who thus described him, said he was looked upon and listened to "with amazement."[4]

Lincoln's six years of association with these two eminent Springfield lawyers were an apprenticeship. Partnering with them in a junior role gave him solid grounding in the profession. When he left Logan in 1844, he was ready to set up business as a senior partner with a junior of his own. The one he chose, rather to that junior's astonishment, was William B. Herndon, who had studied law in the Logan-Lincoln office. Herndon was so junior that he didn't yet have a license to practice. Lincoln always called him Billy, and Billy always called him Mr. Lincoln.[5]

Herndon loved literature of every kind and kept up to the minute on current affairs. He loved to study politics, psychology, phrenology, and human nature in general. He was a social creature, generous, and loving of his fellow man. He was progressive and anti-slavery and his opinions were heated. He was something of a self-confessed radical. Yet he had been elected mayor of Springfield in 1850.[6]

Despite being wildly different, one being conservative and unemotional by nature [Lincoln] and the other radical and hotly emotional [Herndon], they had much in common. They respected one another and entertained similar political sentiments. Both shared a droll sense of humor, a disregard of details, rugged physical frames—although one was inordinately tall and the other of average height—and angular features mirroring a "half tender melancholy."[7]

This somewhat odd legal couple hung out a shingle in a bare stairway over an upstairs office in Springfield that read simply, "Lincoln & Herndon." The office itself was on the second floor of a brick building across from the courthouse. It was a two-room affair in the back of the building with windows overlooking stable rooftops, ash heaps, and littered back yards.[8]

"Here," Herndon said, "is where we expounded the law to our clients, prepared our papers and charged up our fees." The room and its furnishings were as modest as the fees. In the center stood a table. Sagging against the wall was a sofa, and on the opposite side of the room a bookcase. An old wood-burning stove and four or five chairs completed the furnishings. The bookcase held about twenty volumes, and scarcely half of them were law books. The others were a mix of literature, official papers, and statistical reports.[9]

For the most part Lincoln carried his files, bankbook, memorandum-book, and the bulk of his letters in his hat, a high silk plug. "Whenever in his reading or researches he wished to preserve an idea," Herndon said, "he jotted it down on an envelope or stray piece of paper and placed it inside the lining. Afterwards when [it] was needed there was only one place to look for it."[10] This system had its perils. Late answering a friend's letter, Lincoln confessed he had lodged it in his old hat, bought a new one the next day, and the letter missed the transfer.[11]

On the top of the table in the office there was a fall-back file—a bundle of papers into which Lincoln slipped anything he wanted to keep that wouldn't fit in his hat. Atop the stack was a note of explanation: "When you can't find it anywhere else, look in this."[12]

Herndon confessed there was no order in the operation of the office, no books kept. All fees, regardless of which of them had handled the case, were split down the middle, 50-50, without receipts or an entry in any ledger. The ambiance in the office was as informal as the business practices. "Lincoln's favorite position when unraveling some knotty law point," Herndon said, "was to stretch both of his legs at full length upon a chair in front of him. In this position, with books on the table near by and in his lap, he worked up his case."[13]

When Lincoln was in town he arrived at the office in the morning at about nine o'clock. The first thing he did was pick up a newspaper, sit spread-eagle on the sofa, one long leg on a chair, another on the table, often spilling himself over one-quarter of the room, and begin reading it aloud. This habit —reading aloud—Herndon confessed, "used to annoy me almost beyond the point of endurance." It annoyed him so much he often left the office to escape it. Asked why he read that way, Lincoln explained, "I catch the idea by two senses, for when I read aloud I *hear* what is read and I see it; and hence two senses get it and I remember it better, if I do not understand it better."[14]

Lincoln was not a case-reading, precedent-citing lawyer. "Practically," Herndon believed, "he knew nothing of the rules of evidence, of pleading, or practice, as laid down in the text-books, and seemed to care nothing about them." But he had "a keen sense of justice, and struggled for it, throwing aside forms, methods, and rules, until it appeared pure as a ray of light flashing through a fog-bank." When he did have to learn or investigate a subject, Herndon said, "he was thorough and indefatigable in his search. He not only went to the root of the question, but dug up the root, and separated and analyzed every fibre of it." But he never crammed on any question until he had a case in which the question was involved. "He thought slowly and acted slowly," Herndon said; "he must needs have time to analyze all the facts in a case and wind them into a connected story."[15]

Giving advice to a newly elected justice of the peace, Lincoln said, "There is no mystery in this matter, King; when you have a case between neighbors before you, listen well to all the evidence, stripping yourself of all prejudice, if any you have, and throwing away if you can all technical law knowledge, hear the lawyers make their arguments as patiently as you can, and after the evidence and the lawyers' arguments are through, then stop one moment and ask yourself: What is justice in this case? and let that sense of justice be your decision. Law is nothing else but the best reason of wise men applied for ages to the transaction and business of mankind."[16]

David Davis, the judge of the judicial circuit in which he traveled—and his friend—agreed that Lincoln "could hardly be called very learned in his profession, and yet he rarely tried a cause without fully understanding the law applicable to it." Davis agreed with Herndon that Lincoln "*read law books but little,* except when the cause made it necessary."[17]

Lincoln's slow-moving thought processes often annoyed Herndon as much as his reading aloud in the office did. In the courtroom he ought to "speak with more vim, and arouse the jury," Herndon believed "—talk faster and keep them awake." Lincoln tried to explain to Herndon "the long, labored movements of my mind." Comparing a pen knife, which moves quickly but through a small space, to a jackknife, which he fancied himself to be and which cuts deeper and travels farther, he said, "I may not emit ideas as rapidly as others, because I am compelled by nature to speak slowly, but when I do throw off a thought it seems to me, though it comes with some effort, it has force enough to cut its own way and travel a greater distance."[18]

Whatever his system, slow or plodding, penknife or jackknife, Lincoln had a way with juries that not even Herndon's vim could equal. James S. Ewing, a fellow lawyer and friend, said that Lincoln was "a jury lawyer," who "played on the human heart as a master on an instrument."[19] A lawyer who was a stranger to Lincoln and his ways told Usher F. Linder that Lincoln's practice of telling stories to the jury was a waste of time. "Don't lay that flattering unction to your soul," Linder answered; "Lincoln is like Tansey's horse, he 'breaks to win.'"[20]

Davis said Lincoln "was hurtful in denunciation" of oppressors in lawsuits. "When he attacked meanness, fraud, or vice, he was powerful, merciless in his castigation."[21] Henry C. Whitney, a lawyer who traveled much on the circuit with Lincoln, believed him "wise as a serpent in the trial of a cause." But Whitney said he had "too many scars from his [Lincoln's] blows to certify that he was harmless as a dove." "When the whole thing is unraveled," Whitney believed, "the adversary begins to see what he [Lincoln] was so blan[d]ly giving away was simply what he couldn't get & Keep. By giving away 6 points and carrying the 7th"—on which the whole case hung—Lincoln would win.[22]

But Whitney saw nothing wrong in this. He believed Lincoln harbored "no envy, malice, or spite—no ill-feeling of any kind toward anybody; he was deferential but not obsequious; he made no sarcastic remarks. He employed no social tyranny to one in his power; he had no angularity except physically; was not inquisitive about the affairs of others; was disinterested and magnanimous, not supercilious or discourteous; was generous and forgiving to a fault. He was not only sincere and candid, but he assured you by his conduct that he was so."[23]

Herndon said, "If you met Mr. Lincoln on a case and you on one side and [he] on the other, you knew that you met a broadminded and liberal gentleman, honest, fair, and that you would be defeated if you ought to be."[24]

Herndon saw Lincoln as "a severe and persistent thinker,"

believing that even as a boy in Indiana, he studied to see a subject clearly and to express it tersely and strongly. "His conscience, his heart and all the faculties and qualities of his mind bowed submissively to the despotism of his reason." Herndon believed he had "profound analytical power.... He was the strongest man I ever saw, looking at him from the elevated standpoint of reason and logic. He came down from that height with irresistible and crashing force.... His conscience ruled his heart; he was always just before he was generous.... In proportion as he held his conscience subject to his head, he held his heart subject to his head and conscience." Lincoln's mind, Herndon said, "was not exactly a wide, broad, generalizing, and comprehensive mind, nor yet a versatile, quick, and subtle one, bounding here and there as emergencies demanded; but it was deep, enduring, strong, like a majestic machine running in deep iron grooves with heavy flanges on its wheels."

"Mr. Lincoln was a very patient man generally," Herndon said, "but if you wished to be cut off at the knee, just go at Lincoln with abstractions, glittering generalities, indefiniteness, mistiness of idea or expression." His perceptions were "cool, persistent, pitiless in pursuit of an idea, a thing, a fact, a person." Others noticed this practical turn of his mind. "No man living," said another, "has less the visionary. He is a... 'good hater' of cloud-clapped theories."[25]

In notes for a law lecture, Lincoln wrote, "I am not an accomplished lawyer. I find quite as much material for a lecture in those points wherein I have failed, as in those wherein I have been moderately successful." Resolve "to be honest at all events," was his either/or advice to lawyers, "and if in your own judgment you cannot be an honest lawyer, resolve to be honest without being a lawyer."[26]

But Lincoln was a lawyer. And where he enjoyed most being a lawyer was on the Eighth Judicial Circuit, which, with politics now in remission, he pursued with all the vim Herndon wanted him to use with juries.

The lawyers riding the circuit traveled across fourteen counties in central Illinois, from the Illinois River eastward to the Indiana line, and a like distance north and south—11,000 square, often lonely, miles, almost a fifth of the area of the state. For three months twice a year, in the spring and fall, they made this "swing around the circle." There were few rails to ride in Illinois—only 110 miles of track in 1850—so they swung around the circle by buggy or by horseback in the spring, when the roads were muddy, the bridgeless streams high, and the unsettled prairie covered with thick-matted grass. Travel for this "ambulatory bar"—as many as twenty-five or thirty lawyers at a time, led by Judge David Davis in a buggy behind a team of gray mares—was from one county courthouse to the next, across "desolate and solitary prairies, devious roads or no roads at all." Across those desolate miles—twenty to nearly seventy miles between county seats—Lincoln rode in "a rattle trap buggy" pulled by his horse, "Old Buck," at a clip of four to five miles an hour.[27]

The lawyers, and the judge who traveled with them, took room and board where they could find it, in rude country taverns, sleeping in cramped bedrooms often more than one lawyer to a bed. Judge Davis, who loved eating and carried three hundred pounds of avoirdupois to show for it, deplored the food and lodgings in these country taverns. He wrote home to his wife: "This thing of travelling in Illinois and being eaten up by bed bugs and mosquitoes is not what it is cracked up to be."[28]

Day after day the lawyers and the judge set up, three days to a week at a time, in the courthouses in each of the fourteen county seats and tried the cases the local clients brought. This traveling bar was the way the aggrieved got legal justice on the lawyer-bereft prairies. It was a "rough-and-tumble practice," Whitney said, where "advocacy was relied on rather than exact knowledge or application of legal principles."[29]

The circuit was like a road show, wrote Jane Martin Johns, a woman who watched it pass through Decatur twice a year, with its retinue of lawyers, clients, witnesses, itinerant peddlers, showmen, gamblers, and many who followed it just for its entertainment value. Taverns, rough and rude as they were, were crowded, and hospitality was "taxed to the utmost limit." The circuit was a much anticipated, much appreciated event in the county seats through which it drifted.[30]

Judge Davis, who presided over this itinerant legal circus, was a Marylander from the Eastern Shore, who had migrated westward with the immigrant flood. After he launched himself in a promising law career in Illinois in the late 1830s he returned east to marry the pert daughter of a stern New Jersey probate judge. Together they returned and settled in Bloomington, and in 1848 at age 33, after a decade as a lawyer, Davis was elected judge of the Eighth Judicial Circuit.

He was six years younger than Lincoln and twice as heavy. He grew into manhood with a headstrong temperament and a flashing temper. But he was punctilious in his courtesy, particularly toward women. The *Philadelphia Enquirer* wrote of "his rotund corporation, the inexpressible humor of his broad, good-natured countenance, and...roar-like laughter." His dominant trait as a judge was his forthrightness. Lincoln, who took to him—they often roomed together on the circuit—said of him that it was not one of his characteristics to feign anything. Davis was "companionable," Jane Johns in Decatur thought. He "knew the law" and "loved a laugh," and much of his laughter, on the circuit, was triggered by a Lincoln story.[31]

On the Eighth Circuit, laughter and wit were brought to the prairie with the justice—and largely because of Lincoln. The circuit was "the locality *par excellence* when entertainment by storytelling was to be looked for." Whitney said, "Fun by storytelling, was the chief staple of our leisure hours."[32] And the storytelling virtuoso of those leisure hours was Lincoln, with his apparently God-gifted talent for mimicry.

"In this," Herndon said, "he was without a rival." Judge Davis, a connoisseur of Lincoln's storytelling, said his "manner of recital" was "in many respects unique, if not remarkable. His countenance and all his features seemed to take part in the performance. His little gray eyes sparkled; a smile seemed to gather up, curtain like, the corners of his mouth; his frame quivered with suppressed excitement; and when the point—or 'nub' of the story, as he called it—came, no one's laugh was heartier than his."[33]

David Davis believed Lincoln told his stories and made his jokes "to whistle off sadness." Lincoln didn't disagree. He told Herndon, "If it were not for these stories, jokes, jests, I should die; they give vent—are the vents—of my moods and gloom." Another close Lincoln friend, Joseph Gillespie, believed he also used anecdotes "as labour saving contrivances."[34] Good, terse stories could short-circuit elaborate explanations. They could deflect discussion away from somewhere Lincoln didn't want it to be.

He was himself to say of his storytelling, "I believe I have the popular reputation of being a story-teller, but I do not deserve the name in any general sense; for it is not the story itself, but its purpose or effect, that interests me. I often avoid a long and use-less discussion by others, or a laborious explanation on my own part, by a short story that illustrates my point of view. So, too, the sharpness of a refusal or the edge of a rebuke may be blunted by an appropriate story so as to save wounded feeling and yet serve the purpose. No, I am not simply a story-teller, but story-telling as an emollient saves me much friction and distress."[35]

Lawyering on the circuit fit Lincoln's instincts and talents perfectly. His personality, character, appearance—his entire persona and aspect—fit the rough-and-tumble fabric of it perfectly. Whitney thought Lincoln's horse, Old Buck, "as rawboned and weird-looking as himself," and that his buggy matched both the horse and its driver. His attire appeared more fitting a farmer or stockman. His luggage was a battered carpetbag, and the umbrella he carried was weather-worn. He wore a short blue cloak over his rumpled suit that reached no farther down his elongated body than to his waist—the style favored in the Mexican War he so disfavored. Whitney wrote: "Imagine a loose-jointed, carelessly attired, homely man, with a vacant, mischievous look and mien, awkwardly halting along in the suburbs of the little prairie village, in the midst of a crowd of wild, Western lawyers, he towering above the rest, taking in the whole landscape, with an apparent vacuity of stare, but with deep penetration and occult vision." That was Lincoln.[36]

What Lincoln was in the early 1850s, in the view of Jane Johns, was "a semi-obscure lawyer and politician, nowhere towering above his fellows except in stature," with a local reputation as "an honest, kind, genial man, too honest, too kind, too genial ever to become a success in the world. His personal appearance and dress were not sufficiently marked to be remembered, yet I think no man ever knew him and forgot him."

Riding circuit, Lincoln let his political hopes lie dormant, sidetracked in favor of the law. But they were never far from his thought. He was still available when called on to help the Whig cause.

In July 1850, Zachary Taylor died in the midterm of his presidency, in the midst of a clamorous Washington battle to shape a compromise and avoid a war over slavery in the territories. Lincoln was in Chicago for a trial and was asked to deliver Taylor's eulogy at a meeting in city hall on July 25. He was still the voice Whigs called up when there was something important to say.

Lincoln praised Taylor's "dogged incapacity to understand that defeat was possible" and said, "It did not happen to Gen. Taylor once in his life, to fight a battle on equal terms, or on terms advantageous to himself—and yet he was never beaten, and never retreated." Taylor had found the presidency "no bed of roses"—not even the most experienced politicians would. No human being, Lincoln said, can hold that office and escape censure. "Still I hope and believe when Gen. Taylor's official conduct shall come to be viewed in the calm light of history, he will be found to have *deserved* as little as any who have succeeded him." With Taylor's death, Lincoln thought the country might have lost "a degree of confidence and devotion, which will not soon again pertain to any successor." Nonetheless he said he could not "help thinking that the American people, in electing Gen. Taylor to the presidency, thereby showing their high appreciation of his sterling, but unobtrusive qualities, did their *country* a service, and *themselves* an imperishable honor. It is *much* for the young to know, that treading the hard path of duty, as he trod it, *will* be noticed, and *will* lead to high places."[37]

The first two years of this new and troubled decade brought death in high places. Henry Clay, Lincoln's and his party's idol, died in June 1852. Scarcely three months later Daniel Webster died. In March 1850 John C. Calhoun had preceded both in death. When Clay died, his Illinois friends and political foes met at the statehouse in Springfield and appointed Lincoln chairman of a committee to arrange for a suitable memorial service. On July 6, at eleven in the morning, the first shot of a seventy-six-gun salute began to roll over the town—a mournful tattoo for each year of Clay's life. Stores were closed and business suspended. With the final gun, a procession formed and the Reverend Charles Dresser, the Episcopalian priest who had married Lincoln and Mary, read the service for the dead.[38]

In his statehouse eulogy, Lincoln spoke of Clay's birth within a year of the signing of the Declaration of Independence. "The infant nation, and the infant child began the race of life together," Lincoln said. "For three quarters of a century they have traveled hand in hand . . . companions ever." Lincoln praised Clay's colonization solution to the slavery question, the hope of "freeing our land from the dangerous presence of slavery; and at the same time . . . restoring a captive people to their long-lost father-land, with bright prospects for the future; and this too, so gradually, that neither races nor individuals shall have suffered by the change."[39] It was a solution Lincoln himself continued to believe in.

A month later Lincoln was back in the world of the political living, looking again with upraised and furrowed brow at a speech in Richmond by his old rival, Stephen Douglas. In his speech, Douglas, now a national political power center of major magnitude, had attacked Winfield Scott, the Whig candidate for president in the 1852 canvass, and denounced the Whig platform generally.

The canvass was in full fury, Scott against Democrat Franklin Pierce of New Hampshire, another Mexican War hero-general and politician. Lincoln was on the Scott electoral ticket, but he wasn't campaigning as hard as he had in 1840, 1844, and 1848. The Whig cause in Illinois in this latest canvass looked hopeless.[40]

But Lincoln helped organize Scott clubs, and he wasn't about to let what Douglas said go unanswered. In a long speech that the *Illinois Journal* said was "full of keen sarcasm and eloquence," raising "shouts of laughter and approbation," Lincoln said, "I was reminded of old times." Of the times, Lincoln told an audience at the Scott Club in Springfield, "when Judge Douglas was not so much greater man than all the rest of us, as he now is—of the Harrison campaign, twelve years ago, when I used to hear, and *try* to answer many of his speeches." And here Douglas was again, Lincoln said, making speeches "marked with the same species of 'shirks and quirks.'" Lincoln took issue in particular with the Douglas charge that Scott's nomination by the Whigs, "forced on the south by the north, on a sectional issue... is exceedingly perilous to the safety of the Union."[41] He spoke again for Scott in Springfield in late October, one of two Whigs replying to another speech by Douglas delivered earlier in the afternoon. Democrats tried to disrupt the speeches that night, hallooing at the door and firing crackers in the hall. So the meeting adjourned until the following night with three hurrahs for Scott, and Lincoln replied more fully to Douglas two evenings later.[42]

Scott was emphatically defeated, winning only four states, a spare forty-two electoral votes. Franklin Pierce, with 254, was elected the fourteenth president.

This half-hearted foray back into politics done, Lincoln

turned again inward, to the law, to his other life, anticipating the next springtime swing through the judicial circuit, when the matted prairie would again be in bloom, and when justice had to be done and stories had to be told.

16

What He Had Become

THE JUDICIAL CIRCUIT was Lincoln's bethel. In the twenty years that he rode it, he would spend half of every year on it, often not going home to Springfield for weekends, as many lawyers on the circuit did.

Judge David Davis, who knew him better perhaps than anybody who traveled with him, believed Lincoln "was happy—as happy as *he* could be, when on this Circuit—and happy no other place. This was his place of Enjoyment. As a general rule when all the lawyers of a Saturday Evening would go home to see their families & friends ... Lincoln would refuse to go home."[1]

"Refuse" is too harsh a word. Before rails were laid across the circuit, Lincoln often had little opportunity to go home on weekends. Most of the lawyers on the circuit practiced only in counties near their own. Lincoln made the entire round of courthouses—rode the full circle—far and near from Springfield, many of them too far from home for a short weekend. And the weekends were short—Sunday only; court was held on both Saturday and Monday. He could not get home and back for just a day. As the railroad came in, in the fifties, Lincoln's absences from Springfield on weekends grew fewer and fewer.[2]

If home was where the heart is, there was also a little heartburn there for Lincoln as well. Life with Mary had turmoil in it. She loved her husband, but she had a Vesuvian temper, which occasionally erupted. She never seemed entirely satisfied with the hired servants. She had been raised in a slave society in Kentucky and non-slave help didn't always measure up. She had a reputation for hiring a servant and soon firing her in a fit of pique. She once told a friend, "Well, one thing is certain; if Mr. Lincoln should happen to die, his spirit will never find me living outside the boundaries of a slave State."[3]

Mary's eruptions were not enough to bury Pompeii, but at times chased Lincoln from the house. One of his friends believed this ironically worked to the advantage of his political career. "The fact," this friend insisted, "that Mary Todd, by her turbulent nature and unfortunate manner, prevented her husband from becoming a domestic man, operated largely in his favor; for he was thereby kept out in the world of business and politics. Instead of spending his evenings at home, reading the papers and warming his toes at his own fireside, he was constantly out with the common people, was mingling with the politicians, discussing public questions with the farmers who thronged the offices in the courthouse and state house, and exchanging views with the loungers who surrounded the stove of winter evenings in the village store." The result of "this continuous contact with the world," the friend believed, "was, that he was more thoroughly known than any other man in his community." Mary's shrewish ways may have inadvertently translated into votes for Lincoln later.[4]

Whatever dissatisfaction there was in the marriage was not entirely Mary's doing. Although he was seen as a good husband "in his own peculiar way," often Lincoln's laid back, countrified lack of polish ruffled Mary's idea of social decorum. He was not above telling callers when she was dressing that "she will be down as soon as she has all her trotting harness on." He was known to answer the front door himself instead of sending a servant to do it—also a social no-no—and inviting the callers to a seat in the parlor, while he went to "trot the women folks out."[5]

When they went out socially, Lincoln, who generally disliked fashionable society, could be unfashionable. He appreciated the value of such gatherings in promoting a politician's ambitions, but typically, he would annoy the women by starting to tell a story, which had a ripple effect, causing the men to stop dancing to listen. This amused Herndon who said, "Just think of a merry dance going on with music, women, and wine, and 'Old Abe' in the corner of the dancing hall with his eight or ten chums around him telling one of his best," leaving the women partnerless on the dance floor.[6] While socially counterproductive it may have been smart politics, since only the men could vote.

Lincoln also had a way of drifting off into abstract, absent-minded thinking. Sometimes on Sundays in the summertime he could be seen in his shirtsleeves hauling his babies in a little wagon up and down Eighth Street. In the late forties and fifties their family grew—with Edward, born in 1846, but dying in early 1850 of consumption; Willie, born in late 1850; and Thomas, nicknamed "Tad," born in 1853.

So abstracted was Lincoln while pulling his babies that when one would tumble out squalling, he would saunter on, wholly oblivious to what Shakespeare would have called its "piteous plaintings." When somebody called his attention to the tragic drama unraveling behind, Lincoln would turn back, pick the child up, pacify it, return it to the wagon, and proceed up and down the street as distracted as before. Or, when one of them fell out, Lincoln might say, "This puts me in mind of a story that I heard down in New Salem..." Sometimes he could be seen in his long linen duster and stovepipe hat pushing a babe slowly along in a carriage with one hand while holding an open book in the other, studiously reading. "A grotesque figure," a young neighbor girl thought.[7]

His law partner was also occasionally victimized by his absent-mindedness. Herndon testified, "I have met Mr. Lincoln of a morning or evening and said to him; 'Good morning, Mr. Lincoln.' He would be so intensely, so deeply, in thought, working out his problem, his question, that he would not notice me, though his best friend; he would walk along, his hands behind his back, not knowing where he was going nor doing; his system was acting automatically. There was no thought in his actions, he only had *consciousness.* Some hours after he had thus passed me, he, on coming to the office, would say: 'Billy, what did you say to me on the other side of the square this morning as we passed?' I would say: 'I simply said good-morning to you, Mr. Lincoln."[8]

It was Herndon's opinion that Lincoln always meekly accepted Mary as the final authority in domestic matters and "exercised no government of any kind over his household." His children, Herndon said, "did much as they pleased. Many of their antics he approved, and he restrained them in nothing. He never reproved them or gave them a fatherly frown. He was the most indulgent parent I have ever known." Herndon had first-hand evidence of this. Lincoln was in the habit, when at home on Sunday, of bringing Willie and Tad to the office while Mary attended church. There the boys ran wild, "absolutely unrestrained in their amusement."[9]

They soon gutted the room, emptied the shelves of books, rifled the drawers, riddled boxes, battered the points of Herndon's gold pens against the stairs, turned over the inkstands on the law papers, threw pencils into the spittoon, scattered letters over the office, and danced over them. None of this, to Herndon's aggravation, ever "disturbed the serenity of their father's good-nature. Frequently absorbed in thought, he never observed their mischievous but destructive pranks." There was "many and many a time," Herndon said, "that I wanted to wring their little necks."[10]

Lincoln, however, had a fixed philosophy about all this. Mary, who might also have wanted to wring their little necks on occasion, said that Lincoln often said, "It is my pleasure that my children are free—happy and unrestrained by paternal tyranny. Love is the chain whereby to lock a child to its parent."[11]

This *laissez faire* attitude toward child rearing was perhaps part of Lincoln's larger philosophy of life. Mary, who was in a position to know him best of all, said, "Mr. Lincoln's maxim and philosophy was—'What is to be will be and no cares of ours can arrest the decree.'"[12] Herndon had frequently heard Lincoln quote a couplet:

There's a divinity that shapes our ends,
Rough-hew them as we will.

"There are no accidents in my philosophy," Lincoln told Herndon. "Every effect must have its cause. The past is the cause of the present, and the present will be the cause of the future. All these are the links in the endless chain stretching from the finite to the infinite." In short, Lincoln believed that "if it is writ, it is writ."[13] Lincoln's personal appearance and habits rather refortified that predestinarian philosophy. If it covers the body, wear it—if it is stitched it is stitched; if it is food eat it—if it is served it is served.

It was widely conceded that Lincoln had neither the talent for stylish dress, nor the body for it. He was "a tall, ungainly looking man," a friend said; a man of "loose, awkward rigging," another said.[14] Leonard Swett, a fellow lawyer who was to become his close friend, understood how loose and awkward the rigging was from the first day they met. Swett was in Danville and new to the circuit. Directed to Judge Davis's room, he climbed the stairway of the hotel with some trepidation, being brought up to believe judges were men "of more or less gravity," to be approached with "some degree of deference." His timid, uncertain knock was answered with a "come in," uttered almost simultaneously. Swett entered the room and saw Davis and Lincoln in their nightshirts engaged in a pillow fight. Davis, low and heavy-set, was leaning against the foot of the bed puffing "like a lizard." Lincoln who looked to Swett, compared to Davis, to be eight feet tall, was "encased in a long, indescribable garment, yellow as saffron, which reached to his heels, and from beneath which protruded two of the largest feet I had, up to that time, been in the habit of seeing." The only thing keeping the nightshirt from slipping off the tall angular frame was a single button at the throat. "Certainly," Swett later wrote, "the ungodliest figure I had ever seen."[15]

Davis believed Lincoln, by nature, was also somewhat ungodly. Lincoln, Davis said many times, "was a peculiar man,

'None such.'"[16] Herndon believed him to be "a many-*mooded* man," who lived in three worlds—in "the purely reflective and thoughtful," in "the sad, thoughtless, and gloomy," and in "the happy world of his own levities." He was sometimes in one state and then another, and at times changing slowly and gradually from one to the other, sometimes transitioning as "quick, quick as a flash."[17]

Lincoln had a loner mentality, an individualism, which Herndon said, stood him out from the mass of men "like a lone cliff over the plain below." Another friend was struck by how different he really was—"a man widely different from the ordinary man of distinction...a man of marked superiority intellectually...different from any other personality I had ever tried to measure and comprehend....He had an individuality that was singularly impressive."[18]

Lincoln was also a loner in his melancholy, which a young admirer, Joseph Fifer, said seemed "to roll from his shoulders and drip from the ends of his fingers." Herndon believed Lincoln's sadness was "more or less...stamped on him," that his melancholy was "organic." This was but one aspect of his many-sided persona. He also had, Fifer said, a "changeable or flexible" face when he was involved in or committed to something going on, "and you would hardly know it was the same man."[19]

Henry Whitney, observing Lincoln on the circuit, believed there were two Lincolns, "the sober, practical business Lincoln" and the storytelling "'madcap' wag Lincoln," and they were "two totally different and widely contrasted persons." In his business matters, Whitney believed, "he was the incarnation of logic and adaptation; in his life *deshabille,* he was the incarnation of humor." He always impressed Whitney "as commonplace and informal in all externals, but noble and dignified in all the essentials of conduct and affairs."[20] His friend Horace White believed he was "doubly gifted"—the most humorous being I ever met, and also one of the most serious."[21]

Serious reading continued to command Lincoln's sober, practical business side. In his semi-moratorium from politics in the late 1840s and early 1850s, the great issue of slavery was growing larger every year. He saw that clearly from the serenity of the circuit, trying to get his arms around it in his reading and thinking.

He was also reading to feed his soul. He carried Shakespeare with him on the circuit. He loved Robert Burns and could quote his poetry extensively from memory. He read Poe and loved "The Raven," in particular, repeating it over and over. John Stuart said that in the evenings he would strip off his coat and lie down on the bed to read and reflect on and digest what he was reading. After supper he would get into his nightshirt, light a candle, draw up a chair or table and read late into the night.

Lincoln said of himself, "I cannot read generally. I never read text books; for I have no particular motive to drive and whip me to it. As I am constituted, I don't love to read generally, and as I do not love to read, I feel no interest in what is thus read. I don't and can't remember such reading. . . . I know that general reading broadens the mind, makes it universal, but it never makes a precise, deep, clear mind."[22]

Milton Hay believed his friend Lincoln's mind "ran to mathematical exactness about things," that it was "a peculiarity with him."[23] To enhance that peculiarity, to sharpen his own precise, deep, clear thinking, Lincoln carried with him on the circuit the six books of Euclid and mastered them. And with this tightly

disciplined, deeply honed mind he read what he really considered important—newspapers.

Now, on the circuit, out of politics, he was reading newspapers more than anything else, reading them aloud, carefully following the rise and drift of political sentiment over the divisive issue of slavery—reading them more closely, Whitney thought, than anybody he knew.[24]

Where all this reading and thinking was taking him, Lincoln probably didn't know himself. But he believed wherever that might be, "you can't fly a high kite unless you have a long string."[25]

Although despairing of a political future, he continued to believe he might someday fly a higher kite. These years on the circuit, although rewarding in many ways, were "cheerless years" in other important ways. He saw his old rival, Douglas, rising to the heights in the affairs of the nation, his name and fame overspreading the land. He saw himself in total eclipse.[26]

In a fit of despair, he told Herndon, "How hard—oh, how more than hard—it is to die and leave one's country no better for the life of him that lived and died her child!" His reading in the newspapers didn't ease his despair. "The world is dead to hope," he told Herndon, "deaf to its own death struggle made known by a universal cry. What is to be done? Is anything to be done? Who can do anything and how can it be done? Did you ever think on these things?"[27]

Despite his pessimism, his friend Orville Browning thought Lincoln believed there must be something in store for him—that he believed in "presentments," that "even in his early days he had a strong conviction that he was born for better things than then seemed likely or even possible." Browning saw him as "a man of very strong ambition" originating from this conviction that he was "destined for something nobler than he was for the time engaged in.... And I have no doubt that Mr. Lincoln believed that there was a predestined work for him in the world."[28]

If so, from the circuit in the early years of the 1850s—in his exile—it seemed something very dim, very distant, very indistinct.

17

Tempest

As LINCOLN WAS looking inward in Illinois, Douglas was soaring upward in Washington.

Douglas had begun this upward political spiral with President Polk's own rocketing entry into the White House in 1845. As a new-minted Democratic congressman, the Little Giant had ardently defended the president's Mexican War measures against all comers, as vigorously as he had ripped down anti-Jackson handbills in Vermont when he was a teenager. He was soon an often-summoned consultant to the pinnacle of political power. When the Wilmot Proviso sought to ban slavery in all the newly won Mexican territory, Douglas unsheathed his heavy artillery against it. This thrust him for the first time into combat over the slavery issue.

The political steam engine that drove him was often derailed by limitations of the body in which it was housed. Douglas was illness-prone, and in 1849 he was looking for physical panaceas as ardently as political ones. Deadly cholera was raging through the West, but Douglas believed he had the perfect protective nostrum—a wonder pill compounded from three parts sulfur and one part charcoal by his fellow boarder in Chicago, Doctor J. Herman Bird. Douglas called the result "Doct Bird's Sulpher Pills," and he wrote his niece Adelaide Granger that he was taking one a day. "We have all got our Pocketts full of [them]," he wrote Adelaide, "and care no more for the cholera than we do the Itch; for it will cure the cholera in an hour, & it takes all winter sometimes to cure the Itch."[1]

Douglas's uncured political itch was to see America realize its destiny, and he believed that resolving the slavery issue was key. Just as he had chaired the committee on the territories in the House, Douglas chaired its counterpart in the Senate. There, he was one of the major players in the long nine-month struggle of 1850 to hammer out a compromise, averting a civil war over slavery in the territories. In the end, after Henry Clay had failed to push a compromise Omnibus Bill through in the Senate, Douglas took command on the floor, broke down the package's components, got them passed one at a time, and then saw them ratified in the House on their way to a gratified signing by President Millard Fillmore.

The Little Giant believed the compromise had at last put the quietus to "the vexed question of slavery." In 1852 he wrote the editor of the *Washington Union,* "I wish to state that I have determined never to make another speech upon the slavery question; and I will now add the hope that the necessity for it will never exist. I am heartily tired of the controversy, and I know the country is disgusted with it." He believed, "The whole country is acquiescing in the compromise measures—everywhere, North

and South. Nobody proposes to repeal or disturb them." He was unilaterally writing *finis* on "an unprofitable controversy." He was convinced that "So Long as our opponents do not agitate for repeal or modification, why should we agitate for any purpose?"[2]

This made Douglas a very big player on the national stage, on a short list of Democratic candidates for president in 1852. He even put together a slate called "The Tickett," with him for president and Virginia Senator R.M.T. Hunter for vice president. The "tickett" would fall short in the hopelessly deadlocked Democratic convention in 1852, and the party would fall back on a dark horse, Franklin Pierce. But Douglas was still young—not yet forty years old. There was time—and there would likely be opportunity. "I am young," he wrote the editor of the *Boston Times*, "& can afford to wait & am not anxious therefore about the present."[3]

Douglas at age thirty-nine had become the embodiment of a virile new movement in the country called Young America, dedicated to the evangelical political religion of western expansion—railroad building, government land for homesteaders—and a vigorous and aggressive pursuit of the national destiny. These young Americans believed, with Douglas, that "Expansion is the law of our existence; when we cease to grow, we commence to decline."[4] It was a young America ready to sweep aside the "Old Fogies," the older professional politicians who had long run things and who resisted pro-active, aggressive innovation in a new age.[5]

He had also become a committed champion of what he saw as the ultimate solution to the problem of slavery in the territories—the "true doctrine," the "great fundamental principle." His elixir, which he saw as the ultimate cure-all, was "popular sovereignty"—leaving the people of the territories "perfectly free to form and regulate their domestic institutions in their own way, subject only to the Constitution of the United States."[6] In his view that was the democratic way, the way to advance freedom, to defang the slavery issue, and clear the way to what his heart most desired—opening up the limitless West beyond his beloved Illinois, all the way to the Pacific, to white settlement. Douglas was growth-minded, a rampant uncompromising exponent of Manifest Destiny.

He was not pro-slavery *per se*. He believed that his popular sovereignty would not bring more slave states, because most of the new territory was not suited to it. The "laws of climate, and production, and of physical geography," he said, "have excluded slavery from the country."[7] But neither was he anti-slavery enough to forbid it entering any territory where the people did want it, free from congressional intervention. Whether or not slavery was moral or immoral didn't matter to Douglas.

At first he had vigorously championed the Missouri Compromise line, as retained in the Compromise of 1850, believing that it "had become canonised in the hearts of the American people, as a sacred thing, which no ruthless hand would ever be reckless enough to disturb."[8] But by 1854, it was getting in the way of his dream of an intercontinental railroad to the West and limitless expansion. The vast intervening territory had somehow to be organized. "The Indian barrier must be removed," he wrote in December 1853. "The tide of emigration and civilization must be permitted to roll onward until it rushes through the passes of the mountains, and spreads over the plains, and mingles with the waters of the Pacific. Continuous lines of settlements ... are imperiously demanded by the highest national considerations."[9]

First off, the Kansas-Nebraska territory had to be organized—the sooner the better. In January 1854, Douglas introduced a bill—the Kansas-Nebraska Act—to take care of that. At
first the bill had kept the compromise line—all territory above
36°30′ to be left free, all below it permitting slavery. But he was
finding that he could not get the bill enacted without Southern
votes. And the South was demanding that the sacred line—
which they had always detested—be abolished to let their slaves
into territory anywhere north as well as south of it.

This was no problem any longer for Douglas. Although he
suspected it would raise an outcry in the North, the line gone
would also open all territory to what was even more sacred to
him, popular sovereignty. The bill was amended explicitly to
abolish the compromise line, which for thirty-five years had
diminished slavery expansion. The fence restricting slavery and
popular sovereignty was lifted. The reckless, ruthless hand that
had disturbed the sacred thing had been his own.

But in his mind it was worth it. The *"true intent and meaning of the act,"* he wrote, "is NOT to legislate slavery into any
Territory or State. The bill, therefore does not introduce slavery;
does not revive it; does not establish it; does not contain any
clause designed to produce that result, or which by any possible
construction can have that legal effect." It simply legislates
"Non-intervention by Congress with slavery in the States and
Territories," which "opens the country to *freedom* by leaving the
people *perfectly free* to do as they please."[10] He had "brought
forward the bill to blot out the Missouri Compromise line—that
black line which ran across the Continent...in order to substitute in its place the great fundamental principle of self-government,
upon which all our free institutions rest."[11]

Needing to bring heavyweight support into line behind the bill, Douglas strong-armed President Pierce—he had the political muscle now to do that—into signing it. Douglas was satisfied his bill would make everything well. He wrote his friend, Georgia's Howell Cobb, "It will triumph & impart peace to the country & stability to the Union. I am not deterred or affected by the violence & insults of the Northern Whigs & abolitionists. The storm will soon spend its fury, and the people of the north will sustain the measure when they come to understand it.... The great principle of self government is at stake & surely the people of this country are never going to decide that the principle upon which our whole republican system rests is vicious & wrong."[12]

But Douglas underestimated the fury of the Northern protest his bill had triggered. The tempest became so intense through the summer of 1854 that he felt compelled to return to Illinois, where it fiercely raged, to defend the bill. He felt the act was necessary and good, and he was confident he could persuade others to see it his way.

What Douglas saw, on his way home to Illinois, "all along the Western Reserve of Ohio," was "my effigy upon every tree we passed." He said, "I could travel from Boston to Chicago by the light of my own effigy."[13]

What he was about to see and experience in Chicago was even more frightening.

He had been warned against launching his campaign of persuasion with an opening address in Chicago on September 1. But he was persuaded he could deal with whatever came down. These were his people in what was now his home city. He wrote his friend Charles H. Lanphier, the editor of the *Illinois Register,* "I speak to the people of Chicago on Friday next Sept 1st on Nebraska. They threaten a mob but I have no fears."[14]

On the platform on the 1st he could hardly get a word out. As he started to speak he was cut short by shouts, groans, and hisses, the staples of political derision. Every time he tried to regroup and speak again, the tumult heightened. The crowd began hurling "missiles" at the stage. The mayor stepped forward to order police to make arrests. But the crowd would have none of it. This was Chicago, the seat of strong antislavery sentiment. The author of that despicable act was not going to be allowed to speak.

Finally, Douglas lost his temper. He called the crowd a mob and shook his fist at it. The tumult intensified. He attempted to stare the audience into silence. That didn't work either. After two long, uproarious hours, he gave up and stalked off the stage shouting his defiance. Even then he wasn't clear of it. Much of the crowd followed his carriage back to the Tremont House and continued to howl after him. Inside, Douglas was shaken. He was not accustomed to this kind of defeat—a situation that he could not master. It must be countered. He began immediately to schedule an extensive campaign in defense of his bill from one end of the state to the other.[15]

It was going to be a fight after all. But Douglas was a fighter.

PART SEVEN

Clash of the Giants

18

Lincoln Emerges

As DOUGLAS RODE homeward toward Illinois along the track of his fiery effigies and met anger in Chicago, Lincoln was in Springfield waiting.

What had happened in Washington had changed everything. Until then, over the five years on the circuit since he had left Congress, law had all but crowded politics off of Lincoln's plate. But Douglas's repeal of the Missouri Compromise had "aroused him as he had never been before."[1]

The journalist, Horace White, said the effect of its repeal was like a blow on the head, the sort of thing "which causes a man to see stars in the daytime."[2] Lincoln was seeing stars in the daytime.

He had come to believe that slavery was "a poisonous exotic" that had "taken deep root in good soil, where it is crowding out every healthy growth." Lincoln still believed, as he always had, however, that "we can't go into our neighbor's field [into the states where it already exists] and dig it out, but we can and must keep it from spreading into clean soil [into the territories] which is the inheritance of the people."[3]

Lincoln believed that Douglas's popular sovereignty meant that "if one man chooses to enslave another, no third man has a right to object."[4] Young John Hay, the nephew of Lincoln's friend and fellow attorney, Milton Hay, saw Lincoln hurry into his uncle's law office, "waving a newspaper, and fairly quivering with excitement," exclaiming, "'This will never do! Douglas treats it as a matter of indifference, morally, whether slavery is voted down or voted up. I tell you it will never do!'"[5]

Joseph Gillespie thought he knew what his friend Lincoln believed about this exotic poison in the bloodstream of the Union. Gillespie said Lincoln believed slaves to be "the most glittering ostentatious & displaying property in the world," that the love of possessing them was "highly seductive" to "the thoughtless and giddy headed young men who looked upon work as vulgar and ungentlemanly." Lincoln believed slavery "was swallowing up every other mercenary passion," and that "its ownership betokened not only the possession of wealth but indicated the gentleman of leisure who was above and scorned labour." This spirit, Lincoln believed, must be "met and if possible checked," that "slavery was a great & crying injustice an enormous national crime and that we could not expect to escape punishment for it."[6]

What to do about it? Lincoln by his own admission didn't see a clear and easy solution, but he believed something had to be done or slavery would overrun the whole country, now that the dividing line had been erased by Douglas in the Kansas-Nebraska Act. Lincoln believed with his idol, Henry Clay—and before him Thomas Jefferson—that the preferred way of getting rid of slavery was for the government to buy the slaves, set them free, then colonize them out of the country. But that was a hard sell, unpopular with slaveholders and with slaves. He believed that "the framers of our government expected slavery to die out and adapted the system to that," but that "their views were being frustrated by adventitious circumstances." His aim now, he told Gillespie, was to actively oppose its spread and restrict it "to its original design."[7]

The slavery question had been nagging Lincoln for two decades—at least since he and Dan Stone had introduced their dissenting resolution into the Illinois legislature in 1837. But until Douglas's bill repealed the compromise line, he had believed "that God will settle it, and settle it right, and that he will, in some inscrutable way, restrict the spread of so great an evil, but for the present it is our duty to wait."[8]

In 1854 Lincoln would wait no longer. As Douglas rode home toward Illinois, he saw that his duty was now strikingly different. He had been seriously jarred by this knock on the head and he intended to meet head-on this old adversary who had loosed this cataclysm on the country. Lincoln had been, Herndon said, "like a sleeping lion." But now he was awake and fully provoked. He would not, Herndon said, now sit, gather "his robes around him ... waiting for the people to call." He would be Daniel and beard the lion in his den.

In light of Lincoln's ambition, which had also been a sleeping lion, here was an opportunity for his own political resurrection. Herndon believed Lincoln was "always calculating, and always planning." His ambition was that "little engine that knew no rest." With the passage of the Kansas-Nebraska Act, he was ready to step again into the political arena. It had always been where his "restless ambition" drew him. The law was important—his calling, his livelihood, what consumed most of his time—but it had always been a stairway to a higher gratification.[9]

Lincoln was on the circuit when news of the repeal of the Missouri Compromise reached Illinois. Judge Theophilus Lyle Dickey, who was sharing a room with him at a local tavern, said Lincoln sat on the edge of the bed and discussed the situation far into the night. Dickey finally fell asleep, but when he awoke the next morning Lincoln was still sitting up in bed, deep in thought. "I tell you, Dickey," he said, picking up where he had left off the night before, "*this nation cannot exist half-slave and half-free!*"[10]

He told Herndon, "The day of compromise has passed. These two great ideas [slavery and freedom] have been kept apart only by the most artful means. They are like two wild beasts in sight of each other, but chained and held apart. Some day these deadly antagonists will one or the other break their bonds, and then the question will be settled."[11]

Lincoln was more than ready. All of his newspaper reading, all of his Euclid, all of his study and thinking and analyzing for all of those five cheerless politically deprived years, had brought him to this. He was primed, as well informed on the slavery issue and as ready to hammer it into powerful argument as any man, including Douglas.

By July 1, 1854, Lincoln was marshalling his thoughts, writing several pages of "fragments" on the issue. "Although volume upon volume is written to prove slavery a very good thing," one of these fragments said, "we never hear of the man who wishes to take the good of it, *by being a slave himself.*"

Another fragment said:

If A. can prove, however conclusively, that he may, of right, enslave B.—why may not B. snatch the same argument, and prove equally, that he may enslave A? You say A. is white, and B. is black. It is *color,* then; the lighter, having the right to enslave the darker? Take care. By this rule, you are to be slave to the first man you meet, with a fairer skin than your own.

You do not mean *color* exactly?—You mean the whites are *intellectually* the superiors of the blacks, and, therefore have the right to enslave them? Take care again. By this rule, you are to be slave to the first man you meet, with an intellect superior to your own.

But, say you, it is a question of *interest*; and if you can make it your *interest,* you have the right to enslave another. Very well. And if he can make it his interest, he has the right to enslave you.[12]

This year—1854—was not a national election year. But it was an important year in Illinois politics. There were congressmen to elect or reelect, and a legislature to seat, which in turn would pick a U.S. senator—a colleague for Douglas. It was why Douglas was back in Illinois—to campaign for a favorable legislature—and, as Lincoln put it, "to set himself right with his people," for "the great racket the passage of his bill has kicked up."[13] It was clear what the pistol-hot issue was going to be.

On August 9, Lincoln met Richard Yates, a Whig anti-Nebraska congressman returning from Washington, and talked to him about his run for reelection. Lincoln's immediate aim was to help him. He would stump for Yates, hitting hard at the repeal of the compromise line. He wrote his friend John M. Palmer, "how anxious I am that this Nebraska measure shall be rebuked and condemned every where." Soon his rebuking and condemning would be drawing "more marked attention than they had ever before done," and he would be quickly pulled to parts of the state outside of Yates's district.[14]

On August 26 in Winchester, Colonel N. H. Knapp stopped E. G. Miner, a Scott County Whig and longtime Lincoln friend, and his son on the street to tell them Lincoln was at the Akin House, that he had "got up a speech on the Kansas-Nebraska bill which he has never made before and he has come down here to 'try it on the dog' before he delivers it to larger audiences." Lincoln tried it on the dog in the courthouse, standing on the floor in front of the judge's chair. The *Illinois Journal* called it "ably and eloquently" done, a "masterly effort...replete with unanswerable arguments."[15] He spoke again in Carrollton two days later for more than two hours, and again in Jacksonville on September 2.

On September 9 he tested what he had "got up" in the fire of debate—with his old surveying boss and political adversary, John Calhoun, at a public meeting in Springfield. Yates had defeated Calhoun in the campaign for Congress two years before. Three days later, Lincoln was in Bloomington addressing a German anti-Nebraska meeting. He told them, there is "a vast difference" between tolerating slavery in the South—protecting the slaveholder in the rights granted him by the Constitution—and extending it "over a territory already free, and uncontaminated with the institution." This repeal of the Missouri Compromise line, Lincoln charged, "was done without the consent of the people, and against their wishes." It was "got up unexpectedly by the people, hurried through, and now they were called upon to sanction it."[16] On the 26th he was in Bloomington again, honing and sharpening his arguments.

On October 3 the state fair was in progress in Springfield, always a ripe opportunity for political speechmaking. Douglas arrived and spoke in the Hall of Representatives in the state-house. When he finished, Lincoln who had arrived late but heard most of it, rose and announced that he would answer Douglas the next day. The table was set for combat. Lincoln and Douglas were about to go head-to-head once again.

"There was no formal or stated reason why Lincoln should reply," Whitney later wrote, "except from a general recognition of his superior ability to do so; no one else was mentioned in that connection, everybody seemed instinctively to indicate Lincoln as the champion, although he was a private citizen merely, with no political strand to bind him to the debate."[17] But reply he would.

Lincoln relished the coming combat. He told a friend, "I will answer that speech without any trouble, because"—he be-lieved—"Judge Douglas made two misstatements of fact, and upon these two misstatements he built his whole argument. I can show that his facts are not facts, and that will refute his speech."[18]

The next day was a warm one for October, an Indian-summer day, and Lincoln was in his shirtsleeves when he stepped on the platform at two o'clock in the afternoon. He spoke for three hours—covering much of the same ground that he had in Bloomington and in the speeches before Bloomington. His thought on the issue, his fragments of notes, had crystallized into a hard-hitting package.

The *Illinois Journal* on October 5 summarized the speech. In it Lincoln charged that "the new fangled doctrines of popular rights" were invented "to cloak the spread of slavery." The Ordinance of 1787, he argued, declared "that slavery or involuntary servitude...*should never exist* in the territory north and west of the Ohio river—the territory out of which have been succes-sively carved the States of Ohio, Indiana, Illinois, Michigan and

Wisconsin." In effect, he argued, the Founders themselves robbed that territory of the right of self-government in the matter of slavery—deprived it specifically "of the blessings of 'popular sovereignty,' as contained in the Nebraska bill."

The Missouri Compromise a third of a decade later had then barred slavery north of 36°30' in the Louisiana territory. And now this Nebraska bill "breaks down that restriction and opens the door for slavery to enter where before it could not go. This is practically legislating for slavery, recognizing it, endorsing it, propagating it, extending it."

Lincoln attacked Douglas's argument that slavery was not likely to expand into the territories in any event. "Why not?" Lincoln demanded. "What will hinder? Do cattle nibble a pasture right up to a division fence, crop all close under the fence, and even put their necks through and gather what they can reach, over the line, and still refuse to pass over into the next green pasture, even if the fence shall be thrown down?"

He raked the Douglas argument that repeal of the 36°30' line was desirable—that slavery had a constitutional, legal, natural, social, and political right to exist in the territories if the people there wished it. "What constitutional right existed for its repeal?" Lincoln demanded. "Or what *legal* right? Can any one point to a law...that creates the right?" What natural right? "Is it [slavery] not held to be the great wrong of the world?" What social and political right? "The word 'Slavery' is not found in the Constitution. The clause that covers the institution is one that sends it *back* where it exists, not *abroad* where it does not." Lincoln offered other analogies: "It is said that the slaveholder has the same right to take his negroes to Kansas that a freeman has to take his hogs or his horses. This would be true if negroes were property in the same sense that hogs and horses are. But is this the case? It is notoriously not so. Southern men do not treat their negroes as they do their horses."[19]

Douglas had stayed, listening to all of this, interrupting occasionally, and, when Lincoln finished he replied for another two hours. Lincoln was agreeable to this. He said in his introductory remarks, "I willingly give Senator Douglas, who now sits in front of me, the privilege of correcting me where I am wrong in the facts about the whole matter of the Kansas-Nebraska bill." It was, after all, the senator who introduced that "offspring of the ambition and greed of slavery."[20]

The *Illinois Journal* and the *Illinois State Register*—at political loggerheads always—had contrary takes on this quasi-debate. The *Journal* said Douglas's rebuttal was "adroit and plausible, but had not the marble of logic in it." The *Register* said Douglas "pounded [Lincoln] to pumice with his terrible war club of retort and argument."[21]

The *Journal* further reported that Lincoln "attacked the Nebraska Bill with unusual warmth and energy, and all felt that a man of strength was its enemy.... The Nebraska Bill was shivered, and, like a tree of the forest, was torn and rent asunder by the hot bolts of truth.... It was a proud day for Lincoln. His friends will never forget it.... [He] took captive the heart and broke like a sun over the understanding." The pro-Lincoln *Chicago Press and Tribune* wrote: "We deemed it by far the ablest effort of the campaign—from whatever source. The occasion was a great one, and the speaker was every way equal to it. The effect produced on the listeners was magnetic."[22]

Whigs in the state were delighted. Here was just the knight to joust with the Little Giant and his big bad bill. A written petition was circulated for Lincoln to "follow Douglas until he run him into his hole or made him holler."[23]

Lincoln took the petition to heart. When Douglas went to Peoria in the middle of October, Lincoln followed him there.

Indeed, Lincoln had now become part of the show. Even before he started his speech, before the large audience in Peoria, Douglas announced that Lincoln would answer him. Douglas started speaking at two o'clock in the afternoon and didn't finish until five. Lincoln then stood, not to speak, but to reschedule, proposing that all who wanted to stay take a break, eat supper, and reconvene at six-thirty or seven, since his answer was going to take as long as Douglas's speech. By prior agreement Douglas would stack on another hour of rebuttal.[24]

At seven Lincoln began speaking, giving basically the same powerful speech he had delivered twelve days earlier in Springfield, honed to an ever sharper edge.

"It is wrong," Lincoln said of the repeal of the Missouri Compromise; "wrong in its direct effect, letting slavery into Kansas and Nebraska—and wrong in its prospective principle, allowing it to spread to every other part of the wide world, where men can be found inclined to take it."

This "*declared* indifference"—Douglas not caring whether it is taken or not—Lincoln said again, is but a cover for the spread of slavery, and "I can not but hate [it]. I hate it because of the monstrous injustice of slavery itself. I hate it because it deprives our republican example of its just influence in the world—enables the enemies of free institutions, with plausibility, to taunt us as hypocrites—causes the real friends of freedom to doubt our sincerity, and especially because it forces so many really good men amongst ourselves into an open war with the very fundamental principles of civil liberty—criticising the Declaration of Independence, and insisting that there is no right principle of action but *self-interest*."

"Let no one be deceived," Lincoln said. "The spirit of seventy-six and the spirit of Nebraska, are utter antagonisms; and the former is being rapidly displaced by the latter."

Lincoln confessed that he himself was in a quandary over slavery where it existed. He said he could not blame the South "for not doing what I should not know how to do myself. If all earthly power were given me, I should not know what to do, as to the existing institution." He said his first impulse would be "to free all the slaves, and send them to Liberia—to their own native land." But he said that a moment's reflection "would convince me, that whatever of high hope...there may be in this, in the long run, its sudden execution is impossible. If they were all landed there in a day, they would all perish in the next ten days."

What then? "Free them, and make them politically and socially, our equals? My own feelings will not admit of this; and if mine would, we well know that those of the great mass of white people will not....A universal feeling, whether well or ill-founded, can not be safely disregarded."

But what to do about slavery as it exists in the South wasn't the question. Whether to let it spread to the territories was. Lincoln saw its spread, as "the great Behemoth of danger." That *was* something we could do something about. And Lincoln was coming down hard on that, as he had been since emerging to challenge Douglas.

Lincoln denied the rationale Douglas used to repeal the compromise line—that the Kansas-Nebraska country needed a territorial government, that the public demanded repeal, and that repeal was in line with a principle that is intrinsically right.

Could not the Nebraska territory have been organized just as well "without as with the repeal?" Lincoln demanded. Iowa and Minnesota were. Why not Nebraska? The public demanded it?

"I deny that the public ever demanded any such a thing," Lincoln said, that it "ever repudiated the Missouri Compromise—ever commanded its repeal. I deny it, and call for the proof." The repeal, with its avowed principle, is intrinsically right? "I insist that it is not," Lincoln said.

Lincoln homed in, as he had in Bloomington, on what he saw as the core difference between him and Douglas—the right of self-government. "The doctrine of self government is right—absolutely and eternally right," he said, "but it has no just application, as here attempted. Or perhaps I should say that whether it has such just application depends upon whether a negro is *not* or *is* a man. If he is *not* a man, why in that case, he who *is* a man may, as a matter of self-government, do just as he pleases with him. But if the negro *is* a man, is it not to that extent, a total destruction of self-government, to say that he too shall not govern *himself*? When the white man governs himself that is self-government; but when he governs himself, and also governs *another* man, that is *more* than self-government—that is despotism. If the negro is a *man,* why then my ancient faith teaches me that 'all men are created equal;' and that there can be no moral right in connection with one man's making a slave of another." No man, Lincoln said, "is good enough to govern another man, *without that other's consent.* I say this is the leading principle—the sheet anchor of American republicanism."

When this repeal of the compromise fell so suddenly on the country, Lincoln said in Peoria, "all was peace and quiet. The nation was looking to the forming of new bonds of Union; and a long course of peace and prosperity seemed to lie before us. In the whole range of possibility, there scarcely appears to me to have been any thing, out of which the slavery agitation could have been revived, except the very project of repealing the Missouri compromise." But the compromise was repealed, "and here we are, in the midst of a new slavery agitation," more intense and threatening than ever before.

Hand in hand with Lincoln's "ancient faith" in the idea of the Declaration of Independence that all men are created equal—was the faith that the repeal could not stand against moral truth. "Slavery," he said, "is founded in the selfishness of man's nature—opposition to it [in] his love of justice. These principles are an eternal antagonism; and when brought into collision so fiercely, as slavery extension brings them, shocks, and throes, and convulsions must ceaselessly follow. Repeal the Missouri compromise—repeal all compromises—repeal the Declaration of Independence—repeal all past history, you still can not repeal human nature. It still will be the abundance of man's heart, that slavery extension is wrong; and out of the abundance of his heart, his mouth will continue to speak."

"The Missouri Compromise ought to be restored," Lincoln urged. "For the sake of the Union, it ought to be restored. We ought to elect a House of Representatives which will vote its restoration." Lincoln acknowledged that the Senate, where Douglas dominated, "is still against us.... But if at these elections, their several constituencies shall clearly express their will against Nebraska, will these senators disregard their will? Will they neither obey, nor make room for those who will?"

"Let no one be deceived," Lincoln said in Peoria. "The spirit of seventy-six and the spirit of Nebraska, are utter antagonisms; and the former is being rapidly displaced by the latter.... Our republican robe is soiled and trailed in the dust. Let us repurify it. Let us turn and wash it white, in the spirit, if not the blood, of the Revolution. Let us turn slavery from its claims of 'moral right,' back upon its existing legal rights, and its arguments of 'necessity.' Let us return it to the position our fathers gave it; and there let it rest in peace. Let us re-adopt the Declaration of Independence, and with it, the practices, and policy, which harmonize with it. Let north and south—let all Americans—let all lovers of liberty everywhere—join in the great and good work. If we do this, we shall not only have saved the union; but we shall have so saved it, as to make, and to keep it, forever worthy of the saving. We shall have so saved it, that the succeeding millions of free happy people, the world over, shall rise up, and call us blessed, to the latest generations."[25]

If Lincoln wasn't running Douglas into his hole, he was making him holler some. Douglas wasn't comfortable with these impromptu face-offs. He could see that Lincoln understood the territorial question better than all of his opponents in the U.S. Senate.[26] He told a friend he was "deeply troubled" over the way things were going. "I have known Lincoln for many years and have continually met him in debate. I regard him as the most difficult and dangerous opponent that I have ever met, and I have serious misgivings as to what may be the result of this joint debate."[27]

His misgivings were warranted. In the election on November 7 an anti-Nebraska legislature was elected. Democrats were in the majority, but Whigs, with abolitionists and anti-Nebraska Democrats, if acting together, could elect a senator.

The ramifications of this did not escape Lincoln. He was riding a wave of flattering praise for his incisive speechmaking on the Nebraska question. The *Quincy Whig* on November 3 had praised him as one of the "truly great men" of Illinois.[28] This opinion was spreading.

In the hurly-burly of the campaign he had been elected to

the state legislature again—on the ballot to help get Yates re-elected to Congress. But with the thought that he might have a chance to become the senator, he began writing confidential letters, laying pipe, and drumming up support for his candidacy.

"You used to express a great deal of partiality for me," he wrote Charles Hoyt, a prominent Whig merchant and mill owner in Aurora, "and if you are still so, now is the time. Some friends here are really for me, for the U. S. Senate; and I should be very grateful if you could make a mark for me among your members." The next day, November 11, he wrote a similar letter to Jacob Harding of Paris. "I really have some chance," he said.

On November 25 he wrote Noah W. Matheny, clerk of the county court, declining the seat in the legislature, clearing the way for his senate run. Two days later he wrote Thomas J. Henderson, an anti-Nebraska member of the state House of Representatives, "It has come round that a whig may, by possibility, be elected to the U. S. Senate; and I want the chance of being the man."

"I have really got it into my head to try to be United States Senator," he wrote his friend Joseph Gillespie, also a member of the General Assembly, on December 1, "and if I could have your support my chances would be reasonably good."[29]

As he was writing these letters of self-promotion, he was assessing his likely opposition. Douglas's candidate for the seat was fellow pro-Nebraska Democrat, James Shields, the incumbent senator. But Lincoln was keeping a particular eye on Lyman Trumbull, an anti-Nebraska, anti-Douglas man who had just been elected to Congress. Trumbull was Connecticut-born, of an eminent New England family. He was four and a half years younger than Lincoln and a former school teacher, but had come to Illinois as a lawyer. He was above medium height, bespectacled, professorial, spare. He was reserved, standoffish, and abstemious, and as a speaker logical rather than eloquent—anything but a glad-handing politician. Like Lincoln, he had taken a virulent stand against the repeal of the Missouri Compromise.[30]

"Let me know," Lincoln urged Gillespie, "whether Trumbull intends to make a push."[31]

As this maneuvering was going on, Lincoln was trying to mount a concrete action to repeal the Kansas-Nebraska Act. In early January he drafted a set of resolutions. They urged the legislators to "use their best endeavors" to get the law repealed, to prevent the territories of Nebraska and Kansas from ever coming into the Union as slave states, to prevent slavery from ever being established where it did not then legally exist, to resist any attempt to divide part of California into a slave state, and to resist the threatened attempt to revive the African slave trade.[32]

Now Lincoln was counting his likely votes for senator. He wrote his friend Elihu B. Washburne, "I understand myself as having 26 commitals; and I do not think any other one man has ten—may be mistaken though."[33]

A strong wind brought heavy snow into Springfield on January 20. The next day, and for the next three days, the capital was cut off from the world. The fierce storm marooned trains on the prairie, downed telegraph lines, and stopped the mail. Not until the 24th did the first train in four days reach Springfield from Alton. On the 28th a train finally bulled its way into the city from the north, the first from there in more than a week. Not until February 1, only a week before the legislature was to meet to vote for a senator, had traffic from points north resumed in full stream, and then only with difficulty.[34]

When the voting began on February 8, Lincoln polled forty-five votes on the first ballot and Shields forty-one, with fifteen votes scattered—shy of the fifty-one needed to elect. Trumbull had five—all Democrats, adamantly anti-Nebraska but unable to bring themselves to vote for a Whig, not even Lincoln. On the sixth ballot Shields was holding steady with forty-two votes, but Lincoln had slipped to thirty-six. On the seventh ballot the pro-Nebraska Democrats switched from Shields to Governor Joel A. Matteson, whom they now hoped to push over the top.

Matteson was a native New Yorker, half a year older than Lincoln. He was a businessman, a master of finance, heavy on executive ability—and heavy in body—but light on oratorical gifts. He had been elected governor in 1852 for his executive ability, not for his heft and despite his shortcomings on a dais. He was kindly, benevolent, well mannered, respected, and liked to tell how he shared his bed nightly with a rattlesnake when he first came to Illinois and was building a cabin on his government claim. But he was a pro-Douglas, pro-Nebraska Democrat. On the ninth ballot Matteson's votes topped out at forty-seven, three shy of election. Trumbull's five dogged Democrats were standing faithful to him, and without them Matteson couldn't make it.[35]

But neither could Lincoln. Gillespie, one of his backers, asked what they ought to do. Without hesitating, Lincoln said, "You ought to drop me and go for Trumbull. That is the only way you can defeat Matteson." He told Stephen Logan, who wanted to continue toughing it out with him, "I think the cause in this case is to be preferred to men." The Lincoln men switched, though Gillespie later said, "it grieved us to the heart to give up Mr Lincoln."[36]

Trumbull was elected with fifty-one votes, just enough to win. Explaining it all to William H. Henderson of Putnam County, Lincoln said his friends "had to surrender to Trumbull's smaller number, in order to prevent the election of Matteson, which would have been a Douglas victory....I could not...let the whole political result go to ruin, on a point merely personal to myself."[37]

Herndon predicted that Trumbull would be a "Great thorn, rough and poisonous in the heart of Douglas."[38] Lincoln was reconciled to the outcome. He wrote Washburne that the Nebraska men hated Trumbull's election "worse than any thing that could have happened. It is a great consolation to see them worse whipped than I am." He said, "I regret my defeat moderately, but I am not nervous about it," that Matteson's defeat "now gives me more pleasure than my own gives me pain."[39]

The excitement over, he turned again to his law practice and the circuit, both busy and booming, where there was much more pleasure for him than pain.

19

Political Earthquake

THIS TIME, Lincoln's departure from politics and return to the law and the circuit was not the cheerless withdrawal it had been five years earlier. The law was back on his main line after his stint of "dabbling in politics,"[1] but Lincoln's political engine was now stoked and blowing smoke on a sidetrack. It had a successful, hard-charging run on the main line in 1854 and nearly carried him into the U.S. Senate in early 1855.

Douglas was still out there bigger than ever, preaching the gospel of popular sovereignty, and still a comet in the political heavens. A presidential election year loomed in 1856 and the Little Giant was being touted in the Democracy as a more likely candidate than ever. But Lincoln wouldn't lie low, as he had in 1852. In a speech in Decatur in early 1856 he made clear how willing he was "to buckle on his armor" for the approaching canvass.[2]

But there was a problem. Both parties were in ferment and

in trouble. The Whig Party, which Lincoln had embraced from its inception two decades before, was dissolving and slipping away. The slavery issue had split its northern and southern wings. The free soil movement was siphoning off its membership in the North. A new American Party, called the "Know-Nothings," a militant anti-immigrant, anti-Catholic party, had been complicating matters, making inroads North and South. Materializing in the early 1840s and peaking in the early 1850s, it had pulled many Whigs into it, away from their traditional moorings.

By 1856 the Whig party, in the words of one political observer, had "sacrificed both its character and its life on the altar of slavery."[3] A new coalition—the scraping together of the various angry and substantial anti-Kansas-Nebraska elements in the country—was forming and calling itself the Republican Party. But it was just aborning.

The Democratic Party was also showing cracks—big ones—over the Kansas-Nebraska issue, and over a darkening cloud of violence that was gripping Kansas. That territory, the centerpiece of the act that had repealed the Missouri Compromise, had now become a battleground of free-soil sentiment versus slavery. Free soil immigrants were streaming there from the Northeast, and militant pro-slavery Southerners were riding over the border from Missouri, armed and angry, to contest the ground. It was producing violence and putting party-splitting pressure on the Democrats.

That did not surprise Lincoln. He wrote Joshua Speed in August 1855, "I look upon that enactment [of the Kansas-Nebraska law] not as a *law,* but as *violence* from the beginning. It was conceived in violence, passed in violence, is maintained in violence, and is being executed in violence. I say it was *conceived* in violence, because the destruction of the Missouri Compromise, under the circumstances, was nothing less than violence. It was *passed* in violence, because it could not have passed at all but for the votes of many members, in violent disregard of the known will of their constituents. It is *maintained* in violence because the elections since, clearly demand its repeal, and this demand is openly disregarded."[4]

The Whig crackup had left Lincoln without an anchorage. He was unmoored, rudderless, without a political compass, finding himself, as Herndon put it, "drifting about with the disorganized elements that floated together after the angry political waters had subsided." It had become apparent, Herndon said, "that if he expected to figure as a leader he must take a stand himself. Mere hatred of slavery and opposition to the injustice of the Kansas-Nebraska legislation were not all that were required of him. He must be a Democrat, Know-Nothing, Abolitionist, or Republican, or forever float about in the great political sea without compass, rudder, or sail."[5]

Throughout 1855 Lincoln had continued to distill his thinking on the slavery issue. In August he had written an introspective letter to George Robertson, a former member of Congress. Since the Missouri Compromise in 1820, Lincoln wrote "we have had thirty six years of experience, and this experience has demonstrated, I think, that there is no peaceful extinction of slavery in prospect for us. The signal failure of Henry Clay, and other good and great men, in 1849, to effect any thing in favor of gradual emancipation in Kentucky, together with a thousand other signs, extinguishes that hope utterly."

On the question of liberty, as a principle, Lincoln wrote, "we are not what we have been. When we were the political slaves of King George, and wanted to be free, we called the maxim that 'all men are created equal' a self evident truth; but now when we have grown fat, and have lost all dread of being slaves ourselves, we have become so greedy to be *masters* that we call the same maxim 'a self evident lie.'"

Lincoln believed, "That spirit which desired the peaceful extinction of slavery, has itself become extinct." So far as peaceful, voluntary emancipation was concerned, "the condition of the negro slave in America is now as fixed, and hopeless of change for the better, as that of the lost souls of the finally impenitent. The Autocrat of all the Russians will resign his crown, and proclaim his subjects free republicans sooner than will our American masters voluntarily give up their slaves."

Lincoln had come to believe that "our political problem now is 'Can we, as a nation, continue together *permanently—forever—* half slave, and half free?' The problem is too mighty for me. May God, in his mercy, superintend the solution."[6]

Lincoln would probably have welcomed some divine superintending for his own political dilemma—finding his new political home. In late August 1855 when Joshua Speed asked him where he stood politically, Lincoln wrote: "That is a disputed point. I think I am a whig; but others say there are no whigs, and that I am an abolitionist. When I was at Washington I voted for the Wilmot Proviso as good as forty times, and I never heard of any one attempting to unwhig me for that. I now do no more than oppose the extension of slavery."

"I am not a Know-Nothing," Lincoln explained to Speed. "That is certain. How could I be? How can any one who abhors the oppression of negroes, be in favor of degrading classes of white people? Our progress in degeneracy appears to me to be pretty rapid. As a nation, we began by declaring that '*all men are created equal.*' We now practically read it 'all men are created equal, *except negroes.*' When the Know-Nothings get control, it will read 'all men are created equal, except negroes, *and foreigners, and catholics.*' When it comes to this I should prefer emigrating to some country where they make no pretence of loving liberty—to Russia, for instance, where despotism can be taken pure, and without the base alloy of hypocracy."[7]

Becoming a Democrat was out of the question. And although he detested slavery, Lincoln was as uncomfortable being lumped with abolitionists as he was with Know-Nothings. Unlike the Whig Party, the Know-Nothing—American—party still had life. On August 11, Lincoln wrote Owen Lovejoy, Elijah Lovejoy's brother, "Until we can get the elements of this organization [the Know-Nothings], there is not sufficient materials to successfully combat the Nebraska democracy with. We can not get them so long as they cling to a hope of success under their own organization; and I fear an open push by us now, may offend them, and tend to prevent our ever getting them."

The Know-Nothings around Springfield, Lincoln wrote, "are mostly my old political and personal friends; and I have hoped their organization would die out without the painful necessity of my taking an open stand against them. Of their principles I think little better than I do those of the slavery extensionists."[8]

Lincoln was cautiously treading water not immediately jumping the sinking Whig ship. Those aboard the new-floated Republican vessel were being called "fusionists" in Illinois, and the prominence of abolitionists in the fusionist ranks gave Lincoln pause. He was willing to cooperate with them in their anti-Nebraskaism, but not to join them—at least not yet.[9]

The new Republican Party had been launched in Wisconsin and had spread rapidly through Michigan and Ohio. But its entry into Illinois had been slow. For two years, the enemies of the Kansas-Nebraska Act in the state had simply called themselves "anti-Nebraska men." It was not until the spring of 1856 that they united under one umbrella organization and joined the Republican crusade. And it was not until then that Lincoln tied his political destiny to its rising star.

Herndon, who had worried about Lincoln's rudderlessness, forced him into it. Already committed and impassioned—as was his way—Herndon had drawn up a paper calling a county convention in Springfield to select delegates for a forthcoming Republican state convention in Bloomington. Lincoln was absent at the time, attending court in Tazewell County. "Believing I knew what his 'feeling and judgment' on the vital questions of the hour were," Herndon explained, "I took the liberty to sign his name to the call."

The call, with Lincoln's and Herndon's heading the list of 130 names, was published in the *Illinois Journal* on May 10. John Stuart, one of several who had been urging Lincoln not to be too hasty, immediately charged into Herndon's office demanding to know if Lincoln had really signed that "Abolition call." "Did Lincoln authorize you to sign it?" Stuart demanded. "No," Herndon confessed. "Then," Stuart exploded, "you have ruined him."

Herndon, however, was not alarmed. "I thought I understood Lincoln thoroughly," he later explained, "but in order to vindicate myself if assailed I immediately sat down, after Stuart had rushed out of the office, and wrote Lincoln . . . a brief account of what I had done and how much stir it was creating in the ranks of his conservative friends." Herndon asked Lincoln to telegraph him at once whether he approved or disapproved.

In what amounted to an oh-what-the-hell answer, Lincoln wired back: "All right; go ahead. Will meet you—radicals and all."[10]

Two weeks later the called meeting convened in the court-house in Springfield and picked four delegates to the state convention in Bloomington on May 29. Lincoln was one of them. The meeting denounced the repeal of the Missouri Compromise and vowed to "unite with all who are willing to unite with us."[11]

From the start, Lincoln had not objected to fusing with anybody "provided I can fuse on ground which I think is right; and I believe the opponents of slavery extension could now do this, if it were not for this K.N.ism." In speeches he had been urging others to "stand with any body who stands right." He was saying now that he was ready "to follow my own advice."[12]

Lincoln left for Bloomington on May 27 and arrived the next day. There he bought his first pair of reading glasses at a little shop in town, and he was one of several speakers that evening at a pre-convention meeting in front of the Pike House. The convention met on the 29th, gave the new party its "official christening" in Illinois, and adopted a platform "ringing with strong Anti-Nebraska sentiments."[13]

When it was time for speechmaking the delegates called for Lincoln. There were reporters present with pencils ready. But as Lincoln began to speak, his words were so powerful that nobody remembered to take notes, dropping their pencils to listen, mesmerized. One reporter, John L. Scripps of the *Chicago Democratic Press,* could only report that "for an hour and a half he held the assemblage spell-bound by the power of his argument, the intense irony of his invective, and the deep earnestness and fervid brilliancy of his eloquence."[14]

Joseph Medill, editor of the *Chicago Tribune,* was there ready to take notes as well and could only report that it was the greatest speech he had ever listened to, that "at times Lincoln seemed to reach up into the clouds and take out the thunderbolts."

When Lincoln finished and sat down, another who was there said, "Men jumped to their feet; stood on their chairs; they waved hats, they waved handkerchiefs, they waved their canes, anything they had," and rushed to the stage to embrace and congratulate him. Medill looked down at his paper, and there lay his pencil and but a few sentences of the speech. Nobody else had recorded more.[15]

"If Lincoln was six feet, four inches high usually, at Bloomington that day," Herndon said, "he was seven feet, and inspired at that." Herndon was even taller in his enthusiasm. "I have heard or read all of Mr. Lincoln's great speeches," he later wrote, "and I give it as my opinion that the Bloomington speech was the grand effort of this life. Heretofore he had simply argued the slavery question on grounds of policy—the statesman's grounds—never reaching the question of the radical and eternal right. Now he was newly baptized and freshly born; he had the fervor of a new convert; the smothered flame broke out; enthusiasm unusual to him blazed up; his eyes were aglow with an inspiration; he felt justice; his heart was alive to the right; his sympathies, remarkably deep for him, burst forth, and he stood before the throne of the eternal Right."

The speech, as Herndon in his own towering belief in eternal right saw it, "was full of fire and energy and force; it was logic; it was pathos; it was enthusiasm; it was justice, equity, truth, and right set ablaze by the divine fires of a soul maddened by the wrong; it was hard, heavy, knotty, gnarly, backed with wrath." At least that was how he remembered it, confessing that he also had "attempted for about fifteen minutes as was usual with me then to take notes, but at the end of that time I threw pen and paper away and lived only in the inspiration of the hour."[16]

Lincoln's half decade of introspective thinking had come to

an explosive head in this one speech that signaled his moorings in a new political anchorage. It had been a speech, one writer later said, powered by his unrivaled grasp of the issue, and it had reached "the very fountain-head of thought and enforced conviction."[17] And nobody remembered exactly what it said, only that it paralyzed them. It would soon become known as his "lost speech."

Lincoln was riding high for a newcomer to a party—higher than he realized. He was on the circuit in Urbana on June 20 when a Chicago reporter arrived about noon bringing news that he had polled 110 votes for vice president at the first Republican national convention meeting in Philadelphia the day before. "I reckon it's not me," Lincoln said. "There's another Lincoln down in Massachusetts [Levi Lincoln, the Bay State governor]. I've an idea he's the one."[18]

But it was the Illinois Lincoln. William B. Allison of Pennsylvania had been requested to nominate him and did so, saying, to cheers, that he "knew him to be the prince of good fellows, and an old-line Whig." "But can Mr. Lincoln fight?" somebody demanded. "YES SIR," said W. B. Archer of Illinois. "He is a son of Kentucky."[19]

The convention in Philadelphia had picked the young romantic western soldier-explorer, John C. Frémont, as its first-ever nominee for president. His running mate would not be Lincoln, but William L. Dayton of New Jersey.

On the Democratic side, Douglas was deep in the presidential hunt—one of four front-running contenders, with James Buchanan, Franklin Pierce, and Lewis Cass. As Joshua Speed said, Douglas had long "held the reins and controlled the movement of the Democratic chariot" in Illinois. Now he was for grabbing the reins of the national Democratic carriage.[20] It was being said around Washington that this one-time apprentice cabinetmaker was "still a *cabinet-maker,* proficient in *making Cabinets* and *Bureaus.*"[21]

Early on, Buchanan had surged to the front of this quartet by being absent from the country. This kept him above the factional strife that had ravaged the other three; he had been minister to Great Britain during the political turmoil generated by the Kansas-Nebraska Act. He had a long resume in government service—nearly half a century. But that long career had been somewhat lackluster—measured and sane, but unexciting. And his longevity meant that he was getting old. He was sixty-five, and that was a liability. He didn't have the dramatic and emotional allure that galvanized masses. He was what Young America looked on as an old fogie. But he had the avuncular image of a man to trust in these untrustworthy times.

Pierce wanted to be renominated. But he was damaged goods. Cass looked too much like a rerun. Douglas had been in the very vortex of the factional struggle. So when the Democratic convention met on June 2 in Cincinnati, Buchanan was the clear front-runner. But the nomination wouldn't come easily. He had also been the frontrunner in 1852 and hadn't been able to close it out. He led in the first ballot this time, but it was not until the seventeenth, to avoid a deadlock, that he made it over the top and then was unanimously nominated. Douglas virtually withdrew himself from contention, instructing his team at the convention to "let no personal considerations disturb the harmony of the party or endanger the triumph of our principles."[22]

There was to be another wild card in this election, as there so often was of late—a potential spoiler. Fillmore had re-emerged, the candidate of the American Party and looking like a complication for the Republicans. With this cast of candidates in place, the canvass opened: two old political mossbacks, Buchanan and Fillmore, versus the kid, the young soldier—two elder statesmen versus a military man whose party was as green as he was.

Lincoln was an elector, which meant he would be obliged again to stump the state. Herndon said, "He was in demand everywhere," and not just in Illinois. Indiana, Wisconsin, and Iowa were all asking for him. "Lincoln's importance in the conduct of the campaign was apparent to all," Herndon said. His priority would be "to wean away Fillmore's adherents," to strive "to show that in clinging to their candidate they were really aiding the election of Buchanan."[23]

Illinois was to become one of the key battlegrounds of the campaign, and the Lincoln & Herndon law office, Henry Rankin said, "was practically the Republican headquarters."[24] But because of the Fillmore wild card, there was trouble in Illinois. "With the Frémont and Fillmore men united, here in Illinois," Lincoln wrote a friend in Michigan, "we have Mr. Buchanan in the hollow of our hand; but with us divided, as we now are he has us. This is the short and simple truth, as I believe." "Every vote taken from Frémont and given to Fillmore," Lincoln complained, "is just so much in favor of Buchanan." He calculated that as things then stood Frémont had about 78,000 votes in Illinois and Fillmore 21,000. This would give Buchanan the state by 7,000, even though he was in the minority by 14,000. "Our whole trouble," he wrote Trumbull, "has been & is Fillmoreism." In a form letter to Fillmore men in early September he wrote: "Be not deceived. *Buchanan* is the hard horse to beat in this race. Let him have Illinois and nothing can beat him; *and he will get Illinois,* if men persist in throwing away votes upon Mr. Fillmore."[25]

Whether or not Lincoln was making any headway against Fillmore, he was aggravating Democrats. The *Illinois State Register* was calling him "that great high-priest of abolitionism." But a little note of respect was filtering out through the aggravation. The Democratic *Illinois Sentinel* in Jacksonville admitted Lincoln was "a fine speaker... certainly the ablest black republican."[26] An old-time Democrat, leaving an open-air meeting after hearing Lincoln speak, told reporter Noah Brooks, "He's a dangerous man, sir! A damned dangerous man! He makes you believe what he says, in spite of yourself!"[27]

What did Lincoln believe in spite of *himself*? Young Brooks, a Republican partisan, met him for the first time at a mass Frémont-Dayton rally in Ogle County. Privately Lincoln was thinking Frémont could not be elected. "Don't be discouraged if we don't carry the day this year," Lincoln told Brooks. "We can't do it, that's certain. We can't carry Pennsylvania; those old Whigs down there are too strong for us. But we shall, sooner or later, elect our President. I feel confident of that." But when? He felt doubtful even about 1860. "It's doubtful—*very* doubtful," he told Brooks. "Perhaps we shall be able to fetch it by 1864; perhaps not.... It may not be in my day; but it will be in yours, I do really believe."[28]

On a muddy, cold, disagreeable election day in early November, Lincoln was the 226th voter at poll number two in Springfield.[29] He had been right about what he told Brooks. Frémont and Dayton lost the election in Illinois and in the country. But he had done his part. He had made over fifty speeches on their behalf. He had done his part for them, and even more for himself. He came down from the stump in 1856 bigger than ever, more popular than ever, and more important to his new party than ever.

20

At the Crossroads

BILLY HERNDON COULD clearly see that in three short years the passage of the Kansas-Nebraska Act had galvanized all of New England and much of the North. It had armed the abolitionists with new weaponry, incited them to more furious resistance to slavery, killed the Whig Party, "drove together strange, discordant elements" to "fight a common enemy," and thrust to the forefront a leader in Lincoln.[1]

It was apparent that all of Lincoln's new-emerging political prestige and skill, like a surging river seeking a new channel, must cut a new course. And the next turn in the river of his ambition seemed bound to cut directly across the path, once again, of Stephen Douglas.

Douglas was much on Lincoln's mind as 1856 phased into 1857. In a fragment he wrote to himself at year's end Lincoln said:

"Twenty-two years ago Judge Douglas and I first became acquainted. We were both young then; he a trifle younger than I. Even then, we were both ambitious; I, perhaps quite as much so as he. With *me,* the race of ambition has been a failure—a flat failure; with *him* it has been one of splendid success. His name fills the nation; and is not unknown, even, in foreign lands. I affect no contempt for the high eminence he has reached. So reached, that the oppressed of my species, might have shared with me in the elevation, I would rather stand on that eminence, than wear the richest crown that ever pressed a monarch's brow."[2]

More than ever now Lincoln wanted to stand on the political heights where Douglas stood. The Little Giant would be up for reelection to his senate seat in 1858. That seat loomed now as an obvious, attainable target. Lincoln was the obvious Republican to challenge Douglas. It would be nothing new; he had done it so often before. But the stakes had never been so high.

Herndon said that the canvass of 1856 and "the signs of the times indicated, and the result of the [1856] canvass demonstrated, that he alone was powerful enough to meet the redoubtable Little Giant in a greater conflict yet to follow."[3] Herndon was by no means alone in that sentiment. By late May the *Chicago Journal* would be describing Lincoln as "the successor of Stephen A. Douglas in the U. S. Senate."[4]

At this turning point in his political life Lincoln, as he had always been, was *sui generis,* on the stump and off. There was nobody quite like him. And he had honed his oratorical skills to a sharp and cutting edge.

Almost daily, Herndon had studied him closely. He had listened to him many times in the courtroom and on the hustings and believed his finely tuned speaking skill was abetted by a

memory that was "exceedingly retentive, tenacious, and strong."
He could write out a speech, Herndon said, "and then repeat it
word for word without any effort on his part."[5]

Despite his gift of speech, Lincoln did not particularly enjoy
speaking. He told Henry Whitney that every time he was on his
way to making a speech, "I wish it was over...when I have to
make a speech, I always want it over."[6] He rejected looping, eru-
dite speeches larded with classical allusions that so many orators
favored. His words, Herndon said, were "strong, terse, knotty,
gnarly, and compact...driven together as by a sledge hammer."[7]
A friend and fellow attorney, Robert G. Ingersoll, said Lincoln's
words were "candid as mirrors," giving "the perfect image of his
thought."[8] However, cruising along in his slow, high-pitched
cadences, it was said he occasionally broke off for repairs in the
middle of a sentence.[9]

Lincoln spoke, Herndon said, "to move the judgment as well
as the emotions of men." But clarity, at the most fundamental
level, was the heart and soul of his speaking style. He once told
Herndon, "Billy, don't shoot too high—aim lower and the common people will understand you. They are the ones you want to
reach—at least they are the ones you ought to reach. The educated and refined people will understand you any way. If you aim
too high your ideas will go over the heads of the masses, and only
hit those who need no hitting."[10]

Whitney believed his "preeminent greatness lay in the com-
bination of the powers of analysis and synthesis" he brought to
the stump. "Unerringly he constructed from loose facts, principles, morals, ethics, and dialectics, a complete concrete theory."
His study of Euclid had put him in the habit of pursuing "long
trains of ideas" and the ability to stick with them until he had

pierced "through the mazes of sophism [to] discover a latent truth."[11]

Though he was a story-spinner off the stump, Lincoln rarely spun an anecdote when discussing serious matters and in his political speeches. Before the Kansas-Nebraska Act, one of the main weapons in his arsenal had been not only humor, but, very often, biting ridicule and invective. Herndon believed Lincoln had "the gift of satire." But after 1854 ridicule was a weapon he no longer used.[12] His friend, Joseph Gillespie, said Lincoln then believed that in discussions of great questions anecdotes shouldn't "be lugged in as to make weight," and that doing so was contrary "to his notion of *fairness.*"[13]

All of Lincoln's speaking apparatus was driven by the motor of logic seasoned by intense thinking and reasoning. As he always did on any important matter, Lincoln had exhausted every angle of this issue of slavery. Schuyler Colfax, an Indiana congressman, said Lincoln had this "peculiarity" from earliest manhood of habitually studying "the opposite side of every disputed question, of every law case, of every political issue, more exhaustively, if possible, than his own side."[14]

His mind, his thought process, Herndon believed, "working in its accustomed channel, heedless of beauty or awe, followed irresistibly back to the first cause. It was in this light he viewed every question. However great the verbal foliage that concealed the nakedness of a good idea Lincoln stripped it all down till he could see clear the way between cause and effect. If there was any secret in his power this was surely it."[15]

Lincoln saw many things clearly now. He clearly saw the cause and effect of slavery in the territories. He clearly believed that Douglas had turned loose a political modus operandi on the country—popular sovereignty—that threatened to make America a slave nation forever. But he saw that Douglas was vulnerable because of it. Lincoln also doubtless saw that if Douglas were to be beaten, he must be the one to do it. It was to be war again with Douglas, hand-to-hand combat at a highly fierce level.

21

Axe Handles and Wedges

NO MAN HAD yet come to the presidency looking better on paper than James Buchanan. He had nearly half a century of diverse grounding in the art of government. Yet experience in this deepest of confounding problems, slavery, hadn't been prominent on his résumé.

Little more than two years before, in the autumn of 1854, Lincoln had admitted in Peoria that if all earthly power were given him he wouldn't know what to do about slavery in the states where it existed, that his only resolve was to keep it out of the free territories.

Not knowing what to do about it where it existed—except leave it alone, as he believed the Constitution demanded—was double true of James Buchanan. But unlike Lincoln, he rather liked the idea that it existed. Although a Pennsylvanian, he harbored Southern sympathies.

What did bother Buchanan was that this problem of slavery in the territories—the big puzzler—was now his to deal with. And his heart's deepest desire was that it not mess up his administration or the country.

In his inaugural he came down on the side of the Kansas-Nebraska Act and popular sovereignty. He argued that the Missouri Compromise line no longer held, that Congress couldn't rightly interfere with slavery in the territories, that it was up to the people in the territories to decide to enter statehood with slaves or free. Individual slaveholders meanwhile could go anywhere they wanted with their slaves.

Buchanan had been working behind the scenes, before his inauguration, to double-stick an even more emphatic policy along those lines in the nation's political matrix and cement it there. He knew that the Supreme Court was about to decide a case that could settle the distraction once and for all, and hopefully remove it as a threat to the nation—and his presidency.

The matter had to do with a slave named Dred Scott. Scott belonged to an army doctor, who had taken him from Missouri, a slave state, into Minnesota Territory, destined to become a free state, then back to Missouri. Scott construed his living in a free state (above the Missouri Compromise line) as grounds for freedom. A Missouri circuit court had agreed with him, an appeals court had disagreed with the circuit court, and the case had come to the Supreme Court, where it had become a high-profile proceeding with high-powered lawyers arguing on both sides.

President-elect Buchanan saw this case as a chance to forever settle the issue and bring final peace to the country and his administration. A Supreme Court decision on the constitutionality of the Missouri Compromise would be just the thing. In early 1857, just before his inauguration, the court was moving toward a decision. Learning that the justices were split on the issue, and wanting them to make a definitive issue-ending verdict, Buchanan began to interfere. He wrote one of the supposedly wavering justices, urging him to a broader decision. With this presidential prodding as part of the picture, the court finally announced that it had reached a decision.

Knowing this beforehand, Buchanan confidently delivered his inaugural address on March 4, leaking news that the Supreme Court would soon settle the matter. Two days later the court spoke.

There were several issues, nuances, and disagreements on key points among the justices. But eighty-year-old Chief Justice Roger Taney did the talking. He handed down a decision that slaves were forever property and without any rights that white men were bound to respect. No black could be a citizen, nor could a slave sue for his freedom. But it went even farther, where Buchanan had hoped it would go. It declared that Congress had no power to prohibit slavery in the federal territories. The decision opened up all the territories to slavery, sealed that policy in concrete, and made it national.[1]

Buchanan was pleased, confident that with his endorsement the decision would settle the matter for good and quiet the sectional storm. Instead it whipped up a cry of outrage and anguish from the ever-growing, seething body of anti-slavery, anti-Nebraska sentiment in the North. It caused Abraham Lincoln to see stars again in the daytime.

Herndon said, "Since the decision of the 'Dred Scott Case' I have seen calm, cool, philosophic men grit their teeth and— swear." Many of these swearing, teeth-gritting philosophic men—Lincoln among them—feared that with the Dred Scott decision all the legal barriers were down, that it was but one more decision away from making it unlawful for any state to *exclude* slavery. This tide, they urgently believed, had to be stemmed and reversed.[2]

In the spring Lincoln went back on the circuit. But that noxious Supreme Court decision nagged him. So did Douglas's support of it. In early June, the Little Giant delivered a speech in Springfield and Lincoln was there listening, then reading the report of it. On June 26 in a speech of his own he unloaded on both the decision and Douglas.

"We think the Dred Scott decision is erroneous," he said. "We know the court that made it, has often over-ruled its own decisions, and we shall do what we can to have it over-rule this." He said, "We offer no resistance to it," but "when...we find it wanting in...claims to the public confidence, it is not resistance, it is not factious, it is not even disrespectful, to treat it as not having quite established a settled doctrine for the country."

In his speech Douglas had raked Republicans for insisting that the Declaration of Independence included all men, black and white. Then, Lincoln protested, he "boldly denies that it includes negroes at all, and proceeds to argue gravely that all who contend it does, do so only because they want to vote, and eat, and sleep, and marry with negroes! He will have it that they cannot be consistent else."

"Now I protest," Lincoln said, "against that counterfeit logic which concludes that, because I do not want a black woman for a *slave* I must necessarily want her for a *wife*. I need not have her for either, I can just leave her alone. In some respects she certainly is not my equal; but in her natural right to eat the bread she earns with her own hands without asking leave of any one else, she is my equal, and the equal of all others."

In his speech Lincoln blasted Douglas and Taney both for insisting that the authors of the Declaration of Independence did not intend to include Negroes in its born-free largess. But excluding them, Lincoln argued, is doing "obvious violence to the plain unmistakable language of the Declaration. I think the authors of that notable instrument intended to include all men, but they did not intend to declare all men equal *in all respects.* They did not mean to say all were equal in color, size, intellect, moral developments, or social capacity. They defined with tolerable distinctness, in what respects they did consider all men created equal—equal in 'certain inalienable rights, among which are life, liberty, and the pursuit of happiness.' This they said, and this meant."

Lincoln dismissed the Douglas argument that when the Founders said all men are created equal they meant only the white race and that they had framed the Constitution simply to justify the revolution that followed.

"My good friends," Lincoln urged, "read that carefully over some leisure hour, and ponder well upon it—see what a mere wreck—mangled ruin—it makes of our once glorious Declaration." He had thought, he said, the Declaration "promised something better. . . . I had thought the Declaration contemplated the progressive improvement in the condition of all men everywhere; but no, it merely 'was adopted for the purpose of justifying the colonists in the eyes of the civilized world in withdrawing their allegiance from the British crown, and dissolving their connection with the mother country.' Why, that object having been effected some eighty years ago, the Declaration is of no practical use now—mere rubbish—old wadding left to rot on the battle-field after the victory is won."

"I now appeal to all," Lincoln said "—to Democrats as well as others—are you really willing that the Declaration shall be thus frittered away?—thus left no more at most, than an interesting memorial of the dead past? Thus shorn of its vitality, and practical value; and left without the *germ* or even the *suggestion* of the individual rights of man in it?"

The Republicans, Lincoln argued, "inculcate, with whatever of ability they can, that the negro is a man; that his bondage is cruelly wrong, and that the field of his oppression ought not to be enlarged. The Democrats deny his manhood; deny or dwarf to insignificance, the wrong of his bondage; so far as possible, crush all sympathy for him, and cultivate and excite hatred and disgust against him; compliment themselves as Union-savers for doing so; and call the indefinite outspreading of his bondage 'a sacred right of self-government.'"

This "much vaunted" Douglas doctrine of self-government for the territories, Lincoln said flatly, is "a mere deceitful pretense for the benefit of slavery." The combined charge of "Nebraskaism, and Dred Scottism," he believed, "must be repulsed, and rolled back. The deceitful cloak of 'self-government' wherewith 'the sum of all villainies' seeks to protect and adorn itself, must be torn from [its] hateful carcass."[3]

Douglas hoped to keep popular sovereignty from becoming a carcass in the first place. Yet he was having trouble in his own party—not in keeping his idea of self-government alive, but keeping its body from being abused. Douglas was also having a violent disagreement with his party's president over Kansas.

War had been building there since the Kansas-Nebraska Act had cleared the way for its statehood. Free-soil-thinking emigrants from the Northeast were continuing to flock to the territory. Pro-slavery men from Missouri continued to ride over the border to rage against them. Two opposing territorial governments were angrily vying for control. President Pierce had already fired two territorial governors since the act was passed and the entire tableau had become so violent the territory was now being called "bloody Kansas."

Douglas was holding out for untainted popular sovereignty. But Buchanan, siding with the South, as Pierce had, was doing violence of his own to Douglas's ideal. In a highly loaded vote in Lecompton, Kansas, in late 1857, the pro-slavery faction rode roughshod over the popular will in an election heavily stacked in their favor, which put in place a slave code for the territory. Buchanan immediately committed himself to it. Douglas denounced the Lecompton Constitution as blatantly bogus—not popular sovereignty at all, not representing the true majority view in the territory. He said, "there is no satisfactory evidence that the constitution formed at Lecompton is the act and deed of the people of Kansas, or that it embodies their will."[4]

Douglas and Buchanan hadn't been getting on well to begin with. Buchanan had been doing end runs around Douglas on patronage. "At present, I am an outsider," Douglas wrote a friend in February. "My advice is not coveted nor will my wishes probably be regarded. I want nothing [but] fair play. I ask nothing for myself. I want only a fair share for my friends." He vowed, "If… the power of the administration is to be used either for plunder or ambition I shall return every blow they may give."[5]

Now it appeared to Douglas that there was a lack of fair play, and no lack of plunder, in Kansas—"trickery & juggling" he called it, "the Lecompton fraud."[6] Douglas was chairman of the Senate committee on the territories and he wasn't going to stand for it. In an angry interview in the White House, Buchanan threatened Douglas, reminding him, with a nod to his upcoming reelection campaign in Illinois, that Democratic senators who were disloyal to President Jackson had lost elections. Douglas sharply retorted, "Mr. President, Andrew Jackson is dead."[7] Their political enmity had become as bitter, if not as bloody, as the fighting for control in Kansas.

Buchanan by 1858 was trying to put teeth in his threat to undo Douglas in his reelection campaign. His followers in Illinois, called Danites (after the band of Mormons who pledged to do their leader Joseph Smith's bidding regardless of law or morality) pulled little popular weight. But they had a hammerlock on the patronage in Illinois, which made them dangerous.[8]

This high-level warfare within the Democracy was having a curious backlash in the Republican Party in Illinois as the election year 1858 dawned. Douglas's war with Buchanan had almost made many Republicans love him. There was talk, much of it coming from the editorial pages of Horace Greeley's *New York Tribune,* suggesting Republicans in Illinois might well consider supporting Douglas for reelection to the Senate against his likely Republican opponent, Lincoln.

That likely opponent was disturbed by Greeley's apparent defection because he believed "every one of [Greeley's] words seems to weigh about a ton."[9] The *Tribune*'s circulation in Illinois was pushing 20,000. Early in 1858, Lincoln told Herndon, "I think Greeley is not doing me, an old Republican and a tried antislavery man, right. He is talking up for Douglas, an untrue and untried man, a dodger, a wriggler.... I don't feel that it is exactly right to pull me down in order to elevate Douglas. I like Greeley, think he intends right, but I think he errs in this hoisting up of Douglas, while he gives me a downward shove. I wish that someone could put a flea in Greeley's ear...and try and turn the currents in the right directions."[10]

Lincoln wrote Trumbull in Washington: "What does the New-York Tribune mean by it's constant eulogising, and admiring, and magnifying Douglas? Does it, in this, speak the sentiments of the republicans at Washington? Have they concluded that the republican cause, generally, can be best promoted by sacraficing us here in Illinois? If so we would like to know it soon; it will save us a great deal of labor to surrender at once."

Lincoln had not yet heard of a Republican in the state going over to Douglas, but he told Trumbull, "if the Tribune continues to din his praises into the ears of its five or ten thousand republican readers in Illinois, it is more than can be hoped that all will stand firm." Lincoln wrote Charles L. Wilson that Greeley "denies that he directly is taking part in favor of Douglas, and I believe him. Still his *feeling* constantly manifests itself in his paper, which, being so extensively read in Illinois, is, and will continue to be, a drag upon us." He wrote his friend Ward Hill Lamon: "As to the inclination of some Republicans to favor Douglas, that is one of the chances I have to run, and which I intend to run with patience."[11]

In a note for a speech, Lincoln lashed out at Douglas: "He tells us, in this very speech [one Douglas delivered on the floor of the Senate on December 9], expected to be so palatable to Republicans, that he cares not whether slavery is voted down or voted up. His whole effort is devoted to clearing the ring, and giving slavery and freedom a fair fight. With one who considers slavery just as good as freedom, this is perfectly natural and consistent."

But, Lincoln demanded, "have Republicans any sympathy with such a view? They think slavery is wrong; and that, like every other wrong which some men will commit if left alone, it ought to be prohibited by law. They consider it not only morally wrong, but a 'deadly poison' in a government like ours, professedly based on the equality of men. Upon this radical difference of opinion with Judge Douglas, the Republican party was organized. There is all the difference between him and them now that there ever was."[12]

In mid-1858, with an axe handle protruding from the body of the Democracy and a wedge threatening to split Republicans in Illinois, the senatorial campaign got underway. And Lincoln was being introspective. "I can not but regard it as possible that the higher object of this contest may not be completely attained within the term of my natural life," he wrote in a fragment of a note about the struggle against slavery. "But I can not doubt either that it will come in due time. Even in this view, I am proud, in my passing speck of time, to contribute an humble mite to that glorious consummation, which my own poor eyes may not last to see."[13]

22

A House Divided

THE SIREN CALL that was shaking Republican unity was not all that was working against Lincoln.

He was also playing against a stacked apportionment deck. The Democrats, controlling both houses of the legislature, had reshuffled the districts based on a census in 1855 that tilted the balance heavily in their favor. Of this Lincoln said, "We know what a fair apportionment of representation upon that census would give us. We know that it could not if fairly made, fail to give the Republican party from six to ten more members of the Legislature than they can probably get as the law now stands." That meant that "we shall be very hard run to carry the Legislature." And that meant that Lincoln would have a very hard run to win the U.S. Senate seat, no matter how well he fought Douglas in the canvass. "Still, so it is," he sighed; "we have this to contend with."[1]

Herndon agreed. He wrote his friend Theodore Parker, the noted New England theologian and social reformer: "Had we a fair apportionment in this State we Republicans could beat [Douglas]." But "there are some complications.... Our State ticket will be elected without much trouble; but as to Lincoln there may be some doubts." The canvass, he wrote Parker, "opens deep and rich; but we Republicans have a clever villain to combat."[2]

Lincoln knew, as the canvass approached, that there was yet another disadvantage under which he labored. Lincoln was a full foot taller than the clever villain, but Douglas's political stature was stratospheric. "Senator Douglas is of world wide renown," Lincoln admitted. "All the anxious politicians of his party, or who have been of his party for years past, have been looking upon him as certainty, at no distant day, to be the President of the United States.... They rush about him, sustain him, and give him marches, triumphal entries, and receptions." On the contrary, Lincoln said, "nobody has ever expected me to be President. In my poor, lean, lank, face nobody has ever seen any cabbages were spouting out."[3]

Douglas was an acknowledged brutal debater. His arsenal bristled with weapons, and few could stand up to them. Lincoln had virtually no national reputation as a debater. He was reputed for his powerful logic, but it was little known outside Illinois and a few neighboring states. But many overlooked the fact that he and Douglas had pounded one another for a quarter century. Each had measured the other's mettle.[4]

Nevertheless, it was hardly a level playing field. The disadvantages that "Republicans labor under," Lincoln believed, "all, taken together," meant "*We* have to fight this battle upon principle, and upon principle alone.... we have to fight this battle without many—perhaps without any—of the external aids which are brought to bear against us."[5]

Disadvantages or not, the battle between the Little Giant and the lean giant was about to be joined. The path for Lincoln was rocky, and the odds long, but he would bring to it his whole lank body and redoubtable soul. And as Mary said, "Mr. Lincoln may not be as handsome a figure, but the people are perhaps not aware that his heart is as large as his arms are long."[6]

Douglas was endorsed by most of his party at its Illinois convention in April. But it was a potentially divisive meeting. When resolutions approving Douglas's course were introduced, Buchanan's Danites bolted and held a "rump" session in another room, calling for a separate Douglas-divorcing convention to meet in Springfield in June. "We had a great double-headed Democratic meeting here—one Buchanan and the other Douglas," Herndon explained to Parker; "they are deeply inimical, malicious, and withering in their mutual curses. Oh! What a sight!"

The Danite meeting on June 9 drew representatives from less than half the 100 counties in the state. Offices were promised to all who would attend, but nobody showed from fifty-two of the counties. The anti-Douglas movement might not be so threatening after all.[7]

The Republicans met in Springfield a week later, and the favorite in every heart was Lincoln. Herndon called it "the largest delegate convention I ever saw...a grand affair....We all felt like exploding, not with gas, but with electric bolts, shivering what we struck."[8]

Though the atmosphere was electric and hearts were warm, a few minds gathering at the convention were jittery and apprehensive. They knew Lincoln was intent on saying something publicly that could be politically catastrophic. But he had been wanting to say it, preparing to say it, for some time.

Some days before the convention, he locked their law-office door, drew the curtain across its glass panel, and read aloud what he had committed to paper, with Billy Herndon as his audience. He halted after each paragraph to hear his partner's comments.

"If we could first know *where* we are, and *whither* we are tending," Lincoln read, "we could then better judge *what* to do, and *how* to do it.

"We are now far into the *fifth* year, since a policy was initiated, with the *avowed* object and *confident* promise, of putting an end to slavery agitation.

"Under the operation of that policy, that agitation has not only, *not ceased,* but has *constantly augmented.*

"In *my* opinion, it *will* not cease, until a *crisis* shall have been reached and passed.

"'A house divided against itself cannot stand.'"[9]

Here a red flag flew up. Herndon interrupted. "It is true," he said, "but is it wise or politic to say so?"

That expression, Lincoln answered "is a truth of all human experience, 'a house divided against itself cannot stand.' . . . The proposition also is true, and has been for six thousand years. I want to use some universally known figure expressed in simple language as universally well-known, that may strike home to the minds of men in order to raise them up to the peril of the times. I do not believe I would be right in changing or omitting it. I would rather be defeated with this expression in the speech, and uphold and discuss it before the people, than be victorious without it."[10]

Lincoln continued reading: "I believe this government cannot endure, permanently half *slave* and half *free.*

"I do not expect the Union to be *dissolved*—I do not expect the house to *fall*—but I *do* expect it will cease to be divided.

"It will become *all* one thing, or *all* the other.

"Either the *opponents* of slavery, will arrest the further spread of it, and place it where the public mind shall rest in the belief that it is in course of ultimate extinction; or its *advocates* will push it forward, till it shall become alike lawful in *all* the States, *old* as well as *new*—*North* as well as *South*."[11]

There was much more, but that was the heart-stopper. It wasn't new to Herndon. Lincoln had first expressed the idea in his pencil-dropping speech in Bloomington in 1856. But bowing to the emphatic protest of several of his Republican supporters then, who believed that its repetition "would make abolitionists of all the North and slavery propagandists of all the South, and thereby precipitate a struggle which might end in disunion," he agreed not to say it again in that campaign.

But now, Herndon knew, "the situation had changed somewhat. There had been a shifting of scenes, so to speak." He believed the Republican Party had gained some in strength and even more in moral effectiveness and force. Herndon believed nothing could hold Lincoln back any longer from "sentiments of right and truth," and that he was prepared "to give the fullest expression to both in all future cases."[12]

Lincoln held one more rehearsal for his "house divided" doctrine, reading it to a dozen or so of his other political friends in the statehouse library. After he finished, he asked each for his opinion. Not one of them endorsed it. One after another, they condemned it in substance and spirit, particularly the "house divided" opening. They unanimously believed the speech unwise, impolitic, even false. One, whom Herndon thought "more forcible than elegant," called it a "d———d fool utterance."

254 • JOHN C. WAUGH

Another said it was a doctrine "ahead of its time." Yet another argued that it would "drive away a good many voters fresh from the Democrats ranks."

Then Herndon, passionate as usual, sprang to his feet and said, "Lincoln, By—God—deliver it just as it reads. If it is in advance of the times let us—you & I if no one Else—lift the people to the level of this Speech now & higher hereafter. The speech is true—wise & politic; and will succeed—now or in the future. Nay it will aid you—if it will not make you president of the United States."

Lincoln sat quietly for a moment, then rose from his chair, walked back and forth in the room, then stopped and said, "Friends: I have thought about this matter a great deal—have weighed the question well from all corners; and am thoroughly Convinced the time has come when it should be uttered, & if it must be that I must go down because of this speech, then let me go down linked to truth—die in the advocacy of what is right and just. This nation cannot live on injustice—a house divided against itself cannot stand.... I say again & again."[13]

On June 16, the Illinois State Republican Convention met and resolved that he was its "first and only choice" to run against Douglas. It was an unprecedented political move. Never before had a party in any state met in convention and endorsed a candidate for the Senate. It was overstepping into the domain of the state legislature, but these Republicans in Illinois, to counter the Greeleys of the world, wanted it bluntly understood that Lincoln was their man and that Douglas was emphatically their enemy.[14]

Lincoln then delivered the controversial speech as written. He led with the explosive opening about the house divided and backed it up with yet more incendiary cannonading. Under the Dred Scott decision, he said, "*squatter sovereignty*" otherwise called "*sacred right of self government,*" is "squatted out of existence, tumbled down like temporary scaffolding—like the mould at the foundry served through one blast and fell back to loose sand—helped to carry an election, and then was kicked to the winds."

He accused Douglas, Pierce, Taney, and Buchanan of collusion. "We can not absolutely *know* that all these exact adaptations are the result of preconcert," Lincoln said. "But when we see a lot of framed timbers, different portions of which we know have been gotten out at different times and places and by different workmen—Stephen, Franklin, Roger and James ... and when we see these timbers joined together, and see they exactly make the frame of a house or a mill, all the tenons and mortices exactly fitting, and all the lengths and proportions of the different pieces exactly adapted to their respective places, and not a piece too many or too few—not omitting even scaffolding ... in *such* a case, we find it impossible to not *believe* that Stephen and Franklin and Roger and James all understood one another from the beginning, and all worked upon a common *plan* or *draft* drawn up before the first lick was struck."

Put all that framework, "*that* and *that* together," Lincoln charged, "and we have another nice little niche, which we may, ere long, see filled with another Supreme Court decision, declaring that the Constitution of the United States does not permit a *state* to exclude slavery from its limits. And this may especially be expected if the doctrine of 'care not whether slavery be voted *down* or voted *up,*' shall gain upon the public mind sufficiently to give promise that such a decision can be maintained when made."

"Such a decision," Lincoln said, "is all that slavery now lacks of being alike lawful in all the States. Welcome or unwelcome, such decision *is* probably coming, and will soon be upon us, unless the power of the present political dynasty shall be met and overthrown."

Lincoln closed his speech with a searing denunciation of the siren call of eastern Republicans whispering up Republican votes for Douglas in Illinois. Douglas's positions are antithetical to ours, Lincoln said, "How can he oppose the advances of slavery? He don't *care* anything about it.... He is not *now* with us—he does not *pretend* to be—he does not *promise* to *ever* be. Our cause, then, must be intrusted to, and conducted by its own undoubted friends—those whose hands are free, whose hearts are in the work—who *do care* for the results."[15]

Lincoln's friends worried about the speech long after it was delivered. A few days later, a doctor friend came to Lincoln's office and said, "Well, Lincoln that foolish speech of yours will kill you—will defeat you in this Contest—and probably for all offices for all time to come—am sorry—very sorry. I wish it was wiped out of existence—Don't you now wish so?"

Lincoln, who had been intently writing through this lament, stopped, raised his spectacles, put the pen down, looked at the doctor a moment, and said, "Well Doct—if I had to draw a pen across and erase my whole life from existence, & all I did; and I had one poor gift or choice left, as to what I should Save from the wreck, I should choose that speech and leave it to the world unerased."

Nevertheless, one Lincoln friend said, "You could hear from all quarters...Republicans say—'D———n that fool speech; it will be the cause of the death of Lincoln and the republican party—Such folly—such non sense! Is Lincoln crazy? D———n it.'"[16]

Douglas returned from Washington to Illinois on July 9 to

open the campaign, aware of the speech, calling it treasonable and disunionist,[17] and intent on making of it the political death of Lincoln and the Republican Party in the state. He arrived in Chicago to the booming of cannon and the whipping of flags. A military escort marched him to the Tremont House, past balconies and windows full of cheering greeters. That evening he spoke from the hotel balcony and, acknowledging Lincoln in the throng, said, "I take great pleasure in saying that I have known personally and intimately, for about a quarter of a century, the worthy gentleman who has been nominated for my place, and I will say that I regard him as a kind, amiable, and intelligent gentleman, a good citizen and an honorable opponent; and whatever issue I may have with him will be of principle and not involving personalities."[18]

There was a grudging respect between these two men. Lincoln believed Douglas had "very little humor or imagination," but that he was "a very strong logician," and "where he had right on his side very few could make a stronger argument; that he was an exceedingly good judge of human nature, knew the people of the state thoroughly and just how to appeal to the[ir] prejudices and was a powerful opponent, both on and off the stump."[19]

Lincoln probably would have agreed with something Senator William Pitt Fessenden of Maine said about Douglas: "You may drop him in the middle of a morass, from which escape seems impossible, and before your back is turned he will have built a corduroy road across it, and be out again and at you harder than ever."[20]

The following evening in Chicago, Lincoln answered Douglas's speech from the same balcony, covering much of the same ground as his speeches in the weeks preceding this opening shot. He hit Douglas again on the deceptive evil of "squatter sovereignty," assailed the Dred Scott decision and the Lecompton Constitution, defended his "house divided" speech and hammered Douglas's positions generally.[21]

Douglas was immediately off and running. With a carefully worked-out itinerary he set out on his mission of destruction. The Illinois Central Railroad had donated a special car to his campaign. It was luxuriously appointed, trimmed with flags and bunting and accompanied by a flatcar mounting a twelve-pounder cannon to fire salutes from town to town, where committees of distinguished citizens, led by mayors, waited to receive him.[22]

"His tactic just now, in part," Lincoln wrote a friend, "is, to make it appear that he is having a triumphal entry into; and march through the country; but it is all as bombastic and hollow as Napoleon's bulletins sent back from his campaign in Russia.... there is no solid shot in these bombastic parades of his."[23]

As he had in 1854, Lincoln immediately set out on Douglas's tail, intent on answering his speeches, often riding in the same train with the other passengers, minus a tailored car, flatcar, and cannon of his own. Again he lashed out at "their thunderings of cannon, their marching and music, their fizzlegigs and fireworks...the little trappings of the campaign."[24]

Late one afternoon a friend of Lincoln's boarded a train in Bloomington and saw him enter in his familiar linen coat, without a vest, topped by a hat "much the worse for wear," and carrying the "inevitable" faded cotton umbrella. "On his arm," the friend noted, "was the cloak that he was said to have worn when in Congress nine years before." He appeared to have no baggage, no secretary, no companion. Lincoln greeted and talked for a time with his friend and several others he happened to know. As night drew on, "he withdrew to another part of the car where he could occupy a seat by himself. Presently he arose, spread the cloak over the seat, lay down, somehow folded himself up till his long legs and arms were no longer in view, then drew the cloak around him and went to sleep."[25]

Despite his unpretentious travel arrangements that so contrasted with Douglas's lavish ones, Lincoln was intent on being a one-man traveling truth squad. He believed, as he told a friend, "Douglas will tell a lie to ten thousand people one day, even though he knows he may have to deny it to five thousand the next."[26]

It was becoming apparent that this would not be enough. Lincoln had to land faster, harder hits on this moving target, with all its pageantry. He needed to hold Douglas in place and hammer him face to face on the same platform—"closer work" than Douglas had given him so far. Lincoln's friends began urging him to draw the Little Giant into a joint debate.[27]

So on July 24 Lincoln wrote Douglas a letter, and Norman Judd, a Chicago attorney and chairman of the Republican State Committee, delivered it to him that day in Chicago. "My Dear Sir," it began, "Will it be agreeable to you to make an arrangement for you and myself to divide time, and address the same audiences during the present canvass? Mr. Judd, who will hand you this, is authorized to receive your answer; and, if agreeable to you, to enter into the terms of such an agreement."[28]

It was not a letter to bring Douglas joy. Meeting Lincoln in joint debate hadn't been a priority. It wasn't on his carefully mapped-out campaign itinerary. He snapped at Judd, who had hunted him down: "What do you come to me with such a thing as this for?"[29]

Douglas knew that, with the country watching, a debate could elevate Lincoln's political height considerably. "If he gets the best of the debate," Douglas figured, "—and I want to say he is the ablest man the Republicans have got—I shall lose everything and Lincoln will gain everything." He had told friends privately before the canvass opened, "I shall have my hands full. He is the strong man of his party—full of wit, facts, dates—and the best stump speaker, with his droll ways and dry jokes, in the West. He is as honest as he is shrewd, and, if I beat him, my victory will be hardly won."[30]

But ducking the debate was not possible. So Douglas proposed seven debates, all in towns in counties where neither had yet spoken. He suggested Freeport, Ottawa, Galesburg, Quincy, Alton, Jonesboro, and Charleston.[31]

Lincoln wrote back immediately and Douglas answered on July 30 with dates and rules. They would debate in Ottawa on August 21, Freeport on August 27, Jonesboro on September 15, Charleston on September 18, Galesburg on October 7, Quincy on October 13, and Alton on October 15. Douglas proposed that the debates last three hours each, and that at Lincoln's suggestion they alternate openings and closing. Douglas would open at Ottawa for an hour, Lincoln replying for an hour and a half, and Douglas closing for half an hour. Lincoln would open at Freeport, and so it would go, in an alternating order. Lincoln wrote back on July 31 that although Douglas had four openings and closes to his three, he accepted the arrangement.[32]

At Douglas's request Lincoln stopped following him around speaking in the same towns. Between debates they would now follow separate stumping itineraries.

In August leading up to the first debate the two campaigned furiously and separately, drawing huge crowds. Lincoln was now getting some pomp and circumstance into his own campaign. On August 12, he opened in Beardstown, where he was met by several hundred admirers, two bands, and two military companies when he stepped off the steamer from Naples. The next day, residents put him back on the steamer with a rousing sendoff for Helena, where he was met by another large crowd and escort. Delegations were streaming in from other towns to hear him speak. At Lewistown he spoke to some six thousand around the public square.[33]

Chester P. Dewey, a reporter sent to cover the debates by the *New York Evening Post,* wrote in his paper: "Douglas is working like a lion. He is stumping the state, everywhere present and everywhere appealing to his old lieges to stand by him."[34] Douglas had wired his friend and ally Usher F. Linder in August, "The hell-hounds are on my track. For God's sake, Linder, come and help me fight them." From that time forward Linder would be known as "For-God's-Sake-Linder."[35]

Both Lincoln and Douglas would doubtless have agreed with Dewey when he wrote, "Illinois is regarded as the battleground of the year, and the results of this contest are held to be of the highest importance to the welfare of the country and the success of the great contending parties."[36]

On the eve of the debates, Lincoln was also talking to himself, writing down his thoughts, penning fragments of speeches again. On a scrap of paper he wrote: "As I would not be a *slave,* so I would not be a *master.* This expresses my idea of democracy. Whatever differs from this, to the extent of the difference, is no democracy."[37]

In a note for speeches on the eve of the debate, he wrote a long series of thoughts to himself. He was still obsessed with what he "clearly" thought he saw as "a powerful plot to make slavery universal and perpetual in this nation." And he still strongly believed it was a conspiracy. He admitted to himself, as he had earlier in his speech at the Republican state convention at Springfield in June, that "the evidence was circumstantial only; but nevertheless it seemed inconsistent with every hypothesis, save that of the existence of such conspiracy."

Douglas's present course had not lessened Lincoln's belief "in the existence of a purpose to make slavery alike lawful in all the States. This can be done by a Supreme Court decision holding that the United States Constitution forbids a State to exclude slavery.... Slavery can only become extinct by being restricted to its present limits, and dwindling out. It can only become national by a Supreme Court decision. To such a decision, when it comes, Judge Douglas is fully committed."

For its first sixty-five years under the Constitution, Lincoln mused, "the practice of government has been to exclude slavery from the new free Territories. About the end of that period Congress, by the Nebraska bill, resolved to abandon this practice; and this was rapidly succeeded by a Supreme Court decision holding the practice to have always been unconstitutional. Some of us refuse to obey this decision as a political rule. Forthwith Judge Douglas espouses the decision, and denounces all opposition to it in no measured terms. He adheres to it with extraordinary tenacity" on "a ground which commits him as fully to the next decision as to this."[38]

Lincoln armed himself for the coming debates with a four-inch by six-inch leather-covered notebook in which he had pasted newspaper clippings, statistics, and other information and data bearing on the important questions in the campaign. He scribbled a few notes throughout. There were 185 pages in the notebook, beginning with the second paragraph of the Declaration of Independence, and on the same page words by Henry Clay: "I repeat it, sir, I never can and never will and no earthly power will make me look directly or indirectly to spread slavery over territory where it does not exist. Never while reason holds her seat in my brain—never while my heart sends the vital fluid through my veins—NEVER!" On the next page Lincoln inserted the "house divided" statement from his speech to the Republican state convention.

"When this little store house of political information was filled," Herndon said, "Mr. Lincoln fastened the clasp, placed the book in his coat pocket, there to repose during the campaign and to be drawn upon whenever the exigencies of the debate required it." In its pages, Herndon said, was "all the ammunition Mr. Lincoln saw fit to gather in preparation for his battle with Stephen A. Douglas."

Herndon said Lincoln also prepared a second notebook on the subject of slavery, with the same number of newspaper clippings and excerpts as the debate book, but indexed so he could instantly find and quote from it the proper passages supporting his argument on almost any phase of the slavery issue.[39]

Armed and ready, Lincoln spent the night before the first debate in Morris, east of Ottawa. The next morning he caught the train west with a crowd from Cook and Will counties. In Ottawa he was taken from the station to Mansion House to await the opening of the debate that afternoon.[40]

23

The Debates

IT WAS THE ROAD SHOW of the decade, this senatorial battle between the state's two political giants. It was high entertainment, and the audience was flocking into Ottawa, the little town high on the Illinois River, riding in on anything that moved.

During the night before and early in the day, August 21, 1858, the audience came—some 12,000 souls—on trains, in paddlewheelers, canal-boats, wagons, carriages, buggies, and on the backs of horses. Delegations came from up and down the river, from Morris, Joliet, and all the towns on the railroad above and below Ottawa.

As Lincoln was riding the train into town from Morris, Douglas left Peru in a carriage escorted by a retinue of riders on horseback and in vehicles. As his procession swung along, it gathered newcomers at every crossroad and stopping place.

When it reached Ottawa the entourage trailing in his wake stretched for nearly a mile.[1]

By eight in the morning the "unwonted commotion" had raised a tornado of dust; the town resembled "a vast smoke house." Two brass twelve-pounders on the town square pounded away through the dust, overlording the mounting hubbub. Multiple bands played, striving to be heard in the din. "Vanity Fair," the *Chicago Press and Tribune* wrote, "never boiled with madder enthusiasm."[2]

A 2:30 in the afternoon, when Douglas stood to open the debate, the public square was jammed. The sun was beaming down and too few trees were giving precious little shade.[3] The oratorical heat was about to make the day warmer still.

A *New York Times* correspondent described Douglas's "rhetorical assault[s]" as having "nothing of the cavalry slash." Rather, he said, they were akin to "a charge of heavy infantry with fixed bayonet," delivered in a "rich and musical baritone, swelling into occasional clarion-blasts toward the close of each important period."[4]

Douglas was readying a powerful rhetorical assault on Lincoln. His heavy infantry was in place, bayonets fixed. It was to be wondered just what these two powerhouses could say to the people, to each other, and about each other, that they had not already said repeatedly for the past four years. The assaults from both sides of the platform were likely to plow familiar ground. But the drama would be unprecedented.

Douglas gazed out on "this vast concourse of people" and said in his rich and musical baritone that he desired "to address myself to your judgment, your understanding, and your consciences, and not to your passions or your enthusiasm." His theme, he said, was to be the sanctity of popular sovereignty in the Kansas-Nebraska Act. "It is the true intent and meaning of this act," Douglas said, in his signature refrain, "not to legislate slavery into any State or Territory, or to exclude it therefrom, but to leave the people thereof perfectly free to form and regulate their domestic institutions in their own way, subject only to the federal constitution."

That was the American way, Douglas insisted, the way of true democracy. "If we will only act conscientiously and rigidly upon [it] . . . which guarantees to each State and Territory the right to do as it pleases on all things local and domestic instead of Congress interfering, we will continue at peace with one another." The government, he said, had flourished for seventy years on this principle.

Douglas called Lincoln a rank abolitionist masked in a Republican guise. He charged that Lincoln stood with every other Black Republican pledged against the popular will. He denounced Lincoln's "house divided" speech as "revolutionary and destructive of the existence of this government," that it was a doctrine that would "dissolve the Union if it succeeds." Why, he demanded "can it [this government] not exist divided into free and slave states. . . . Why can it not exist on the same principles on which our fathers made it?"

He insisted that the Founding Fathers created a Union embracing both slavery and freedom. And now Lincoln wanted to rip it apart. He decried Lincoln's contention that when the Declaration of Independence said all men are created equal, it meant all men, black as well as white. For his part, Douglas said, as he had said so many times before, that he would never accept a black man as *his* equal—that by "all men" the Founding Fathers had clearly meant only white men of European descent. Douglas also told Lincoln what he believed the Almighty had intended and hadn't intended. God had never intended the black man to be the equal of the white man, Douglas argued. He "belongs to an inferior race, and must always occupy an inferior position."

Countering Douglas's assault in his hour and a half, Lincoln said, as he also had often said before, that he agreed the white man should always be superior, but that the black man "in the right to eat the bread, without leave of anybody else, which his own hand earns, he is my equal and the equal of Judge Douglas, and the equal of every living man."

More than ever Lincoln believed the difference between them was a moral one, that Douglas's indifference whether slavery was voted up or down was morally wrong. That was to be his theme in these debates, just as the sanctity of popular sovereignty was to be Douglas's. He charged that Douglas in every way was denying the black man his right as a man.

Lincoln denounced the Dred Scott decision, arguing as always that it emphatically opened the door to slavery in all the territories. The decision held in effect that the people of a territory cannot *prevent* the establishment of slavery in their midst, so the inevitable next step would be to *make* slavery perpetual and universal throughout the Union—and Douglas was a conspirator working to make this happen.

Lincoln injected Henry Clay into the debate, recalling that Clay "once said of a class of men who would repress all tendencies to liberty and ultimate emancipation, that they must, if they would do this, go back to the era of our Independence, and muzzle the cannon which thunders its annual joyous return; they must blow out the moral lights around us; they must penetrate the human soul, and eradicate there the love of liberty; and then and not till then, could they perpetuate slavery in this country!"

To Lincoln's way of thinking, "Judge Douglas is, by his example and vast influence, doing that very thing in this community, when he says that the negro has nothing in the Declaration of Independence. Henry Clay plainly understood the contrary. Judge Douglas is going back to the era of our Revolution, and to the extent of his ability, muzzling the cannon which thunders its annual joyous return. When he invites any people to have slavery, to establish it, he is blowing out the moral lights around us. When he says he 'cares not whether slavery is voted down or voted up,'—that it is a sacred right of self government—he is in my judgment penetrating the human soul and eradicating the light of reason and the love of liberty in this American people."[5]

And so it ended. The next day Lincoln wrote Joseph O. Cunningham, editor of the *Urbana Union,* "Douglas and I, for the first time this canvass, crossed swords here yesterday; the fire flew some, and I am glad to know I am yet alive."[6]

The press reaction to this first debate, as always, mirrored the newspaper's political bias. The Democratic press claimed Lincoln was so thoroughly outdone that it was doubtful he was still politically alive. The fiercely pro-Douglas *Chicago Times* ran a string of headlines telling how Lincoln had been whipped, his heart, legs, tongue, arms, all failing him, and the battle fought and won, with Douglas emerging as "the champion of the people."[7]

The other end of the spectrum was just as lopsided in its assessment. The pro-Lincoln *Chicago Press and Tribune* describing Douglas, wrote: "He howled, he ranted, he bellowed, he pawed the dirt, he shook his head, he turned livid in the face, he struck his right hand with his left, he foamed at the mouth, he anathematized, he cursed, he exulted, he domineered—he played Douglas."[8]

The *New York Evening Post*'s Chester P. Dewey took the first debate as an opportunity to take a close look at Lincoln. "In repose," Dewey wrote, "I must confess that 'long Abe's' appearance is not comely. But stir him up and the fire of his genius plays on every feature. His eye glows and sparkles, every lineament, not so illformed, grows brilliant and expressive, and you have before you a man of rare power and magnetic influence. He takes the people every time, and there is no getting away from his sturdy good sense, his unaffected sincerity, and the unceasing play of his good humor, which accompanies his close logic, and smooths the way to conviction. Listening to him on Saturday, calmly and unprejudiced, I was convinced that he had no superior as a stump speaker. He is clear, concise, and logical; his language is eloquent and at perfect command. He is, altogether a more fluent speaker than Douglas, and in all the arts of debate fully his equal."[9]

Lincoln's friends were cheered. Horace White, covering the debates for the *Chicago Press and Tribune,* said, "The Ottawa debate gave great satisfaction to our side. Mr. Lincoln, we thought, had the better of the argument, and we all came away encouraged."[10]

Unlike dust-choked Ottawa, the weather in Freeport six days later was chilly and dismal—damp, cloudy, lowering. A yet vaster concourse of people—an estimated 15,000—swarmed to the little town near the Wisconsin line. They rode in from towns and hamlets for a radius of forty miles, organizing into delegations that rallied at convenient points and formed processions of wagons, carriages, and horses. Some started for Freeport the night before, escorted by bands, with flags and banners snapping and hats and handkerchiefs waving.[11]

Douglas arrived in a coach drawn by four gaily caparisoned horses. Lincoln arrived by special train. At two o'clock in the afternoon he was wheeled to the debate site, a grove not far from the center of town, in a Conestoga wagon drawn by six white horses. His thick wiry black hair was in its usual unkempt bird-nest condition, and he was dressed in a rusty-black Prince Albert coat with somewhat abbreviated sleeves. His short black trousers were equally abbreviated, giving an exaggerated dimension to his feet. "He wore a high stove-pipe hat, somewhat the worse for wear," an observer noted, "and he carried a gray woolen shawl, a garment much worn in those days instead of an overcoat."[12]

This was upper-tier Illinois, Republican country. Like Ottawa, it was in the heart of the strongest anti-slavery sentiment in the state, and it was Lincoln's turn to open the debate. He immediately addressed seven questions Douglas had asked him in Ottawa. That out of the way—decidedly not to the Little Giant's entire satisfaction—Lincoln said he now had four questions he wanted to ask Douglas.

The first, third, and fourth questions didn't make much of a stir. The second question of the four that Lincoln asked, however, was loaded: "Can the people of a United States Territory, in any lawful way, against the wish of any citizen of the United States, exclude slavery from its limits prior to the formation of a State Constitution?"

That question put Douglas between a rock and a hard place. If he answered "no, it can't exclude slavery then," which is what the Dred Scott decision demanded, he would alienate the free-soil North. If he answered "yes, a state can exclude it then," he was in effect rejecting the Dred Scott decision, which he professed to support, and would further alienate the slaveholding South.

Douglas didn't flinch. "I answer emphatically, as Mr. Lincoln has heard me answer a hundred times [indeed, Douglas claimed, since 1850] from every stump in Illinois, that in my opinion the people of a territory can, by lawful means, exclude slavery from their limits prior to the formation of a State Constitution." Although he had said this before, Southerners were not going to be happy to hear it again. It would add flame to the Southern fire he had brought down on himself when he spurned the Lecompton constitution.

That answer to that question was the centerpost of this second debate, and it was a telling turn. It became immediately and widely known as the Freeport Doctrine, and for better or worse Douglas was stuck with it.[13]

It would be twenty-five days, nearly a month, before the third debate on September 15 in Jonesboro at the other end of the state—the Democratic end—hard on the Kentucky line in what they called Little Egypt. The two debaters meanwhile went stumping their separate ways.

Herndon was sending occasional updates on the campaign to his friend Theodore Parker, the abolitionist, theologian, and social reformer in Boston. "The politics now in our State are in the blue-hot condition," he wrote Parker on August 31; "it has ceased to sparkle, but now it burns. Mr. Lincoln and Senator Douglas have had two 'hitches.'"

Our State, Herndon explained to Parker, "is a peculiar one politically: first, we have a north which is all intelligence, all for freedom. Secondly, we have a South, people from the sand hills of the South, poor white folks. These are pro-slavery and ignorant 'up to the hub.' And thirdly, we have a belt of land, seventy-five miles in width, running from the east bank of the Mississippi to the Wabash—to Indiana; and running north and south, from Bloomington to Alton."

In this middle belt of land, Herndon explained, "this 'great battle' between Lincoln and Douglas is to be fought and victory won. On this belt there are three classes of individuals: first, Yankees; secondly, intelligent Southerners; and thirdly, poor whites. I now speak sectionally. Again: on this belt are four political shades of party politics: first, Republicans; second, Americans (old Whigs); third, Douglas Democrats; and fourth, National Democrats, Buchanan men. 'Quite a muss.'"14

Lincoln arrived in Jonesboro the evening before the debate, and the night sky was sending omens. Donati's comet, the brightest celestial phenomenon of the century, appeared in the night sky, riveting all eyes to the heavens. Horace White, who had known Lincoln since 1854 and was with him constantly, covering the debates for the *Chicago Press and Tribune,* wrote that "Mr. Lincoln greatly admired this strange visitor, and he and I sat for an hour or more in front of the hotel looking at it."15

Douglas came up from Cairo the next morning on the train in the company of carloads of supporters, his cannon booming and band blaring, a show to rival Donati's comet. This was his country. The halloing in this debate in this region of "dog day" temperatures would be heavily weighted in his favor.16

He opened this one on the fairgrounds north of town, talking of the "great revolution" in political parties of this decade. Now, he said, they were no longer divided on national principles, but by a geographical line—a large party in the North arrayed under a Republican banner (read abolition banner)— a sectional party hostile to the Southern states, its people, and its institutions. He charged that Lincoln was further dividing the Union, "inviting a warfare between the North and the South."

He again came down hard for white supremacy and for "preserving this government as our fathers made it"—"for the benefit of white men and their posterity forever...I do not believe that the Almighty made the negro capable of self-government."

In his hour and a half Lincoln challenged Douglas's view of the government "as our fathers made it." That, Lincoln said, "is the exact difficulty between us." He charged that Douglas and his friends have skewed the intentions of the fathers. "I say when this government was first established it was the policy of its founders to prohibit the spread of slavery into the new Territories of the United States, where it had not existed. But Judge Douglas and his fiends have broken up that policy and placed it upon a new basis by which it is to become national and perpetual. All I have asked or desired anywhere is that it should be placed back again upon the basis that the fathers of our government originally placed it upon." He had no doubt it would eventually become extinct, "for all time to come."[17]

Three days later, on September 18, the debate was joined again for the fourth time, in Charleston on the state's eastern side—in that middle swing belt of the state, and it was Lincoln's turn to open. Giant processions escorted both men to Charleston from Mattoon. The streets were jammed "with a perfect tide of humanity, surging to and fro." Immediately after dinner the tide surged out to the county fair grounds, where Lincoln took the stand at a quarter to three o'clock in the afternoon.[18]

Lincoln in this fourth debate decried the absence of peace and tranquility that the issue of slavery had brought to the country. "Have we ever had any peace on this slavery question?" he asked. "When are we to have peace upon it if it is kept in the position it now occupies? How are we ever to have peace upon it?" To Lincoln, this was an essential question. "To be sure if we will all stop and allow Judge Douglas and his friends to march on in their present career until they plant the institution all over the nation, here and wherever else our flag waves, and we acquiesce in it, there will be peace. But let me ask Judge Douglas how he is going to get the people to do that? They have been wrangling over this question for at least forty years."

This, Lincoln said, "was the cause of the agitation resulting in the Missouri Compromise—this produced the troubles at the annexation of Texas, in the acquisition of the territory acquired in the Mexican war. Again, this was the trouble which was quieted by the Compromise of 1850, when it was settled '*forever*,' as both the great political parties declared in their National Conventions. That 'forever' turned out to be just four years, *when Judge Douglas himself re-opened it*."[19]

In the days following the debate in Charleston, Lincoln was optimistic. Believing he had more than held his own against the Little Giant, he thought "the skies are bright and the prospects good." He wrote Norman Judd, "I believe we have the gentleman, unless they overcome us by fraudulent voting" which he considered a real possibility considering the rather loose voting practices in the state.[20] But Lincoln was weary. "If it were not for one thing," he told a friend, "I would retire from the contest. I know that if Mr. Douglas's doctrine prevails, it will not be fifteen years before Illinois itself will be a slave state."[21]

The fifth debate was not until October 7, and early in the month, in a whirl of crowd-studded separate campaigning, Lincoln was talking to himself again. In a fragment on pro-slavery ideology, he wrote, "Suppose it is true, that the negro is inferior to the white, in the gifts of nature; is it not the exact reverse justice that the white should, for that reason, take from the negro, any part of the little which has been given him? '*Give* to him that is needy' is the christian rule of charity; but 'Take from him that is needy' is the rule of slavery."

It seemed to Lincoln that "the sum of pro-slavery ideology seems to be this: 'Slavery is not universally *right,* nor yet universally *wrong*; it is better for *some* people to be slaves; and, in such cases, it is the Will of God that they be such." Now, Lincoln reasoned, "No one thinks of asking Sambo's opinion on it." As a good thing, Lincoln mused, "slavery is strikingly peculiar, in this, that it is the only good thing which no man ever seeks the good of, *for himself.*"

Senator Douglas, Lincoln told himself in yet another introspective fragment, "regularly argues against the doctrine of the equality of men; and while he does not draw the conclusion that the superiors ought to enslave the inferiors, he evidently wishes his hearers to draw that conclusion." The common object, Lincoln concluded, "is to subvert, in the public mind, and in practical administration, our old and only standard of free government, that 'all men are created equal,' and substitute for it some different standard. What that substitute is to be is not difficult to perceive. It is to deny the equality of men, and to assert the natural, moral, and religious right of one class to enslave another."[22]

But as Lincoln said a few days later in a speech in Pekin, as the fifth debate approached, he "had known Douglas for twenty-five years, and was not now astonished by any statement which he might make, no matter what it might be."[23]

This two-decades-long rivalry between the two, Herndon explained to Theodore Parker in another update, "for weal or woe was being fought all over the wide prairies of Illinois." Occasionally Lincoln swung from the prairie into Springfield, Herndon said—a pit stop of sorts—"to consult with his friends or to post himself up on questions that occurred during the canvass. He kept me busy hunting up old speeches and gathering facts and statistics at the State library."[24]

Douglas arrived in Galesburg about ten in the morning on the day of the fifth debate, October 7, on the train from Burlington. At noon the Republicans went with a military contingent to the station to meet Lincoln, and the two debaters were driven to the meeting ground at Knox College, wheel to wheel, in separate four-horse carriages. A reporter marveled at the "Great outpouring of people. Twenty thousand persons present." The crowd was "immense notwithstanding the remarkable heavy rains of the day previous, and the sudden change during the night to a fierce blowing, cutting wind, which lasted during the whole day, ripping and tearing banners and sending signs pell mell all over the town. At early dawn our gunners announced the opening of day and at an early hour the people began to pour in from every direction in wagons, on horseback and on foot."[25]

Douglas opened the debate in Galesburg to three rousing hurrahs and said, up front, that he still carried "the banner of Popular Sovereignty aloft," never allowing it "to trail in the dust." In fact, none of the repeated themes was allowed to trail in the dust. Their polar differences on what the Declaration of Independence meant also surfaced again. "I tell you," Douglas raged, "that this Chicago doctrine of Lincoln's—declaring that the negro and the white man are made equal by the Declaration of Independence and by Divine Providence—is a monstrous heresy." Not so, Lincoln answered. "I believe the entire records of the world...may be searched in vain for one single affirmation, from one single man, that the negro was not included in the Declaration of Independence. I think I may defy Judge Douglas to show that he ever said so, that Washington ever said so, that any President ever said so, that any member of Congress ever said so, or that any living man upon the whole earth ever said so, until the necessities of the present policy of the Democratic party, in regard to slavery, had to invent that affirmation."

Lincoln again addressed the morality of not caring whether slavery is voted down or up. "I confess myself," he said, "as belonging to that class in the country who contemplate slavery as a moral, social, and political evil," looking "hopefully to the time when as a wrong it may come to an end."

He said, "I believe that the right of property in a slave *is not* distinctly and expressly affirmed in the Constitution, and Judge Douglas thinks it *is*. I believe that the Supreme Court and the advocates of [the Dred Scott] decision may search in vain for the place in the Constitution where the right of property in a slave is distinctly and expressly affirmed."[26]

Not only were the two debaters repeating themselves, neither one was winning the other to his point of view. How much of the audience was won over nobody knew.

Following that fifth debate in Galesburg, the two men continued campaigning in opposite directions, geographically and ideologically, before meeting again in the sixth debate in Quincy six days later on October 13. With the seventh looming in Alton on October 15, the debates were sprinting toward the finish line.

Lincoln arrived in Quincy on the morning train from Macomb under a clear sky that had redeemed Illinois from a series of cold and dismal storms. Like Douglas, his arrivals were now being announced by thundering cannon.[27]

There was little left but repetition. Lincoln again denied being a party to offensive Republican resolutions passed in 1854 as Douglas had charged, and refuted claims that he said different things in the northern and southern ends of the state. He

Lincoln studying on the banks of the Sangamon: "It didn't seem natural, nohow, to see a feller read like that." *Courtesy of the Library of Congress, LC-USZ62-123260*

Lawyer Lincoln: His bethel was the circuit. *Courtesy of the Library of Congress, LC-USZ62-121969*

Mary Lincoln in her "trotting harness." *Courtesy of the Library of Congress, LC-DIG-cwpbh-01027*

LINCOLN'S LAST WARNING.

Lincoln hacking at the slavery tree. Lincoln's Last Warning. "Now, if you don't come down, I'll cut the Tree from under you." *Courtesy of the Library of Congress, LC-USZ62-48218*

FORCING SLAVERY DOWN THE THROAT OF A FREESOILER

Political antislavery cartoon: Forcing Slavery Down the Throat of a Freesoiler. *Courtesy of the Library of Congress, LC-USZ62-92043*

William H. Herndon—as true to
Lincoln as the "needle to the pole."
*Courtesy of the Library of Congress,
LC-USZ62-68409*

Stephen A. Douglas—a Little Giant
fixated on popular sovereignty.
*Courtesy of the Library of Congress,
LC-USZ61-2039*

Lincoln on the stump, Springfield, 1858. He became a pretty good "stump speaker and corner-grocery debater." *Courtesy of the Library of Congress, LC-USZ62-12951*

Lincoln returning home after the debates: "It hurts too much to laugh and I am too big to cry." *Courtesy of the Library of Congress, LC-USZ6-301*

The presidential footrace—Lincoln and Douglas, the long and short of it. *Courtesy of the Library of Congress, LC-USZ62-14834*

Election day at the polling place. *Courtesy of the Library of Congress, LC-USZ62-118012*

Buchanan escorting Lincoln to his inaugural—the procession is passing the gate of the Capitol grounds. *Courtesy of the Library of Congress, LC-USZ62-331*

Lincoln's inauguration, March 4, 1861—bayonets in the crowd and cannon at both ends of Pennsylvania Avenue. *Courtesy of the Library of Congress, LC-USZ62-48090*

underlined again the moral difference between him and Douglas and their two parties, insisting that the Dred Scott decision would spread evil into all the states. Douglas again pounded his themes—demanding answers to questions when he thought Lincoln was evasive and vehemently denying the social and political equality of whites and blacks while holding high the banner of popular sovereignty. And they disagreed again on the intent of the founding fathers.[28]

Two days later the two debaters were in Alton in the strongly Democratic end of the state for their "final passage of arms." The two gladiators arrived together on the steamer *City of St. Louis* from Quincy. Another steamer, the *White Cloud,* brought several hundred from St. Louis, across the river. Others, among them Mary Lincoln, streamed in from Springfield and Carlinville on a special train to witness this final debate. The fair weather was holding. It was one of the prettiest of October days.

Douglas opened the debate in front of City Hall on a specially erected platform at the base of the town's two hills, addressing a crowd of 4,000 to 5,000 to "a great tumult of cheering." The arena was jammed with people for several blocks. Douglas was hoarse, suffering from a cold. One observer said from a distance his voice sounded like a mastiff giving off short quick barks.[29]

Douglas summed up the four months since the canvass opened. "In my speeches," he said, "I confined myself closely to those three positions which he [Lincoln] had taken controverting his proposition that this Union could not exist as our fathers made it, divided into free and slave States, controverting his proposition of a crusade against the Supreme Court because of the Dred Scott decision, and controverting his proposition that the Declaration of Independence included and meant the negroes as well as the white men, when it declared all men to be created equal." These propositions, Douglas said, "constituted a distinct issue between us."

Time after time, Douglas said, "I have enumerated the territories, one after another, putting the same question to him with reference to each, and he has not said, and will not say, whether, if elected to Congress, he will vote to admit any territory now in existence with such a constitution as her people may adopt. He invents a case which does not exist, and cannot exist under this government, and answers it; but he will not answer the question I put to him in connection with any of the territories now in existence."

"Why," Douglas demanded, "can he not say whether he is willing to allow the people of each state to have slavery or not as they please...."

Lincoln answered, his long arms rising and falling in gestures throughout. Frequently he paused and turned to Douglas, to say, "Is that not so, Judge Douglas; is not that so?"[30] He said again what he had been saying from the beginning about slavery.

In summing up he struck again the moral chord: "You may turn over everything in the Democratic policy from beginning to end, whether in the shape it takes on the statute book, in the shape it takes in the Dred Scott decision, in the shape it takes in conversation or the shape it takes in short maxim-like arguments—it everywhere carefully excludes the idea that there is anything wrong in it."

Then Lincoln said:

That is the real issue. That is the issue that will continue in this country when these poor tongues of Judge Douglas and myself shall be silent. It is the eternal struggle between these two principles—right and wrong—throughout the world. They are the two principles that have stood face to face from the beginning of time; and will ever continue to struggle. The one is the common right of humanity and the other the divine right of kings. It is the same principle in whatever shape it develops itself. It is the same spirit that says, 'You work and toil and earn bread, and I'll eat it.' No matter in what shape it comes, whether from the mouth of a king who seeks to bestride the people of his own nation and live by the fruit of their labor, or from one race of men as an apology for enslaving another race, it is the same tyrannical principle.[31]

Thus did Lincoln and Douglas distill their thoughts in the forty-two long hours of seven long debates.

They continued to campaign separately toward election day. In his last speech of the campaign, at a giant Republican canvass-ending rally in Springfield on October 30, Lincoln said, "The planting and the culture are over; and there remains but the preparation, and the harvest.... I have borne a laborious, and, in some respects to myself, a painful part in the contest." He said, "today could the Missouri restriction be restored, and the whole slavery question replaced on the old ground of 'toleration' by *necessity* where it exists, with unyielding hostility to the spread of it, on principle, I would, in consideration, gladly agree, that Judge Douglas should never be *out,* and I never *in,* an office, so long as we both or either, live."[32]

Finally it was over. Both men had campaigned their hearts out across a combined 10,000 miles up and down and across Illinois, mostly by rail, from June to November. Lincoln had covered 4,000 of those miles and had delivered sixty-three major speeches, running two to three hours long, and made unnumbered other appearances, in addition to his seven debates with the Little Giant.[33]

It was now up to the voters, and election day was November 2. The following day the *Illinois State Journal* in Springfield wrote, "We are gratified to state that the election ... passed off as usual, without any disturbance." It reported there had not been as many street fights as expected, even though by sundown the city prison was nearly full.[34] A drenching rain fell across the northern end of the state all day as far south as Vandalia. It was dry, however, in lower Egypt. The weather was something of a metaphor for the outcome—a shower of votes for Lincoln where he was strongest, dry where he wasn't. Statewide, Republican candidates outpolled Democrats by some 4,000 votes. But it didn't matter. The redistricting had done its work. The Democrats carried the legislature and when it met two months later to elect a senator it elected Douglas by nine votes, 54 to 46.

The pro-Lincoln *Chicago Press and Tribune* wrote, "Mr. Lincoln is beaten.... No man could have done more." From Pennsylvania the *Reading Journal* wrote that the newspaper believed Lincoln had "made for himself a reputation as a great statesman and popular debater, as extensive as the country itself." The inconstant Horace Greeley conceded that Lincoln's speeches were "of a very high order. They were pungent without bitterness and powerful without harshness," and that the address in Springfield opening the canvass had been "a model of compactness, lucidity and logic."[35] The pro-Republican *Louisville Journal* said of them that they were "searching, scathing, stunning ... the tomahawking species."[36]

The *Illinois State Journal,* unshakeable Lincoln ally since its early days as the *Sangamo Journal,* called the campaign "the event most remarkable and most exciting...which the people of Illinois have ever witnessed or taken part in," the longest ever and "fought with a fierceness which never lagged for a moment." The paper said, "Mr. Lincoln...has gained for himself a reputation as an orator and a statesman, which is henceforth National in its character...a man whom the Republicans not only of Illinois but of the whole Union can rally around as 'a leader.'"[37]

Even David R. Locke, the humorist who wrote under the nom de plume of Petroleum V. Nasby was serious for a moment, calling the debates "the greatest political struggle this country ever witnessed." He had interviewed Lincoln after the final debate in Alton and Lincoln had predicted that he would win the popular vote, but Douglas would be elected because of the redistricting. "You can't overturn a pyramid," Lincoln told Locke, "but you can undermine it; that's what I have been trying to do."[38]

Lincoln told Charles S. Zane, a Springfield lawyer, "It hurts too much to laugh and I am too big to cry."[39] He wrote his friend Anson G. Henry on November 19, "Of course I *wished,* but did not much *expect* a better result." He said, "I am glad I made the late race. It gave me a hearing on the great and durable question of the age, which I could have had in no other way; and though I now sink out of view, and shall be forgotten, I believe I have made some marks which will tell for the cause of civil liberty long after I am gone."[40]

The day the legislature met and voted Douglas in, Henry C. Whitney found Lincoln in his law office alone. "I never saw a man so depressed," Whitney said. "He was simply steeped in gloom.... 'Well,' Lincoln said, 'whatever happens I expect everyone to desert me now, but Billy Herndon.'"[41]

For his part, Douglas was spent. He called the contest "fierce," requiring him "to perform more speaking than was

either agreeable to my wishes, or consistent with my strength."
He told a newspaperman in Washington after the debates that
Lincoln was "the greatest debater I have ever met, either here or
anywhere else"—"the hardest fellow to handle I have ever encountered yet," he told a fellow senator.[42] Lincoln later said of
Douglas, that he was a man of "great hardihood, pertinacity and
magnetic power." Of all the men he had ever seen, Lincoln said,
"he has the most audacity in maintaining an untenable position,"
and has "bamboozled thousands into believing him."[43]

There was still mutual admiration there—of sorts.

On the Glory Road

PART EIGHT

On the Glory Road

24

Spreading the Gospel

AFTER THE DEBATES in which he was bathed in Douglas's fierce "reflected light," Lincoln had become "visible to the nation"—something of a national figure with the ratcheted up reputation of a man who could go head-to-head with the Little Giant and come out "neither dead nor dying."[1]

On Lincoln's mind in the wake of the debates, however, was not his upward soaring reputation, but follow-up and never-give-up. In the remaining days of 1858 he sprayed letters to fellow Republicans, saying "The fight must go on"—"The cause of civil liberty must not be surrendered at the end of *one,* or even, one *hundred* defeats"—"Let no one falter. The *question* is not half settled"—"We are right, and can not finally fail. There will be another blow-up in the so-called democratic party before long."[2] Into the next year he was still rallying the faithful. "Yes,

Archie," he told Archibald Williams in January, "Douglas has taken this trick, but the game is not played out."[3]

In a letter to Lyman Trumbull in early December, Lincoln surveyed the post-debate landscape. "Douglas has gone South," Lincoln wrote Trumbull, "making characteristic speeches, and seeking to re-instate himself in that section. The majority of the democratic politicians of the nation mean to kill him; but I doubt whether they will adopt the aptest way to do it."

The aptest way to handle him, said Lincoln, who had extensive experience in Douglas-handling, "is to present him with no new test, let him into the Charleston Convention [the Democratic national convention in 1860], and then outvote him, and nominate another." Under that scenario, Lincoln said, "he will have no pretext for bolting the nomination, and will be as powerless as they can wish."

"On the other hand"—and this is what worried Lincoln— "if they push a Slave code upon him, as a test, he will bolt at once, turn upon us, as in the case of Lecompton, and claim that all Northern men shall make common cause in electing him President as the best means of breaking down the Slave power. In that case, the democratic party go into a minority inevitably; and the struggle in the whole North will be, as it was in Illinois last summer and fall, whether the Republican party can maintain [its] identity, or be broken up to form the tail of Douglas' new kite."

The truth of the matter is, Lincoln told Trumbull, "the Republican principle can, in no wise live with Douglas; and it is arrant folly now, as it was last Spring, to waste time, and scatter labor already performed, in dallying with him."[4]

In Chicago on March 1, in his first political speech since the campaign, Lincoln said, "I do not wish to be misunderstood upon this subject of slavery in the country. I suppose it may long exist, [in the states where it now exists] and perhaps the best way for it to come to an end peaceably is for it to exist for a length of time. But I say that the spread and strengthening and perpetuation of it is an entirely different proposition. There we should in every way resist it as a wrong, treating it as a wrong, with the fixed idea that it must and will come to an end."[5]

Lincoln wanted to fix that idea as widely as possible. Throughout 1859, when his law practice permitted and his schedule could bear it, he began to export it into neighboring states. He delivered some eighteen speeches outside of Illinois. He spoke in Wisconsin to the north—in Milwaukee, Janesville, and Beloit. He spoke in Indiana which was one of the three important "October" states, where state elections were held the month before and inevitably seemed to precurse the outcomes of presidential elections. He spoke in Columbus, Hamilton, Dayton, and Cincinnati, in Ohio, another of the key October states (the third was Pennsylvania). He went to Iowa on personal business, and delivered a political speech in Council Bluffs while he was there. He even ventured onto the field of bloody violence itself, Kansas Territory, speaking in Elwood, Troy, Doniphan, Atchison, and Leavenworth.

In these sorties he delivered his gospel vigorously. An observer in Milwaukee, watching him being emphatic—raising both arms to one side as far as he could reach, then bringing them down in an arc as low as he could reach, and then swinging them up as high as he could reach on the other side—was reminded of "the sweep of great elms in a storm."[6]

At most of these out-of-state stops Lincoln's ascending reputation caused him to be treated as visiting political royalty, being met at the depot and escorted to his hotel—a procedure he had become accustomed to in the debates. A reporter in Council Bluffs wrote, "He was listened to with much attention, for his Waterloo defeat by Douglas has magnified him into quite a lion here."[7] Such was his reputation that he had to turn down more speeches than he could accept. They came in a stream. Turning down one in Boston, he nonetheless attached a long reply—something of a mailed-in speech—which was widely circulated in the Republican press. In it he rang major chords of his anti-slavery litany.[8]

The major chords of that litany were still tuned to the music of Stephen A. Douglas. He seemed always to be addressing Douglas. These forays in 1859 were, in effect, Debates, Part 2. In September 1859, Douglas wrote an article for *Harper's New Monthly Magazine*, the most prestigious literary journal in the country. It ran for eighteen tightly packaged pages sandwiched between a poem, "A Homely Song of Toil" and the latest serial-ized excerpt from *The Virginians*, a novel by William Makepeace Thackeray. The article was a spirited, definitive defense of his solution to the slavery problem, titled, "The Dividing Line be-tween Federal and Local Authority: Popular Sovereignty in the Territories." In it Douglas argued his own well-worn litany. Lin-coln read it and said, "This will never do. He puts the moral ele-ment out of this question. It won't stay out."[9]

Nor would the moral question stay out of what Lincoln was telling out-of-staters. After the article came out, Douglas went to Ohio to promote his "great principle," and Lincoln followed him. It was like old times—same hounding after him, same themes, different venues.

In Columbus, in his first speech before an Ohio audience, Lincoln argued, "Douglas's proposition is to establish that the leading men of the revolution were for his great principle of non-intervention by the government in the question of slavery in the territories; while history shows that they decided in the cases actually brought before them, in exactly the contrary way, and he knows it."

"Not only did they so decide at that time," Lincoln said, "but they stuck to it during sixty years, through thick and thin, as long as there was one of the revolutionary heroes upon the stage of political action. Through their whole course, from first to last, they clung to freedom. And now he asks the community to believe that the men of the revolution were in favor of his great principle, when we have the naked history that they themselves dealt with this very subject matter of his principle, and utterly repudiated his principle, acting upon a precisely contrary ground."[10]

In Cincinnati Lincoln cited the favorite Douglas thesis, "that these states [Ohio, Indiana, Illinois] are free upon his 'great principle' of Popular Sovereignty, because the people of those several states have chosen to make them so." But, Lincoln asked the Ohioans, "Pray what was it that made you free? What kept you free? Did you not find your country free when you came to decide that Ohio should be a Free State?" Kentucky is separated from Ohio by a river not a mile wide. Yet "Kentucky is entirely covered with slavery—Ohio is entirely free from it." So what is the difference? Not climate nor soil. "The Ordinance of '87 kept it out of Ohio," Lincoln insisted. And it is the same case with Indiana and Kentucky, the same with Illinois and Missouri. "I think all these facts," Lincoln said, "most abundantly prove that my friend Judge Douglas' proposition, that the Ordinance of '87 or the national restriction of slavery, never had a tendency to make a Free State, is a fallacy—a proposition without the shadow or substance of truth about it."[11]

Summing up the central theme of all of his out-of-state speaking in Beloit, Wisconsin, in early October, Lincoln again called popular sovereignty "that stupendous humbug," and said that the hatred of slavery in all its aspects, moral, social, and political, "is the foundation of the Republican party—its active, life-giving principle." The Republicans can't do anything about it in the states where it exists, he said, as he had many times before, "but when it attempts to overleap its present limits and fasten itself upon free territory, they would resist and force it back." This, he said "was what the Republican party was now trying to do."[12]

Lincoln's spreading of the word to neighboring states about his party's aspirations heightened his own reputation. Riding that reputation, he began reaching out to national Republican leaders on what he saw as an urgent party problem. He was concerned in particular about the danger the Fugitive Slave Law posed for the party. "It is ungodly; it is ungodly; no doubt it is ungodly!" he told a friend in early 1860. "But it is the law of the land, and we must obey it as we find it."[13]

When the Republican state convention in Ohio adopted a platform with a plank to repeal the law, Lincoln wrote Salmon P. Chase a worried letter. "This is already damaging us here," he wrote. "I have no doubt that if that plank be even *introduced* into the next Republican National convention, it will explode it"—the convention and the party.

He wrote Congressman Schuler Colfax of Indiana deploring the Ohio plank, the effort in New Hampshire to make obedience to the law punishable as a crime, and the movement against foreigners in Massachusetts. In these things—in "these apples of discord," he told Colfax, "there is explosive matter enough to blow up half a dozen national conventions."

He was trying to tell his fellow Republicans that everything should be avoided in local party conventions and in the national convention that would cripple party members elsewhere—as he believed efforts to repeal the Fugitive Slave Law would do in Illinois. "In every locality," he said, "we should look beyond our noses."[14]

During all this outreach, something from far away—and highly tantalizing—suddenly landed under his own nose.

25

Cooper Union

THE HARD-TO-REFUSE invitation came in the mail in October 1859 and was from out-of-staters who mattered more than most—New Yorkers.

William Cullen Bryant, the editor of the *New York Evening Post,* who moonlighted as one of the nation's premier poets, had been worried. There was no question that the New York delegation would go to the Republican national convention next year solidly pledged to their favorite son and the party's front-runner for president, their senator and former governor, William H. Seward. But what if the Western delegations would not accept Seward or any Eastern candidate? There was talk to that effect. The nomination then might go to some candidate repugnant to New Yorkers.

So Bryant called a meeting in his office to see that the delegation had a qualified fallback choice, an acceptable westerner—if there was such a thing. The editor-poet suggested that—among others—they take a look at the lanky lawyer from Illinois, who had shown up so well in his debates with Douglas—indeed shown an exceptional grasp of "the grave issues pending" and who had "a power to influence public opinion." Bryant reminded the others that he had sent Chester Dewey to cover the debates in Illinois, and Dewey's dispatches had left Bryant with a high opinion of Lincoln. He suggested they send him an invitation to speak in New York so they might make an up-close, first-hand evaluation.[1]

So the invitation had gone out to Lincoln on October 12 from James A. Briggs, a New York–based political activist and member of the arrangement committee. The idea was for Lincoln to speak in Henry Ward Beecher's famed Plymouth Church in Brooklyn on or about November 19, on any subject he pleased, for $200. The fee was generous, higher than any Lincoln had ever earned for a speech of any kind anytime, anywhere.[2]

Lincoln hesitated at first. He had never spoken in New York before. He told friends, "I don't know whether I shall be adequate to the situation; I have never appeared before such an audience as may possibly assemble to hear me. I am appalled by the magnitude of the undertaking."[3] He was not enough appalled, however, to turn it down. Indeed, here was an opportunity to move and shake the movers and shakers. Besides, Lincoln figured "it was worth a visit...to New York to make the acquaintance of such a man as William Cullen Bryant."[4] Lincoln had a weakness for poetry, particularly morose verse. He resonated in particular with the clanging sentiments of "Thanatopsis," Bryant's meditation on death, which he had years earlier memorized.[5]

———

Lincoln accepted the invitation from New York if the committee would accept a February date instead of November, and if it would agree to a "political" speech.[6] They agreed. Lincoln started to put together what he doubtless believed was the speech of his political career. This one would take more research than he had ever put into a political address.

He began logging time in the state library, combing dusty volumes of congressional proceedings and digging into political history. He concentrated on the Founders, plumbing their thinking deeper than he ever had before. He read letters and writings of the leaders. Who these men were, and what they thought, were important to him. Where they stood on the slavery question particularly keyed his research. There, he believed, was the true antidote to Douglas's arguments for popular sovereignty. He closely studied the proceedings of the constitutional convention in Philadelphia in 1787 when the Founders passed the Northwest Ordinance.

Jumping out at him from all this concentrated research was pertinent documentation: Of the thirty-eight signers of the Constitution, twenty-three had showed in their votes that they believed the federal government had the power to regulate slavery in the territories—contrary to what Douglas said in his *Harper's* piece. This proved to Lincoln conclusively what he had always believed—that they had in mind slavery's ultimate extinction and that popular sovereignty was not their idea of how to do it. When the time to leave for New York approached, he had in his valise a speech written in his own hand on blue foolscap, fine-tuned with a few interlineations.[7]

Since he knew he would be under a critical microscope in New York, he wanted to look his best, so he went to a clothing store in Springfield to buy a new outfit. Since no ready-made suit ever had any hope of fitting him, he bought a black one for $100 and had it retooled to approximate the shape of his angular, outsized body—also a hopeless strategy. So that the trousers would appear long enough, he had them loosely braced, which brought on a compensating bagginess about the waist and thighs. To make the waistcoat appear respectable, he opted for tails that were too short and the rest of it too full. He then packed it in a valise, which consigned the entire project to wrinkled disarray.[8] But he had done the best he could with the body he had.

He left the house in Springfield on Wednesday morning, February 22, unattended, without fanfare, and without advance notice, walking to the depot to board the train just as the city was beginning its celebration of George Washington's birthday. He was wearing a pair of boots, new-bought like the suit, a tad too short and pinching his feet. He was carrying $50 in cash and a $50 draft to cover travel expenses.[9]

The *Illinois State Register* took sardonic note of his departure. It wrote: "The Honorable Abraham Lincoln departs today for Brooklyn under an engagement to deliver a lecture...in Beecher's Church. Subject, not known. Consideration, $200 and expenses. Object, presidential capital. Effect, disappointment."[10]

The 1,200-mile trip would have exhausted Homer's Ulysses. It took half a dozen different trains, three days with three middle-of-the-night transfers—running to catch some, waiting interminably for others—before arriving sleep-deprived in New York City on Saturday, February 25.[11]

Henry C. Bowen, who had played a role in promoting the invitation, knew the speaker was on his way. Bowen had never met Lincoln, but he had worked to get him there and was happy he was coming. He was the editor of the *New York Independent,* an influential anti-slavery Congregationalist weekly, which the Lincolns subscribed to in Springfield. He was working alone in his office that Saturday afternoon when there was a rap on his door. He supposed it was a late-arriving messenger, so without turning around he shouted, "Come in." He heard someone enter, but occupied at his desk, he didn't bother looking up. After a short elapsed silence, a voice asked: "Is this Mr. Henry C. Bowen?" Still not looking up, Bowen owned up to it, and the voice said, "I am Abraham Lincoln."

That got Bowen's attention. Swiveling about immediately, as he later testified, "I faced a very tall man wearing a high hat and carrying an old-fashioned comical-looking carpet-bag.... My heart went into my boots as I greeted this tall stranger. His clothes were travel-stained and he looked tired and woebegone and there was nothing in my first hasty view of the man that was at all prepossessing." Bowen had the "disheartening and appalling thought" that the whole event he had worked so hard to induce, was doomed to disaster.

"For an instant," he said, "I felt sick at heart over the prospect, and could not greet my visitor with any warmth of manner, though I tried very hard to suppress any manifestation of my thoughts." But Lincoln eased his "tension of dismay and surprise" somewhat when he spoke in "a most kindly and genial voice."

"Mr. Bowen," he said, "I am just in from Springfield, Illinois, and I am very tired. If you have no objection I will lie down on your lounge here and you can tell me about the arrangements for Monday night."

"There was such a blend of dignity and gentleness in the stranger's voice and words," Bowen later wrote, "such an absence of all self-consciousness, or embarrassment, that there came a degree of relief to the tension of my first disagreeable and disappointing impressions."

After the few moments of talk that followed Bowen began to see, beyond the hayseed veneer, the powerful and winning personality of this unkempt giant of a visitor sprawled on his office couch. His fears about Monday night eased and soon vanished. He began to think the opposite of what he first thought. He began to feel "exultant in prospect of a triumph" Monday night.[12]

Lincoln checked in to a ground-floor room at the Astor House, a palatial hotel with a celebrated courtyard and equally celebrated indoor plumbing. The room cost about two dollars a night, meals included.[13]

The Young Men's Republican Union had assumed sponsorship of Lincoln's speech, and he had learned for the first time that the lecture—to draw a larger audience—had been switched from Beecher's church in Brooklyn to the hall of the year-old Cooper Union for the Advancement of Science and Art in New York City. Worried that what he had prepared for the Beecher audience might—like his suit—not fit just right in this new setting, he spent much of the rest of Saturday reviewing his speech and making more interlineations on the foolscap.[14]

Monday night the big auditorium at Cooper Union, on Seventh Street at the foot of the Bowery, was ablaze with lights. All 168 gas burners in its twenty-seven crystal chandeliers were hissing and throwing brilliant reflections against the mirrors lining the walls in the hall. The crowd, as Lincoln knew would be the case, was "the pick and flower of New York culture," all "the noted men—all the learned and cultured of [Lincoln's] party, editors, clergymen, lawyers, merchants, critics." Some 1,500 had paid twenty-five cents a head to be there and they filled three-quarters of the huge hall.[15]

Bryant rose and strode to the podium to introduce the speaker. "I have only, my friends," he began, "to pronounce the name of Abraham Lincoln of Illinois, I have only to pronounce his name to secure your profoundest attention."[16] Attention was likely. There was indeed "a curiosity," one witness said, "to see and hear the man who had dared 'To beard the lion in his den, the Douglas in his hall.'"[17]

When Bryant sat down, Lincoln found himself standing before a velvet-covered, gold-tasseled, slant-topped iron lectern.[18] He was a sight. His baggy new western suit, just out of his valise and fully wrinkled for the occasion, "presented a series of ridges and valleys like the inequalities of a washboard." Its "telltale creases" put it wholly out of sync with the tailored, trim-fitting suits of Bryant and the other dignitaries on the platform.[19]

He was "an awkward specimen indeed," one man thought. He was "tall, tall—oh how tall, and so angular and awkward that I had, for an instant, a feeling of pity for so ungainly a man," a reporter wrote. "His clothes were black and ill-fitting, badly wrinkled." He began in his high shrill voice—as was generally the case before it gradually descended to a lower register when the flow of his speech began to kick in. When he lifted his arm to gesture, the collar of his coat on the right side flew up. Another unconvinced witness looking at him, listening to this antic beginning, concluded that there was in him "not a trace of the smooth-tongued orator."[20]

"The first impression of the man from the West," another wrote, "did nothing to contradict the expectation of something weird, rough, and uncultivated. The long, ungainly figure, upon which hung clothes that while new for the trip, were evidently the work of an unskillful tailor; the large feet; the clumsy hands, of which, at the outset at least, the orator seemed to be unduly conscious; the long, gaunt head capped by a shock of hair that seemed not to have been thoroughly brushed out made a picture which did not fit in with New York's conception of a finished statesman."[21]

But as his speech gathered momentum Lincoln forgot the audience, his wrinkled suit, his flying collar, and his awkwardness, and became, he later said, as much at ease as if delivering a speech at home in Springfield.[22]

He began his speech immediately refuting Douglas. He pulled from his research in the state library the proof that the Fathers had intended to take control of slavery, setting it on a course to ultimate extinction, and had consistently acted accordingly. "The sum of the whole is," he said, "that of our thirty-nine fathers who framed the original Constitution, twenty-one— a clear majority of the whole—certainly understood that no proper division of local from federal authority, nor any part of the Constitution, forbade the Federal Government to control slavery in the federal territories; while all the rest probably had the same understanding."

Lincoln pointed out that in 1789 the first Congress sitting under the new Constitution passed an act to enforce the ordinance of 1787 outlawing slavery in the Northwest Territories. The act went through all its stages without a word of opposition, Lincoln said, through both branches without yeas and nays, the equivalent of unanimous passage. President Washington, one of the original thirty-nine signers of the Constitution, signed the act.

All that Republicans ask, Lincoln told the New Yorkers, all they desire—in relation to slavery—was this: *"As those fathers marked it, so let it be again marked, as an evil not to be extended, but to be tolerated and protected only because of and so far as its actual presence among us make that toleration and protection a necessity. Let all the guaranties those fathers gave it, be, not grudgingly, but fully and fairly maintained."*

Then Lincoln spoke to the South. "You say we are sectional," he said. "We deny it. That makes an issue; and the burden of proof is upon you. You produce your proof; and what is it? Why, that our party has no existence in your section." But your proof, he said, "does not touch the issue. The fact that we get no votes in your section, is a fact of your making, and not of ours." We, he said, "stick to, contend for, the identical old policy which was adopted by 'our fathers who framed the Government under which we live;' while you with one accord reject, and scout, and spit upon that old policy, and insist upon substituting something new."

Hammering the point home, he said, "you say we have made the slavery question more prominent than it formerly was. We deny it. We admit that it is more prominent, but we deny that we made it so. It was not we, but you, who discarded the old policy of the fathers. We resisted, and still resist, your innovation; and thence comes the greater prominence of the question."

He scored the South for threatening to break up the Union rather than have its assumed rights under the Constitution denied—the right to take slaves into the federal territories, and to hold them there as property. "But no such right is specifically written in the Constitution," Lincoln argued. "That instrument is literally silent about any such right. We, on the contrary, deny that such a right has any existence in the Constitution, even by implication. Your purpose, then, plainly stated, is, that you will destroy the Government, unless you be allowed to construe and enforce the Constitution as you please, on all points in dispute between you and us. You will rule or ruin in all events."

You, Lincoln said, still addressing the South, say "you will not abide the election of a Republican President! In that supposed event, you say, you will destroy the Union; and then, you say, the great crime of having destroyed it will be upon us! That is cool. A highwayman holds a pistol to my ear, and mutters through his teeth, 'Stand and deliver, or I, shall kill you, and then you will be a murderer!'"

Having spoken to the South, Lincoln now spoke to Republicans. *"It is exceedingly desirable,"* he said, *"that all parts of this great Confederacy shall be at peace, and in harmony, one with another. Let us Republicans do our part to have it so. Even though much provoked, let us do nothing through passion and ill temper. Even though the southern people will not so much as listen to us, let us calmly consider their demands, and yield to them, if, in our deliberate view of our duty, we possibly can."*

Coming to the end of his speech, Lincoln said of the South, "Holding, as they do, that slavery is morally right, and socially elevating, they cannot cease to demand a full national recognition of it, as a legal right, and a social blessing." All they ask, he said, "we could readily grant, if we thought slavery right; all we ask, they could as readily grant, if they thought it wrong. Their thinking it right, and our thinking it wrong, is the precise fact upon which depends the whole controversy. Thinking it right, as they do, they are not to blame for desiring its full recognition, as being right; but, thinking it wrong, as we do, can we yield to them? Can we cast our votes with their view, and against our own? In view of our moral, social, and political responsibilities, can we do this?"

Lincoln then closed his speech under the hissing gaslights with this:

> If our sense of duty forbids this, then let us stand by our duty, fearlessly and effectively. Let us be diverted by none of those sophistical contrivances wherewith we are so industriously plied and belabored—contrivances such as groping for some middle ground between the right and the wrong, vain as the search for a man who should be neither a living man nor a dead man—such as a policy of "don't care" on a question about which all true men do care—such as Union appeals beseeching true Union men to yield to Disunionists, reversing the divine rule, and calling, not the sinners, but the righteous to repentance—such as invocations to Washington, imploring men to unsay what Washington said, and undo what Washington did. Neither let us be slandered from our duty by false accusations against us, nor frightened from it by menaces of destruction to the Government nor of dungeons to ourselves. LET US HAVE FAITH THAT RIGHT MAKES MIGHT, AND IN THAT FAITH, LET US, TO THE END, DARE TO DO OUR DUTY AS WE UNDERSTAND IT.[23]

Four New York newspapers the next day printed the speech—the *Tribune, Times, Herald,* and Bryant's *Evening Post.* It would soon be broadcast far beyond New York as a pamphlet—a stone dropped in the waters with a wide political ripple effect. Greeley was lavish in praise in the *Tribune.* "Since the days of Clay and Webster," he wrote, "no man has spoken to a larger assemblage of the intellect and mental culture of our

City. Mr. Lincoln is one of Nature's orators.... No man ever before made such an impression on his first appeal to a New-York audience."[24]

The tall sucker from the Illinois prairie had conquered the big city.

The next day he headed north into New England. It was intended as a visit with his son Robert, a student at Phillips Exeter Academy in New Hampshire. But it became a speechmaking odyssey. Over the next eleven days he delivered eleven more speeches, zigzagging north, back again south, north again, and finally south once more through three New England states, in heavy demand, going wherever he was invited and could go. Everywhere he went, he reshopped the gist of his Cooper Union address.[25]

When he spoke in Exeter Town Hall on March 3, Robert's classmates turned out to see and hear him. They experienced the same emotional gyrations Lincoln seemed to trigger in every first-time audience. Robert Atkins saw him enter the Town Hall from the rear and thought, "What a darned fool I've been to walk up here through the mud to hear *that* man speak." Warren Prescott was equally appalled, watching Lincoln sit on the platform as he waited to speak. "He sat all hunched up, legs crossed," Prescott said, "and honestly I think his foot was as long as the end of the little table on the platform." When Lincoln rose, Prescott said to himself, "I wish I was at home." Marshall Snow was likewise put off. "His hair was rumpled," Snow noted, "his neckwear was all awry, he sat somewhat bent in the chair, and altogether presented a very remarkable, and, to us, disappointing appearance." They were all feeling sorry for the son because of the father. "We sat and stared at Mr. Lincoln,"

Snow said. "We whispered to each other: 'Isn't it too bad Bob's father is so homely? Don't you feel sorry for him?'"

But when Lincoln "untangled those long legs from their contact with the rounds of the chair," and drew himself to his full towering height and launched into his speech, everything changed. Within the usual elapsed ten minutes, Atkins said, "I was glad I was there." Prescott, too, felt he "wouldn't have been anywhere else but in that hall." Snow said, "not ten minutes had passed before his uncouth appearance was absolutely forgotten by us boys.... His face lighted up and the man was changed; it seemed absolutely like another person speaking to us.... There was no more pity for our friend Bob; we were proud of his father." When the speech ended, Atkins said, "the cheers nearly raised the roof."[26]

Half a dozen speeches later a weary Lincoln caught a night express out of Bridgeport for New York on March 10.[27]

It had been an exhausting run, and Lincoln had turned down probably as many speeches as he had accepted. Finding new ways to phrase his message was a challenge. From Exeter he wrote Mary, "I have been unable to escape this toil. If I had foreseen it, I think I would not have come east at all. The speech at New York, being within my calculation before I started, went off passably well and gave me no trouble whatever. The difficulty was to make nine others, before reading audiences who had already seen all my ideas in print."[28]

On March 12 he turned at last toward home. Gabriel Lewis Smith, a New York lawyer and one of the founders of the Republican Party in the Elmira area, ran into him on a train. Smith noted that Lincoln unfolded in sections, "like a carpenter's rule." He asked Lincoln about Douglas and the prospects for the

Democratic Party in the coming presidential canvass. Lincoln pondered a moment, and then said: "Judge Douglas, with great ability and great ambition, has no superior in making the worse appear the better reason, but he is without moral sense so far as concerns the slavery question, and he has split his party wide open by the repeal of the Missouri Compromise and his nostrum of squatter sovereignty. The Southern Democrats will refuse to support him for President this year, and he cannot hope to win without them. Four years ago I could see no prospect of the Republican Party winning before 1864 at the earliest; now I believe that with the right candidate on the right platform we shall win an easy victory in November."[29]

What Smith didn't ask was what Lincoln's prospects were in that Republican Party during the coming canvass. But it had now become a relevant question.

26

Reaching for the Brass Ring

LINCOLN IN EARLY 1860 was now like Donati's comet, a sudden shooting star visible in the political night sky. He had grown an illustrious tail and was being linked in Republican minds and in public print to that ultimate political apogee, the presidency.

Previously, the prospect had seemed to be pie-in-the-sky fantasy. During the 1858 debates with Douglas, he confessed to the journalist Henry Villard that he had some doubts about his ability to be a senator, much less president. "Just think," he mused, breaking off into a roar of laughter, "of such a sucker as me as President."[1]

Others were thinking that way and not laughing. The buzz had started following the debates in late 1858. Jeriah Bonham, editor of the *Illinois Gazette,* reporting the election results and writing "hastily" on deadline, editorialized: "What man now fills the full measure of public expectation as the statesman of to-day and of the near future, as does Abraham Lincoln? And in writing our own preference for him, we believe we but express the wish of a large majority of the people that he should be the standard-bearer of the Republican party for the presidency in 1860." The editorial ran on November 8, 1858.[2] The buzz had been in the air in Illinois ever since.

In the fall of 1858 Jesse Fell, his friend from Bloomington, raised the idea of the presidency directly with Lincoln. "Oh, Fell," Lincoln told him, "what's the use of talking of me for the presidency, whilst we have such men as Seward, Chase, and others, who are so much better known to the people and whose names are so intimately associated with the principles of the Republican party. Everybody knows them; nobody, scarcely, outside of Illinois, knows me. Besides, is it not, as a matter of justice, due to such men, who have carried this movement forward to its present status, in spite of fearful opposition, personal abuse, and hard names? I really think so."

But Fell wouldn't let up. He persisted, asking Lincoln for information about his life. Pressed on the matter, Lincoln said, "I admit the force of much that you say, and admit that I am ambitious and would like to be president. I am not insensible to the compliment you pay me and the interest you manifest in the matter, but there is no such good luck in store for me as the presidency of these United States. Besides, there is nothing in my early history that would interest you or anybody else, and, as Judge Davis says, 'It won't pay.'"[3] Lincoln rather believed his friends were chasing rainbows.

In the middle of April 1859, Thomas J. Pickett, editor of the *Rock Island Register,* wrote Lincoln that he would like to engineer a simultaneous acclamation of him for president in all of the

Republican papers in the state. Lincoln answered, "I must, in candor, say I do not think myself fit for the Presidency."[4]

In late April, Lincoln was in the office of the *Central Illinois Gazette* in Champaign when its editor, Will O. Stoddard, suggested his candidacy. Lincoln demurred, just as he had with Fell earlier. But on May 4 Stoddard wrote in his paper anyway, "it is the firm and fixed belief of our citizens that...no man will be so sure to consolidate the party vote of this State, or will carry the great Mississippi Valley with a more irresistible rush of popular enthusiasm, than our distinguished fellow citizen ABRAHAM LINCOLN."[5]

On December 7, Stoddard's *Gazette* ran another article backing him, and on December 21 it started running his name at the head of its editorial columns.

In the autumn of 1859, the *Chicago Press and Tribune* began to mention Lincoln's name when it spoke of presidential "possibilities and probabilities," also touting him as the most "available" candidate.[6] On February 16 the paper became emphatic. It extravagantly praised Lincoln as "a man of great breadth and great acuteness of intellect," even "executive capacity"—a reach, because he had never been in a position to demonstrate any such capacity. The paper outright urged his nomination. Since the *Press and Tribune* was the most influential Republican newspaper in the state, this meant he was no longer just a possible candidate for the nomination. By no stretch was he the favorite of all the candidates, but he was in effect in the race, the anointed favorite son of Illinois.[7]

Returning from New York and New England in the middle of March, Lincoln himself had become something of a believer. Edward Judd, Norman Judd's son, later wrote that he returned "with a growing belief that there was a fair chance that in the end he might be the Republican nominee for President. Seward and Chase then bulked largest in the popular mind, but there was a possibility, so shrewd a politician as Mr. Lincoln was quick to foresee, that they might kill one another off, when their followers came to close quarters in the convention, and thus the way be opened for him to secure Republican leadership in the nation."

With such a scenario in mind, young Judd recounted, "Mr. Lincoln as soon as he was back in his Springfield office, resumed in a quiet but effective way the work he had begun before his Eastern trip to secure an Illinois delegation to the national convention, fully and definitely committed to his candidacy." Even before he left for the East, Lincoln had written young Judd's father "in characteristic fashion that while he was in a position where it would not hurt much for him not to be placed on the national ticket, it would be harmful to him not to secure the Illinois delegates to the convention."[8]

The stars were in a peculiar alignment just then for the candidacy of "such a sucker" as Lincoln. The state had emerged on the frontier as one of the most demographically and politically powerful in the Union. Its population had doubled in the decade of the Fifties—a bigger spike upward proportionately than the country as a whole. By 1860 it had lapped seven other states to become the fourth largest in the Union in population and wealth. Its lush prairies, long since under the plow, had elevated it into first place in the Union in wheat and corn production. It had more acres of cultivated farmland—thirteen million—than any state save New York. Its 2,900 miles of railroad track was exceeded only by Ohio.[9]

It was now a political powerhouse with thirteen congressmen, nearly double the seven it had in 1850. And Lincoln had become the preeminent Republican in that now powerful state. If there was to be a favorite son candidate for Illinois, he was obviously it. He appeared to have more "availability"—which meant electability—than the leading candidates.

Being a relative unknown nationally also had an upside. Despite his single term in Congress, he had not stirred much animosity. Low on the political horizon, he had not been a target. A rundown of all the names generally mentioned for the Republican nomination showed the wear and tear of familiarity. Seward was thought too radical on the slavery issue and unlikely to carry the important doubtful states. Chase, far more radical, could not even count on the undivided support of his own state. Edward Bates of Missouri was well liked by conservatives in the party, but he had been a Know-Nothing and would stir revolt in the powerful German electorate. John McLean, a justice of the U.S. Supreme Court, could carry the doubtful states, but he was getting along in years and was about as politically exciting as watching paint dry.[10]

In early April Lincoln was busily assessing the field from the Illinois perspective. "I think Mr. Seward is the very best candidate we could have for the North of Illinois," he wrote Richard M. Corwine. a Cincinnati lawyer, "and the very *worst* for the South of it. The estimate of Gov. Chase here is neither better nor worse than that of Seward, except that he is a newer man. They are regarded as being almost the same, seniority giving Seward the inside track. Mr. Bates, I think, would be the best man for the South of our State, and the worst for the North of it."

Lincoln told Corwine that if McLean were fifteen, or even ten years younger, dull or not, he might be strongest statewide, "but his great age, and the recollection of the deaths of Harrison and Taylor have, so far, prevented his being much spoken of here." All that said, Lincoln believed Republicans could carry the state "for any one who may be nominated; but doubtless it would be easier to do it with some than with others."

How about for Lincoln? "I feel myself disqualified to speak of myself in this matter," he told Corwine.[11]

However, to others he *was* speaking of himself in that matter. In a letter to Columbus attorney Samuel Galloway in late March he wrote, "My name is new in the field; and I suppose I am not the *first* choice of a very great many. Our policy, then, is to give no offence to others—leave them in a mood to come to us, if they shall be compelled to give up their first love. This, too, is dealing justly with all, and leaving us in a mood to support heartily whoever shall be nominated." He wrote newspaper editor James F. Babcock about this same time, saying, "As to the Presidential nomination, claiming no greater exemption from selfishness than is common, I still feel that my whole aspiration should be, and therefore must be, to be placed anywhere, or nowhere, as may appear most likely to advance our cause." Lincoln had admitted to Corwine, however, "when not a very great man begins to be mentioned for a very great position, his head is very likely to be a little turned." To Lyman Trumbull he wrote, "I will be perfectly frank. The taste *is* in my mouth a little."[12]

By the first of May, when he wrote Corwine another letter giving him more "lay of the land," Lincoln was speaking openly of himself and his chances. "I think the Illinois delegation will be unanimous for me at the start," he told Corwine; "and no other delegation will. A few individuals in other delegations would like to go for me at the start, but may be restrained by their colleagues. It is represented to me, by men who ought to know, that the whole of Indiana might not be difficult to get. You know how it is in Ohio. I am certainly not the first choice there; and yet I have not heard that any one makes any positive objection to me. It is just so everywhere so far as I can perceive. Everywhere, except in Illinois, and possibly Indiana, one or another is preferred to me, but there is no positive objection. This is the ground as it now appears."[13]

Decatur was in the geographical middle of Illinois, mutually convenient—or inconvenient, depending on where you were coming from—to either end and either side of the state. It had been the destination of the Lincolns when they migrated to Illinois from Indiana thirty years before. In those three decades the rough little settlement had grown into a bustling town of seven or eight thousand citizens. On May 6, 1860, it was packed with "most of the choice political spirits of Illinois of the Republican party,"[14] coming to pick a delegation to the national convention—and the candidate the delegation would be pledged to vote for in Chicago.

A temporary makeshift structure called "The Wigwam" had been erected on Park Street with a roof so low on its south side that Lincoln's head would have grazed the canvas ceiling. To many, his name was far higher than the ceiling—especially to Richard J. Oglesby from Decatur. Inspired by the success of Harrison's log cabin and hard cider campaign of 1840, Oglesby believed Lincoln needed something like that—some catchy slogan on which to anchor a bid for the nomination. And he believed he knew what that might be.

Being well acquainted with people around Decatur, he went to John Hanks, Lincoln's cousin, who told him about the rails he and Lincoln had split when clearing the land a dozen miles west of town thirty years before.

Oglesby and Hanks drove down to the old clearing in a

buggy. Hanks examined the rails and found the same kind—hewn from black walnut and honey locust.

"There they are," John said, after chipping at the rails of an old fence with his penknife. "They are the identical rails we made."

They then found the stumps they had cut them from, took two of the rails, tied them under the hind axle of the buggy, and started for town. Oglesby stored them in his barn to await the convention.

On May 6, after the convention was underway, Oglesby rose and announced that "an old Democrat had something he wished to present to this meeting." The shout went up, "What is it! What is it!" "Receive it! Receive it!"

Hanks was ushered in with the two rails attached to a banner that read:

ABRAHAM LINCOLN, THE RAILSPLITTER CANDIDATE, FOR
PRESIDENT IN 1860. TWO RAILS FROM A LOT OF 3,000 MADE
IN 1830 BY JOHN HANKS AND ABE LINCOLN.

In the stir this created, John H. Palmer, a Lincoln man, leaped to his feet with a resolution saying, "Abraham Lincoln is the first choice of the Republican Party of Illinois for the presidency," and instructing the delegates to the Chicago convention "to use all honorable means to secure the nomination and to cast the vote of the state as a unit for him."

This was bitterly opposed by the Seward men present, but it was nonetheless adopted amid a din of applause, much jumping, screaming and howling, and hurling of hats, canes, books, and papers into the air until part of the canvas roof covering the makeshift "Wigwam" fell in over their heads. The roof had been "literally cheered off the building."

The effort to nominate anybody else collapsed with it— under the weight of the two fence rails. "The Seward boom was dead," one observer wrote. "'Dick' Oglesby and old John Hanks and two fence rails had killed it." And a slogan worthy of log cabins and hard cider—and just as appealing to the common man—had been born. Lincoln had become "the Railsplitter candidate."[15]

When the tempest subsided, someone yelled out, "Abe, did you split them rails?" Lincoln rose and said, "Gentlemen, I Suppose you want to know something about those things. Well, the truth is John Hanks and I did make rails in the Sangamon Bottom. I don't know whether we made those rails or not.... But I do know this. I made rails then—and I think I could make better ones than these now!"[16]

Soon after the convention adjourned, Lincoln was asked about his chances of being nominated. He said, "I reckon I'll get about a hundred votes at Chicago, and I have a notion that will be the high water mark for me." Also asked if he would be attending the convention, opening in less than a week, he said, "I am a little too much of a candidate to go, and not quite enough of a candidate to stay away; but upon the whole I believe I will not go."[17]

But ready to go was a team of Lincoln's closest political friends and fellow lawyers—Judge David Davis, Norman Judd, Jesse Fell, Leonard Swett, O. H. Browning, Stephen T. Logan, Ward Hill Lamon, William H. Herndon. They were highly skilled, and they were headed for Chicago to make their tall friend very much a candidate.

27

Chicago

A "WIGWAM" HAD BECOME the favored structure of choice
for Republican convention halls. And in May 1860, the biggest
one ever built hugged the shoreline of Lake Michigan in
Chicago. Like the Illinois prairie, it was massive and barnlike,
hewn from rough timber. It was a $7,000 pavilion built for one
purpose—the hour of a momentous nomination. It was aflutter
with flags, banners, bunting, pennants, and streamers. It was, the
reporter from the *New York Tribune* wrote, "the first of its kind,
and itself something of a wonder." It was to house what was then
"the greatest show on earth"—the second Republican National
Convention.

The party faithful flocking to it would number in the thousands—it was built to hold 10,000. Its delegates and observers
would give it the largest audience ever assembled within doors

in the country. It was as ready as the delegates themselves, with acoustics that would carry a speaker's voice to every part of the hall.[1]

The Republican royalty flocking there believed this was their year. The holdover signs from the canvass four years before augured success. Even with John C. Frémont, their candidate on that first canvass, green and virtually unschooled in politics, they had carried nearly every state in the North except Illinois, Indiana, Pennsylvania and New Jersey. Even in those four critical states their vote, teamed with the American Party's, had about equaled the Democratic vote.[2]

But what was happening this election year in the Democratic Party stirred even greater optimism among Republicans. The Democrats had met in Charleston, South Carolina, only days before—on the last day of April—and slivered into two pieces. South Carolina was perhaps the worst state imaginable for nominating the party's front-runner, Stephen A. Douglas. He and his candidacy, burdened with the Freeport Doctrine, which was anathema to the South, sought validation in the most firebrand, slave-loving, disunion-prone of Southern cities. The convention had splintered over the platform, over Douglas, and over his popular sovereignty, which Southerners didn't believe went far enough in their favor. Delegates of seven Southern states, denouncing a platform that fell short of all-out sanction for the peculiar institution, had bolted the convention and set up shop on their own. Unable to nominate Douglas because of the defections, the faithful Democrats had adjourned, agreeing to reconvene in Baltimore in June for a second try at nominating the Little Giant.

Lincoln had called the Democratic convention "the Charleston Fandango."[3] And it looked to the Republicans from the shore of Lake Michigan that, blessed by this devastating Democratic dance of disintegration, the election of their man—whoever he might be—was a likely thing. Choosing him was therefore critical and worrisome.

Contrary to Charleston, an ill fit for Stephen Douglas, there could hardly have been a better fit than Chicago and the dark-horse Republican candidacy of Abraham Lincoln. It had been picked over all the eastern possibilities as the convention site thanks to Norman Judd, the Illinois representative on the Republican National Committee. He had persuaded his eastern colleagues that this big-shouldered, dynamic young western city was just the place for their big, growing party's nominating convention.

Judd, a transplanted easterner, had been a member of the Illinois Senate for several years. He had been one of the resolute and unmovable backers of Lyman Trumbull in the reach for the U.S. Senate seat that eluded Lincoln in 1855. Trumbull had recommended Judd to Lincoln as "the shrewdest politician...in the State." Some thought him a "trimmer." Lincoln had even called him that. He was seen as "sly, cat-like, and mysterious," his talents more suited to the politician than the statesman.[4] But he was a valuable man who packed political punch and he was a key member of Lincoln's 1860 team.

Judd had had a late-night pre-convention epiphany. Returning home two or three days before the convention met on May 16, he lit a lamp on a table in the far corner of the bedroom where Mrs. Judd was already retired, and busied himself with pencil and paper. After about half an hour, Mrs. Judd rose from bed and crossed the room to see what he was doing. As she approached, Judd said, "By cracky, Abe's nominated."

Flourishing the paper he had been writing on Judd said:

"The national committee met this afternoon and assigned to me the seating of the delegates in the convention, and as sure as shooting, Abe's nominated."

He had diagrammed a plan to seat the state delegations committed to Seward in the front of the hall. He would seat the delegations favorable to Lincoln, in whole or in part, in the center of the hall. Delegates supporting other candidates, or still in doubt, would be assigned to the rearmost rows of seats wherever possible. This arrangement would isolate the Seward delegations from the doubtful or undecided, situating the Lincoln camp ideally for swaying them in the heat of the nominating process. To Judd this was looking like a sure-thing seating arrangement for a Lincoln nomination.[5]

The on-site wheeling and dealing was in full flower before the convention convened. Wired by Judge Davis that they could have Simon Cameron's delegates from Pennsylvania if they would promise Cameron the Treasury Department in the cabinet, Lincoln wired back, "I authorize no bargains and will be bound by none." The day before the nominations the editor of the *Illinois Journal* arrived from Springfield carrying a copy of the *Missouri Democrat*. In its margins Lincoln had scribbled notes relating to Seward's positions on slavery. He also had written, in words heavily underscored, "*Make no contracts that will bind me.*" When the paper was brought into the room and read to Davis, Judd, Logan, and Herndon, Davis is reported to have said, "Lincoln ain't here, and don't know what we have to meet, so we will go ahead, as if we hadn't heard from him, and he must ratify it." That said, the dealing for votes continued and Lincoln's admonition was ignored.[6]

Leonard Swett, another player on the Lincoln team, later wrote, "The lawyers of our circuit went there determined to leave no stone unturned, and really they, aided by some of our State officers and a half dozen men from various portions of the State, were the only tireless, sleepless, unwavering, and ever-vigilant friends he had."

The first delegation this sleepless team approached was Indiana, which was about equally divided between Bates and McLean. "Saturday, Sunday, and Monday were spent upon her," Swett explained, and "finally she came to us unitedly with twenty-six votes, and from that time acted efficiently with us."

Seward, Swett said, "came there with very nearly strength enough to nominate him, that is, men who intended to vote for him. Bates was the next strongest but that element was an opposition to Seward because he was not available in the doubtful States and would, as we well knew, come to the winning man in opposition to him."

Pennsylvania, Swett also knew, believed Seward could not carry their state. That delegation backed Cameron, their favorite son. The Lincoln men's leading argument was thus gained: "the united assertion of the four doubtful States, Pennsylvania, New Jersey, Indiana, and Illinois, that Seward would be defeated."

The situation, then, Swett explained, was this: "Indiana and Illinois for Lincoln, and against Seward: Pennsylvania for Cameron and against Seward; New Jersey for her own man but against Seward. Calling upon the delegations as they concluded Seward could not be elected, we succeeded in getting them for our man; with Pennsylvania we did nothing but get them for us as a second choice."

Swett said they let *New York Tribune* editor Horace Greeley, busy intervening everywhere, run his pro-Bates machine. But behind the scenes they also got most of the Bates delegates lined up for Lincoln as a fallback choice. Vermont, Delaware, and New

Hampshire had also agreed to give Lincoln their second vote. "Our programme," Swett wrote, "was to give Lincoln 100 votes on the first ballot, with a certain increase afterward, so that in the convention our fortunes might seem to be rising and thus catch the doubtful." When the third day of the convention dawned—nominating day—the preliminary work was done and this strategy was firmly in place.[7]

The strategy notwithstanding, doubts that he could carry key states in the West notwithstanding, Seward was still the clear frontrunner as the convention opened. The mighty New York delegation was for him, to the man, for as long as it took. There was no shrewder political operator than New York's Thurlow Weed, and he was as busy as the Lincoln team in the preconvention hours putting together combinations and striking bargains.

The convention was called to order on May 16 by the temporary chairman, David Wilmot of Pennsylvania, who appointed a committee to usher the permanent chairman, George Ashmun of Massachusetts, to the podium. Ashmun was a congressman, the epitome of a conservative old-line Whig, a handsome and dignified presence with winning manners. He "looked the Puritan" and had been an intimate and confidential friend of the late great Daniel Webster. After Ashmun's opening speech the convention adjourned for the day.[8]

On the second day the main item of business was adopting a platform. One was crafted from basic Republican beliefs, but settled largely, Isaac Bromley of the *New York Tribune* thought, "not so much on their merits as on the probable effect on a Seward and Anti-Seward canvass." In nearly all of this, Bromley reported, the Seward men, "playing the game very cleverly, won." The resolutions sailed through by acclamation at about six in the evening and "amid whirlwinds of noise that exceeded all previous demonstrations, the convention adjourned till next day."

Bromley didn't believe there was much sleep for anybody that night. Nominating day was next, and the streets were alive through the night "with processions and brass bands," with "oratory on tap" and "in constant eruption." The real business of the night, however—the wheeling and dealing for ballots the next day—went on quietly in the hallways and rooms inside.[9]

Political conventions were shouting affairs, opportunities for men with leather lungs. Every good politician knew this and tried to play it to his advantage, wanting to be the candidate in the hall who could rally the most and loudest voices to back his candidacy. No man knew that better than Ward Hill Lamon, the big strapping Illinois lawyer who occasionally partnered with Lincoln on the circuit and who was leather-lunged himself. Lamon knew the Seward camp had come to Chicago armed with outsiders in ample quantity with voices of high-quality leather. They were a crowd hired and financed by Weed on behalf of Seward and led by the noted professional boxer Tom Hyer. The Seward backers had been operating a "torchlight, brass-band, and Roman-candle business," filling the days with processions and the nights with music punctuated by oratory from hotel balconies, with loud, aggressive, boisterous, high-decibel backing.[10]

The *Cincinnati Commercial's* Murat Halstead figured these New Yorkers could "drink as much whiskey, swear as loud and long, sing as bad songs, and 'get up and howl' as ferociously as any crowd of Democrats you ever heard, or heard of." Such as they were, they paraded about Chicago's dusty streets in columns four-abreast, their gaily bedizened band marching in front banging out, "*O isn't he a darling.*"[11]

Seward's hired howlers and cheerleaders had filled the Wigwam toward evening on the second day expecting that the balloting for a nominee would be then. But platform crafting had taken up the entire time before adjournment. They would have to await the third day. But Illinois also had in-state world-class shouters, screamers, and howlers—one, it was said, who could shout loud enough to be heard clear across Lake Michigan, another a long-distance bellowing champion.[12] And Lamon had a plan.

Teaming with Alexander Conner, a lawyer and editor of an Indianapolis newspaper, who had come to Chicago to give whatever aid he could to the Lincoln cause, Lamon set the plan in motion. Conner was on friendly footing with the printer of the convention hall's admission tickets, having known him in Indianapolis. They had him print a large supply of extra tickets and recruited men to spend the night signing them with the names of the officers of the convention. The counterfeit tickets were then distributed to Lincoln shouters, who filed into the seats in the Wigwam at an early hour the next morning before the Seward sympathizers, loudly and proudly parading through the streets, arrived. There many of them found they couldn't get into the over-packed hall. Lamon and Conner, however, could, and they sat on the platform ready to lead "rafter-shaking cheers" for Lincoln at any mention of his name.[13]

It was a matter of pride, this howling combat. "The idea of us Hoosiers and Suckers being out screamed," Swett said, "would have been as bad to them as the loss of their man."[14]

The Wigwam was jammed, every square foot of it, with somebody—12,000 somebodies, those with true tickets and those with bogus tickets. The streets on all sides of the big hall were crammed with people, thousands more, tense with excitement, anticipating the nominating and balloting inside. Because everyone was on edge there were few preliminaries. The scene inside was dazzling, aflame with decorations and heaving with constant movement. The buzz of voices and the hum of conversation, thought the *New York Tribune*'s Isaac Bromley, "bewildered the sense." He found it difficult to untangle himself from its mesmeric rhythms and keep it in perspective.[15]

The nominations and their seconds began, each generating a tornado of howls and applause. True to what everybody expected, the uproar for Seward and Lincoln raised the roof. The audience went wild when their names were entered. Leonard Swett, watching with an admittedly prejudiced eye when Norman Judd nominated Lincoln, said, "No mortal ever before saw such a scene.... Five thousand people at once leaped to their feet, women not wanting in the number, and the wild yell made soft vesper breathings of all that had preceded. No language can describe it. A thousand steam whistles, ten acres of hotel gongs, a tribe of Comanches, headed by a choice vanguard from pandemonium, might have mingled in the scene unnoticed."[16]

Or as verse had it:

At once there rose so wild a yell,
Within that dark and narrow dell;
As all the fiends from heaven that fell
Had peeled the banner cry of hell.[17]

"One might have supposed that the choice between them [Lincoln and Seward] was to be governed by volume of sound," Bromley wrote.

Maine led off the voting, a tense opening shot, since the votes of the New England states were thought critical and would be anxiously watched. Seward was counting on a solid majority from that section. Maine gave ten of its votes to Seward, but six to Lincoln, not much of an edge. New Hampshire was a shocker, only one for Seward and seven for Lincoln. All of Vermont's ten votes on this first ballot went to its favorite son, Jacob Collamer—a courtesy vote, everyone knew. With each of these votes Seward's hopes ebbed and Lincoln's surged. Even the vote of Massachusetts was mildly disappointing for Seward—twenty-one votes for him, but four for Lincoln. They had expected a solid vote. When New England's eighty-one votes were all in, Seward had thirty-two of them, Lincoln had nineteen, and thirty were scattered.

New York cast its seventy votes solidly for Seward, and the hall for several minutes shook with a deafening roar. New Jersey and Pennsylvania were solid, or nearly so, for their favorite sons. Virginia stunned the Seward camp when it gave fourteen of its votes to Lincoln and only eight to their man. Indiana was another shocker for Seward, going solidly for Lincoln, fruit of the preconvention logrolling. Good news for Seward came from Michigan, however, which gave him all of its twelve votes. Illinois went solidly for Lincoln. As expected, Wisconsin, California, Minnesota, and Kansas voted solidly for Seward. That, his camp thought, was more like it.

When the first ballot was counted, Seward had 173-and-a-half votes, some sixty short of the 233 needed to nominate. Lincoln had 102, and the rest of the 465 votes were split among ten candidates. The Lincoln camp was gratified. Its first-ballot quota had been met. It was clear now that either Seward or Lincoln was going to be nominated. The only question was whether Seward could detach the sixty votes he needed from the other candidates before Lincoln could put together his combinations.

The second round of balloting riveted the intense attention of everyone in the hall. Vermont led off, transferring her solid vote from Collamer to Lincoln, and when the New England vote was in Lincoln had surged ahead of Seward in the region, thirty-six to thirty-three, a dramatic shift. Pennsylvania, true to its bargain, threw forty-eight Cameron votes into the Lincoln column. When the second round ended Seward was still forty-nine votes short of a majority and Lincoln was only three-and-a-half votes behind him.

Pencils, including Bromley's own, ran rapidly up and down the list of states. The most acute of the vote counters realized that the forty-nine votes for Seward seemed harder to get than the fifty-two for Lincoln. It was now only a question of one more breathtaking ballot, two at most.

"While the third ballot was in progress," Bromley wrote, "there was a great deal of hurrying back and forth, swift consultations, pulling and hauling, and hubbub generally." The demonstrations now were strangely muted. "The excitement was too intense, the nervous strain too severe," Bromley thought, "to relieve itself in noise."

New England continued to sheer away from Seward, upping Lincoln's edge there forty-two to thirty-one. There was no major change in blocks of votes, only "a gradual crumbling away of support from the scattering candidates and a drawing toward Lincoln." When the last delegation voted, the running count of half a dozen reporters in the hall had Lincoln with 231-and-a-half votes, short only a vote and a half from the nomination. Ohio still had fifteen in reserve, holding for Chase, and Missouri eighteen still holding for Bates. In an instant, Bromley reported, "there was a scramble to get in on the winner."

David K. Cartter, a congressman and celebrated stutterer

from Ohio, who had been bobbing up and down throughout the entire convention, was first out of the gate, stammering, "I-I a-a-arise, Mr. Chairman, to a-a-anounce the c-c-change of f-four votes, from Mr. Chase to Abraham Lincoln."[18]

Nearly every delegation in the hall was instantly on its feet, "shrieking a change of votes, none of which except Ohio's was ever recorded." Few now cared. Lincoln had been nominated. The hall exploded. However, the New Yorkers, Bromley reported, "sat dumb" and "made no stir," and part of the Massachusetts delegation also sat the tumult out—"oases of silence," Bromley wrote, "in a Sahara of sound."

"I thought I had heard noise and seen wild excitement before," Bromley wrote, "but this was the grand climacteric. On the platform near me Henry S. Lane [of Indiana] was executing a war dance with some other dignified delegate as partner; the Indiana men generally were smashing hats and hugging each other; the Illinois men did everything except stand on their heads; hands were flying wildly in the air, everybody's mouth was open, and bedlam seemed loose."

Bromley had "seen conventions carried off their feet before... but never anything like that. I was so overcome with the spectacle that the contagion of it took no hold. I could not shout, I simply caught my breath and stared at it. It seemed as if it never would stop."

Over the desk of the reading clerk was an open skylight. On the roof, men had been transmitting news of the proceedings to the waiting thousands who milled about outside the hall. A loaded cannon had been wheeled into place on the roof to announce the news whenever it happened and whatever it was. The four votes switching from Chase to Lincoln in Ohio had hardly come stammering from Cartter's mouth than the gun belched fire.

The cry, "Lincoln is nominated!" floated from the roof out into the streets, and the crowd outside also went wild. Bromley noted that when the tempest inside waned for an instant the roar from the outside rolled in like an echo, and the storm inside broke again. "The waves of noise," he wrote, "rolled back and forth till from sheer weariness the shouters sank into their seats."

After a time an almost painful silence fell as the chairman pounded for order with his gavel. Looking toward the New York delegation, followed by all eyes, Ashmun called out, "The gentleman from New York." As the hushed hall listened with profound attention, William M. Evarts, the chairman of the New York delegation, moved that the nomination be made unanimous. It was seconded by John A. Andrew of Massachusetts, Carl Schurz of Wisconsin and Austin Blair of Michigan, "in speeches that contained more sadness than exultation." The motion was passed and another wave of tumult swept the hall.[19]

The man who had been not enough of a candidate to stay away from the convention and too much of one to go waited out the day in Springfield. About nine in the morning Christopher C. Brown, a fellow lawyer, came into Lincoln's office and found him lying on the sofa. "Well, Brown," Lincoln asked, "have you heard any thing?" About ten o'clock they walked to the *Illinois State Journal* office where, by arrangement, dispatches from the convention floor were coming in.[20]

The wait was likely to be a long one. But a common expression of the day seemed pertinent: "You'll know more when the steamer gets in."[21] Lincoln was nervous and fidgety. To burn it off, as they waited, he told stories and played "Fives," a kind of handball, against the wall of a three-story building at the end of an alley near the *Journal* office. He said the game made his shoulders feel good—worked the tension out. A friend watching said his "suppleness, leaps and strides to strike the ball were comical in the extreme."[22]

The editor of the *Journal* came in with two telegrams. One said the delegates were filing into the convention hall. The other said that the names of the candidates for nomination had been put before the convention and Lincoln's name had been received "with the greatest enthusiasm." Charles S. Zane, another young Springfield lawyer waiting with Lincoln in the *Journal* office, later wrote that Lincoln believed "if Mr. Seward did not get the nomination on the first ballot or come very near to it he would not be likely to get it at all."[23] The results of the first ballot telegraphed to Springfield had Seward some sixty votes short.

When the operator handed the results of the second ballot to Lincoln, showing Seward still fifty votes short and Lincoln only three-and-a-half votes behind him, Zane saw a look of satisfaction pass over Lincoln's face.[24]

As Lincoln sat folded up in an armchair in the *Journal* office waiting with the small group of men for results of the third ballot, conversation became slow and desultory. There was tension in the room. Finally a boy banged through the door and handed a scrap of paper to Lincoln, who stared at it, expressionless, for what seemed hours to the others in the room. Then he said, "I knew this would come when I saw the second ballot." The message read, "Mr. Lincoln, you are nominated on the third ballot." He uncoiled from the armchair and said, quietly, "I must go home; there is a little short woman there that is more interested in this Matter than I am."[25]

Lincoln knew better than anybody that Mary had been a paramount player in getting him to this hour in this day in his career. His old law partner, Mary's kin John Stuart, knew it too. "She had the fire—the will and ambition," Stuart said. It was Mary who had repeatedly vowed when she was but a girl that she would marry a man who would become president. And here she was on the cusp of fulfilling that premonition. "Lincoln's talent & his wifes Ambition," Stuart knew, "did the deed." The marriage was "a policy Match all around."[26] And Lincoln's policy at this moment was to share the victory with her.

Someone in the room said, "Mr. Lincoln, I suppose we will soon have a book containing your life now." Lincoln said, "there is not much in my past life about which to write a book as it seems to me." He then left the second-floor office and strode out onto the sidewalk, where a crowd of friends and neighbors had gathered.[27]

Bedlam followed him to the house on the corner of Eighth and Jackson. As he reached it, the first shots of a hundred-gun salute were rattling windows in town. Around the square, men shouted, shook hands, and slapped one another on the back. At the statehouse, the Republican headquarters, and the *Journal* office, they broke out flags. Soon bells all over town were tolling, and pistol shots were ringing out. Friend after friend followed Lincoln into his parlor to congratulate him.

That evening a crowd gathered at the statehouse to hear speeches, but the excitement was too exuberant for talk. The meeting adjourned and the crowd, trooping behind a band and "growing like a rolling snowball," started for Lincoln's house. There, responding to their shouts, he appeared at the doorway and spoke a few words, saying the demonstration was more a tribute to the cause than to himself. He invited as many in as the house could hold, and a voice shouted, "We will give you a larger house on the fourth of next March!"[28]

After Lincoln's nomination, a second ballot nominated Hannibal Hamlin, the popular U.S. Senator from Maine, to run for vice president on the ticket. Hamlin, his first name a hand-me-down from the famed Carthaginian general of two centuries before Christ, was a long-time Democrat who had broken from his party over the Kansas-Nebraska Act and was now a Republican. For that past pedigree, and because he was an easterner and a friend of Seward—politically and geographically well suited—it was thought he would balance the ticket.

Hamlin, however, was less than enthusiastic. He loved being a senator. He was playing cards in his Washington hotel room when political friends burst in to tell him he had been nominated. This irritated him. He didn't relish the honor, figuring he would go from being a powerful senator to a likely "fifth wheel on a coach." He grumped at the intruders, "You people have spoiled a good lone hand I held." He wrote his wife, "I neither expected or desired it, but it has been made and as a faithful man to the cause, it leaves me no alternative but to accept it."[29]

The wheeling, dealing, and bargaining of the Lincoln team had worked. But so had chance and situation.

The day after the convention adjourned, a hand-picked committee of party leaders, led by Ashmun, boarded a train to Springfield. Its members, some of them with a heavy heart, went to notify Lincoln formally that he had been nominated. Many of them had never met this outsider whom they knew only dimly as the "railsplitter," a "plain ungainly man, a *homespun* candidate," once a member of Congress, but otherwise "unacquainted with public affairs." He had risen in "a ground-swell of public opinion...like the tides of the sea" and swept all before him at the convention. For better or worse, he was their nominee and the likely next president. And he needed to be officially notified. About thirty men, including correspondents, were in the single passenger car drawn by one of the Illinois Central's swiftest locomotives as it glided out of Chicago's Grand Central Station.[30]

The train arrived in Springfield on a beautiful May evening as the sun was setting. After supper, the delegates, escorted by an excited knot of well-wishers, started for Lincoln's house. Two of Lincoln's boys, Willie and Tad, were seated on the steps as they reached the gate.

"Are you Mr. Lincoln's son?" William Evarts asked Willie, the older of the two.

"Yes, sir," he said.

"Then let's shake hands," Evarts said.

Tad spoke up and said, "I'm a Lincoln too!"

Laughing, the delegates mounted the steps and knocked on the door.

They gathered in the room to the left of the hall, across from the parlor, where Lincoln stood in front of the fireplace wearing a black frock coat. He bowed to the committee, not gracefully— which seemed out of the question given his angularities—and then stood stiffly erect with eyes downcast. The delegation arranged itself around three sides of the room. Ashmun advanced a pace or two and briefly stated what the convention had done and their errand.

It was evident to one of the committee members, William D. Kelley of Pennsylvania, that Ashmun's words were receiving Lincoln's intense attention, that he "had no eye nor ear for any other object." When Ashmun finished, "the bowed head rose as by an electric movement, the broad mouth, which had been so firmly drawn together, opened with a genial smile, and the eyes that had been shaded, beamed with intelligence and the exhilaration of the occasion." Kelley noted that Lincoln's response "flowed in a pleasant voice, and, though without marked emphasis, each syllable was uttered with perfect clearness."[31]

Lincoln said: "Mr. Chairman and gentlemen of the committee, I tender you, and through you the Republican National Convention, and all the people represented in it, my profoundest thanks for the high honor done me, which you now formally announce. Deeply, and even painfully sensible of the great responsibility which is inseparable from that honor—a responsibility which I could almost wish had fallen upon some one of the far more eminent men and experienced statesmen whose distinguished names were before the Convention, I shall, by your leave, consider more fully the resolutions of the Convention, denominated the platform, and without unseasonable delay, respond to you, Mr. Chairman, in writing—not doubting now, that the platform will be found satisfactory and the nomination accepted."

Lincoln then said, "And now, I will no longer defer the pleasure of taking you, and each of you, by the hand."[32] Ashmun began introducing members of the committee, until tiring of that and asking them to present themselves. Norman Judd called out, "Come up, gentlemen, it's nobody but Old Abe Lincoln!"[33]

That is what those in the room who had never met him were beginning to see. "I was afraid I should meet a gigantic railsplitter, with the manners of a flatboatman, and the ugliest face in creation," one was heard to say; "and he's a complete gentleman."[34]

Lincoln approached New York Governor and Chairman of the Republican Executive Committee Edward D. Morgan, the most physically commanding figure in the party, and greeted him. Morgan, a taciturn man, made no audible response. Determined to draw him out, Lincoln asked, "Pray, Governor, how tall may you be?" Lincoln liked to ask that of men who appeared as tall as he. He even liked standing back-to-back with them to see who was taller.

"Nearly six feet three," Morgan said, lapsing again into silence.

Kelley, standing beside Morgan, himself a giant, interposed. "And pray, Mr. Lincoln, how tall may you be?"

"Six feet four," Lincoln said.

Kelley bowed and said: "Pennsylvania bows humbly before New York, but still more humbly before Illinois. Mr. Lincoln, is it not curious that I, who for the last twelve years have yearned for a president to whom I might look up, should have found one here in a State where so many people believe they grow nothing but 'Little Giants?'"[35]

After the delegates were presented to Mrs. Lincoln, the short little woman waiting in the parlor, they started back to the hotel—past houses lit from basements to attics, past corners bright with bonfires. Cannon boomed at intervals and the night sky was ablaze with rockets. Oratory was pouring out to an overflow audience in the statehouse.[36]

The act was over, but the shouting wasn't.

From Ballots to Bullets

From Ballots to Bullets

28

The Four-Legged Race

IT WAS NOT OVER between Lincoln and Douglas. Now, at the end of a quarter century of going head-to-head in Illinois, they were about to go head-to-head on the biggest stage for the biggest prize all—president of the United States.

The faithful wing of the Democratic Party nominated the Little Giant on the first ballot in Baltimore in June, following the misfire in Charleston in April. For his running mate the Democrats picked a still-faithful ex-governor of Georgia, Herschel J. Johnson.

This time the Lincoln-Douglas rivalry would not be one-on-one, as it had been all those previous years. This was a time of intense alienation. Southern Democrats, alienated from Northern Democrats over slavery—and from Douglas in particular—had re-convened their separate convention in Baltimore and nominated an opposition ticket headed by John C. Breckinridge of

Kentucky, Buchanan's vice president, and picked Joseph Lane of Oregon to run with him. This Southern ticket would have the backing of both ex-president Franklin Pierce and outgoing president and ardent Douglas hater, James Buchanan. A party could scarcely be more deeply, bitterly divided.

Yet another alienated spinoff was also in the race—a Union-loving segment of the body politic styling itself the Constitutional Union Party. Deeply deploring disunion, it was alienated from the Democrats and Republicans both. Meeting also in Baltimore, it nominated a ticket of its own, headed by former Speaker of the House and U.S. Senator John Bell of Tennessee. A reporter, Charles Coffin, described that makeshift party as a "raking together" of "the embers of a dying political organization"—the Whigs—and a file of disgruntled Know-Nothings. Their convention, Coffin wrote, was "appropriately held in an old church from which worshipers had forever departed." For vice president it nominated Edward Everett of Massachusetts, the celebrated orator, former governor, former congressman, former senator, former secretary of state. He was far more distinguished and a greater statesman than Bell. One editor called its slate the "kangaroo" ticket, because its hind legs were longest. Sara Pryor, the wife of firebrand Virginia Congressman Roger Pryor, called them the "ruffled-shirt gentry."[1]

If Lincoln and Douglas wondered what they had gotten themselves into, it would be understandable. When Lincoln was nominated, his exultation was soberly tempered by forebodings of the trouble that might lie ahead. But he was resolved "to abide the consequences, whatever they might be."[2]

Lincoln had worked something of a party-crafting miracle in Illinois since 1858. Following the senatorial election that year, the elements in his party were in unholy disarray. Conservative

Free Soilers hated the abolitionists in the party, the Germans despised the Know-Nothings, and old-line Whigs scorned the refugee anti-Nebraska Democrats flocking into the new party, resenting them as repugnant Johnny-come-latelys; in their view Democrats of any stripe were not to be trusted, or welcomed in—they were but a bunch of locofocos. Lincoln had struggled mightily to keep these diverse elements from one another's throats, urging them to work together to a common end. He had succeeded, and his success had elevated him to undisputed leadership in the party, won him loyal support of these divisive elements, and got him nominated for president in Chicago.

Douglas had the Southern bolters to worry about. They couldn't win the election but they could cut deeply into his votes and kill his chances. Lincoln had the party of the ruffled-shirt gentry to worry about, which also couldn't win, but could scatter the vote in the crucial states he needed to win. They, and not Douglas this time, appeared to be Lincoln's true opposition. It was widely believed that he could win if he could unite and dazzle the Know-Nothings of the American Party who had voted for Fillmore in 1856. If he couldn't, he would lose.[3]

Lincoln desperately needed unity in his own party, because he would not be on any ballot in the South. In 1856, states in the Deep South had vowed that if a Black Republican—John C. Frémont then—was elected president they would secede. They appeared even more ready to leave the Union if one was elected this time.

Faced with a similarly disastrous split in his party and the excess of tickets in the canvass, Douglas's chances were far more iffy and doom-ridden than Lincoln's. And here was Lincoln, his old rival and nemesis of a quarter-century, in his face once again. Douglas was in the Senate Chamber in Washington when news of Lincoln's nomination reached him. He walked over from the chamber to the House of Representatives with Massachusetts Congressman John B. Alley and there a small group of Republicans gathered around to hear him read the telegram. After reading it, Douglas paused for a moment and then said, "Well, gentlemen, you have nominated a very able and a very honest man."[4] That did not mean, however, that Douglas was glad about it.

The campaign went on the march, literally. Cadres of Wide Awakes, young Republican partisans in red military caps and shiny blue capes, marched for Lincoln to the light of torches, the beat of drums, and the mesmeric cadence of tramping feet. Their flickering torches dropped hot oil on their slickers and left a lingering odor of kerosene hanging on the night air.[5]

In towns and cities across the country Republican headquarters were shaped into wigwams. Symbols from Lincoln's past—axes and split rails—were everywhere, carried to the beat of the drums and visible in the light of the torches. There were rallies, barbecues, and parades, with much flag-waving and cannonading. The party's leading politicians hit the stump, haranguing enormous crowds.

The air was electric with political excesses. A Republican newspaper, *The Rail-splitter*, spit out a steady rain of pro-Lincoln propaganda. Bands played, and glee clubs sang, "Old Abe Lincoln came out of the wilderness," to the tune of "The Old Gray Mare," and "Ain't I glad I joined the Republicans, / Joined the Republicans, joined the Republicans, / Ain't I glad I joined the Republicans / Down in Illinois."[6] It was a campaign that brought to mind, for those who could remember, the ballyhoo canvass of 1840.

On August 8 there was a giant rally and "ratification" meeting in Springfield. A light breeze soon cleared away the fog that had early blocked the morning sun, and guns saluted the sight. The roads leading into Springfield were jammed. Special trains brought in 180 carloads of riotous partisans primed for a political show. The capital was soon awash in seething humanity—some 70,000, wave upon wave. At ten o'clock a procession began to form, teeming with Wide Awakes and clogged with floats—flatboats and log cabins on wheels, twenty-three oxen drawing an immense wagon peopled with blacksmiths, wheelwrights, and railsplitters at work. The parade stretched in a line eight to ten miles long. Snaking past Lincoln's house it seemed endless. Not until two in the afternoon did all of it reach the fairgrounds west of town. There, from five speaker stands, orators stirred up the faithful. In the evening, a torchlight procession carried the crowd to the Springfield wigwam, where there were more speeches for those able to get inside and for the thousands who stood outside fruitlessly yearning to get in.

When Lincoln arrived on the grounds in the afternoon, there was a stampede to his carriage. He was lifted from it and bodily carried by the mob to one of the stands, where, in the face of the acclaim, he said, "Well, I am right end up!" and declared himself a non-speaker.[7]

"I appear among you upon this occasion," he said, "with no intention of making a speech. It has been my purpose, since I have been placed in my present position, to make no speeches... it is my wish that you will hear this public discussion by other of our friends who are present for the purpose of addressing you and let me be silent." As the expectant crowd massed around the carriage following these brief words, Lincoln escaped on horseback.

The pro-Lincoln newspapers described it all in a lavish out-pouring of headlines. "THE PRAIRIES ON FIRE / FOR LINCOLN!" one cried. The *Illinois Journal* devoted three columns to it. The reporter from the *Cincinnati Gazette* believed "immense" was the only word to describe it. "The enthusiasm was beyond all bounds," he wrote. "I never saw so dense and large a crowd.... Mr. Lincoln's bearing to-day, under such a tribute of personal popularity and admiration as I have never before seen paid to any human being, more and more convinces me of the real great-ness of his character."[8]

Since 1854, when he had reentered politics riding the crest of the anti-Nebraska wave, Lincoln had made some 175 speeches on the subject of slavery.[9] Now, as he said on the stand at the giant rally at the fairgrounds, he was making none.

Saying nothing was standard expected procedure for candi-dates for the presidency, embedded now in the concrete of tradi-tion. Lincoln was making it an unbending rule. He was deflecting all requests for his political opinions with a form letter, written and signed by John G. Nicolay, a young former editor and clerk for the Illinois secretary of state, who had been appointed his pri-vate secretary to handle his ballooning correspondence.

"Dear Sir," Nicolay wrote in his generic letter, "Your letter to Mr. Lincoln of [blank] and by which you seek to obtain his opin-ions on certain political points, has been received by him. He has received others of a similar character; but he also has a greater number of the exactly opposite character. The latter class be-seech him to write nothing whatever upon any point of political doctrine. They say his positions were well known when he was nominated, and that he must not now embarrass the canvass by undertaking to shift or modify them. He regrets that he can not oblige all, but you perceive it is impossible for him to do so."[10]

That was the nub of the matter. Lincoln in those 175 speeches since 1854 had said everything he was going to say. Saying anything more might indeed not only embarrass the canvass but inflame passions at this incendiary time. For the first time in a quarter of a century, Lincoln's voice would not be heard in a political campaign in Illinois. His ideas, however, continued to have an abundant shelf life; the party's orators, stumping in every state, borrowed from them liberally.[11]

Sudden celebrity was washing over Lincoln, and he was not ready for this overnight elevation to national prominence. "He could not understand," William Herndon said, "why people should make so much over him."[12] He soon found he couldn't, even with Nicolay's help, answer all the mail pouring in. Not willing to say or write anything of substance, he was, however, willing to sign his autograph for those who asked for it. In another form letter, signed by himself, he wrote: "Dear Sir: You request an autograph, and here it is."[13]

Lincoln was not speaking out, and he was not going anywhere either. He wrote Congressman Elihu B. Washburne, "I expect to be at home all summer."[14]

After his nomination he had moved his headquarters to the governor's room in the statehouse, a room rarely used, and generally only in the legislative session. It was next door to the office of the state superintendent of public instruction, Newton Bateman, who worried that callers in his office would disturb the nominee. But Lincoln said, "If you can stand my noise, I can stand yours."[15]

The governor's room soon became what Nicolay described as "a perfect museum of symbolic presents" from visiting well-wishers and others—axes, mauls, wedges, log chains and other "paraphernalia." Lincoln and Nicolay spent their days there amid that collection, coping with the correspondence and receiving a flood of visitors.[16]

Lincoln arrived at his commandeered reception room by nine or ten o'clock in the morning—sometimes earlier—and the flood never let up. They were coming from everywhere, every imaginable kind of person, great and small, for every kind of reason. Townsmen came, folk from the country, friends, relatives, artists, photographers, biographers, journalists, politicians, and those who just wanted to stare at a live presidential candidate.[17]

Generally anybody who wanted to see Lincoln could. But by mid-July he was writing these ground rules for Nicolay:

> Ascertain what he wants.
> On what subjects he would converse with me,
> And the particulars if he will give them.
> Is an interview indispensable?
> Tell him my motto is "Fairness to all,"
> But commit me to nothing.[18]

Being committed to nothing especially mattered during a visit from Thurlow Weed, that political wizard from New York, who was fresh from seeing his protégé Seward defeated at Chicago. This made many Republicans nervous, for Weed was a notorious engineer of political deals and commitments. Lincoln wrote Trumbull after Weed's visit, "Remembering that Peter denied his Lord with an oath, after most solemnly protesting that he never would, I will not swear I will make no committals; but I do think I will not."[19]

A friend of Lincoln's told a New York editor, Ellis Henry Roberts, "You New Yorkers do not know our glorious standard bearer. You think him a mere rough diamond, a slang-whanging stump speaker, who lacks the ease and polish of the well-bred gentleman." Well, the friend said, come see for yourself. And Roberts did.[20]

Noteworthy among the visitors was the flood of journalists, reporters, and editors such as Roberts. But Lincoln was also approached by another kind of writer—biographers. These included the Chicago newsman John L. Scripps, wanting to write a campaign biography, and James Q. Howard, collecting material for another biography that the journalist William Dean Howells would write. Lincoln rather bridled at all this deep searching into his past life, claiming it was barren ground. "Why Scripps," he said, "it is a great piece of folly to attempt to make anything out of my early life. It can all be condensed into a single sentence, and that sentence you will find in Gray's 'Elegy': 'The short and simple annals of the poor.' That's my life, and that's all you or any one else can make of it."[21]

Portrait artists also came, bent on capturing Lincoln's essence for a public that only dimly knew what he looked like. One of these, Charles A. Barry, commissioned by Governor John A. Andrew and other prominent Massachusetts Republicans to make a portrait of Lincoln, arrived in early June. After ten days of sitting sporadically for Barry, Lincoln looked at the finished crayon portrait and said, "Even my enemies must declare that to be a true likeness of Old Abe."

When the work was exhibited in the New York studio of George Ward Nichols, "a short, thick-set gentleman" walked in and paused before it. He didn't speak to Barry and Barry didn't speak to him. "He stood for a little while a short distance from the picture," Barry later recounted. "Then he stepped forward and, folding his arms across his breast, said slowly with clear utterance: 'An honest man, God knows.' The next instant he passed out of the room." Barry later learned that the visitor was Douglas.[22]

In the middle of July Lincoln thought he should make an effort to get in touch with Hannibal Hamlin, his running mate, whom he believed he had never met. "It appears to me," Lincoln wrote Hamlin, "that you and I ought to be acquainted, and accordingly I write this as a sort of introduction of myself to you. You first entered the Senate during the single term I was a member of the House of Representatives, but I have no recollection that we were introduced. I shall be pleased to receive a line from you." Lincoln told Hamlin, "The prospect of Republican success now appears very flattering, as far as I can perceive. Do you see any thing to the contrary?" Hamlin answered in late July that although he wasn't certain, he thought they had been formally introduced at one time or another in the past. He reported that Maine would do her duty and that New England looked good.[23]

When a visitor said to him, "Well—how do you do, Mr. President," Lincoln said, "Not yet President—better not count the chickens till they are hatched."[24] But the unhatched eggs had warmth and were clearly incubating. By July 4 Lincoln was writing his friend Anson G. Henry, "to-day, it looks as if the Chicago ticket will be elected." A month later he was writing Simeon Francis, who in 1859 had moved to Portland, Oregon, to publish *The Oregon Farmer*: "I hesitate to say it, but it really appears now, as if the success of the Republican ticket is inevitable. We have no reason to doubt any of the states which voted for Frémont. Add to these Minnesota, Pennsylvania, and New Jersey, and the thing is done."

In late August Simon Cameron wrote Lincoln, "You may as well be getting your inaugeral address ready, so as to have plenty of time to make it short. If possible we are daily becoming stronger in Pennsylvania, and in New-Jersey all is right." Joseph Medill of the *Chicago Tribune* wrote Lincoln, "We are stirring up Northern Illinois, and will give you the Frémont majority in 30 Northern counties." In late September Lincoln wrote Henry again, "Besides what we see in the newspapers, I have a good deal of private correspondence; and, without giving details, I will only say, it all looks very favorable to our success."[25]

The elections for lesser offices in the bellwether October states indicated that the eggs were all but hatched. An earlier visitor from Pennsylvania told Lincoln that although Buchanan had carried his state in 1856, in 1860 it "will turn the biggest summerset you ever heard of."[26]

On October 10, as the state election results were coming in, Lincoln wrote Herndon, "it is entirely certain that Pennsylvania and Indiana have gone Republican very largely, Penn 25,000 & Indiana 5 to 10. Ohio of course is safe." He wrote Seward two days later, "I have had no fears of New-York recently.... It now really looks as if the Government is about to fall into our hands. Pennsylvania, Ohio, and Indiana have surpassed all expectations, even the most extravagant." The next day he wrote another friend, "We are indulged in much rejoicing over the late splendid victories in Pennsylvania, Indiana, and Ohio, which seem to foreshadow the certain success of the Republican cause in November."[27]

From the start of the campaign, Douglas had been falling between the stools of two sectional extremes. He could not win the election without strong Southern support. But if he veered too far southward politically he risked sheering off necessary Northern support. And there was Breckinridge, digging deep into his Southern potential.

There was a political principle Douglas would not forsake for any vote, and that was his popular sovereignty. One reporter covering the campaign wrote, "He has staked so much on the Squatter Sovereignty doctrine that he seems to be falling into a monomania about it, and drags it about the country with him with as much assiduity as if it were a change of linen or a toothbrush."[28]

Indeed, Douglas was literally dragging a campaign around the country, relentlessly attacking disunion. While Lincoln stayed in Springfield saying nothing and going nowhere, as became a presidential candidate by tradition, Douglas was violating that custom wholesale, going everywhere—into twenty-three states before the agony ended—trying to turn the tide.

When the worst happened and the Republicans carried the October states, he clearly saw that no amount of hard traveling and hard talking—no matter how good his balancing act—none of it was now going to win it for him. He said to his secretary, James B. Sheridan, "Mr. Lincoln is the next President. We must try to save the Union. I will go South."[29]

And he went South, on this mission impossible, throwing out every consideration for his foredoomed candidacy, and saying things Southern leaders didn't want to hear, appealing directly to the common people, appealing for Union. There he met mostly animosity. "The bloated visage of Stephen A. Douglas," a Memphis newspaper wrote as he set out, "is now turned toward the South. He commences his tramp to-day, and like an itinerant peddler of Yankee notions, will soon be hawking his pinchbeck principles over the South. He comes in our midst with no worthier motives than the incendiary."[30]

One of his eleventh-hour outcries was from the steps of the Alabama state capitol in Montgomery on November 2, in midday, in the very heat of Southern anger. He chanted again his mantra of popular sovereignty, non-intervention, as the heavyweight solution that will "crush out Northern abolitionism and Southern disunion." On election day, four days later, he was in Mobile, still vainly hawking union.[31]

Cannon fire greeted the rising sun in Springfield that day, November 6. Tranquility never got a foothold thereafter. When the cannonading stopped, another brand of commotion set in. The "out-door tumult," the *New York Tribune* correspondent reported, stirred "whatever sluggish spirits there might be" and awakened "all slumbering resolutions."

On the evening before, the *Tribune* reporter saw Lincoln standing alone before his post office box and marveled at his "extent"—the word for height in the West. To the reporter, Lincoln's extent seemed only "somewhat less than a steeple." But on this election-day morning Lincoln was in the governor's room at the statehouse, his extent jackknifed into an ample armchair. He seemed exceedingly composed and comfortable, rising now and then to greet some new visiting delegation.[32]

It seemed to Samuel R. Weed, a reporter from a St. Louis newspaper, that while Lincoln had a lively interest in the election's outcome, he seemed more concerned with the fortunes of local candidates than his own. One "would have concluded," Weed thought, "that the district attorneyship of a county in Illinois was of far more importance than the Presidency itself." Lincoln mentioned a legislative candidate he favored and thought would be elected "if he didn't find Abe Lincoln too heavy a load to carry on the same ticket." At another time, he compared elections to boils, causing much pain before they came to a head but, after passing, leaving the body healthier than before. He said he hoped the bitterness of this canvass would pass away "as easily as the core of a boil."

Although Weed wrote that seriousness dominated Lincoln's demeanor, his humor hadn't deserted him. At one point in the evening Lincoln said it was lucky for him that "the women couldn't vote," otherwise the monstrous portraits of him that had been circulating during the canvass would surely defeat him.[33]

About four o'clock, estimates of results began filtering in, among them a dispatch from Charleston. It quoted a former South Carolina congressman as saying that he hoped Lincoln was elected, for then South Carolina "would soon be free." Such secession talk was not new to Lincoln. He had seen letters of the same tenor before. By five o'clock the few scattered returns included word that Massachusetts had racked up 50,000 votes for the Republicans. Lincoln called that "a clear case of the Dutch taking Holland."[34]

About nine in the evening, Lincoln and his friends, along with the reporters, trooped from the statehouse to the small second-story room occupied by the Western Union Telegraph office on the other side of the public square. There Lincoln settled himself in easy reach of the telegraphers. About the same time, Springfield's Republican partisans began filling the Hall of Representatives in the statehouse, to await the returns there.[35]

By ten o'clock it was noticed there had been no report from all-important New York. Lincoln reportedly said that "the news will come quick enough if it was good, and if bad, he was not in any hurry to hear it." Conditional good news arrived about half past ten in a message from Thurlow Weed: "We are encouraged at this hour to believe you have carried this State." Lincoln read it in silence, then aloud, and said the news was satisfactory, but not conclusive.[36] By eleven o'clock reports coming from New Jersey were not good. But reports from New England, beginning to arrive in profusion, were. As the telegrams trickled in, Lincoln read them against an ever-rising wave of hurrahs floating in from across the square.[37]

Worry over New York continued to nag him. For the second time in the evening the reporter Weed thought him anxious. "It became more and more evident," Weed wrote, "that New York was indeed the 'pivotal' state." About eleven thirty Simeon Draper, chairman of the New York state committee reported, "We have made steady gains everywhere throughout the State, but the city returns are not sufficiently forward to make us sure of the result, although we are quite sanguine a great victory has been won." New York had a habit of being a nail biter, returns from New York City often canceling out the returns from greater New York state.

Lincoln was cautious, but few others were. Lyman Trumbull, who had been speech-making for Lincoln in Illinois for the past two months, rushed into the room after hearing the Draper dispatch and shouted, "Uncle Abe, you're the next President, and I know it!" The crowd at the statehouse had heard it, too. They "surged into the street and began cheering, yelling and shouting," Weed reported, "like a thousand madmen suddenly let loose from their keepers. It was hard to maintain even a commonplace dignity inside the telegraph office while so much noise and excitement was going on outside." Only Lincoln remained composed, folded up in his chair. "Not too fast, my friends," he cautioned. "Not too fast, it may not be over yet."

Messages continued to pour in, including New York, all so favorable that state auditor Jesse DuBois asked, "Well, Uncle

Abe, are you satisfied now?" Lincoln smiled, "Well, the agony is most over, and you will soon be able to go to bed." The agony indeed looked to be put to bed shortly when the telegraph manager reported in high excitement, "Mr. Lincoln, here is news which will do you good."

The message was from Draper in New York and like the first one, addressed privately to Lincoln. It was dated midnight and said, "The [Democratic] majorities in New York and Brooklyn will not exceed 35,000"—not enough to offset the pro-Lincoln vote in the rest of the state. "We tender you our congratulations upon this magnificent victory." Inside the telegraph office there was much hearty handshaking and congratulations. The telegraph operators left their instruments to join in. Weed reported that Lincoln at last showed pleasure. It sealed the election. "He would have been a more remarkable man than Abraham Lincoln who could have concealed his pleasure upon such an occasion." When the celebrating had died somewhat, Lincoln asked for the Draper dispatch, put it into his pocket and said it was about time he "went home and told the news to a little woman who was sitting up for him."[38]

The victory message was read from the telegraph office to the crowd waiting in the statehouse and milling in the street, and "as its last echoes rang out upon the midnight air a shout went up which was carried from street to street like the rush of many waters." It seemed, Weed reported, "to startle men and women from their beds and many a window in Springfield was lifted" to see what the ruckus was about. A church bell tolled and campaign songs swelled again from hundreds of excited voices. One celebrant described the scene as "perfectly *wild*. While the votes were being counted the Republicans were at the Representatives

hall *singing, yelling! shouting*!!...dancing....Old men, young, middle aged, clergymen and *all*!"[39]

Springfield continued to rock through the night. The reporter from the *New York Tribune* reported the meetings at the statehouse "were not adjourned until dawn, and the popular feeling became so uncontrollable at about four in the morning that there was nothing to satisfy it but to bring out the big gun and make it thunder rejoicings for the crowd." This left part of the city "consequently in somewhat shattered condition of nerve" by morning light, but "still ready for any emergency of cheering or hand-shaking that might occur."[40]

Weed reported that by eight o'clock cannon were booming again. Early trains and hundreds of farm wagons and vehicles of all kinds began rolling into town, filled with people anxious to wish Lincoln well. He was in his quarters in the governor's room by mid-morning surrounded by old friends and neighbors. He greeted all with pleasure and his accustomed good nature. But more than one in the room noted a line of melancholy in his otherwise genial face. He sat for a time in the big armchair with his feet on a lower rung of the large stove and said half a dozen times in two hours, "Well, boys, your troubles are over now, but mine have just begun." He conducted a regular levee in the swelling crowd, taking hold of every hand.

One of the hands was of an old gray-haired and grizzled farmer, who said, "Uncle Abe, I didn't vote for yer, but I am mighty glad yer elected just the same."

"Well, my old friend," Lincoln said, "when a man has been tried and pronounced not guilty he hasn't any right to find fault with the jury."[41]

The canvass had riveted the nation. Nearly 4.7 million voters went to the polls—eighty percent of those eligible to vote. Lincoln didn't win a majority of the popular vote—only forty percent of it. It would have been a miracle had he done so; he was not even on the ballot in ten Southern states. Six of every ten voters had voted against him. But he had rolled up a decisive electoral vote—180 to Breckinridge's 72 and Bell's 39. Douglas, fighting a lost cause to the last, polled the second highest popular vote—1,365,976 to Lincoln's 1,857,610. But this translated into only twelve electoral votes from two states, New Jersey and Missouri.[42]

Later, Lincoln reportedly said he was "accidently elected president of the United States."[43]

Accidents do happen. This one had monumental significance.

29

Firebell in the Night

IN 1820, Thomas Jefferson called the problem over slavery in the Missouri territory "the most portentous" that had yet threatened the young Union. It was a problem twisting like an angry tornado across the American psyche. In the gloomiest moment of the Revolutionary War, Jefferson said, he had not had "apprehensions equal to what I feel from this source." He called it "a firebell in the night," that awakened him and filled him with terror.[1]

Abraham Lincoln's election forty years later set off another firebell in the night—the South's insistent call to secession. And this time it could not be silenced by compromise. For the firebrands in the South the rise to the presidency of a "Black Republican"—"that ogre Lincoln"—[2] could not be tolerated. It gave them the lever they had long sought to wrest the South free from the North and its odious abolitionism. That lever now needed only to be pulled.

It was pulled on December 20, 1860, by South Carolina, the most pro-slavery, Black Republican-hating state in the South. "Nobody," one South Carolina diarist wrote, "could live in this state unless he were a fire-eater."[3] In Charleston a special convention—169 delegates—met and unanimously passed an ordinance of secession, unilaterally dissolving its tie to the Union. Over the next month-and-a-half six other Deep South states followed with secession ordinances of their own—Mississippi on January 9, 1861, Florida on January 10, Alabama on January 11, Georgia on January 19, Louisiana on January 26, and Texas on February 1.

South Carolina, ever the flywheel in this stunning spin-away of states, invited the six others to send delegations to Montgomery, Alabama, to organize a Confederate Government. They met on February 4 and within the week, meeting in secret session, adopted a constitution, elected a provisional president—Jefferson Davis of Mississippi—and were in business.

In Washington the Buchanan administration was reeling. Buchanan himself, with his strong pro-Southern sentiments, pressured and browbeaten by advisers, seemed paralyzed.

The cabinet began to fall apart. First to leave was Secretary of State Lewis Cass of Michigan. He said he represented a Northern and loyal constituency, and could not longer remain in "such treasonable surroundings." On some mornings, Joseph Holt of Kentucky, then Buchanan's secretary of war replacing the secession-minded Virginian, John B. Floyd, who had resigned December 29, would see the unhappy president not bearing up under the pressure, looking "as pale and haggard and worn out as if he had been tramping on a treadmill all night."[4]

Lincoln was in disbelief. Nearly a decade before, in his eulogy to Henry Clay, he had said, "We...look for, and are not much

shocked by, political eccentricities and heresies in South Carolina."[5] But, Herndon said of him, "he could not in his heart believe that the South designed the overthrow of the government."[6]
Lincoln wrote in a letter to a former fellow Whig congressman,
Peter H. Silvester, "The political horizon looks dark and lowering; but the people, under Providence, will set all right."[7]

Lincoln saw no new law or new interpretation of an old law
that Southerners could complain of, "no speciality whatever,
nothing but the naked desire to go out of the Union."[8] Asked in
December if he thought Southerners would carry out their
threats to secede, he had said: "I do not think they will. A number from different sections of the South pass through here daily,
and all that call appear pleasant and seem to go away apparently
satisfied, and if they only give me an opportunity, I will convince
them that I do not wish to interfere with them in any way, but
protect them in everything that they are entitled to. But if they
do, the question will be and must be settled, come what may."[9]

A visiting Ohio journalist and politician, Donn Piatt, said the
president-elect "did not believe, could not be made to believe,
that the South meant secession and war." Piatt, begging to disagree, told him that "in ninety days the land would be whitened
with tents."

"Well," Lincoln replied, "we won't jump that ditch until we
come to it," and after a short pause, "I must run the machine as
I find it."[10]

The question now was, in what condition was he going to
find it?

For four years Lincoln and Herndon, "student-like," had
steadfastly kept up on national affairs, diligently mining various
sources. Henry B. Rankin, who was apprenticing in their law office, watched them "reviewing and sifting all conflicting opinions

on national questions that came to their office table from North and South, East and West." Lincoln's preparation, Rankin believed "could not have been more thorough, exact, and comprehensive." He was reading both Northern and Southern newspapers. "Let us have both sides on our table," Lincoln said, "each is entitled to its 'day in court.'"[11]

But now, armed with both sides of the question, he felt powerless. He told his friend Joseph Gillespie, "Gillespie, I would willingly take out of my life a period in years equal to the two months which intervene between now and my inauguration to take the oath of office now." Every hour, he told Gillespie, "adds to the difficulties I am called upon to meet, and the present Administration does nothing to check the tendency toward dissolution. I, who have been called to meet this awful responsibility, am compelled to remain here, doing nothing to avert it or lessen its force when it comes to me."[12]

Earlier, when John Nicolay told him that Buchanan had ordered Major Robert Anderson, commanding the small Union garrison in Charleston harbor, to surrender Fort Moultrie if attacked, Lincoln had exploded. "If that is true," he said, "they ought to hang him." Lincoln told Nicolay that he had sent a confidential message to Winfield Scott, the general-in-chief of the army, saying to be prepared, "immediately after my inauguration, to make arrangements at once to hold the forts, or if they have been taken, to take them back again." That, he told Herndon, "is good ground to live and to die by."[13]

"It is not of myself I complain," Lincoln told Gillespie, who had never heard him speak with more bitterness, "but every day adds to the difficulty of the situation and makes the outcome more gloomy. Secession is being fostered rather than repressed, and if the doctrine meets with general acceptance in the Border States it will be a great blow to the Government."

He told Gillespie, "I have read, upon my knees, the story of Gethsemane, where the Son of God prayed in vain that the cup of bitterness might pass from him. I am in the Garden of Gethsemane now, and my cup of bitterness is full and overflowing."

He said, "Joe, I suppose you will never forget that trial down in Montgomery County, where the lawyer associated with you gave away the whole case in his opening speech. I saw you signaling to him, but you couldn't stop him. Now, that's just the way with me and Buchanan. He is giving away the case, and I have nothing to say, and can't stop him."[14]

In Washington, Buchanan was saying that secession was unconstitutional; the framers, "never intended to implant in its bosom the seeds of its own destruction," but that if a state decided to secede there was nothing the government could legally do to stop it.[15] William Seward said this position meant no state had the right to secede—unless it wanted to—and the government must save the Union—unless somebody opposed it.[16]

Lincoln was appalled. It was clear to him that "the Union must be preserved at all hazards."[17] The very existence of a national government, he believed, "implies the legal power, right, and duty" of maintaining itself whole, a notion that, "if not expressed, is at least implied in the Constitution." His impression—"leaving myself room to modify the opinion if, upon further investigation, I should see fit to do so"—was "that this government possesses both the authority and the power to maintain its own integrity. That, however, is not the ugly point in this matter. The ugly point is the necessity of keeping the government together by force, as ours should be a government of fraternity."

The right of a state to secede, he believed, "is not an open or debatable question. It was fully discussed in Jackson's time and denied not only by him, but by the vote of Congress. It is the duty of a president to execute the laws and maintain the existing government. He cannot entertain any proposition for dissolution or dismemberment. He was not elected for any such purpose."[18] And no state, he believed, "can, in any way lawfully, get out of the Union, without the consent of the others."[19]

Lincoln refused to say publicly any more than he had said before his nomination and election. But he longed for the South to be reassured that he—and all true Republicans—did not wish to interfere with the domestic institutions of any state, nor did they advocate Negro equality. Not wanting to say that again now, he had it written into a speech by Lyman Trumbull.[20]

Lincoln was also shocked that the South could think his election alone was an aggressive act. He wrote his old congressional friend, Georgia's Alexander Stephens, a letter *"For your own eye only."* In it he said: "Do the people of the South really entertain fears that a Republican administration would, *directly,* or *indirectly,* interfere with their slaves, or with them, about their slaves? If they do, I wish to assure you, as once a friend, and still, I hope, not an enemy, that there is no cause for such fears. The South would be in no more danger in this respect, than it was in the days of Washington."[21]

Even before Lincoln was writing to Stephens, Douglas agreed, saying "No man in America regrets the election of Mr. Lincoln more than I do; none made more strenuous exertions to defeat him; none differ with him more radically and irreconcileably upon all the great issues involved in the contest. No man living is [more] prepared to resist, by all legitimate means, sanctioned by the Constitution and laws of our country, the aggressive policy which he and his party are understood to represent. But, while I say this, I am bound, as a good citizen and law-abiding man, to declare my conscientious conviction that the mere election of any man to the Presidency by the American people, in accordance with the Constitution and the laws, does not of itself furnish any just cause or reasonable ground for dissolving the Federal Union."[22]

There was metaphor for all of this in a passing incident in Springfield after the election. Lincoln was attacked on the street by a goat that some boys had been teasing. Holding the goat by the horns, Lincoln tried reasoning with it. "I didn't bother you," the president-elect said to the goat. "It was the boys. Why don't you go and butt the boys? I wouldn't trouble you."[23]

As he waited in Springfield, Lincoln was riding out a tsunami of demands. Since his nomination, his friend Leonard Swett said, he had "made himself the Mecca to which all politicians made pilgrimages. He told them all a story, said nothing, and sent them away."[24]

The visitors to the governor's room in the statehouse were running 100 to 150 a day. "The influx of politicians is so great," wrote the young reporter Henry Villard, who was monitoring events, "that a large number are nightly obliged to seek shelter in sleeping cars."[25] Herndon reported that "individuals, deputations, and delegations from all quarters pressed in upon him in a manner that might have killed a man of less robust constitution. The hotels of Springfield were filled with gentlemen who came with light baggage and heavy schemes. The party had never been in office. A clean sweep of the 'ins' was expected, and all the 'outs' were patriotically anxious to take the vacant places. It was a party that had never fed; and it was vigorously hungry."[26]

Lincoln told Richard C. Parsons, an Ohio lawyer and legislator, that most of his visitors badly wanted something. "No sooner was my election certain," he told another friend, "than I became the prey of hundreds of hungry, persistent applicants for office, whose highest ambition is to feed at the government crib." He told the German, Carl Schurz, an ardent Seward man now supporting Lincoln, "Men like you, who have real merit and do the work, are always too proud to ask for anything. Those who do nothing are always the most clamorous for office and very often get it, because it is the only way to get rid of them."[27]

He seemed to be bearing up well enough, however. Horace White reported that "when sitting for a photo & putting on his most serious look," he appeared "as though he had been just sentenced to death."[28] But a reporter for the *Lexington* (Illinois) *Weekly Globe,* seeing him, wrote: "Old Abe looks as though the campaign had worn lightly on him. He is commencing to raise a beautiful pair of whiskers, and looks younger than usual. Still there is no disguising the fact that he is homely."[29]

The whiskers Lincoln was growing, after a lifetime with a beardless face, were the doing of Grace Bedell, an eleven-year-old girl from Westfield, New York. After his nomination and before his election she wrote to him, "I have got 4 brother's," she explained, "and part of them will vote for you any way and if you will let your whiskers grow I will try and get the rest of them to vote for you[.] you would look a great deal better for your face is so thin. All the ladies like whiskers and they would tease their husband's to vote for you and then you would be President. My father is a going to vote for you and if I was a man I would vote for you to but I will try to get everyone to vote for you that I can[.]"

Lincoln was charmed. "As to the whiskers," he wrote her,

"having never worn any, do you not think people would call it a piece of silly affection if I were to begin it now?"[30] But despite what people might think, he was now growing a set.

Not all of Lincoln's worries were washing over him from the riptide of visitors. He was troubled by premonitions. Herndon believed that Lincoln feared for his life. "I feel as if I should meet with some terrible end," he told Herndon.[31]

Death threats had been coming from Baltimore and other points around Washington, with predictions that he would not reach the capital alive, or that his inauguration would be prevented. Lincoln wrote to Winfield Scott, recounting the threats and inquiring about the risk.[32]

Thomas Mather, adjutant-general of Illinois, was dispatched to deliver the letter to Washington. Mather found Scott propped up in bed by "an embankment of pillows," weak from a chronic illness and trembling perceptibly. However, there was no trembling in his response. "General Mather," Scott said, greatly agitated, "present my compliments to Mr. Lincoln when you return to Springfield, and tell him I expect him to come to Washington as soon as he is ready. Say to him that I'll look after those Maryland and Virginia rangers [secessionist sympathizers] myself; I'll plant cannon at both ends of Pennsylvania Avenue, and if any of them show their heads or raise a finger I'll blow them to hell." Mather returned to Springfield and hurried to assure Lincoln that if Scott were alive on inauguration day, there need be no fear.[33]

William Seward urged Lincoln to come to Washington early. In late December he wrote Lincoln of a plot to seize the capital on or before inauguration day, March 4. "I am not giving you opinions and rumors," Seward wrote. "Believe that I know what I write. . . . I therefore renew my suggestion of your coming here earlier than you otherwise would—and coming in by surprise—without announcement." Seward also suggested that if he had chosen secretaries of war and navy, they should hurry to Washington too.

Lincoln said he didn't expect to leave for Washington before the middle of February, "because I expect they will drive me insane after I get there, and I want to keep tolerably sane, at least until after the inauguration."[34] However, he would go to Chicago before then. Wanting at last to meet his vice president–elect, he wrote Hamlin, "I am anxious for a personal interview with you at as early a day as possible. Can you, without much inconvenience, meet me at Chicago?"[35]

Hamlin could, and Lincoln and Mary left for Chicago on November 21. In Springfield and again in Lincoln, Bloomington, and Lexington en route, he made brief statements, in which he said in effect he wasn't going to make any statements. He just said he wasn't "in the habit of making speeches now."

Leaving Springfield, however, he did say, "let us neither express, nor cherish, any harsh feeling towards any citizen who, by his vote, has differed with us. Let us at all times remember that all American citizens are brothers of a common country, and should dwell together in the bonds of fraternal feeling." In Bloomington he said, "We will try to do well by them in all parts of the country, North and South, with entire confidence that all will be well with all of us."[36] Then the Deep South began seceding in December.

Two tasks were weighing on Lincoln's mind and taking his time as the day approached for his trip to Washington—writing his inaugural speech and shaping a cabinet.

He began working on his address in late January. He asked

Herndon to dig out Henry Clay's speech on the Senate floor during the debates on the compromise in 1850, Andrew Jackson's proclamation against nullification in the early 1830s, Webster's monumental reply to South Carolina's Senator Robert Y. Hayne during that crisis, and a copy of the Constitution. These in hand, Lincoln locked himself in the counting room over a store across the street from the statehouse owned by one of his brothers-in-law, Clark Moulton Smith.[37]

Lincoln wished to keep the speech under wraps until he delivered it. "Neither his own house nor the office where he received his numerous daily visitors could be used for this work," John Nicolay explained. "He needed a retreat completely safe from prying inquisition." In the counting room over Smith's store, Lincoln wrote, copied what he wrote, and destroyed every fragment of leftover manuscript.

When he finished, the text was handed to the publisher of the *Illinois State Journal.* Taking with him a trusted compositor and a case of type, the publisher "locked himself in a room of the *Journal* office, and remained there until the document was set up, the necessary proofs taken, and the form secure in the office safe until Mr. Lincoln could correct and revise the proofs."

A second and third revision called for slight changes. Then about a dozen copies were printed and the type disbursed— "all," Nicolay said, "under the eyes of the publisher. Perfect secrecy was maintained, perfect faith was kept."[38]

Lincoln knew it was not the final word. He wrote George D. Prentice, editor of the *Louisville* (Kentucky) *Journal,* who requested a copy, "I have the document already blocked out; but in the now rapidly shifting scenes, I shall have to hold it subject to revision up to near the time of delivery."[39]

To get the manuscript from Springfield to Washington in an unviolated state, "through all the delay, hurly-burly, and confusion incident to such a trip," Nicolay believed, would be "no easy problem."[40]

But that problem could wait. Pressing Lincoln now was cabinet-making. He wanted the best men he could find, and they seemed to comprise his opposition for the nomination. George W. Julian, a Whig-cum-Free Soiler-cum-Republican congressman from Indiana, believed this inclination of Lincoln's "illustrated the natural tendency of his mind to mediate between opposing forces," which he called "the balancing of matters."[41]

Lincoln had started the process on the night he was elected: "When I finally bade my friends good-night and left that room," he later said, "I had substantially completed the framework of my cabinet."[42] Whether it would finally work out was another matter.

He above all wanted William Seward, writing to him on December 8, in a message delivered by Hamlin: "With your permission, I shall at the proper time, nominate you to the Senate, for confirmation, as Secretary of State." In a longer, private letter written that same day and delivered by the same hand, Lincoln told Seward, "it has been my purpose, from the day of the nomination at Chicago, to assign you, by your leave, this place in the administration. I have delayed so long to communicate that purpose, in deference to what appeared to me to be a proper caution in the case... and now I offer you the place, in the hope that you will accept it, and with the belief that your position in the public eye, your integrity, ability, learning, and great experience, all combine to render it an appointment pre-eminently fit to be made."[43]

Seward answered on December 13, asking for "a little time to consider whether I possess the qualifications and temper of a minister and whether it is in such a capacity that my friends

would prefer that I should act if I am to continue at all in the public service." Fifteen days later Seward wrote Lincoln a brief letter, accepting the appointment. Lincoln wrote Seward, again privately, "Your selection for the State Department having become public, I am happy to find scarcely any objection to it. I shall have trouble with every other Northern cabinet appointment—so much so that I shall have to defer them as long as possible, to avoid being teased to insanity to make changes."[44]

Lincoln also wanted Chase. He had in mind the treasury portfolio. On the last day of the year he wrote Chase, "In these troublous times, I would [much] like a conference with you. Please visit me here at once." On January 5 they conferred, Lincoln made an offer, and Chase left having neither accepted or rejected it.[45]

As Chase was leaving, John W. Bunn, one of Lincoln's longtime friends, a Springfield businessman, passed him on the stairs. Greatly agitated, Bunn said abruptly, "You don't want to put that man in your cabinet."

Lincoln wasn't offended by the abruptness or impertinence, but he asked, "Why do you say that?"

"Because, he thinks he is a great deal bigger than you are."

Lincoln also believed in Chase's bigness. He had told Charles H. Ray, editor of the *Chicago Press and Tribune,* "Take [Chase] all in all, he is the foremost man in the party."

But Lincoln asked Bunn, "Well, do you know of any other men who think they are bigger than I am?"

"I do not know that I do," Bunn replied, "but why do you ask me that?"

"Because," said Lincoln, "I want to put them all in my cabinet."[46]

Chase eventually accepted the appointment.

Lincoln also wanted the third of his three major rivals for the nomination, Edward Bates, an eminent lawyer. In a December interview with the Missourian, he offered him the attorney-generalship. Bates's friends had asked that he be named secretary of state, the first place in the cabinet, but Lincoln wanted Seward in that position. Bates accepted the appointment, and Lincoln immediately put him to work. He asked his attorney-general-to-be "to examine very thoroughly and make himself familiar with the Constitution and the laws relating to the question of secession, so as to be prepared to give a definite opinion upon the various aspects of the question." Lincoln wanted this done before the inauguration.[47]

The president-elect thus far was getting what he wanted, a cabinet, of "all the talents and all the popularities."[48]

He continued working in Springfield to add the rest of the best to this power-packed core trio. In his visit with Hamlin in Chicago, Lincoln told his running mate, "I need a man of Democratic antecedents from New England." Hamlin recommended Gideon Welles, a Connecticut editor and politician, saying he had "no hesitation in saying that...Mr. Welles is the better man for New England."[49] Lincoln ticketed Welles for secretary of the navy.

Lincoln also had his eye on Montgomery Blair, a West Point graduate and noted Washington lawyer, "but I can not, as yet, be committed on the matter, to any extent whatever." Trumbull recommended him for secretary of war, but Blair would become Lincoln's postmaster general.[50]

Lincoln confided to Herndon that he "wanted to give the South, by way of placation," a place in the cabinet, "that a fair division of the country entitled the southern states to a reasonable representation." He first asked his old friend Joshua Speed, now a prominent Kentucky businessman, to accept a position. When Speed refused, Lincoln asked him to sound out fellow Kentuckian James Guthrie, the secretary of the treasury under Pierce. Lincoln had him in mind for secretary of war, but that didn't work out.[51]

Lincoln also wanted to placate Indiana, which had been so crucial to the nomination. Lincoln told two Indianans proposing Caleb B. Smith for a place, that he did not want to "embarrass himself with promises," and "could only say that he saw no insuperable objections to Indiana's having a man, nor to Smith's being that man."[52] Smith, a former Whig congressman, would become secretary of the interior.

Simon Cameron was Lincoln's biggest cabinet headache. Despite his warning to his wheeler-dealing team at the convention to entangle him in no pledges, they had made big promises to Cameron to get Pennsylvania's vote. Now Lincoln was in trouble because of it.

"Lincoln is in a fix," Herndon wrote Trumbull. "Cameron's appointment to an office in his Cabinet bothers him. If Lincoln do appoint Cameron he gets a fight on his hands, and if he do not he gets a quarrel deep, abiding, & lasting. . . . So this political world wags. Poor Lincoln! God help him! Pshaw what a scramble for office! What angry looks & growls for bones that have fat & meat on them."[53]

Cameron was shady at best, with a reputation for less-than-honest dealings. But he was the most powerful political force in Pennsylvania, that most powerful of states. Lincoln told two of Cameron's supporters, "All through the campaign my friends have been calling me 'Honest Old Abe,' and I have been elected mainly on that cry. What will be thought now if the first thing I do is to appoint Cameron, whose very name stinks in the nostrils of the people for his corruption?"[54]

When Gustave P. Koerner, a political leader and power in the German community, and Norman Judd urged him not to include Cameron, Lincoln said, "There has been delegation after delegation from Pennsylvania, hundreds of letters, and the cry is 'Cameron, Cameron!' Besides, you know I have already fixed on Chase, Seward, and Bates.... The Pennsylvania people say: 'If you leave out Cameron you disgrace him.' Is there not something in that?"

When Koerner protested Cameron's corrupt reputation, Lincoln said, "I know, I know, but can I get along if that state should oppose my administration?"[55]

Finally, on the last day of December, Lincoln wrote Cameron saying he would "at the proper time, nominate you to the U.S. Senate, for confirmation as Secretary of the Treasury, or as Secretary of War—which of the two, I have not yet definitely decided." But Lincoln still waffled. Three days later he took back the offer. "Things have developed," he wrote Cameron, "which make it impossible to take you into the cabinet."[56]

Lincoln wanted Chase as secretary of treasury, assuring Trumbull that Cameron had not been offered the job and "I think, will not be. It seems to me not only highly proper, but a necessity that Gov. Chase shall take that place." Lincoln told Trumbull that Cameron "must be brought to co-operate" and would readily take the war department. "But then," Lincoln complained, "comes the fierce opposition to his having any Department, threatening even to send charges into the Senate to procure his rejection by that body. Now, what I would most like, and what I think he should prefer too, under the circumstances, would be to retain his place in the Senate." Lincoln told Trumbull that despite the "very fierce opposition" to him, "he is more amply recommended for a place in the cabinet, than any other man."[57]

The pressure to appoint him was too much. Figuratively holding his nose, Lincoln added Cameron to the list of names he would submit for Senate confirmation after he was inaugurated. Cameron was to be his secretary of war.[58]

The time for leaving for Washington was fast approaching. There was one remaining thing Lincoln felt he must do—pay a farewell visit to Sarah Bush Lincoln, that "good and kind mother."[59] She was a widow now. Lincoln's father had died a decade before, and she was living with her daughter Matilda in Farmington in Coles County.

Sarah had not wanted her stepson to run for president. "I... was afraid Somehow or other—" she later said, "felt in my heart that Something would happen to him...and that I should see him no more."[60]

Lincoln left to visit her on a very cold January 30. The next day, after breakfast in Charleston, he left in a buggy for Farmington with August H. Chapman, who had married into the Hanks side of Lincoln's family. They had difficulty crossing the Kickapoo, a little stream three miles south of Charleston, because of ice. On the way Lincoln told Chapman that Sarah had been his best friend in this world and that no son could love a mother more than he loved her.

Lincoln spent the day with her, and as he prepared to leave and they embraced, her fears for him welled up again. She told him she despaired of ever seeing him again, that his enemies would assassinate him. Though Lincoln tended to believe she might be right, he hurried to reassure her.

"No No, Mama," he said, "they will not do that. Trust in the Lord and all will be well. We will See each other again."

Lincoln then visited his father's grave. Back in Charleston, the clamor to see him was so insistent that he authorized a public reception at the town hall for that evening. At seven o'clock he was there greeting the crowd. Asked to speak, he would only say that "the time for a public definition of the policy of his administration had not come, and that he could but express his gratification at seeing so many of his friends and give them a hearty greeting." The next day he returned to Springfield.[61]

There was not now much time. Soon he must leave for Washington.

30

Getting There

NOBODY HAD BEEN THERE for Lincoln more than Billy Herndon. Through all the years of stumping, the long days on the circuit, more than 5,000 law cases, all the head-to-heads with Douglas, Herndon had been "as true to Lincoln as the 'needle to the pole.'"[1] Lincoln owed him—owed himself—a quiet time together before he left. That time had come. By early February Lincoln had his affairs in order. He and Mary had disposed of their household goods and furniture and rented out the house at Eighth and Jackson Streets. On the 6th they held a farewell soiree, and on the afternoon before his departure he went to the office to examine papers and confer with his partner. When business was done, Lincoln threw himself down on the old sagging sofa. He lay quietly for some moments, looking up at the ceiling. Neither man spoke.

Then, Lincoln asked, "Billy, how long have we been together?"

"Over sixteen years," Herndon answered.

"We've never had a cross word during all that time, have we?"

"No, indeed we have not." Herndon was positive about that.

Lincoln then remembered some incidents of his early practice and laughed at some ludicrous times. Herndon had never seen him more cheerful.

After a time, Lincoln gathered a bundle of books and papers that he wished to take with him and started to leave. But then he remembered the signboard, "Lincoln & Herndon," that swung on rusty hinges over the stairway.

"Leave it hang there undisturbed," he told Herndon. "Give our clients to understand that the election of a President makes no change in the firm of Lincoln and Herndon. If I live I'm coming back some time, and then we'll go right on practicing law as if nothing had ever happened."

Lincoln was finding it hard to leave. He tarried for a moment to take one last look around, then passed through the door into the narrow hallway. Herndon accompanied him downstairs.

"I am sick of office-holding already," he told Herndon, "and I shudder when I think of the tasks that are still ahead."

He talked of the sadness of parting from old friends and associates, saying the sorrow of it was deeper than most persons would imagine. It was more marked in his case, he told Herndon, because of the irrepressible feeling he had—shared with Sarah—that he would never return alive.

Herndon protested, calling his premonition an illusory notion not in harmony or keeping with the popular ideal of a president.

"But it is in keeping with my philosophy," Lincoln said.

As they walked along, the conversation was frequently interrupted by passersby. Finally he said, "I am decided; my course is fixed; my path is blazed; the Union and the Constitution shall be preserved, and the laws enforced at every and at all hazards. I expect the people to sustain me. They have never yet forsaken any true man." Those were the very last words Herndon remembered him saying before Lincoln grasped his hand warmly and with a fervent "Good-bye," disappeared down the street.[2]

The next morning, February 11, the sky was leaden in Springfield and the air wet with mist, as Lincoln made his way to the Wabash Station on the Great Western Railway.[3] Long before the special train was scheduled to depart, a nonpartisan crowd had gathered around the tracks to see him off. At precisely five minutes to eight, Lincoln left his room in the station and moved through the crush of people toward his car.

On the rear platform, before stepping into the car, Lincoln turned toward them, paused several seconds to control his emotions, then began to say his own final farewell:[4]

My friends—No one, not in my situation, can appreciate my feeling of sadness at this parting. To this place, and the kindness of these people, I owe every thing. Here I have lived a quarter of a century, and have passed from a young to an old man. Here my children have been born, and one is buried. I now leave, not knowing when, or whether ever, I may return, with a task before me greater than that which rested upon Washington. Without the assistance of that Divine Being, who ever attended him, I cannot succeed. With that assistance I cannot fail. Trusting in Him, who can go with me, and remain with you and be every where for good, let us confidently hope that all will yet be well. To His care commending you, as I hope in your prayers you will commend me, I bid you an affectionate farewell.[5]

It was raining now, but the *Illinois Journal* reporting the event, said "every hat was lifted, and every head bent forward to catch the last words of the departing chief," and as he finished "there was an uncontrollable burst of applause." A young observer wrote in his diary that day that an "audible good bye & God speed followed him as the train disappeared."

The *Journal* called it "a most impressive scene. We have known Mr. Lincoln for many years; we have heard him speak upon a hundred different occasions; but we never saw him so profoundly affected, nor did he ever utter an address, which seemed to us as full of simple and touching eloquence, so exactly adopted to the occasion, so worthy of the man and the hour."[6]

As the special train moved out of the station eastward Lincoln stood on the rear platform until the houses of Springfield receded and the train was traveling past open fields and farms.[7]

Inside the car, beginning the journey with him, were a mix of relatives, friends, and associates, among them Lincoln's brother-in-law William Wallace, Judge David Davis, Norman Judd, Ward Hill Lamon, Orville Browning, and Governor Richard Yates. His two secretaries, John G. Nicolay and John Hay (recently brought on), were in the car. Army Colonel Edwin V. (Bull) Sumner was aboard as a military escort, with Lincoln's young friend, Elmer Ellsworth, the sprightly commander of a company of spit-and-polish Zouaves. Not all of these would go all the way to Washington with him; some would be dropped off at points along the way, others doubtless would board for stretches of time as the train moved toward Washington. In charge of the party was a New Yorker, William S. Wood, recommended to Lincoln by Seward.[8]

The locomotive pulled a baggage car and three passenger cars, one of them beautifully appointed, carpeted, curtained, and upholstered for the presidential party. The journey would resemble a milk run, halting at whistle stops all along the track, and pulling into major stations for longer stops in Indiana, Ohio, Pennsylvania, New York, New Jersey, and Maryland.[9]

Committees "innumerable" would be waiting at every stop— at every state line, in every state capital. Flocking to greet him on his way would be governors, legislators, squads of Wide Awakes—and just plain citizens—eager to see him and if possible shake his hand. Even at way stations where no stops were scheduled and the train simply whistled by, crowds gathered to watch him pass.[10] There were major towns, such as Dayton, Ohio, where his schedule would not let him stop, where he could only "bow to the friends there" as the train sped on.[11]

Despite the comfort of the car, it was going to be an uncomfortable trip. Lincoln was expected to say something at every stop. But he resolved that he would have "nothing to say to the American people until his inaugural address."[12]

Yet there was an urgent longing in the American people to hear him say something to reassure them in the shattering epidemic of seceding states. The people wanted to know that "even as the crisis had come so also had come the MAN."[13]

After the election Lincoln had written a politician who urged him to make a public statement, "I could say nothing which I have not already said, and which is in print, and open for the inspection of all. To press a repetition of this upon those who *have* listened, is useless; to press it upon those who have *refused* to listen, and still refuse, would be wanting in self-respect, and would have an appearance of sycophancy and timidity, which would excite the contempt of good men, and encourage bad ones to clamor the more loudly." To the editor of the *Missouri Republican,* he wrote, "I am not at liberty to shift my ground—that is out of the question."[14]

Lincoln was not the sort, his friend Henry Whitney said, who could talk effectively about nothing. "He must have something to say," Whitney believed, "and somebody to convince."[15]

In Decatur, Lincoln moved quickly through the crowd shaking hands. In Tolono, still in Illinois, he spoke briefly, echoing the theme of his Springfield farewell. "I am leaving you," he told the crowed gathered at the station, "on an errand of national importance, attended, as you are aware, with considerable difficulties. Let us believe, as some poet has expressed it: Behind the cloud the sun is still shining."[16]

His train crossed the Indiana line out of Illinois at half past twelve in the afternoon to a salute of thirty-four guns, and in Lafayette, Indiana, he marveled at the fast pace of life. "When I first came to the west, some 44 or 45 years ago, at sundown," he told the crowd, "you had completed a journey of some 30 miles which you had commenced at sunrise, and thought you had done well. Now only six hours have elapsed since I left my home in Illinois."[17]

At Thorntown, Indiana, he was telling a story and had neared the comic ending when the train abruptly pulled out of the station, leaving the crowd to wonder not only about the crisis, but about the punch line. It was said in jest that some of the Thorntown folks followed the train on foot to the next stop to hear the rest of the story.[18]

In Indianapolis, greeted by another thirty-four guns, Lincoln responded briefly to Governor Oliver P. Morton's train-side wel-come. "While I do not expect, upon this occasion, or on any oc-casion, till after I get to Washington, to attempt any lengthy speech," Lincoln said, "I will only say that to the salvation of this Union there needs but one single thing—the hearts of a people like yours." He told them, "I... am but an accidental instru-ment, temporary, and to serve but for a limited time, but I appeal to you again to constantly bear in mind that with you, and not with politicians, not with Presidents, not with office-seekers, but with you, is the question, 'Shall the Union and shall the liberties of this country be preserved to the latest generation.'"[19]

That evening in Indianapolis he spoke briefly from the bal-cony of the Bates House, about "coercion." The word, he said, is "in great use about these days," but "if the Government... simply insists upon holding its own forts, or retaking those forts which belong to it—or the enforcement of the laws of the United States... would any or all of these things be coercion?" By "what principle or original right," he asked, "is it that one-fiftieth or one-ninetieth of a great nation, by calling themselves a State, have the right to break up and ruin that nation as a matter of original principle?... to play tyrant over all its own citizens, and deny the authority of everything greater than itself."[20]

When they left Springfield Lincoln had put his inaugural ad-dress and other papers in a small, old-fashioned black oilcloth carpetbag, which he had entrusted to his oldest son Robert for safekeeping. However, he failed to tell the eighteen-year-old that it contained the precious speech. As with most teenagers Robert had his mind on more compelling things than looking after a carpetbag. This was a triumphal tour; he was excited and forget-ful. The press was calling him "The Prince of Rails," and at al-most every stop boys his own age were ready to pounce on him to "do him the honors after their own capricious whims." And here they were at the first pounceable stop, Indianapolis.

When Lincoln reached his room at the Bates House he remembered the carpetbag and its top-secret contents. He called urgently for Robert only to learn that he had been snatched away by "The Boys" for a tour of Indianapolis. When finally found and brought in, he blandly told his father he had handed the carpetbag to the clerk at the hotel.

"And what did the clerk do with it?" demanded his father.

"Set it on the floor behind the counter," Robert answered.

John Nicolay, a witness to all of this, saw a "look of stupefaction" pass over Lincoln's face, with "visions of that Inaugural in all the next morning's newspapers" floating "through his imagination." Without a word, Nicolay recounted, "he opened the door of his room, forced his way through the crowded corridor down to the office, where, with a single stride of his long legs, he swung himself across the clerk's counter, behind which a small mountain of carpetbags of all colors had accumulated. Then drawing a little key out of his pocket he began delving for the black ones, and opened one by one those that the key would unlock, to the great surprise and amusement of the clerk and bystanders, as their miscellaneous contents came to light. Fortune favored the President-elect, for after the first half dozen trials, he found his treasures."

Robert was somewhat sternly admonished, but there was an upside. For the rest of the trip he no longer had to watch over the carpetbag. Lincoln would keep it under his own charge.[21]

The next day, February 12, was Lincoln's fifty-second birthday. At Lawrenceburg on the Indiana line, just before passing into Ohio, he said, "I have been selected to fill an important office for a brief period, and am now, in your eyes, invested with an influence which will soon pass away; but should my administration prove to be a very wicked one, or what is more probable, a very foolish one, if you, the PEOPLE, are but true to yourselves and to the Constitution, there is but little harm I can do, *thank God!*"[22]

In Cincinnati later in the day he was "overwhelmed" by the turnout. In a speech that evening he continued to sound the transitory theme: "In a few short years," he said, "I and every other individual man who is now living will pass away. I hope that our national difficulties will also pass away, and I hope we shall see in the streets of Cincinnati—good old Cincinnati—for centuries to come, once every four years her people give such a reception as this to the constitutionally elected President of the whole United States."[23]

In Columbus the next day, Lincoln offered the Ohio legislature words of wishful thinking—"a few broken remarks"—that rang hollow and were bound to fall with disbelief on skeptical ears. "I have not maintained silence from any want of real anxiety," he said. "It is a good thing that there is no more than anxiety, for there is nothing going wrong. It is a consoling circumstance that when we look out there is nothing that really hurts anybody. We entertain different views upon political questions, but nobody is suffering anything. This is a most consoling circumstance, and from it we may conclude that all we want is time, patience, and a reliance on that God who has never forsaken this people."[24]

In Steubenville the next day, February 14, on the banks of the Ohio River, "this majestic stream," he was still thinking and speaking self-deprecating, wishful words. "Though the majority may be wrong, and I will not undertake to say that they were not wrong in electing me, yet we must adhere to the principle that the majority shall rule. By your Constitution you have another chance in four years. No great harm can be done by us in that time—in that time there can be nobody hurt. If anything goes wrong, however, and you find you have made a mistake, elect a better man next time. There are plenty of them."[25]

Later that day his train passed into Pennsylvania. It was raining hard when it arrived in Pittsburgh—too hard for a speech. The best he could do was a few impromptu remarks standing on a chair in the lobby of the Monongahela House. The next day he continued preaching the gospel that there was no real problem. "Notwithstanding the trouble across the river," he said, pointing southward and smiling, "there is really no crisis, springing from anything in the government itself. In plain words, there is really no crisis except an *artificial* one! What is there now to warrant the condition of affairs presented by our friends 'over the river?' Take even their own view of the questions involved, and there is nothing to justify the course which they are pursuing. I repeat it, then—*there is no crisis,* excepting such a one as may be gotten up at any time by designing politicians. My advice, then, under such circumstances, is to keep cool. If the great American people will only keep their temper, on both sides of the line, the troubles will come to an end, and the question which now distracts the country will be settled just as surely as all other difficulties of like character which have originated in this government have been adjusted."[26]

That day, February 15, his train doubled back into Cleveland, Ohio, where it was snowing and raining and the streets were buried in mud. "The large numbers that have turned out under these circumstances," Lincoln told the crowd, "testify that you are in earnest about something or other." Again he reassured them there was "no occasion for any excitement," that the crisis was artificial. With a nod again toward the South, he said, "Have they not all their rights now as they ever had? Do they not have their fugitive slaves returned now as ever? Have they not the same constitution that they have lived under for seventy-odd years? Have they not a position as citizens of this common country, and have we any power to change that position? What then is the matter with them? Why all this excitement? Why all these complaints? As I said before, this crisis is all artificial. It has no foundation in facts. It was not argued up, as the saying is, and cannot, therefore, be argued down. Let it alone and it will go down by itself."[27]

By now, trying to speak without saying anything, he had grown hoarse—and tired. It was not until they reached Westfield, New York, on February 16, that Lincoln found an occasion to warm his heart. There he said, "I have a correspondent in this place, a little girl, her name is Grace Bedell, and I would like to see her."

A small boy mounted on a post, pointed to a beautiful girl with black eyes who was "blushing all over her fair face," and cried out, "there she is, Mr. Lincoln!" Lincoln left the car, and the crowd made room for him. When he reached Grace, he said, "You see I have let these whiskers grow for you, Grace." He kissed her, shook her hand, returned to the car, and was soon gone.[28]

In Dunkirk, New York, later that day some 12,000 to 15,000 turned out to welcome him. A triumphal arch had been erected over the track, inscribed with Union mottoes. Bands played and ladies waved handkerchiefs as Lincoln stepped from the train on to a velvet-carpeted platform under a Union flag. As the tumult subsided, he said, "I am glad to meet you all; I regret I cannot stop to speak to you, but were I to stop and make a speech at every station, I would not reach Washington until after the inauguration. *Standing as I do, with my hand upon this staff, and under the folds of the American flag,* I ASK YOU TO STAND BY ME SO LONG AS I STAND BY IT."[29]

For the next two days Lincoln's train crossed New York, making multiple stops along the track from Dunkirk to Buffalo—where he was hosted by ex-president Millard Fillmore—to Rochester to Syracuse to Albany, and through Troy, Poughkeepsie, Fishkill, and Peekskill into New York City. At the Astor House, he mounted a platform in a reception room that in its time had received Webster and Clay. There he stated what he had said "several times upon this journey, and I now repeat it to you, that when the time does come I shall then take the ground that I think is right—the ground I think is right for the North, for the South, for the East, for the West, for the whole country. And in doing so I hope to feel no necessity pressing upon me to say anything in conflict with the constitution, in conflict with the continued union of these States—in conflict with the perpetuation of the liberties of these people—or anything in conflict with anything whatever that I have ever given you reason to expect from me."[30]

On February 21, after two days in New York City and various stops in New Jersey, Lincoln was in Philadelphia. Replying to the welcome from Mayor Alexander Henry, he said, "I bring to the work a sincere heart. Whether I will bring a head equal to that heart, will be for future time to determine."

The next day, he raised a flag in Independence Hall, and said: "I am filled with deep emotion at finding myself standing here in the place where were collected together the wisdom, the patriotism, the devotion to principle, from which sprang the institutions under which we live. You have kindly suggested to me that in my hands is the task of restoring peace to our distracted country. I can say in return...that all the political sentiments I entertain have been drawn, so far as I have been able to draw them, from the sentiments which originated, and were given to the world from this hall in which we stand. I have never had a feeling politically that did not spring from the sentiments embodied in the Declaration of Independence." There "is no need of bloodshed and war," he said. "There is no necessity for it... there will be no blood shed unless it be forced upon the Government. The Government will not use force unless force is used against it."[31]

Later that day at Leaman Place, Pennsylvania, Lincoln told the crowd that he had merely come out to see them and let them see him, and to tell them he thought *"he had the best of the bargain!"* To loud calls for Mary, Lincoln brought her out and said, "[Here is] the long and the short of it!"[32]

These little "offhand speeches" that Lincoln was making along the tracks to Washington showed Herndon back in Springfield that he intended "to keep his own secrets and make no blunders, excite no hate, arouse no bad feelings, say nothing that would bind him till the development of the last fact in the great drama in which he was to take part." Some critics were calling his speeches "Lincoln's last jokes." Edward Everett, a connoisseur of elegant speechmaking, had followed them in disgust. He wrote in his diary, "These speeches thus far have been of the most ordinary kind, destitute of everything, not merely of felicity and grace, but of common pertinence. He is evidently a person of very inferior cast of character, wholly unequal to the crisis."[33]

The entire trip had been frenetic. The committees that met Lincoln from city to city seemed to John Nicolay to be "consumed by a demon of impatience. They would sometimes tumble pell-mell into a car and almost drag Mr. Lincoln out before the train had even stopped, and habitually... before the proper police or military guards could be stationed about a depot or stopping place to secure necessary space and order for a comfortable open path to the waiting carriages."

In Buffalo the local newspaper wrote that the crowd, "in its crazed eagerness to get nearer to the distinguished visitor...became an ungoverned mob, making an irresistible rush towards him which swept the soldiers [Lincoln's escorts and guard] from their lines, and threw everything into the wildest confusion that we ever witnessed in our lives."

Another newspaper reported, "The vital history of that day's ride is to be written in three words: 'Crowds, cannon and cheers.' Such crowds—surging through long arches, cursing the military and blessing Old Abe; swinging hats, banners, handkerchiefs, and every possible variety of festival bunting; and standing with open mouths as the train, relentlessly punctual, moved away."

The history of one, the newspaper wrote, "is the history of all; depots in waves, as if the multitudinous sea had been let loose, and its billows transformed into patriots, clinging along roofs and balconies and pillars, fringing long embankments, swarming upon adjacent trains of motionless cars, shouting, bellowing, shrieking, howling; all were boisterous; all bubbling with patriotism. The enthusiasm for the President was spontaneous and universal."[34]

Lincoln was well tired of it all. He confessed to Ward Hill Lamon that "he had not done much hard work in his life, but to make speeches day after day, with the object of speaking and saying nothing, was the hardest work he had ever done." He said, "I wish that this thing were through with and I could find peace and quiet somewhere."[35]

By the time Lincoln reached Harrisburg, the Pennsylvania capital, he was more concerned with bullets. He had been told there was a plot afoot to assassinate him before he reached Washington.

Ahead of Lincoln down the track, Allan Pinkerton was worried. A Chartist refugee from Scotland, Pinkerton had a cloak-and-dagger mentality. As a sheriff's deputy in Chicago, he evolved into the first detective in that city's newly formed police force. In 1850 he founded one of the first private detective agencies in the country, from which he had built himself a national reputation by 1861.

His agency had been hired by S. M. Felton, president of the Philadelphia, Wilmington and Baltimore Railroad, to investigate a threat. It was rumored that secessionists in Maryland intended to seize a large steamer the railroad used to ferry its trains across the Susquehanna River at Havre de Grace, burning the company's bridges.

Pinkerton began the investigation in January, locating his headquarters in Baltimore under the alias of John H. Hutchinson, a stockbroker. As he snooped undercover he began stumbling across information wholly unrelated to the railroad—a plot against the life of the president-elect. A man named Luckett remarked to Pinkerton-alias-Hutchinson that Lincoln may pass through Baltimore quietly "but I doubt it."

Luckett told Pinkerton that an Italian named Cypriano Ferrandini, "a true friend to the South," was ready to give his life to the cause if necessary and had hatched a plot to prevent Lincoln from passing through alive.

"I was looking for nothing of the Kind," Pinkerton later reported, "and had certainly not the slightest idea of it." Alarmed, he moved on to Ferrandini himself, and found him "a man well calculated for controlling and directing the ardent minded," an "enthusiast" who believed that "murder of any kind is justifiable and right to save the rights of the Southern People." He told Pinkerton that Lincoln shall "never, never" be president, and he would willingly give his life for Lincoln's. He told Pinkerton, "*If I alone must do it, I shall—Lincoln shall die in this City.*"

Gradually the details of the plot came into focus for Pinkerton as Lincoln was departing Springfield. It was clear that the attempt was to be made during his passage through Baltimore. The president-elect's itinerary was to land him at the city's Calvert Street Station. By carriage, he would transfer to the Camden Street Station and board the Baltimore and Ohio cars for Washington. The distance between the two stations was a little over a mile. The assassination attempt would occur as Lincoln passed through the narrow vestibule of the Calvert Street Station to enter his carriage. A row or fight was to be started by the plotters outside the station. The few policemen, under the charge of police chief George P. Kane, himself a "rabid Rebel," would rush out to quell it, leaving Lincoln unprotected.

A secessionist named Springer told Pinkerton agent Timothy Walker that a thousand men in Baltimore were organized to kill Lincoln. Pinkerton believed that was a wild exaggeration, but Lincoln had to be told.[36]

Pinkerton wrote a letter to Norman Judd at the Burnet House in Cincinnati, telling him about the plot. Judd told no one on the Lincoln train, but he urged Pinkerton to keep probing. In Buffalo, Judd received another letter from Pinkerton assuring him that the investigation was continuing. At the Astor House in New York, Judd was called away to an upstairs room, where yet another letter introduced him to a woman waiting there. She was

Kate Warne, alias M. Barley, head of Pinkerton's female detective department. She told him a meeting would be arranged with Pinkerton when Judd reached Philadephia.

In Philadelphia Judd found Pinkerton waiting for him under an assumed name, accompanied by Felton, the railroad president. The two men were persuasive. Judd left the meeting satisfied that "a well-matured and organized plot" did indeed exist.[37]

Meanwhile, corroborating evidence had come from William Seward and Winfield Scott in Washington. Also having word of a Baltimore plot, they had hired a handful of New York police officers to ferret it out. Like Pinkerton they became convinced that there was grave danger to Lincoln if he followed the schedule that had been mapped out and widely published. Seward sent his son Frederick to Lincoln with a communication urging him to change his itinerary.[38]

On February 21, with all this in hand, Judd arranged to meet with Pinkerton in his room at the Continental Hotel at 10:15, with Lincoln present. Pinkerton laid the whole plot before the president-elect and strongly urged him to forego the rest of his schedule and secretly travel, that very night, from Philadelphia directly to Washington.

Lincoln was quiet for a few moments after hearing all this. Finally Judd broke the silence, asking if he would accept the new plan.

"No," Lincoln said. "I cannot consent to this, I shall hoist the Flag on Independence Hall to-morrow morning"—Washington's birthday—"and go to Harrisburg to-morrow, then I have fulfilled all my engagements, and if you and Allan think there is positive danger in my attempting to go through Baltimore openly according to the published programe—if you can arrange any way to carry out your views, I shall endeavor to get away quietly from the people at Harrisburgh to-morrow evening and shall place myself in your [hands]."[39]

Lincoln fulfilled his schedule in Philadelphia the next day, and the train moved on to Harrisburg, where he addressed the Pennsylvania state legislature.

After the meeting with Lincoln in Philadelphia, Judd set plans in motion. He conferred with officials of both railways, the telegraph people, and Pinkerton. Between them they drew up a new schedule. Accompanied only by Ward Hill Lamon, his strapping, well armed friend and fellow attorney, Lincoln would leave Harrisburg, unannounced, for Philadelphia on a special train at six o'clock that evening. At that hour the telegraph lines would be cut at Harrisburg. The Baltimore train would be held at Philadelphia until Lincoln arrived and was safely aboard. Pinkerton would meet them there and accompany them the rest of the way. He would have Kate Warne book passage from Philadelphia to Washington in the rear of the sleeping car, and Lincoln would occupy the compartments in the guise of an invalid. Judd sent word back to Seward through his son that the president would arrive in Washington the next morning, February 23, at six o'clock.

When Judd disclosed the final plan to Lincoln in Harrisburg the president-elect appeared "perfectly unexcited," but agreeable. Lincoln told David Davis and other key members of his entourage, "I've thought the matter over fully and reckon I had better do as Judd says. The facts come from two different and reliable sources, and I don't consider it right to disregard both."[40]

In Philadelphia, Lincoln threw an overcoat loosely over his shoulders and donned a black Kossuth hat—named for Louis Kossuth, the hero of the Hungarian revolution. Lincoln rode to the waiting Baltimore train in a carriage with Lamon and Pinkerton. Henry F. Kenney, superintendent of the Philadelphia, Wilmington and Baltimore Railroad, sat with the driver. The train for Baltimore was being held by the engineer ostensibly to await a package destined for E. J. Allen, who was Pinkerton under yet another alias, at Willard's Hotel in Washington.

In a dark, unlit spot a short distance from the depot, the party left the carriage. Lincoln, the presumed invalid, leaned on Pinkerton's arm and stooped considerably to hide his giveaway height. Lamon followed a few paces to the rear. They passed rapidly through the depot and entered the designated sleeping car. Kenney delivered the bogus package to the engineer and the train pulled out of the station bound for Baltimore, where the party had to wait about half an hour before starting the final leg into Washington.[41]

The only three men in Washington who were in on this stealth were the two Sewards and Lincoln's friend Elihu Washburne, the Republican congressman from Illinois. When the train arrived in Washington, Washburne was planted behind one of the pillars where he could see without being seen. He watched as every car emptied—and still no Lincoln. He was in despair and about to leave when he saw three figures emerge from the last sleeping car. He couldn't mistake the "long, lank form" of the president-elect, even though it was hunched. "My heart," Washburne later said, "bounded with joy and gratitude." He believed anyone who knew Lincoln could not have failed to recognize him at once, though "he looked more like a well-to-do farmer from one of the back towns of Jo Daviess County coming to Washington to see the city, take out his land warrant and get the patent for his farm, than the President of the United States."[42]

When the party was well on the platform, Washburne stepped out from behind his pillar and said, "Abe you can't play that on me." The three travelers were startled. Pinkerton hit Washburne with his elbow, staggering him. As Pinkerton drew back his fist to hit him again, Lincoln grabbed his arm and said, "Don't strike him, Allan, don't strike him—that is my friend Washburne."[43]

After they had all exchanged congratulations, they walked out to the front of the station, where Washburne had a carriage waiting. They drove rapidly to Willard's Hotel, where Lincoln and his family were to stay, and entered on 14th Street. It was not yet daylight. The porter showed them to the little receiving room at the head of the stairs and then at Washburne's direction, went to the office to have Lincoln assigned a room. They had not been in the hotel more than two minutes before Seward hurriedly rushed in, chagrined that he hadn't met them at the train.[44]

But no matter, now all was well. Lincoln was safely in Washington. As Washburne left the hotel, his vigil over, the Irish porter smiled and said, "And by faith it is you who have brought us a Prisidint."[45]

31

The War Comes

LINCOLN'S OVERNIGHT RUN from Harrisburg into Washington was less than triumphal. But it had avoided making either him or Ferrandini a martyr.

The Democratic press was merciless, portraying it as a clandestine sneak into Washington unworthy of the city's great presidential namesake. Some took to calling it "that smuggling business."[1]

Lincoln was not proud of it and had some regret that he had let Judd and Pinkerton talk him into it. "I did not then, nor do I now believe," he later told Illinois Congressman Isaac N. Arnold, "I should have been assassinated had I gone through Baltimore as first contemplated, but I thought it wise to run no risk where no risk was necessary."[2]

But what people thought of that escapade was now the least of his worries. He was in Washington safe—but safe could not be said of the Union. Like a ripe watermelon split by a knife, it was cracking across the Deep South from South Carolina to Texas. A rebellious Confederate government was up and running in the seven seceded states. The border states from Virginia and North Carolina to Missouri were trembling uncertainly on the edge.

"The simple fact," young Charles Francis Adams of the Massachusetts Adamses, later wrote, "was that the ship was drifting on the rocks of a lee shore." The Union was clinging "to a delusive hope that the coming change of commanders would alter the whole aspect of the situation, and we would work clear." Lincoln, the new commander, Adams moaned, "was an absolutely unknown quantity; and yet he was the one possible *Deus ex machina*!"[3]

Only a few days before leaving Springfield, Lincoln had told Joseph Gillespie, "I only wish I could have got there to lock the door before the horse was stolen. But when I get to the spot I can find the tracks."[4] The tracks were muddied at best. But men were trying to prevent and reverse the split. Kentucky's John J. Crittenden, the venerable and highly respected successor to Henry Clay's U.S. Senate seat, had been tirelessly trying. In the final days of his Senate term he was reminiscent of Clay, desperately pushing a compromise in a peace conference in Washington that would extend the Missouri Compromise farther across the troubled continent to the Pacific. But it was far too late for that.

Lincoln had little hope for the conference, then being held in Willard's Hotel, and believed it ought to adjourn. He rejected any compromise that sanctioned the spread of slavery into the territories, believing the Union could not be saved by nationalizing and extending slavery in any fashion.[5] Herndon in Springfield reported to a friend that Lincoln's answer to compromisers was "Away—off—begone! If the nation wants to back down, let it—not I."[6]

In December after the election, in a private and confidential letter to Trumbull, Lincoln had said, "Let there be no compromise on the question of *extending* slavery. If there be, all our labor is lost, and, ere long, must be done again. The dangerous ground—that into which some of our friends have a hankering to run—is Pop. Sov. Have none of it. Stand firm. The tug has come, & better now, than any time hereafter."

From Illinois he had spread that word in private and confidential letters to others who might have a say in Congress. He wrote Washburne: "Prevent, as far as possible, any of our friends from demoralizing themselves, and our cause, by entertaining propositions for compromise of any sort, on '*slavery extention.*' There is no possible compromise upon it, but which puts us under again, and leaves all our work to do over again. Whether it be a Mo. line, or...Pop. Sov. it is all the same. Let either be done, & immediately filibustering and extending slavery recommences. On that point hold firm, as with a chain of steel."[7]

Now, in Washington early in March, hours before his inaugural, he was not budging from that position.

It rankled Lincoln that the South was so blatantly and violently running roughshod over the democratic process. "We have just carried an election on principles fairly stated to the people," he wrote Pennsylvania Republican Congressman James T. Hale in January. "Now we are told in advance, the government shall be broken up, unless we surrender to those we have beaten, before we take the offices. In this they are either attempting to play upon us, or they are in dead earnest. Either way, if we surrender, it is the end of us, and of the government. They will repeat the experiment upon us *ad libitum.*"[8]

In an interview widely reported in the press a few days later, Lincoln said, "I will suffer death before I will consent or will advise my friends to consent to any concession or compromise which looks like buying the privilege of taking possession of this government to which we have a constitutional right."[9]

Even so, Lincoln was still trying to soothe the South, yet not give ground on that important point. Serenaded by the U.S. Marine Band at a levee on March 1, Lincoln said, "I hope that if things shall go along as prosperously as I believe we all desire they may, I may have it my power to remove something of this misunderstanding—that I may be able to convince you, and the people of your section of the country, that we regard you as in all things being our equals—in all things entitled to the same respect and to the same treatment that we claim for ourselves—that we are in no wise disposed, if it were in our power, to oppress or deprive you of any of your rights under the constitution, or even narrowly to split hairs with you in regard to these rights."[10]

In the two weeks between his arrival in Washington and the eve of his inauguration, an uninterrupted flood of visitors streamed to his quarters in Willard's Hotel, most of them seeking office for themselves or their friends or relatives. The young reporter Henry Villard called such seekers "place-wanting cormorants."[11]

It appeared to Lincoln that, "Sitting here, where all the avenues to public patronage seem to come together in a knot, it does seem to me that our people are fast approaching the point where it can be said that seven-eighths of them were trying to find how to live at the expense of the other eighth."[12]

One seeker at the knot said, "The political caldron has been in a dreadful boil since I came." Accommodations were tight.

On the night before the inauguration Willard's had 1,500 guests booked in its 500 rooms.[13]

Sunday, March 4, was clear and somewhat blustery with a rasping dust-laden wind. The Capitol, where Lincoln was to be inaugurated, was in an unfinished condition, being outfitted with a new cast-iron dome. Derricks jutted from it and from both the House and Senate wings. From the eastern portico, a square temporary platform had been built with benches for distinguished inaugural spectators. Thousands of the less distinguished were already jammed in, waiting to witness the hopefully peaceful shift of power that had characterized this democracy.[14]

"Never since the formation of the government," the *New York Herald* wrote that morning, "was an inauguration day invested with so much of gloom.... the little cloud 'the size of a man's hand' which appeared in the Southern horizon on the morning after the 6th of November [the day Lincoln was elected] has grown and spread and become darker and darker, till now the whole Southern heavens are overcast, and tempest seems almost inevitable."

"The clouds at the North, too," the *Herald* wrote, "have been ever since gathering and growing blacker, and moving forward in dense masses charged with electricity. It only needs a word and a blow from one man to produce a collision and make the theory of the irrepressible conflict a fearful practical reality. A word alone may be sufficient to precipitate the antagonistic elements upon each other, but, followed up by a blow, the result is certain." No President of the United States, the *Herald* wrote, "has ever been inaugurated under such circumstances before."[15]

Charles Aldrich, a young westerner from Iowa, had traveled more than a hundred miles by stage from Webster City, then caught a train for the long ride to the inaugural. He too felt the gathering storm. "It was a solemn and almost gloomy time," he later wrote, "because there was a universal consciousness that we were just on the outbreak of war."[16]

A crowd had also gathered at a side entrance to Willard's Hotel. Near noon, an open barouche drove up and its only occupant stepped out—"a large, heavy, awkward-moving man," an observer said of him, "far advanced in years, short and thin gray hair, full face, plentifully seamed and wrinkled, head curiously inclined to the left shoulder." He wore "a low-crowned, broad brimmed silk hat, an immense white cravat like a poultice, thrusting the old-fashioned standing collar up to the ears, dressed in black throughout, with swallow-tail coat not of the newest style."

It was President Buchanan, sad faced and glad to be handing this impossible job to somebody else, even if it was a Republican. The past six weeks had been almost more than he could bear. He had arrived at the Willard's that morning to escort his successor to the Capitol. He entered the hotel and soon reappeared arm-in-arm with Lincoln as a band struck up "Hail to the Chief." The two took seats side-by-side in the barouche and it rolled slowly up the avenue toward the Capitol.[17]

True to his word, General Scott intended to make this change of guard an uninterrupted one. He had marshaled every soldier in the city into a force to protect the incoming president. More than 650 of them were hardened army regulars. A hand-picked body of men, sappers and miners from West Point, marched ahead of the presidential carriage. A squadron of District cavalry rode on either side of the barouche, and infantry companies of militia marched behind. The main force of the regulars under Scott himself flanked the movement on F Street.

Scott had stationed one battery of artillery near the Treasury building, and two outside the north entrance to the Capitol grounds. When he had assured Mather that he would blow to hell any secessionist who showed a head or finger, he had meant it. On the rooftops along the route he stationed militia sharp-shooters ready to open fire on any suspect movement below. At daybreak, following a rumor of a planned attempt to blow up the platform at the east portico, Scott stationed a battalion of District troops in a semicircle around the foot of the steps.[18]

At the Capitol the inaugural party entered by the north door. They passed through a narrow corridor bracketed by a high board fence guarded by marines, to the Senate chamber across the rotunda from the east portico. There they watched as Hannibal Hamlin took the oath as vice president.[19]

Just before Lincoln appeared on the platform on the east portico, a file of soldiers marched in front and moved slowly through the crowd. Their bayonets could be seen, cold and steely, jutting above the heads of the people. Charles Aldrich, watching from his vantage point, understood that several hundred other men armed with revolvers were scattered in the crowd to protect the president. [20]

At last Lincoln stepped onto the east portico, tall and gaunt, towering above all around him. He was wearing a black suit coat and black pantaloons, a black tie under a turned-down collar, a black vest, and the tall black hat that exaggerated his great height. His hand gripped a long ebony gold-headed cane. White-haired Oregon Senator Edward Baker, Lincoln's long-time friend and political ally—for whom his deceased son was named—introduced him to the crowd. At the front of the platform was a table holding a Bible and a pitcher of water. Lincoln stood the cane in a corner of the railing, but was momentarily perplexed about where to put his hat. After a brief, uncertain moment, Douglas took it and held it.

Lincoln put on his reading glasses, drew out the carefully crafted manuscript, and began to speak in his high-pitched but clear, distinct, and resonant voice.[21]

"Fellow citizens of the United States," he began. He did not know exactly who that now included. But he wanted immediately to reassure the seceded South that he still viewed them that way. He proclaimed, as he had repeatedly said in nearly all of his published speeches, "I have no purpose, directly or indirectly, to interfere with the institution of slavery in the States where it exists. I believe I have no lawful right to do so, and I have no inclination to do so."

He wanted to "press upon the public attention" the most conclusive possible evidence that "the property, peace and security of no section are to be in anywise endangered by the now incoming Administration." All the protection consistent "with the Constitution and the laws" that can be given, will be "cheerfully given . . . when lawfully demanded, for whatever cause—as cheerfully to one section, as to another," including, he said, enforcement of the Fugitive Slave Law.

"I now enter," Lincoln said, "upon the same task [as the fifteen presidents before him] for the brief constitutional term of four years, under great and peculiar difficulty. A disruption of the Federal Union heretofore only menaced, is now formidably attempted."

He said, "I hold, that in contemplation of universal law, and the Constitution, the Union of these States is perpetual. Perpetuity is implied, if not expressed, in the fundamental law of all national governments. It is safe to assert that no government proper, ever had a provision in its organic law for its own termination."

It therefore followed, Lincoln said, that "no State, upon its own mere motion, can lawfully get out of the Union—that *resolves* and *ordinances* to that effect are legally void; and that acts of violence, within any State or States, against the authority of the United States, are insurrectionary or revolutionary."

Therefore, Lincoln said, "in view of the Constitution and the laws, the Union is unbroken," and that he was enjoined "to the extent of my ability" to faithfully execute those laws in all the states. This he would do as "a simple duty on my part," and he trusted his doing so "will not be regarded as a menace, but only as the declared purpose of the Union that it *will* constitutionally defend, and maintain itself.

"In doing this," he said, "there needs to be no bloodshed or violence; and there shall be none, unless it be forced upon the national authority." He vowed he would use the power entrusted to him "to hold, occupy, and possess the property, and places belonging to the government, and to collect the duties and imposts; but beyond what may be necessary for these objects, there will be no invasion—no using of force against, or among the people anywhere."

He said, "Plainly, the central idea of secession, is the essence of anarchy," and when the principle of the rule of the majority is rejected, "anarchy, or despotism in some form, is all that is left." One section of our country, Lincoln said, "believes slavery is *right* and ought to be extended, while the other believes it is wrong, and ought not to be extended. This is the only substantial dispute." But physically, he said, "we cannot separate. We cannot remove our respective sections from each other, nor build an impassable wall between them." Unlike a divorced man and wife, the two sections "cannot but remain face to face; and intercourse, either amicable or hostile, must continue between them. Is it possible then to make that intercourse more advantageous, or more satisfactory, *after* separation than *before*? ... Suppose you go to war, you cannot fight always; and when, after much loss on both sides, and no gain on either, you cease fighting, the identical old questions, as to terms of intercourse, are again upon you."

Lincoln urged the South to "think calmly and *well,* upon this whole subject. Nothing valuable can be lost by taking time."

Then he ended with this coda:

In *your* hands, my dissatisfied fellow countrymen, and not in *mine,* is the momentous issue of civil war. The government will not assail *you.* You can have no conflict, without being yourselves the aggressors. *You* have no oath registered in Heaven to destroy the government, while *I* shall have the most solemn one to "preserve, protect and defend" it.

I am loth to close. We are not enemies, but friends. We must not be enemies. Though passion may have strained, it must not break our bonds of affection. The mystic chords of memory, stretching from every battlefield, and patriot grave, to every living heart and hearthstone, all over this broad land, will yet swell the chorus of the Union, when again touched, as surely they will be, by the better angels of our nature.[22]

It was an apt ending for a man whom one reporter said "always touched sympathetic chords."[23]

When Lincoln finished, Chief Justice Taney, his frail figure enveloped in his black robes, looking to one observer like "a galvanized corpse" and dwarfed by this long western giant, administered the oath of office. Lincoln kissed the Bible, and the dignitaries on the platform rose and slowly filed back into the Capitol, none of them knowing whether to peace or to war.[24]

It was likely that Henry Watterson, a young Southern newsman covering the inaugural, was thinking what most of the South was thinking when he said of the inaugural address, "To me it meant war."[25]

It was soon apparent to Lincoln that the tracks he had hoped to pick up after he came to Washington were rapidly taking him where he didn't want to go, a destination he found unbelievable.

The tracks were leading to a Union fort called Sumter in South Carolina's Charleston Harbor. A ring of cannon, primed to fire, had been positioned and leveled on the fort and its small undermanned United States army garrison commanded by Major Robert Anderson. But for the Confederacy to take it by force and cannon fire meant starting a war. To Lincoln giving it up was to lose everything. He had hardly been inaugurated when he learned that the flash point for a Union-shattering explosion was closer than he thought, much closer. The very first paper put into his hands after he was sworn in was a letter from Major Anderson, saying that the garrison's provisions would be exhausted before an expedition could be sent to relieve them.[26]

Lincoln called his fire-new cabinet into session and put three questions to General Scott:

"1st To what point of time can Major Anderson maintain his position at Fort Sumpter, without fresh supplies or reinforcement?

"2d. Can you, with all the means now in your control, supply or re-inforce Fort Sumpter within that time?

"3d If not, what amount of means and of what description, in addition to that already at your control, would enable you to supply and reinforce that fortress within the time?"

Scott soon answered, (1) "He has hard bread, flour & rice for about 26 days, & salt meat...for about 48....How long he could hold out...cannot be answered with absolute accuracy. (2) "No: Not within many months." (3) "A fleet of war vessels & transports, 5,000 additional regular troops & 20,000 volunteers.... would require new acts of congress & from six to eight months."[27]

This was a depressing answer with unreasonable parameters. But by the end of March, Lincoln had decided to attempt to re-provision Anderson anyway. He ordered Secretary of the Navy Gideon Welles to mount an expedition "to move by sea," and to "be got ready to sail as early as the 6th of April next."

The steam warships *Pocahontas* at Norfolk, *Pawnee* at Washington, and the revenue cutter *Harriet Lane* in New York were ordered to prepare to steam to Charleston at the head of a small fleet with a month's worth of stores. The expedition was to carry two hundred soldiers in the event the garrison at Fort Sumter needed to be relieved or reinforced.[28]

Lincoln's cabinet was split on sending the expedition.[29] But Lincoln had the final word; the expedition would go. He had pledged in his inaugural to hold, occupy, and possess the property of the government. There was little other choice.

"Hoping still that you will be able to sustain yourself till the 11th or 12th," Secretary of War Simon Cameron wrote Anderson on April 4, and "finding your flag flying...[it] will attempt to provision you; and in case the effort is resisted, will endeavor to reinforce you." It was a message that would never reach the beleaguered garrison.[30]

Lincoln also sent a state department emissary to inform South Carolina Governor Francis Pickens of his intention—that there would be an attempt to supply Fort Sumter with provisions only, and that, if such an attempt was not resisted, there would be no effort to throw in men, arms, or ammunition.[31]

Lincoln was in a pressure cooker. He was now thinking that the agonies he was going through were "so great that could I have anticipated them, I would not have believed it possible to survive them."[32] The pressure on the new administration, Indiana congressman George W. Julian wrote, was "utterly unprecedented and beggared all description." It was "a sort of epidemic," that at the time "perfectly appalled" Lincoln, gave him no relief, "but pursued him remorselessly night and day."[33]

Asked what his policy was, Lincoln said, "I have none. I pass my life in preventing the storm from blowing down the tent, and I drive in pegs as fast as they are pulled up."[34]

It was still difficult for Lincoln to believe all this was happening, that the Union really was dissolving. Wasn't there any reservoir of resistance to this in the South? William Seward believed there was strong Union sentiment still, even in South Carolina. Lincoln sent his friend Stephen A. Hurlbut to Charleston to see if it was so, but Hurlbut reported that it wasn't. Attorney James Louis Petigru, one of the few remaining Unionists in the state, along with others, told Hurlbut that the secessionists had an iron grip, that there were no Union people there. "There was no mistaking the entire unanimity and earnestness of the secession sentiment," Hurlbut told Lincoln.[35]

On April 1, William Seward wrote to the president, believing still in his heart that he, and not Lincoln, ought to be making a policy and implementing it. The gist of his letter was that there must be a policy and that someone must "pursue and direct it incessantly. Either the President must do it himself...or Devolve it on some member of his Cabinet." He assured Lincoln, "I neither seek to evade nor assume responsibility." But it was implied in his letter that he hoped for such responsibility. Lincoln quickly disabused Seward about what was required and who was to do it. "I must do it," he made Seward understand.[36] The question of who was running the show was emphatically answered. Lincoln was to be the boss of this administration, such as it was.

The situation quickly rushed to a climax. Before the Union fleet could assemble outside Charleston Harbor, the new Confederate government, now running things and getting no satisfactory pledge from Anderson to surrender, opened fire on the hapless fort at 4:30 A.M. on April 12. Two days later Anderson surrendered.

The fat was finally in the fire. For Lincoln it was either fight, or accept the rebellion as a fait accompli and do as Horace Greeley had suggested in December 1860: "If the cotton states shall become satisfied that they can do better out of the Union than in it, we insist on letting them go in peace....We hope never to live in a Republic whereof one section is pinned to another by bayonets."[37]

Neither did Lincoln want anything to do with bayonets. But he couldn't let the cotton states go, either. On April 15, he issued a proclamation: "Whereas the laws of the United States have been for some time past, and now are opposed, and the execution thereof obstructed...by combinations too powerful to be suppressed by the ordinary course of judicial proceedings, or by the powers vested in the Marshals by law....I...hereby do call forth, the militia of the several States of the Union, to the aggregate number of seventy-five thousand, in order to suppress said combinations, and to cause the laws to be duly executed."[38]

When this call for 75,000 militia went out to march against the South, four angry border states—Virginia, North Carolina, Tennessee, and Arkansas—set in motion ordinances of secession. This for them was coercion, and it was unendurable. Soon they would be joining their sisters, the seven original deep-South states, in the new Confederacy now rushing to arms. "The days come and go," the writer-poet Henry Wadsworth Longfellow wrote in his journal, "with a trouble in the air, and in the hearts of men." The times, he mourned, "have such a gunpowder flavor."[39]

Disunion and civil war—which both Lincoln and Douglas had fought for so long to prevent—had come. The road had not only been long, but contentious, and its end calamitous. It was the last thing either man had wanted.

Twilight of the Little Giant

IMMEDIATELY AFTER the firing on Fort Sumter and after what appeared to be an irreversible plunge into civil war, George Ashmun, the congressman from Massachusetts who had chaired Lincoln's nominating convention in the Wigwam, wanted to do one more important thing for this novice president.

He felt the situation "was one which demanded prompt action and the cordial support of the whole people of the North" across the political spectrum. He must somehow rally Douglas behind this man whom the Little Giant had fought from platform to platform and stump to stump in Illinois for a quarter of a century. He was the leader of the Democracy, the opposition, the one man who might rally it to Lincoln's side.

Ashmun went to Douglas and said he "desired him to go with me at once to the President, and make a declaration of his determination to sustain him in the needful measures which the exigency of the hour demanded to put down the rebellion." At first Douglas would have none of it. He told Ashmun, "Mr. Lincoln has dealt harshly with me, in removing some of my friends from office, and I don't know as he wants my advice or aid."

But Ashmun would not be put off. He finally persuaded the Little Giant to go with him to the White House.

"We fortunately found Mr. Lincoln alone," Ashmun later recounted, "and upon my stating the errand on which we had come, he was most cordial in his welcome." The president took from a drawer and read to the two men the draft of the proclamation for the 75,000 volunteers to serve three months to put down the rebellion. The proclamation also summoned Congress to a special session on July 4. Lincoln said he intended to issue it the next morning.

When the reading ended, Douglas said, "Mr. President, I cordially concur in every word of that document, except that instead of a call for 75,000 men I would make it 200,000. You do not know the dishonest purposes of those men [the rebels] as well as I do." He turned to a map that hung at one end of the president's room. In detail he pointed to the principal strategic points he thought ought to be strengthened at once—Washington itself, Fortress Monroe at Hampton Roads in Virginia, Harpers Ferry on the Baltimore and Ohio Railroad at the confluence of the Shenandoah and Potomac Rivers, and Cairo in his and Lincoln's Illinois. Turning strategist, Douglas enlarged at length on the "firm, warlike footing" he believed the situation demanded.

Lincoln listened intently to the Little Giant. This seemed to Ashmun more even than he had hoped for. "I venture to say," he indeed did say, "that no two men in the United States parted that

night with a more cordial feeling of a united, friendly, and patri-
otic purpose than Mr. Lincoln and Mr. Douglas."

The meeting lasted two hours. When it ended, again at Ashmun's urging Douglas wrote out a dispatch for the Associated
Press. In it he said, "Mr. Douglas called on the President this
evening and had an interesting conversation on the present condition of the country. The substance of the conversation was that
while Mr. Douglas was unalterably opposed to the administration on all its political issues, he was prepared to sustain the
President in the exercise of his constitutional functions to preserve the Union, and maintain the government and defend the
Federal capital." In his dispatch, Douglas called for a firm policy and prompt action. "The capital of our country was in danger," he said, "and must be defended at all hazards, and at any
expense of men and money." He said he "spoke of the present
and future without reference to the past."[1]

This was not the last thing Douglas would do for Lincoln.
Their state must rally behind his erstwhile rival in this life or
death moment for the Union. In late April, he returned to Illinois. When word came down that he would be in Springfield on
the 25th to address a joint session of the legislature, that he was
ready with a comprehensive statement of his position, the capital—and all the North—waited in a state of high anticipation.

The hall of the House of Representatives in Springfield was
packed that night. When the Little Giant rose to speak, as he
had so many times in his career, applause rocked the hall. His
message was that secession was unjustifiable and it was treason,
and all men, whatever their party, must support the government
to put it down.

"For the first time since the adoption of the Federal constitution," he said, "a widespread conspiracy exists to destroy the

best government the sun of heaven ever shed its rays upon. Hostile armies are now marching upon the Federal capital, with a view of planting a revolutionary flag upon its dome; seizing the national archives; taking captive the president elected by the votes of the people, in the hands of secessionists and disunionists. A war of aggression and of extermination is being waged against the government established by our fathers. The boast has gone forth by the secretary of war of this revolutionary government, that on the first day of May the revolutionary flag shall float from the walls of the capitol at Washington, and that on the fourth day of July the revolutionary army shall hold possession of the Hall of Independence in Philadelphia."

The question this presents, Douglas said, "is whether we will wait for the enemy to carry out his boast of making war upon our soil; or whether we will rush as one man to the defence of the government and its capital, to defend it from the hands of all assailants who have threatened to destroy it!"

Douglas said, sadly, that he had tried to prevent all this. "So long as there was a hope of peaceful solution," he said, "I prayed and implored for compromise. I can appeal to my countrymen with confidence that I have spared no effort, omitted no opportunity to adapt a peaceful solution of all these troubles, and thus restore peace, happiness and fraternity to this country. When all propositions of peace fail, there is but one course left for the patriot, and that is to rally under that flag which has waved over the Capitol from the days of Washington, and around the government established by Washington, Jefferson, Hamilton and their compeers.

"My friends," Douglas said finally, "I can say no more. To discuss these topics is the most painful duty of my life. It is with a sad heart—with a grief that I have never before experienced, that I have to contemplate this fearful struggle; but I believe in my conscience that it is a duty we owe to ourselves and our children, and our God, to protect this government and that flag from every assailant, be he who he may."

Douglas was not feeling well. He had always, in his life, struggled with illness. Now, exhausted by the strain of impending war, of travel, and of speaking, he checked into the Tremont House in Chicago to fight that old assailant once again. This time he would lose. A severe attack of rheumatism deprived him of the use of his arms. Then he fell gravely ill. Typhoid seemed to set in, and an ulcerated sore throat and jaundice. It was all too much. After a month-long struggle, he died on June 3. He had just turned forty-eight years old. At least when death came, it came in his beloved Illinois.

Church bells tolled the unhappy news and all business was suspended. Flags were lowered to half-mast and crepe hung from hundreds of homes. The young man in Springfield who had told his diary about Lincoln's farewell for Washington in February now wrote: "The providence of God has today brought about an event that fills a nation with sorrow; and a great people mourns the death of a gifted statesman, a wise senator, a patriot and a great man. Stephen Arnold Douglas is no more."

On June 7, the day of Douglas's funeral, businesses again shut down and stores and public buildings were dressed in black. Except for a single cannon, roaring at half-hour intervals, the day, a Sabbath, was still. In Springfield hearts were sad, and the sorrow was non-partisan.[2]

In Washington the White House was shrouded in mourning. Only Lincoln, perhaps, knew what this loss of his longtime friend and foe was to him personally, and to the country. However he felt, for the first time in his political life he would be without Douglas.

As Lincoln faced the future without the Little Giant, he told Lot M. Morrill, the new U.S. senator from Maine: "I don't know but that God has created some one man great enough to comprehend the whole of this stupendous crisis and transaction from beginning to end, and endowed him with sufficient wisdom to manage and direct it. I confess I do not fully understand, and foresee it all. But I am placed here where I am obliged to the best of my poor ability to deal with it. And that being the case I can only go just as fast as I can see how to go."[3]

But there he was, Henry Rankin later wrote, "a tall, homely gentle, strong man, heroic and sad," come "from the valley of the Father of Waters," to take "the helm of state in time of revolution."[4] He was the living half of that remarkable tandem of Lincoln and Douglas in which he had been tried and tempered in the heat of the most intense political fire.

Because he had been so tried and tempered—and had triumphed—he was perhaps after all, that one man great enough.

IN APPRECIATION

Writing a book, particularly a work of history, is at the same time one of the loneliest of professional callings, but of necessity also one of the most help-filled. It calls for endless hours alone with a word processor or typewriter or a pen or pencil, sitting down or standing up—however it is you operate. But it also requires help upon help of all kinds from many sources.

Good editors are absolutely essential for putting a book together. For this book I again have had the help and comfort of three outstanding ones. I have been fortunate, falling twice into the hands of editors at Harcourt; this is my second book for them. This time the manuscript profited enormously from the attention of senior editor Jenna Johnson, whose very careful and sensitive reading helped separate the chaff from the wheat. Waiting in the wings—as he was in my first book for Harcourt (*Surviving the Confederacy*)—was David Hough who, with copy editor Amy Root, went over what Jenna and I had produced with a fine-toothed comb, pulling at the snags, constantly doing so many little things to make the book better. I can't thank that trio enough. They have done a wonderful job helping make this book what it is.

Three great Lincoln scholars and historians read the manuscript and offered invaluable suggestions—Edwin Cole Bearss, a walking encyclopedia of virtually every aspect of the American past, and Frank Williams and Harold Holzer, two of the most esteemed of Lincoln scholars. Their advice and suggestions, which I have eagerly embraced, and their help and friendship—not only in this, but over the years—have been treasures to me in my professional life.

A work of history also calls for extended time in libraries. No historian can write a book without libraries and archives and librarians and archivists. This book has profited from them enormously. It is perhaps, in part, a generational thing that the Internet seems to be the point of first reference for those far younger than I. When my grandkids begin to think research they will doubtless think Internet first. But it isn't and can't be the first place a historian—particularly one of my age—thinks to go for information. Libraries and archives continue to be my frontline—and any historian's, young or old—for accurate research.

I am particularly indebted for this book to the librarians and archivists at the Abraham Lincoln Presidential Library in Springfield, Illinois. There I had the benefit of the expertise of Thomas F. Schwartz, the Illinois State Historian, and his estimable staff. In particular I want to thank Kathryn M. Harris, the library services director, Dennis E. Suttles, the genealogical research librarian, Jan Perone and her staff in the newspaper division, and Glenna Schroeder-Lein, of the manuscripts division.

As I have in every book I have written since living in Texas these past thirteen years, I must thank the staffs at the three great university libraries in the Dallas-Fort Worth metroplex—Texas Christian, Southern Methodist, and the University of Texas at Arlington. As ever, their collections have been invaluable and their librarians indispensable. The staff in the Prints and Photographs Division of the Library of Congress was also of great help in collecting photos for the book. Two librarians at the Arlington public library have been particular godsends—as always: Priscilla Cardwell, the interlibrary loan librarian, and Trudi Ensey.

No end of appreciation is also due my literary agent, Mike Hamilburg, and his invaluable associate, Joanie Kern. And finally, there has been my wife, Kathleen Lively, always there, waiting to welcome me back from my daily visits to the nineteenth century with an indulgent smile and support without end.

For all of these wonderful people, and for others too many to list, my sincerest thanks.

NOTES

Each of these notes lists a short summary of the source referenced—the author or editor's last name, short title of the work, and page or pages cited. The full listings are presented in alphabetical order under Sources Cited, which follows this section.

Prologue: The Uncoiling of the Serpent

1 The plastered ambiance is described in the *Illinois State Register,* 15 December 1836, in Baringer, *Lincoln's Vandalia,* 88–89.
2 From the *Illinois House Journal,* quoted in Miers, *Lincoln Day by Day,* 1:65.
3 Lincoln, *Collected Works,* 1:75n.
4 Quoted in Winkle, *The Young Eagle,* 253.
5 Lincoln, *Collected Works,* 7:281.
6 Ibid., 1:74–75.

Chapter 1: The Dark and Bloody Ground

1 Kinkaid, *The Wilderness Road,* 32.
2 Speed, *The Wilderness Road,* 25.
3 Ibid., 41.
4 Whitney, *Lincoln the Citizen,* 4.
5 Kinkaid, *The Wilderness Road,* 186.
6 Channing, *Kentucky,* 3.
7 Arnold, *The Life of Abraham Lincoln,* 14, 15–16; Warren, *Lincoln's Parentage and Childhood,* 8.
8 Whitney, *Lincoln the Citizen,* 33.
9 For this description I am indebted to Wilson and Davis, *Herndon's Informants,* 5, 37, 67; Tarbell, *Early Life of Abraham Lincoln,* 233; and Wilson, *Lincoln Among His Friends,* 24.

10 Wilson and Davis, *Herndon's Informants*, 5, 37, 454.

11 Barton, *The Paternity of Abraham Lincoln*, 272–73.

12 The wedding and infare are described in Tarbell, *Abraham Lincoln and His Ancestors*, 75, 89; Baber, *Nancy Hanks*, 84; and Warren, *Lincoln's Parentage and Childhood*, 69–70, 71.

13 Beveridge, *Abraham Lincoln*, 1:3, 3n, 4.

14 Quoted in Wilson, *Lincoln Among His Friends*, 20.

15 This description of the Knob Creek place is an amalgam stitched from Tarbell, *Abraham Lincoln and His Ancestors*, 99, 102; Miers, *Lincoln Day by Day*, 1:4; Wilson and Davis, *Herndon's Informants*, 257; and Beveridge, *Abraham Lincoln*, 1:26.

16 Hitchcock, *Nancy Hanks*, 57.

17 Wilson, *Lincoln Among His Friends*, 22.

Chapter 2: The Hoosier Years

1 This picture of Indiana when it became a state is taken from Levering, *Historic Indiana*, 141, 142.

2 Quoted in Thomas, *Abraham Lincoln*, 9. See also Wilson and Davis, *Herndon's Informants*, 111.

3 Angle, *"Here I Have Lived,"* 10.

4 Lincoln, *Collected Works*, 1:386.

5 Wilson, *Lincoln Among His Friends*, 22.

6 Ibid., 29.

7 Barton, *The Paternity of Abraham Lincoln*, 273.

8 Warren, *Lincoln's Youth*, 54, 55.

9 Wilson, *Lincoln Among His Friends*, 23, 24.

10 Wilson and Davis, *Herndon's Informants*, 85.

11 Wilson, *Lincoln Among His Friends*, 24.

12 Ibid., 25.

13 The description of Sarah is stitched from Herndon and Weik, *Herndon's Life of Lincoln*, 29–30; Wilson and Davis, *Herndon's Informants*, 113; and Tarbell, *Abraham Lincoln and His Ancestors*, 128.

14 Wilson, *Lincoln Among His Friends*, 25.

15 Warren, *Lincoln's Youth*, 37–38; McLaren, "Reminiscences of Pioneer Life in Illinois, 1830–1860," no page number.

16 Wilson, "There I Grew Up," 98, 10l; Dennis Hanks in Wilson and Davis, *Herndon's Informants*, 40.

17 Wilson, *Lincoln Among His Friends*, 28.

18 Lincoln, *Collected Works*, 4:62.

19 Wilson and Davis, *Herndon's Informants*, 107, 108, 104.

20 Ibid., 120, 503.

21 Ibid., 108, 113.

22 Ibid., 108, 120.

23 Ibid., 132, 114, 241.

24 Eggleston, *The First of the Hoosiers,* 87.

25 Lincoln, *Collected Works,* 4:62, 3:511.

26 Wilson and Davis, *Herndon's Informants,* 106–7.

27 Wilson, *Lincoln Among His Friends,* 26; Wilson and Davis, *Herndon's Informants,* 41.

28 Nicolay and Hay, *Abraham Lincoln,* 1:36.

29 Winkle, *The Young Eagle,* 18.

30 Tarbell, *Abraham Lincoln and His Ancestors,* 149.

31 Moses, *Illinois, Historical and Statistical,* 1:233.

32 The listing of books Lincoln read in his growing-up years is taken variously from Wilson and Davis, *Herndon's Informants,* 107, 112; Tarbell, *Abraham Lincoln and His Ancestors,* 145–46, 149; Wilson, *What Lincoln Read,* 20, 23–24, 28, 30–31; Beveridge, *Abraham Lincoln,* 1:75.

33 Lincoln, *Collected Works,* 1:1.

34 Joseph C. Richardson in Wilson and Davis, *Herndon's Informants,* 119.

35 Sarah Bush Johnston in ibid., 106, 107; Scripps, *Life of Abraham Lincoln,* 55.

36 Wilson and Davis, *Herndon's Informants,* 42, 104, 105, 107, 109.

37 Wilson, *Lincoln Among His Friends,* 30.

38 Ibid., 29.

39 Ibid., 30.

40 Miers, *Lincoln Day by Day,* 1:13.

41 Angle, *"Here I Have Lived,"* 33–34.

42 The riding the freshet image is by Lincoln's friend William G. Greene in Wilson and Davis, *Herndon's Informants,* 12.

43 Lincoln, *Collected Works,* 4:63–64.

44 Miers, *Lincoln Day by Day,* 1:15.

Chapter 3: New Salem

1 Moses, *Illinois, Historical and Statistical,* 1: 17, 18, 282; Tillson, *A Woman's Story of Pioneer Illinois,* vix.

2 Moses, *Illinois, Historical and Statistical,* 1:18–19; Stuart, *Three Years in North America,* 369.

3 Moses, *Illinois, Historical and Statistical,* 1:268, 269, 270.

4 Scripps, *Life of Abraham Lincoln,* 41; Ford, *A History of Illinois,* 1:142–43; Blanchard, *History of Illinois,* 46; Johanssen, *Stephen A. Douglas,* 36–37; Oliver, *Eight Months in Illinois,* 97; Stuart, *Three Years in North America,* 2:399.

5 Speed, *Reminiscences of Abraham Lincoln,* 16.

6 Winkle, *The Young Eagle,* 52.

7 Angle, *"Here I Have Lived,"* 4; Nicolay and Hay, *Abraham Lincoln,* 1:59; Wilson and Davis, *Herndon's Informants,* 202.

8   This three-paragraph description of New Salem and its demographics owes much to Reep, *Lincoln at New Salem*, 9, 11, 13, 15, 17, 128; Thomas, *Lincoln's New Salem*, 24, 38, 45, 50; and Wilson and Davis, *Herndon's Informants*, 73.

9   What Lincoln looked like is distilled from Wilson and Davis, *Herndon's Informants*, 72, 170, 201; and Wilson, *Lincoln Among His Friends*, 91, 175.

10 Herndon and Weik, *Herndon's Life of Lincoln*, 490.

11 Lincoln, *Collected Works*, 1:320; Fehrenbacher, *Recollected Words of Abraham Lincoln*, 90, 92, 126; Mearns, *Lincoln Papers*, 1:151.

12 Wilson, *Honor's Voice*, 54, 55, 67.

13 Wilson and Davis, *Herndon's Informants*, 11, 161.

14 Ibid., 13, 18, 73.

15 Winkle, *The Young Eagle*, 52, 55.

16 Lincoln, *Collected Works*, 4:65; Herndon and Weik, *Herndon's Life of Lincoln*, 90; Pratt, *The Personal Finances of Abraham Lincoln*, 14. According to Lincoln historian Thomas F. Schwartz, how, when, and whether Lincoln paid off the entire debt is still a puzzle. For a detailed discussion of this, see Schwartz's *Finding the Missing Link: A Promissory Note and the Lost Town of Pappsville.*

17 Lincoln, *Collected Works*, 4:65.

18 Nicolay and Hay, *Abraham Lincoln*, 1:78n.

19 Thomas, *Lincoln's New Salem*, 98.

20 Wilson and Davis, *Herndon's Informants*, 7, 91.

21 Ibid., 73, 80, 369, 370, 386, 402.

22 Wilson, *What Lincoln Read*, 42–44; Scripps, *Life of Abraham Lincoln*, 66n.

23 Wilson, *Honor's Voice*, 61–62; Wilson, *What Lincoln Read*, 42.

24 Reep, *Lincoln at New Salem*, 31–32

25 Benjamin F. Irwin in Wilson and Davis, *Herndon's Informants*, 353.

26 Herndon and Weik, *Herndon's Life of Lincoln*, 77–78.

27 Lincoln, *Collected Works*, 1:510.

Chapter 4: "Politics"

1   Wilson, *Lincoln Among His Friends*, 27.

2   J. Rowan Herndon in Wilson and Davis, *Herndon's Informants*, 7–8; Nicolay and Hay, *Abraham Lincoln*, 1:103n; Logan, "Stephen T. Logan Talks About Lincoln," 2.

3   This reputedly first public political speech by Lincoln is reported in Johns, *Personal Recollections of Early Decatur*, 60–61.

4   Wilson, *Lincoln Among His Friends*, 29.

5   *History of Fayette County*, 31.

6   Lincoln, *Collected Works*, 8–9.

7   Abner Y. Ellis in Wilson and Davis, *Herndon's Informants*, 171.

8   Nicolay, *An Oral History of Abraham Lincoln*, 34.

9   Herndon and Weik, *Herndon's Life of Lincoln*, 85–86; Thomas, *Lincoln's New Salem*, 84–85.

10 Herndon and Weik, *Herndon's Life of Lincoln*, 86; Wilson and Davis, *Herndon's Informants*, 171.

11 Pease, *Illinois Election Returns*, 262. For a discussion of New Salem's Whig coloration see *Lincoln Lore*, No. 1715, January 1981, pp. 1–3.

12 Herndon and Weik, *Herndon's Life of Lincoln*, 103–4.

13 Rice, *Reminiscences of Abraham Lincoln*, xix.

14 Herndon and Davis, *Herndon's Informants*, 259.

15 Ibid., 8n, 8.

16 Pease, *Illinois Election Returns*, 275.

17 Wilson and Davis, *Herndon's Informants*, 254; Fehrenbacher, *Recollected Words of Abraham Lincoln*, 439.

18 Miers, *Lincoln Day by Day*. 1:41. For the idea that no tailor alive could perfectly fit cloth to Lincoln's frame see Wilson, *Lincoln Among His Friends*, 62.

Chapter 5: Vandalia

1 For a succinct history of the siting and fate of the capitol and new statehouse in Vandalia see Ross, *Historical Souvenir of Vandalia*, 9–13. The origins of Vandalia's name comes from Moses, *Illinois, Historical and Statistical*, 1:297.

2 French, "Men and Manners of the Early Days in Illinois," 71.

3 Douglas, *The Letters of Stephen A. Douglas*, 11.

4 Lincoln, *Collected Works*, 1:48.

5 Nicolay, *An Oral History of Abraham Lincoln*, 12.

6 Pease, *Illinois Election Returns*, 299.

7 Herndon and Weik, *Herndon's Life of Lincoln*, 138; Arnold, *The Life of Abraham Lincoln*, 50.

8 Wilson and Davis, *Herndon's Informants*, 476.

9 Herndon and Weik, *Herndon's Life of Lincoln*, 142.

10 Nicolay, *An Oral History of Abraham Lincoln*, 13.

11 Just how much log rolling and vote trading there was is open to some speculation. Most historians believe it was intense. But for a contrary opinion, see Davis, "I Shall Consider the Whole People of Sangamon My Constituents," 16–18.

12 Wilson quoted in Whitney, *Lincoln the Citizen*, 140.

13 *Sangamo Journal*, 28 January 1837, quoted in Mitgang, *Lincoln as They Saw Him*, 11.

Chapter 6: Death in Alton

1 This brief summary of party lines owes much to Winkle, *The Young Eagle*. 186–87.

2 Shakespeare, *As You Like It*, act 4. sc. 3, line 113.

3 Horton and Horton, *Slavery and the Making of America*, 139, 143–44.

4 Quoted in Harris, *The History of Negro Servitude in Illinois*, 63n–64n.

5 Horton and Horton, *Slavery and the Making of America,* 144; Tanner, *The Martyrdom of Lovejoy,* 19.

6 Lovejoy, *Memoir of Lovejoy,* 296–97; Tanner, *The Martyrdom of Lovejoy,* 22.

7 Lovejoy, *Memoir of Lovejoy,* 19, 23, 32, 37–38, 43; Simon, *Freedom's Champion,* 18–20; Tanner, *The Martyrdom of Lovejoy,* 21.

8 Lovejoy, *Memoir of Lovejoy,* 43, 60, 67; Simon, *Freedom's Champion,* 21–22, 24.

9 Tanner, *The Martyrdom of Lovejoy,* 23.

10 Ibid., 51.

11 Lovejoy, *Memoir of Lovejoy,* 136–37; Tanner, *The Martyrdom of Lovejoy,* 51–52.

12 Simon, *Freedom's Champion,* 45–48.

13 Lovejoy, *Memoir of Lovejoy,* 155–56.

14 Taylor, *Haunted Alton,* 20, 22; Simon, *Freedom's Champion,* 59.

15 Tanner, *The Martyrdom of Lovejoy,* 86–87.

16 Ibid., 100.

17 Quoted in Lovejoy, *Memoir of Lovejoy,* 230; Tanner, *The Martyrdom of Lovejoy,* 122.

18 Tanner, *The Martyrdom of Lovejoy,* 124; Lovejoy, *Memoir of Lovejoy,* 232.

19 Lovejoy, *Memoir of Lovejoy,* 250–51; Tanner, *The Martyrdom of Lovejoy,* 125, 128–29.

20 Lovejoy, *Memoir of Lovejoy,* 258–60.

21 The quoted descriptions of excitement are from Reynolds, *My Own Times,* 319.

22 Tanner, *The Martyrdom of Lovejoy,* 155; Lovejoy, *Memoir of Lovejoy,* 283–84; Simon, *Freedom's Champion,* 118–19, 123.

23 Tanner, *The Martyrdom of Lovejoy,* 155, 149–50.

24 Ibid., 150–51; Lovejoy, *Memoir of Lovejoy,* 290–91.

25 Tanner, *The Martyrdom of Lovejoy,* 156, 156n; Simon, *Freedom's Champion,* 130.

26 Tanner, *The Martyrdom of Lovejoy,* 151–52, Lovejoy, *Memoir of Lovejoy,* 291–92; Simon, *Freedom's Champion,* 133. In this description of the events of Lovejoy's death I have relied mainly on the eyewitness account of Tanner, who was one of the score of defenders in the warehouse.

27 Tanner, *The Martyrdom of Lovejoy,* 152; Simon, *Freedom's Champion,* 135.

28 Tanner, *The Martyrdom of Lovejoy,* 157, 160–61.

29 Putnam, "The Life and Services of Joseph Duncan," 160.

30 From Lincoln's Lyceum address in *Collected Works,* 1:109–12.

31 Simon, *Freedom's Champion,* 49.

32 *Sangamo Journal,* 28 October 1837.

Chapter 7: Springfield

1 Mitgang, *Lincoln as They Saw Him,* 12; Angle, "Here I Have Lived," 57.

2 Miers, *Lincoln Day by Day,* 1:77; Mitgang, *Lincoln as They Saw Him,* 11–13.

3 William Herndon quotes Lincoln along this line in Fehrenbacher, *Recollected Words of Abraham Lincoln,* 242.

4   This description of Stuart owes much to Winkle, *The Young Eagle,* 162, 164; and to Thomas, "Lincoln and the Courts," 68–69.

5   Basler, "James Quay Howard's Notes on Lincoln," 390.

6   Speed, *Reminiscences of Abraham Lincoln,* 21.

7   The quote is Lincoln's as remembered by Thomas Lewis, a Springfield lawyer and businessman, in Fehrenbacher, *Recollected Words of Abraham Lincoln,* 296. The rundown of his entry into law is from Lincoln's own brief biographical sketch in *Collected Works,* 4:65. The newspaper announcement of the partnership is in the *Sangamo Journal,* 22 April 1837.

8   The quotes are from Nicolay and Hay, *Abraham Lincoln,* 1:59, and Winkle, *The Young Eagle,* 30.

9   Moses, *Illinois, Historical and Statistical,* 1:27.

10 The quote about the lawyers is by Speed, in his *Reminiscences of Abraham Lincoln,* 20. The summary of Springfield's growth is from Winkle, *The Young Eagle,* 156, 157, 176, 216.

11 Angle, *"Here I Have Lived,"* 91–92.

12 Ibid., 92.

13 Ibid., 85, 93; Donald, *"We Are Lincoln Men,"* 40; King, *Lincoln's Manager,* 74.

14 This rundown on Joshua Speed owes much to Donald, *"We Are Lincoln Men,"* 30–33.

15 Speed, *Reminiscences of Abraham Lincoln,* 21–22. Speed also recounts this first meeting in a slightly varying version in Wilson and Davis, *Herndon's Informants,* 590. Speed said Lincoln came to his store carrying two saddlebags. Lincoln reminiscing on his move much later said that he carried everything to Springfield in a carpetbag. See Fehrenbacher, *Recollected Words of Abraham Lincoln,* 296.

16 This comparison of Speed and Lincoln and reasons for Lincoln's melancholy draws from Wilson, *Honor's Voice.* 245, 187.

17 Herndon and Weik, *Herndon's Life of Lincoln,* 473, xv.

18 Speed's further impressions of Lincoln are in Wilson and Davis, *Herndon's Informants,"* 498–99.

19 Lincoln, *Collected Works,* 1:77–78.

20 Wilson, *What Lincoln Read,* 47–48.

21 Wilson and Davis, *Herndon's Informants,* 59.

22 Angle, *"Here I Have Lived,"* 65.

23 Speed, *Reminiscences of Abraham Lincoln,* 23.

Chapter 8: Young Hickory

1   Herndon and Weik, *Herndon's Life of Lincoln,* 131.

2   Johnson, *Stephen A. Douglas,* 5.

3   Ibid., 24; Stevens, "Life of Stephen A. Douglas," 283; McConnell, "Recollections of Stephen A. Douglas," 41.

4   Johannsen, *Stephen A. Douglas,* 6.

5 *New York Times,* 2 August 1860.

6 Autobiographical Sketch in *The Letters of Stephen A. Douglas,* 57.

7 Flint, *Life of Stephen A. Douglas,* 21.

8 Douglas, Autobiographical Sketch in *The Letters of Stephen A. Douglas,* 58.

9 Sheahan, *Life of Stephen A. Douglas,* 6; Johannsen, *Stephen A. Douglas,* 9.

10 Douglas, Autobiographical Sketch in *The Letters of Stephen A. Douglas,* 58; Johannsen, *Stephen A. Douglas,* 10.

11 Douglas, Autobiographical Sketch in *The Letters of Stephen A. Douglas,* 58–59; Johannsen, *Stephen A. Douglas,* 11. The political "pole star" and "saint" analogy is from Stevens, "Life of Stephen A. Douglas," 270, 282.

12 Douglas, *The Letters of Stephen A. Douglas,* 59; and Johannsen, *Stephen A. Douglas,* 14–15.

13 Henry David Thoreau, quoted in Holbrook, "Why Did They Go Away?" 33.

14 Douglas, Autobiographical Sketch in *The Letters of Stephen A. Douglas,* 59; Capers, *Stephen A. Douglas,* 6.

15 Douglas, Autobiographical Sketch in *The Letters of Stephen A. Douglas,* 59, 60.

16 Ibid., 60, 61.

17 These encomiums to Illinois are from Stuart, *Three Years in North America,* 368–69, 372, 424.

18 Douglas, Autobiographical Sketch in *The Letters of Stephen A. Douglas,* 61.

19 Carr, *Stephen A. Douglas,* 7; Douglas, *The Letters of Stephen A. Douglas,* 3.

20 Flint, *Life of Stephen A. Douglas,* 17.

21 Pratt, "Stephen A. Douglas, Lawyer, Legislator, Register and Judge," part 1, p. 12.

22 Douglas, Autobiographical Sketch in *The Letters of Stephen A. Douglas,* 63.

23 Stevens, "Life of Stephen A. Douglas," 285; Johannsen, *Stephen A. Douglas,* 25.

24 Johannsen, *Stephen A. Douglas,* 23.

25 Douglas, Autobiographical Sketch in *The Letters of Stephen A. Douglas,* 64–65.

26 Douglas, *Letters of Stephen A. Douglas,* 12, 12n, 16–17, 12.

27 Quoted in Pratt, "Stephen A. Douglas, Lawyer, Legislator, Register and Judge," part 1, p. 12.

28 Stevens, "Life of Stephen A. Douglas," 298.

29 Douglas, *The Letters of Stephen A. Douglas,* 37.

30 Douglas, Autobiographical Sketch in ibid., 67–68.

31 Johnson, *Stephen A. Douglas,* 26.

32 Stevens, "Life of Stephen A. Douglas," 296.

33 *Sangamo Journal,* 18 April 1835.

34 Ibid., 3 February 1838.

35 Stevens, "Life of Stephen A. Douglas," 311; Sheahan, *Life of Stephen A. Douglas,* 34; Lorant, *The Glorious Burden,* 153.

36 Sheahan, *Life of Stephen A. Douglas,* 36–37; Stevens, "Life of Stephen A. Douglas," 317.

37 Miers, *Lincoln Day by Day,* 1:89.

38 Ibid., 93.

39 Pease, *Illinois Election Returns,* 109.
40 Lincoln, *Collected Works,* 1:159; Johannsen, *Stephen A. Douglas,* 73–74; Sheahan, *Life of Stephen A. Douglas,* 39.

Chapter 9: The Ballyhoo Campaign

1   Schlesinger, *History of American Presidential Elections,* 1:578.
2   Ibid., 584, 588.
3   Lorant, *The Glorious Burden,* 144.
4   In these descriptions of Harrison and Van Buren I have leaned on Freidel, *Our Country's Presidents,* 65, 66, 69–71; McPherson, *"To the Best of My Ability,"* 66, 72–74; Roseboom, *A History of Presidential Elections,* 114, 119; and Kunhardt, *The American President,* 91.
5   Wilson, *Honor's Voice,* 210.
6   Douglas L. Wilson describes Lincoln's anonymous "attack journalism" quite admirably in his excellent book, *Honor's Voice,* 298–302.
7   Miers, *Lincoln Day by Day,* 1:117–18; *Illinois State Register,* 12 October 1839.
8   Speed, *Reminiscences of Abraham Lincoln,* 23. Speed says the gauntlet was thrown one evening in December, but the first debates began November 19, followed by another round in late December. See Wilson and Davis, *Herndon's Informants,* 476; Herndon and Weik, *Herndon's Life of Lincoln,* 153–54.
9   "Tournament" is what Herndon called it in *Herndon's Life of Lincoln,* 154.
10 Miers, *Lincoln Day by Day,* 1:121.
11 *Illinois State Register,* 23 November 1839.
12 Wilson and Davis, *Herndon's Informants,* 181.
13 Rice, *Reminiscences of Abraham Lincoln,* 9, 19.
14 This capsule assessment of Calhoun is framed from descriptions by Herndon in Herndon and Weik, *Herndon's Life of Lincoln,* 98; and Hertz, *The Hidden Lincoln,* 79.
15 Lincoln, *Collected Works,* 1:155.
16 Ibid., 159, 159n, 158, 160. Also see Wilson, *Honor's Voice,* 200–1.
17 Lincoln, *Collected Works,* 1:178. The full text of Lincoln's December 26th speech runs for twenty pages in ibid., 159–79.
18 Wilson and Davis, *Herndon's Informants,* 181.
19 Kinkaid, *The Wilderness Road,* 217; Lorant, *The Glorious Burden,* 154.
20 Roseboom, *A History of Presidential Elections,* 120.
21 Schlesinger, *History of American Presidential Elections,* 1:678.
22 Quoted in Wilson, *Honor's Voice,* 203.
23 Roseboom, *A History of Presidential Elections,* 121; Kunhardt, *The American President,* 21; Lorant, *The Glorious Burden,* 158–60; McPherson, *"To the Best of My Ability,"* 76; Wilson, *Honor's Voice,* 213–14.
24 Kunhardt, *The American President,* 21; Lorant, *The Glorious Burden,* 165; Schlesinger, *History of American Presidential Elections,* 1:670.
25 Wead, *Diary,* 1.

26 Schlesinger, *History of American Presidential Elections,* 1:643.
27 This packaged image of Harrison is stitched from Kunhardt, *The American President,* 21; Roseboom, *A History of Presidential Elections,* 120; Freidel, *Our Country's Presidents,* 69; and Lorant, *The Glorious Burden,* 157–158.
28 Roseboom, *A History of Presidential Elections,* 120; Lorant, *The Glorious Burden,* 167; Freidel, *Our Country's Presidents,* 66,
29 Wilson, *Honor's Voice,* 203.
30 Speed, *Reminiscences of Abraham Lincoln,* 25.
31 Wilson, *Intimate Memories of Lincoln,* 120.
32 Lincoln, *Collected Works,* 1:184.
33 Ibid., 201; Miers, *Lincoln Day by Day,* 1:130.
34 Lincoln, *Collected Works,* 1:206.
35 Miers, *Lincoln Day by Day,* 134.
36 The hybrid phrase is borrowed from "Recollections of Lincoln: Three Letters of Intimate Friends," 7.
37 Miers, *Lincoln Day by Day,* 1:137.
38 Alexander, *A Political History of the State of New York,* 2:16; Ford, *A History of Illinois,* 1:311n; King, *Lincoln's Manager,* 42; Lorant, *The Glorious Burden,* 147–48; Roseboom, *A History of Presidential Elections,* 115.
39 Miers, *Lincoln Day by Day* 1:138; Tarbell, *The Life of Abraham Lincoln,* 1:166; Wilson, *Honor's Voice,* 212.
40 Moses, *Illinois Historical and Statistical,* 1:438.
41 Andrew S. Kirk in Wilson and Davis, *Herndon's Informants,* 602–3.
42 H. H. Hoagland in Ibid., 603,
43 *Illinois State Register,* 21 August 1840; Miers, *Lincoln Day by Day,* 1:142–43.
44 *Illinois State Register,* 16 October 1840.
45 Carr, *Stephen A. Douglas,* 11.
46 Winkle, *The Young Eagle,* 195; Elihu B. Washburne in Rice, *Reminiscences of Abraham Lincoln,* 10, 6–7.
47 Quoted in Roseboom, *A History of Presidential Elections,* 122.
48 Sheahan, *Life of Stephen A. Douglas,* 42–43.
49 Schlesinger, *History of American Presidential Elections,* 1:644, 672; Roseboom, *A History of Presidential Elections,* 122; Wilson and Davis, *Herndon's Informants,* 60–61.
50 Ibid., 169; Kunhardt, *The American President,* 22; Jones, "The Thirty-One-Day Presidency," 50, 52.
51 Kunhardt, *The American President,* 23; Ferris, *The Presidents,* 111.

Chapter 10: Lincoln in Love

1 Pond, "Intellectual New Salem in Lincoln's Day," 14.
2 Wilson, *Lincoln Among His Friends,* 35.
3 Wilson and Davis, *Herndon's Informants,* 91, 170.
4 Ibid., 443.

5   Wilson, *Honor's Voice*, 235.

6   McLaren, "Reminiscences of Pioneer Life in Illinois, 1830–1860," unnumbered page.

7   Wilson and Davis, *Herndon's Informants*, 534; Hammond, "Memories of the Rutledge Family of New Salem, Illinois," 3; and Reep, *Lincoln at New Salem*, 48–49.

8   Wilson and Davis, *Herndon's Informants*, 402–3; Wilson, *Honor's Voice*, 117–18.

9   Herndon and Weik, *Herndon's Life of Lincoln*, 112n.

10   Wilson and Davis, *Herndon's Informants*, 243, 250, 527. Lincoln's description of Mary Owens as a fair match for Falstaff is in *Collected Works*, 1:118.

11   Wilson and Davis, *Herndon's Informants*, 611, 601, 256.

12   Lincoln, *Collected Works*, 1:119.

13   This rundown on the background of the Todds and Edwardses and their establishment in Springfield borrows from Winkle, *The Young Eagle*, 161–163.

14   Ibid., 149, 165.

15   Donald, *"We Are Lincoln Men,"* 40,

16   James and Temple, *Mrs. Lincoln's Clothing*, 56, 63, 55, 64.

17   The general description of Mary—and Elizabeth's misgivings about a marriage with Lincoln—are from Helm, *Mary, Wife of Lincoln*, 55, 44–45, 84, 119; Wilson and Davis, *Herndon's Informants*, 443, 444; and Rankin, *Personal Recollections*, 160–61. For Mary's nickname see Wilson, *Honor's Voice*, 248.

18   Helm, *Mary, Wife of Lincoln*, 41. Also see Wilson, *Honor's Voice*, 216.

19   Herndon and Weik, *Herndon's Life of Lincoln*, 165, 166, 182. Herndon's and Mary's assessments of Lincoln's dancing skills are in Wilson, *Honor's Voice*, 216; and Helm, *Mary, Wife of Lincoln*, 74.

20   Johannsen, *Stephen A. Douglas*, 72–73.

21   For this chain of events leading to Lincoln's engagement to Mary I am indebted to Wilson, *Honor's Voice*, 217, 219–21.

22   Ibid., 221; Wilson, *Lincoln Before Washington*, 104.

23   Joshua Speed in Wilson and Davis, *Herndon's Informants*, 430.

24   Wilson, *Lincoln Before Washington*, 103; Wilson and Davis, *Herndon's Informants*, 477, 475, 133, 444.

25   Wilson and Davis, *Herndon's Informants*, 444.

26   Wilson, *Honor's Voice*, 235, 236, 284; Wilson and Davis, *Herndon's Informants*, 133, 475.

27   Lincoln, *Collected Works*, 1:228, 229.

28   Nicolay, *An Oral History of Abraham Lincoln*, 1.

29   Lincoln, *Collected Works*, 1:254n, 282.

30   Ibid., 289.

31   Wilson, *Honor's Voice*, 290.

32   Herndon and Weik, *Herndon's Life of Lincoln*, 179.

33   Wilson and Davis, *Herndon's Informants*, 251; Herndon and Weik, *Herndon's Life of Lincoln*, 180.

34 Temple, *Mrs. Mary Edwards Brown Tells Story of Lincoln's Wedding*, 3, 4.

35 This description of the Globe Tavern is distilled from Winkle, *The Young Eagle*, 219; Wilson, *Intimate Memories of Lincoln*, 61; Angle, *"Here I Have Lived*," 87; and Temple, *"The Taste Is in My Mouth*," 29.

36 Lincoln, *Collected Works*, 1:305. Anyone writing about Lincoln's Illinois years, and especially of his three problematic courtships, owes a great debt to the work of Douglas L. Wilson. I have drawn heavily, in this chapter particularly, on his three books, *Lincoln Before Washington, Honor's Voice*, and the landmark work, *Herndon's Informants*, edited with Rodney O. Davis.

Chapter 11: The Steam Engine in Breeches and the Engine that Knew No Rest

1 "Embrigglement," the word describing the Mary Todd fiasco is attributed to Lincoln's friend Jesse K. Dubois in "Recollections of Lincoln: Three Letters of Intimate Friends," 9.

2 Lincoln speaks of this "savoury remembrance" in a letter to Mary Speed on 27 September 1841, in Lincoln, *Collected Works*, 1:261

3 Ibid, 260.

4 Ibid., 279.

5 Herndon and Weik, *Herndon's Life of Lincoln*, 207–8; Miers, *Lincoln Day by Day*, 1:186.

6 *Illinois State Register*, 24 June 1842.

7 Carter, "Lincoln and Douglas as Lawyers," 223.

8 Wead, Diary, 8, 13–14.

9 Quoted in Pratt, "Stephen A. Douglas, Lawyer, Legislator, Register and Judge," part 2, 40.

10 Wead, Diary, 13; Carter, "Lincoln and Douglas as Lawyers," 224–25.

11 Faragher, *Sugar Creek: Life on the Illinois Prairie*, 153.

12 Wead, Diary, 13.

13 Quoted in Johannsen, *Stephen A. Douglas*, 120, 111.

14 Wead, Diary, 15.

15 Browning in U. S. Congress, *Addresses on the Death of Hon. Stephen A. Douglas*, 26–27.

16 Herndon and Weik, *Herndon's Life of Lincoln*, 304.

17 Lincoln, *Collected Works*, 1:306, 307.

18 Miers, *Lincoln Day by Day*, 1:203, 206; Lincoln, *Collected Works*, 1:319, 322.

19 Pease, *Illinois Election Returns*, 139.

20 Augustus K. Riggin in Wilson and Davis, *Herndon's Informants*, 603.

Chapter 12: Who Is James K. Polk?

1 Kunhardt, *The American President*, 211.

2 Freidel, *Our Country's Presidents*, 74.

3   Quoted in Lorant, *The Glorious Burden,* 171.
4   The grist for this description of Tyler is culled from McPherson, *"To the Best of My Ability,"* 78–79; see also Kunhardt, *The American President,* 211.
5   Kunhardt, *The American President,* 211.
6   Schlesinger, *History of American Presidential Elections,* 1:664.
7   Ibid., 770.
8   Quoted in Kunhardt, *The American President,* 212.
9   Dickens, *American Notes,* 125.
10 Schlesinger, *History of American Presidential Elections,* 1:749.
11 Ibid., 760.
12 This chain of events is admirably told in Roseboom, *A History of Presidential Elections,* 127–29, from which I have crafted my own version.
13 Ibid., 130.
14 Ibid., 130–31.
15 Quoted in Kunhardt, *The American President,* 410.
16 This summary draws from Roseboom, *A History of Presidential Elections,* 130.
17 Freidel, *Our Country's Presidents,* 77–78.
18 Lorant, *The Glorious Burden,* 182; Roseboom, *A History of Presidential Elections,* 132; McPherson, *"To the Best of My Ability,"* 90.
19 McPherson, *"To the Best of My Ability,"* 82.
20 Roseboom, *A History of Presidential Elections,* 131–32. The quote from the Liberal Party platform is from Lorant, *The Glorious Burden,* 180, 182.
21 Lorant, *The Glorious Burden,* 182.
22 Miers, *Lincoln Day by Day,* 1:210.
23 Lincoln, *Collected Works,* 1:316–18.
24 Ibid., 331, 331n; Winkle, *The Young Eagle,* 220–22; Temple, *"The Taste Is in My Mouth,"* 29.
25 *Illinois State Register,* 16 February 1844, quoted in Miers, *Lincoln Day by Day,* 1:222–23.
26 William Butler to John J. Hardin, Hardin Papers, quoted in Ibid., 223.
27 *Sangamo Journal,* 28 March 1844, in Lincoln, *Collected Works,* 1:333.
28 Quoted in Miers, *Lincoln Day by Day,* 1:227.
29 Lincoln, *Collected Works,* 1:337. 347–48.
30 Ibid., 378.
31 The full text of the verse is in ibid., 367–70
32 This rundown of election results owes much to Roseboom, *A History of Presidential Elections,* 133, 133n; See also Lorant, *The Glorious Burden,* 183.
33 Quoted in Lorant, *The Glorious Burden,* 183.
34 Ibid.; Ferris, *The Presidents,* 119–20; Kunhardt, *The American President,* 212; McPherson, *"To the Best of My Ability,"* 81–82.
35 Kunhardt, *The American President,* 214; McPherson, *"To the Best of My Ability,"* 82.

Chapter 13: Laying Congressional Pipe

1   I owe Winkle, *The Young Eagle,* 236, in part, for the context of this analysis.
2   Lincoln, *Collected Works,* 1:348.
3   Ibid., 349.
4   Ibid., 350, 353.
5   Hardin's plan is in ibid., 358n.
6   Ibid., 355–56.
7   Ibid., 356.
8   Ibid., 354.
9   Miers, *Lincoln Day by Day,* 1:267, 268.
10 *Sangamo Journal,* 7 May 1846.
11 Cartwright, *Autobiography,* 48.
12 This picture of Cartwright is drawn from Herndon and Weik, *Herndon's Life of Lincoln,* 218; Watters, *Peter Cartwright,* 31, 24; Levering, *Historic Indiana,* 169–70; McLaren, "Reminiscences of Pioneer Life in Illinois, 1830–1860" unnumbered page; Cartwright, *Autobiography,* 5, 444; Wilson, *Lincoln Before Washington,* 63, 66; Moses, *Illinois, Historical and Statistical,* 1:395n.
13 Quoted in Rankin, *Personal Recollections,* 282.
14 Cartwright, *Autobiography,* 17; Watters, *Peter Cartwright,* 9.
15 *Illinois Daily Journal,* 30 January 1850, quoted in Miers, *Lincoln Day by Day,* 1:30; Boggess, *The Settlement of Illinois,* 191.
16 Cartwright, *Autobiography,* 7.
17 Quoted in Faragher, *Sugar Creek: Life on the Illinois Prairie,* 160–61.
18 Watters, *Peter Cartwright,* 44; Faragher, *Sugar Creek: Life on the Illinois Prairie,* 161.
19 Boggess, *The Settlement of Illinois,* 191–92.
20 Lincoln, *Collected Works,* 1:383.
21 Ibid., 382.
22 Herndon and Weik, *Herndon's Life of Lincoln,* 355.
23 This story is told in Tarbell, *Abraham Lincoln and His Ancestors,* 270–71.
24 Pease, *Illinois Election Returns,* 159.
25 Lincoln, *Collected Works,* 1:391.
26 French, "Men and Manners of the Early Days in Illinois," 73–74.
27 Quoted in Mitgang, *Lincoln as They Saw Him,* 50.
28 Ibid., 52.
29 The Lincoln itinerary to Washington is in Miers, *Lincoln Day by Day,* 1:294–296.

Chapter 14: Seeing Spots

1   Ford, *A History of Illinois,* 1:85–86.
2   Reynolds, *My Own Times,* 169.

3   Temple, *"The Taste Is in My Mouth",* 38–39. "Suckerdom" is borrowed from a quote in Thomas, "Lincoln and the Courts," 91.

4   *New York Tribune,* 11 December 1847, quoted in Mitgang, *Lincoln as They Saw Him,* 52.

5   Benjamin Perley Poore, in Rice, *Reminiscences of Abraham Lincoln,* 217.

6   Herndon and Weik, *Herndon's Life of Lincoln,* 220, 221; Lincoln, *Collected Works,* 1:420.

7   Townsend, *Lincoln and His Wife's Home Town,* 152–55.

8   Lincoln's resolutions are in *Collected Works,* 1:420–22, 420n.

9   Ibid., 432, 433, 435, 439, 439n. The full text of Lincoln's January 12 speech is in ibid., 431–42.

10   These reactions are quoted in Mitgang, *Lincoln as They Saw Him,* 54–55, 58.

11   Lincoln, *Collected Works,* 1:446–47.

12   Ibid., 474, 468, 477, 452.

13   Morgan, *Our Presidents,* 105.

14   Bauer, *Zachary Taylor,* 216.

15   Hamilton, *Zachary Taylor,* 39–40.

16   Dyer, *Zachary Taylor,* 280.

17   Moses, *Illinois, Historical and Statistical,* 2:561.

18   This story is told by Benjamin Perley Poore in Rice, *Reminiscences of Abraham Lincoln,* 219–21.

19   *Delaware State Journal,* 13 June 1848, in Lincoln, *Collected Works,* 1:475.

20   Lincoln, *Collected Works,* 2:1–5.

21   Ibid., 1:454.

22   Ibid., 2:1, 5.

23   Wilson and Davis, *Herndon's Informants,* 699.

24   *Boston Atlas,* 16 September 1848, in Lincoln, *Collected Works,* 2:5.

25   Quoted in Miers, *Lincoln Day by Day,* 1:320.

26   Lincoln, *Collected Works,* 2:6.

27   Quoted in ibid. 7.

28   Wilson and Davis, *Herndon's Informants,* 691, 699.

29   Lincoln, *Collected Works,* 2:11.

30   Herndon and Weik, *Herndon's Life of Lincoln,* 233.

31   Lincoln's proposed legislation is in *Collected Works,* 2:20–22.

32   Fehrenbacher, *Recollected Words of Abraham Lincoln,* 260; Lincoln, *Collected Works,* 2:22n; Miers, *Lincoln Day by Day,* 2:4n.

33   Lincoln, *Collected Works,* 1:431. Also see letter to Richard S. Thomas, page 455.

34   Ibid., 2:22–23.

Chapter 15: Lincoln's Other Life

1   Lincoln, *Collected Works,* 2:10–11.

2   Hertz, *The Hidden Lincoln,* 96.

3   Lincoln, *Collected Works,* 3:512.
4   This description of Logan is a tapestry woven from Elihu B. Washburne in Rice, *Reminiscences of Abraham Lincoln,* 11, and Newton, *Lincoln and Herndon,* 16.
5   Herndon and Weik, *Herndon's Life of Lincoln,* xvi, 211.
6   Hertz, *The Hidden Lincoln,* 395–96.
7   Newton, *Lincoln and Herndon,* 21.
8   Ibid., 1, 42.
9   Weik, *The Real Lincoln,* 4–5.
10 Herndon and Weik, *Herndon's Life of Lincoln,* 254.
11 Lincoln, *Collected Works,* 2:80.
12 Herndon and Weik, *Herndon's Life of Lincoln,* 254.
13 Ibid., 256.
14 Ibid., 268; Hertz, *The Hidden Lincoln,* 95.
15 Herndon and Weik, *Herndon's Life of Lincoln,* 271–72.
16 Hertz, *The Hidden Lincoln,* 428.
17 Ibid., 148.
18 Herndon and Weik, *Herndon's Life of Lincoln,* 273.
19 Quoted in Angle, *Abraham Lincoln by Some Men Who Knew Him,* 39.
20 Quoted in Hertz, *Lincoln Talks,* 22.
21 Herndon and Weik, *Herndon's Life of Lincoln,* 274.
22 Wilson and Davis, *Herndon's Informants,* 636.
23 Whitney, *Lincoln the Citizen,* 170.
24 Hertz, *The Hidden Lincoln,* 431.
25 These various perceptions of Lincoln's mind are from Herndon and Weik, *Herndon's Life of Lincoln,* 342, 480–82, 488; Hertz, *The Hidden Lincoln,* 132, 133, 416; and Wilson, *Intimate Memories of Lincoln,* 302.
26 Lincoln, *Collected Works,* 2:81, 82.
27 Nicolay, *Personal Traits of Abraham Lincoln,* 80; Current, "Lincoln and the Eighth Circuit," 11; Wilson, *Lincoln Among His Friends,* 105, 114, 122; Weik, *The Real Lincoln,* 188; Lufkin, "Mr. Lincoln's Light from Under a Bushel—1850," p. 5.
28 King, *Lincoln's Manager,* 77.
29 Whitney, *Lincoln the Citizen,* 173.
30 Johns, *Personal Recollections of Early Decatur,* 62–63.
31 King, *Lincoln's Manager,* 3n, 7,177–78, 114, 119. Johns's opinion of Davis is from her *Personal Recollections of Early Decatur,* 62.
32 Whitney, *Lincoln the Citizen,* 194.
33 Thomas, "Lincoln's Humor," 63, 64, 62.
34 The Davis and Gillespie opinions are from Wilson and Davis, *Herndon's Informants,* 348, 187. Lincoln's quote to Herndon is in Fehrenbacher, *Recollected Words of Abraham Lincoln,* 252.
35 Quoted in Angle, *Abraham Lincoln by Some Men Who Knew Him,* 24.
36 Whitney, *Lincoln the Citizen,* 189, 191.

37 Lincoln, *Collected Works,* 2:86–87, 89. The full text of Lincoln's eulogy is on pages 83–90.
38 Angle, *"Here I Have Lived,"* 208.
39 Lincoln, *Collected Works,* 2:121–22, 132. The complete text of Lincoln's eulogy to Clay is on pages 121–32.
40 Ibid., 4:67.
41 *Illinois Daily Journal,* 17 August 1852; Lincoln, *Collected Works,* 2:136–38.
42 Miers, *Lincoln Day by Day,* 2:86–87.

Chapter 16: What He Had Become

1 Wilson and Davis, *Herndon's Informants,* 349.
2 Herndon and Weik, *Herndon's Life of Lincoln,* 249n.
3 John S. Bradford in Wilson and Davis, *Herndon's Informants,* 729.
4 Herndon and Weik, *Herndon's Life of Lincoln,* 349–50.
5 Ibid., 342, 385n, 345.
6 Ibid., 342–43; Hertz, *The Hidden Lincoln,* 215.
7 Hertz, *The Hidden Lincoln,* 104–5. Wilson, *Intimate Memories of Lincoln,* 134. The Shakespeare phrase is from *Comedy of Errors,* act. 1, scene 1, line 72.
8 Hertz, *The Hidden Lincoln,* 99.
9 Herndon and Weik, *Herndon's Life of Lincoln,* 343–44.
10 Ibid., 344; Hertz, *The Hidden Lincoln,* 129, 105.
11 Mary Todd Lincoln in Wilson and Davis, *Herndon's Informants,* 357.
12 Ibid., 358.
13 Herndon and Weik, *Herndon's Life of Lincoln,* 352, 352n, 354; Hertz, *The Hidden Lincoln,* 122.
14 Whitney, *Lincoln the Citizen,* 233; Wilson, *Intimate Memories of Lincoln,* 167; Villard, *Lincoln on the Eve of '61,* p. 55.
15 Wilson and Davis, *Herndon's Informants,* 732.
16 Ibid., 349.
17 Hertz, *The Hidden Lincoln,* 123–24.
18 Ibid., 169; Angle, *Abraham Lincoln by Some Men Who Knew Him,* 21.
19 Wilson, *Intimate Memories of Lincoln,* 155; Hertz, *The Hidden Lincoln,* 52, 64.
20 Whitney, *Lincoln the Citizen,* 220–21.
21 White, *Abraham Lincoln in 1854,* 20.
22 Quoted in Fehrenbacher, *Recollected Words of Abraham Lincoln,* 242.
23 From Nicolay, *An Oral History of Abraham Lincoln,* 26.
24 Whitney, *Lincoln the Citizen,* 189–90.
25 Fehrenbacher, *Recollected Words of Abraham Lincoln,* 263.
26 This opinion is Cincinnati lawyer William Martin Dickson's, in Wilson, *Intimate Memories of Lincoln,* 147.
27 Fehrenbacher, *Recollected Words of Abraham Lincoln,* 241; Hertz, *The Hidden Lincoln,* 75.
28 Browning is quoted in Nicolay, *An Oral History of Abraham Lincoln,* 6–7.

Chapter 17: Tempest

1   Douglas, *Letters of Stephen A. Douglas,* 170–71, 171n.
2   Ibid., 207, 243.
3   Ibid., 219n, 231.
4   Douglas, *Speeches of Senator S. A. Douglas,* 10.
5   For a definition of "Old Fogies," see Johannsen, *Stephen A. Douglas,* 346.
6   Ibid., 248; Douglas, *The Letters of Stephen A. Douglas,* 285.
7   Douglas, *The Letters of Stephen A. Douglas,* 289.
8   Johannsen, *Stephen A. Douglas,* 255.
9   Douglas, *The Letters of Stephen A. Douglas,* 270.
10   Ibid., 288.
11   Douglas, *Speeches of Senator S. A. Douglas,* 15.
12   Douglas, *The Letters of Stephen A. Douglas,* 300.
13   Johannsen, *Stephen A. Douglas,* 451.
14   Douglas, *The Letters of Stephen A. Douglas,* 327.
15   I took my version of this rough up of Douglas in Chicago mainly from Johannsen, *Stephen A. Douglas,* 453–55.

Chapter 18: Lincoln Emerges

1   Lincoln, *Collected Works,* 4:67.
2   White, *Abraham Lincoln in 1854,* 6.
3   Quoted in Johns, *Personal Recollections of Early Decatur,* 71.
4   Herndon and Weik, *Herndon's Life of Lincoln,* 334.
5   Nicolay, *Personal Traits of Abraham Lincoln,* 117.
6   Wilson and Davis, *Herndon's Informants,* 183.
7   Ibid., 183–84.
8   Fehrenbacher, *Recollected Words of Abraham Lincoln,* 61.
9   Herndon and Weik, *Herndon's Life of Lincoln,* 292, 304, 270.
10   Newton recounts this story in *Lincoln and Herndon,* 57.
11   Fehrenbacher, *Recollected Words of Abraham Lincoln,* 245.
12   Lincoln, *Collected Works,* 2:222–23.
13   Quoted in Fehrenbacher, *Recollected Words of Abraham Lincoln,* 154.
14   Lincoln, *Collected Works,* 2:228, 4:67.
15   Wilson, *Intimate Memories of Lincoln,* 165; *Illinois Daily Journal,* 2 September 1854 in Lincoln, *Collected Works,* 2:227.
16   Lincoln, *Collected Works,* 2:230–31, 232–33.
17   Whitney, *Lincoln the Citizen,* 251.
18   Quoted in Fehrenbacher, *Recollected Words of Abraham Lincoln,* 70.
19   Lincoln, *Collected Works,* 2:240–45. Also see White, "Abraham Lincoln in 1854," 10.
20   Quoted in Fehrenbacher, *Recollected Words of Abraham Lincoln,* 245.
21   Lincoln, *Collected Works,* 2:240n.

22 Quoted in Scripps, *Life of Abraham Lincoln,* 110–11.

23 Wilson and Douglas, *Herndon's Informants,* 198.

24 Lincoln, *Collected Works,* 2:247–48.

25 Lincoln's Peoria speech is printed in full in ibid., 247–83. My summary draws specifically from pages 255, 256, 257, 259, 261, 265, 266, 270, 271, 272, 273, 275, 276.

26 Wilson and Davis, *Herndon's Informants,* 211.

27 Wilson, *Lincoln Among His Friends,* 171.

28 Lincoln, *Collected Works,* 2:286.

29 These various letters seeking backing for his run for the Senate are in ibid, 286–90.

30 The description of Trumbull is from Moses, *Illinois, Historical and Statistical,* 2:593–94.

31 Lincoln, *Collected Works,* 2:290.

32 Ibid, 300–1.

33 Ibid., 304.

34 Storm coverage is in the *Illinois Daily Journal,* 23 January–2 February, 1855.

35 The account of the voting is from Lincoln, *Collected Works,* 2:304–5; King, *Lincoln's Manager,* 107; and Johns, *Personal Recollections of Early Decatur,* 74–75. The description of Matteson is from Moses, *Illinois, Historical and Statistical,* 2:583, and Bonham, *Fifty Years' Recollections,* 77–79.

36 Wilson and Davis, *Herndon's Informants,* 183.

37 Lincoln, *Collected Works,* 2:306–7.

38 Herndon is quoted in Newton, *Lincoln and Herndon,* 76.

39 Lincoln, *Collected Works,* 2:306.

Chapter 19: Political Earthquake

1 Lincoln, *Collected Works,* 2:308.

2 Ibid., 333.

3 George W. Julian in Rice, *Reminiscences of Abraham Lincoln,* 47.

4 Lincoln, *Collected Works,* 2:321.

5 Herndon and Weik, *Herndon's Life of Lincoln,* 311.

6 This introspection is from Lincoln, *Collected Works,* 2:318.

7 Ibid., 322–23.

8 Ibid., 316.

9 Ibid., 288n.

10 The account of Lincoln's railroading into the Republican ranks is from Herndon and Weik, *Herndon's Life of Lincoln,* 311–12.

11 Angle, *"Here I Have Lived,"* 215.

12 Lincoln, *Collected Works,* 2:316–17.

13 Purchase of the spectacles is reported by Henry C. Whitney in Wilson and

Davis, *Herndon's Informants,* 631; the quotes are from Herndon and Weik, *Herndon's Life of Lincoln,* 312.

14 Quoted in Mitgang, *Lincoln as They Saw Him,* 78.

15 Wilson, *Intimate Memories of Lincoln,* 154–55.

16 Herndon and Weik, *Herndon's Life of Lincoln,* 312–13.

17 Moses, *Illinois, Historical and Statistical,* 2:600.

18 Wilson and Davis, *Herndon's Informants,* 734.

19 Mitgang, *Lincoln as They Saw Him,* 79.

20 Wilson, *Intimate Memories of Lincoln,* 24.

21 Carr, *Stephen A. Douglas,* 3.

22 Douglas, *The Letters of Stephen A. Douglas,* 361.

23 Herndon and Weik, *Herndon's Life of Lincoln,* 315–17.

24 Rankin, *Personal Recollections of Abraham Lincoln,* 27.

25 Lincoln, *Collected Works,* 2:358, 360, 374.

26 Quoted in ibid., 366, 373.

27 Quoted in Wilson, *Intimate Memories of Lincoln,* 205.

28 Ibid., 206.

29 Miers, *Lincoln Day by Day,* 2:183.

Chapter 20: At the Crossroads

1 Herndon and Weik, *Herndon's Life of Lincoln,* 294.

2 Lincoln, *Collected Works,* 2:382–83.

3 Herndon and Weik, *Herndon's Life of Lincoln,* 318.

4 *Chicago Journal,* 22 May 1857, in Miers, *Lincoln Day by Day,* 2:194.

5 Hertz, *The Hidden Lincoln,* 416.

6 Wilson and Davis, *Herndon's Informants,* 407.

7 Hertz, *The Hidden Lincoln,* 196.

8 Rice, *Reminiscences of Abraham Lincoln,* 310.

9 Morris, *Lincoln: A Foreigner's Quest,* 57.

10 Herndon and Weik, *Herndon's Life of Lincoln,* 332, 262.

11 Whitney, *Lincoln the Citizen,* 223, 226.

12 Thomas, "Lincoln's Humor," 76, 78; Herndon and Weik, *Herndon's Life of Lincoln,* 44. For an essay on Lincoln's early use of satire and invective, see Bray, "'The Power to Hurt,'" 39–58.

13 Wilson and Davis, *Herndon's Informants,* 181.

14 Rice, *Reminiscences of Abraham Lincoln,* 333.

15 Herndon and Weik, *Herndon's Life of Lincoln,* 239.

Chapter 21: Axe Handles and Wedges

1 The definitive work on the Dred Scott case is Fehrenbacher, *The Dred Scott Case: Its Significance in American Law and Politics.*

2 Newton, *Lincoln and Herndon*, 111, 169.
3 Lincoln's address is in *Collected Works*, 2:398–410. Specific material used here is from pages 401, 405–7, 409, 399. The "hateful carcass" quote is from a fragment of a speech written later, ibid., 454.
4 Douglas, *Report of Senator Douglas, of Illinois, on the Kansas-Lecompton Constitution*, 1.
5 Douglas, *The Letters of Stephen A. Douglas*, 372.
6 Ibid., 403, 405.
7 Nichols, *The Disruption of American Democracy*, 130.
8 Angle, *"Here I Have Lived,"* 227–28, 227n.
9 Fehrenbacher, *Recollected Words of Abraham Lincoln*, 123.
10 Ibid., 250. The Tribune's circulation in Illinois reached 20,000 by 1860. See Fehrenbacher, *Prelude to Greatness*, 10–11.
11 Lincoln, *Collected Works*, 2:430, 457, 459.
12 Ibid., 449.
13 Ibid., 482.

Chapter 22: A House Divided

1 Lincoln, *Collected Works*, 505, 472, 506.
2 Newton, *Lincoln and Herndon*, 178–79, 186.
3 Lincoln, *Collected Works*, 2:506.
4 For the thoughts expressed in this paragraph I am indebted to Angle, *Abraham Lincoln by Some Men Who Knew Him*, 33.
5 Lincoln, *Collected Works*, 2:506.
6 Quoted in Herndon and Weik, *Herndon's Life of Lincoln*, 238.
7 Newton, *Lincoln and Herndon*, 161–62, 167.
8 William Herndon to LymanTrumbull in Pratt, *Concerning Mr. Lincoln*, 10.
9 Herndon and Weik, *Herndon's Life of Lincoln*, 325; Lincoln, *Collected Works*, 2:461.
10 Herndon and Weik, *Herndon's Life of Lincoln*, 325.
11 Lincoln, *Collected Works*, 2:461–62.
12 Herndon and Weik, *Herndon's Life of Lincoln*, 325–26.
13 My rendering of Lincoln's pre-speech review is an amalgam of Herndon's account in ibid., 326, and John Armstrong's in Wilson and Davis, *Herndon's Informants*, 574–75.
14 Fehrenbacher, "The Nomination of Lincoln in 1858," p. 24. For an excellent discussion of the unprecedented nature and reason for the resolution endorsing Lincoln, see the chapter on Lincoln's senatorial nomination in Frehrenbacher, *Prelude to Greatness*, 48–69.
15 Lincoln, *Collected Works*, 2:462, 464, 465–66, 467, 468. The complete text of the speech is in pp. 461–69.
16 This continuing angst of Lincoln's friends is reported by Armstrong in Wilson and Davis, *Herndon's Informants*, 575.

17 Lincoln, *Collected Works,* 2:507.
18 Newton, *Lincoln and Herndon,* 179–80.
19 Fehrenbacher, *Recollected Words of Abraham Lincoln,* 371.
20 Quoted in Wilson, *Lincoln Among His Friends,* 172.
21 The text of Lincoln's July 10 speech is in Lincoln, *Collected Works,* 2:484–502.
22 Newton, *Lincoln and Herndon,* 182.
23 Lincoln, *Collected Works,* 2:502–3.
24 Ibid., 507.
25 Wilson, *Intimate Memories of Lincoln,* 108.
26 Wilson and Davis, *Herndon's Informants,* 731.
27 Herndon and Weik, *Herndon's Life of Lincoln,* 328; Bonham, *Fifty Years' Recollections,* 169.
28 Lincoln, *Collected Works,* 2:522.
29 Nicolay, *An Oral History of Abraham Lincoln,* 44.
30 Newton, *Lincoln and Herndon,* 184.
31 Lincoln, *Collected Works,* 2:529n.
32 Ibid., 531–32n, 531.
33 Miers, *Lincoln Day by Day,* 2:224–25.
34 Dewey in Mitgang, *Lincoln as They Saw Him,* 105, 106.
35 Douglas, *The Letters of Stephen A. Douglas,* 427, 427n.
36 Mitgang, *Lincoln as They Saw Him,* 105.
37 Lincoln, *Collected Works,* 2:532.
38 These thoughts are from a fragment in ibid., 548–49, 550, 551–52.
39 The two notebooks are described by Herndon in Hertz, *The Hidden Lincoln,* 20–21.
40 Miers, Lincoln, *Day by Day,* 2:225.

Chapter 23: The Debates

1 This description of crowds and the two candidates arriving in Ottawa on debate day is shaped from an account of the *Chicago Times,* 22 August 1858, reprinted in Mitgang, *Lincoln as They Saw Him,* 108.
2 *Chicago Press and Tribune,* 23 August 1858.
3 *Chicago Times,* 22 August 1858, in Mitgang, *Lincoln as They Saw Him,* 108.
4 Quoted in Flint, *Life of Stephen A. Douglas,* 19.
5 The full text of the first debate is in Lincoln, *Collected Works,* 3:1-37.
6 Ibid., 37.
7 Mitgang, *Lincoln as They Saw Him,* 107.
8 Quoted in Whitney, *Lincoln the Citizen,* 276n.
9 Quoted in King, *Lincoln's Manager,* 122.
10 Mitgang, *Lincoln as They Saw Him,* 107.
11 *Chicago Press and Tribune,* 30 August 1858; Martin P. S. Rindllaub in Wilson, *Intimate Memories of Lincoln,* 182–83.
12 *Illinois State Journal,* 30 August 1858; *Chicago Press and Tribune,* 30 August

1858; Lincoln is described by Rindlaub in Wilson, *Intimate Memories of Lincoln,* 183–84.

13 The text of the Freeport debate is in Lincoln, *Collected Works,* 3:38–76.

14 Newton, *Lincoln and Herndon,* 203.

15 *Chicago Press and Tribune,* 17 September 1858.

16 Ibid.

17 The text of the Jonesboro debate is in Lincoln, *Collected Works,* 3:102–44.

18 *Illinois State Journal,* 23 September 1858.

19 The full text of the Charleston debate is in Lincoln, *Collected Works,* 3:145–201.

20 Ibid., 203, 202.

21 Fehrenbacher, *Recollected Words of Abraham Lincoln,* 432.

22 Lincoln's fragments are in Lincoln, *Collected Works* 3:204–5.

23 Ibid., 206.

24 Newton, *Lincoln and Herndon,* 223; Herndon and Weik, *Herndon's Life of Lincoln,* 336.

25 *Galesburg Democrat,* 8 and 9 October 1858.

26 The text of the Galesburg debate is in Lincoln, *Collected Works,* 3:207–44.

27 *Chicago Press and Tribune,* 15 October 1858.

28 The text of the Quincy debate is in Lincoln, *Collected Works,* 3:245–83.

29 *Chicago Press and Tribune,* 18 October, 1858; Henry Guest McPike in Wilson, *Intimate Memories of Lincoln,* 174.

30 McPike in Wilson, *Intimate Memories of Lincoln,* 175.

31 The text of the final debate in Alton is in Lincoln, *Collected Works,* 3:283–325.

32 Ibid., 334.

33 This convenient rundown of Lincoln's campaign output is borrowed from Davis, "Abraham Lincoln, Esq." 29. For total miles traveled see Fehrenbacher, *Prelude to Greatness,* 8

34 *Illinois State Journal,* 3 November 1858, quoted in Miers, *Lincoln Day by Day,* 2:235.

35 Quoted in Mitgang, *Lincoln as They Saw Him,* 127, 135, 132.

36 Ibid., 112.

37 *Illinois State Journal,* 3 November 1858.

38 Rice, *Reminiscences of Abraham Lincoln,* 439, 441, 443.

39 Fehrenbacher, *Recollected Words of Abraham Lincoln,* 510.

40 Lincoln, *Collected Works,* 3:339.

41 Hertz, *The Hidden Lincoln,* 10.

42 Douglas, *Speeches of Senator S. A. Douglas,* 5; Wilson, *Lincoln Among His Friends,* 287; Chesnut, *Mary Chesnut's Civil War,* 25.

43 Wilson, *Intimate Memories of Lincoln,* 302.

Chapter 24: Spreading the Gospel

1 Pillsbury, *Lincoln and Slavery,* 39–40; Lincoln, *Collected Works,* 3:346.

2 Lincoln, *Collected Works,* 3:336, 339, 340, 341, 342.

3   Wilson, *Lincoln Among His Friends,* 134.
4   Lincoln's letter to Trumbull, written on 11 December 1858, is in Lincoln, *Collected Works,* 3:345.
5   Ibid., 370.
6   Charles Caverno in Wilson, *Intimate Memories of Lincoln,* 211–12.
7   Lincoln, *Collected Works,* 3:396.
8   Lincoln's reply to the Boston invitation is in ibid., 374–376. Also see 376n.
9   Fehrenbacher, *Recollected Words of Abraham Lincoln,* 203–4.
10 Lincoln, *Collected Works,* 3: 416.
11 Ibid., 454–55, 457.
12 Ibid., 482.
13 Fehrenbacher, *Recollected Words of Abraham Lincoln,* 188.
14 These concerns over the Fugitive Slave Law and other matters are from Lincoln, *Collected Works,* 3:384, 386, 390–91, 394.

Chapter 25: Cooper Union

1   The origin of the invitation to Lincoln to speak in New York is from an account from George Haven Putnam in Wilson, *Intimate Memories of Lincoln,* 256–57.
2   Holzer, *Lincoln at Cooper Union,* 9–10, 12.
3   Lawrence Weldon in Rice, *Reminiscences of Abraham Lincoln,* 207.
4   Fehrenbacher, *Recollected Words of Abraham Lincoln,* 40.
5   Helm, *Mary, Wife of Lincoln,* 101.
6   Lincoln, *Collected Works,* 3:494n.
7   These paragraphs on what Lincoln studied, what he was getting out of it, and the final manuscript owe much to Holzer's excellent *Lincoln at Cooper Union,* 50–53, 56. Also see Wilson, *Intimate Memories of Lincoln,* 251.
8   This description of Lincoln's suit is a reshaping of a description from Whitney, *Lincoln the Citizen,* 280; and Holzer, *Lincoln at Cooper Union,* 57.
9   Wilson, *Lincoln Among His Friends,* 218; Holzer, *Lincoln at Cooper Union,* 57, 58.
10 Quoted in Holzer, *Lincoln at Cooper Union,* 59.
11 Ibid., 60–61, 64.
12 Bowen's encounter with Lincoln is recounted in Wilson, *Lincoln Among His Friends,* 218–20. See also, Holzer, *Lincoln at Cooper Union,* 74.
13 Holzer, *Lincoln at Cooper Union,* 72.
14 Ibid, 73, 103; Warren, "Lincoln's $200 speech," *Lincoln Lore,* No. 1878 (5 September 1955).
15 This description of the hall at Cooper Union that night borrows from Holzer, *Lincoln at Cooper Union,* 103, 105. Also see Mitgang, *Lincoln as They Saw Him,* 156.
16 Mitgang, *Lincoln as They Saw Him,* 156.
17 Richard Cunningham McCormick in Wilson, *Intimate Memories of Lincoln,* 252.

18 This description of the lecturn is from Holzer, *Lincoln at Cooper Union,* 108.
19 Whitney, *Lincoln the Citizen,* 280.
20 Holzer, *Lincoln at Cooper Union,* 110, 113; Herndon and Weik, *Herndon's Life of Lincoln,* 369.
21 Wilson, *Intimate Memories of Lincoln,* 258.
22 Putnam in Wilson, *Lincoln Among His Friends,* 221.
23 Lincoln's Cooper Union speech is in Lincoln, *Collected Works,* 3:522–50. Pages cited: 532, 527, 535, 536, 537, 538, 542, 543, 546, 547, 548, 549, 550. The emphasis in the last sentence is Lincoln's.
24 *New York Tribune,* 28 February 1860, quoted in Mitgang, *Lincoln as They Saw Him,* 158.
25 Holzer, *Lincoln at Cooper Union,* 175, 176.
26 I am entirely indebted to Holzer, 187, for all of these accounts by Robert's classmates.
27 Miers, *Lincoln Day by Day,* 2:275.
28 Lincoln, *Collected Works,* 3:555.
29 Gabriel Lewis Smith in Wilson, *Intimate Memories of Lincoln,* 215, 216.

Chapter 26: Reaching for the Brass Ring

1   Villard, *Memoirs of Henry Villard,* 1:97.
2   Bonham, *Fifty Years' Recollections,* 528, 530.
3   The exchange with Fell is from Fehrenbacher, *Recollected Words of Abraham Lincoln,* 154–55.
4   Lincoln, *Collected Works,* 3:337n, 377.
5   Whitney, *Lincoln the Citizen,* 264–65.
6   Bonham, *Fifty Years' Recollections,* 178.
7   Holzer, *Lincoln at Cooper Union,* 49. 56.
8   Wilson, *Intimate Memories of Lincoln,* 3–4.
9   Moses, *Illinois, Historical and Statistical,* 2:629; Fehrenbacher, *Prelude to Greatness,* 5.
10 This assessment of Lincoln relative to the other candidates is from Angle, *"Here I Have Lived,"* 237–38.
11 Lincoln's letter to Corwine is in Lincoln, *Collected Works,* 4:36.
12 Ibid., 34, 43, 36, 45.
13 Ibid., 47.
14 Johnson (no first name) in Wilson and Davis, *Herndon's Informants,* 462.
15 The story of Oglesby and the rails is weaved from Johns, *Personal Recollections of Early Decatur,* 80–82, and Johnson in Wilson and Davis, *Herndon's Informants,* 463.
16 Wilson, *Lincoln Among His Friends,* 187; Johnson in Wilson and Davis, *Herndon's Informants,* 463.
17 Wilson, *Intimate Memories of Lincoln,* 264; Lawrence Weldon in Rice, *Reminiscences of Abraham Lincoln,* 208–9.

Chapter 27: Chicago

1   This description of the Wigwam borrows from Isaac Hill Bromley of the *Tribune* in Wilson, *Intimate Memories of Lincoln,* 276–77; and Halstead, *Three Against Lincoln,* 143.

2   King, *Lincoln's Manager,* 145–46.

3   Lincoln, *Collected Works,* 3:509.

4   This description of Judd is from King, *Lincoln's Manager,* 128.

5   Judd's son Edward describes this epiphany in Wilson, *Intimate Memories of Lincoln,* 4.

6   Whitney, *Lincoln the Citizen,* 289; Herndon and Weik, *Herndon's Life of Lincoln,* 373–74. Also see Lincoln, *Collected Works,* 4:50, 50n.

7   Leonard Swett in Wilson, *Intimate Memories of Lincoln,* 294–95.

8   Isaac Hill Bromley in Wilson, *Intimate Memories of Lincoln,* 283.

9   Ibid., 283, 286.

10 Ibid., 279.

11 Halstead, *Three Against Lincoln,* 159, 149.

12 Baringer, "Campaign Technique in Illinois," 237.

13 This underhanded ploy to stack the hall with Lincoln howlers is described by Edward Judd and Henry M. Russel in Wilson, *Intimate Memories of Lincoln,* 5, 125.

14 Leonard Swett in ibid., 295.

15 Bromley in ibid., 287; Halstead, *Three Against Lincoln,* 164.

16 Swett in Wilson, *Intimate Memories of Lincoln,* 295.

17 Halstead, *Three Against Lincoln,* 165. Also see Baringer, "Campaign Technique in Illinois," 238.

18 Baringer, "Campaign Technique in Illinois," 239.

19 The description of all that happened inside the Wigwam in the several paragraphs above, unless otherwise cited, is crafted from Bromley's vivid report in Wilson, *Intimate Memories of Lincoln,* 287–90, 282–83.

20 Christopher C. Brown in Wilson and Davis, *Herndon's Informants,* 438; Charles Zane in Wilson, *Lincoln Among His Friends,* 136.

21 Fehrenbacher, *Recollected Words of Abraham Lincoln,* 396.

22 Christopher C. Brown, James Gourley, and Charles Zane in Wilson and Davis, *Herndon's Informants,* 437, 438, 453, 492; Joseph D. Ropers, in Wilson, *Intimate Memories of Lincoln,* 141.

23 Charles Zane in Wilson, *Lincoln Among His Friends,* 136, and in Wilson and Davis, *Herndon's Informants,* 491.

24 Zane in Wilson, *Lincoln Among His Friends,* 136.

25 The scene describing the arrival of news that Lincoln had been nominated is stitched from Angle, *"Here I Have Lived,"* 236; from Zane in Wilson, *Lincoln Among His Friends,* 137; and in Wilson and Davis, *Herndon's Informants,* 492.

26 John T. Stuart in Wilson and Davis, *Herndon's Informants,* 63, 64.

27 Zane in ibid., 491.

28 The description of the celebration in Springfield following the nomination draws from Angle, *"Here I Have Lived,"* 236–37; and Lincoln, *Collected Works,* 4:50.

29 Hatfield, *Vice Presidents of the United States,* 206, 207; Also see Baker, *200 Notable Days,* 65.

30 This is taken, with considerable switching about, from Charles Coffin in Rice, *Reminiscences of Abraham Lincoln,* 164–65, 168.

31 The committee's departure to Springfield, arrival at Lincoln's house, and scene inside are stitched from Coffin in Rice, *Reminiscences of Abraham Lincoln,* 168; William D. Kelley in ibid., 256–59; and Angle, *"Here I Have Lived,"* 239.

32 Lincoln, *Collected Works,* 4:51.

33 *New York Tribune,* 25 May 1860, quoted in Segal, *Conversations with Lincoln,* 32.

34 Angle, *"Here I Have Lived,"* 239.

35 Kelley in Rice, *Reminiscences of Abraham Lincoln,* 259. This dialogue is also reported by Coffin in ibid., 169–70, and by the *New York Tribune* correspondent on 25 May 1860, in Segal, *Conversations with Lincoln,* 31–32. Both of those two accounts have Lincoln asking this not of Morgan, but of Kelley himself. I have used Kelley's account, because he was a direct participant.

36 Angle, *"Here I Have Lived,"* 239–40.

Chapter 28: The Four-Legged Race

1 Charles Coffin in Rice, *Reminiscences of Abraham Lincoln,* 162; Pryor, *Reminiscences of Peace and War,* 104.

2 John A. Dahlgren in Fehrenbacher, *Recollected Words of Abraham Lincoln,* 128.

3 Thanks to King, *Lincoln's Manager,* 127, 146, for the analysis in these two paragraphs.

4 John B. Alley in Rice, *Reminiscences of Abraham Lincoln,* 575.

5 Wilson, *Lincoln Among His Friends,* 93, 94.

6 Segal, *Conversations with Lincoln,* 39–40; Angle, *"Here I Have Lived,"* 245.

7 Angle, *"Here I Have Lived,"* 246–47; "The Presidential Candidate Attends a Rally," 123, 124.

8 Lincoln, *Collected Works,* 4:91, 91–92n.

9 Morris, *Lincoln: A Foreigner's Quest,* 91.

10 Lincoln, *Collected Works,* 4:60.

11 Moses, *Illinois, Historical and Statistical,* 2:634.

12 Herndon and Weik, *Herndon's Life of Lincoln,* 1.

13 Lincoln, *Collected Works,* 4:68.

14 Ibid., 77.

15 Fehrenbacher, *Recollected Words of Abraham Lincoln,* 24.

16 Nicolay, *An Oral History of Abraham Lincoln,* 103.

17 Wilson and Davis, *Herndon's Informants,* 436. Segal, *Conversations with Lincoln, 33.*

18 Lincoln, *Collected Works,* 4:83. Also see Nicolay, *An Oral History of Abraham Lincoln,* 91.

19 Lincoln, *Collected Works,* 4:71.

20 Ellis Henry Roberts in Wilson, *Intimate Memories of Lincoln,* 300.

21 John L. Scripps in Wilson and Davis, *Herndon's Informants,* 57.

22 Charles A. Barry in Wilson, *Intimate Memories of Lincoln,* 307, 310.

23 Lincoln, *Collected Works,* 4:84, 85n.

24 Newton Batemen in Wilson and Davis, *Herndon's Informants,* 437.

25 These letters are in Lincoln, *Collected Works,* 4:82, 90, 110, 111n, 118.

26 Benjamin F. Irwin, in Wilson and Davis, *Herndon's Informants,* 462.

27 Lincoln, *Collected Works,* 4:126–27.

28 Quoted in Johannsen, *Stephen A. Douglas,* 780.

29 Ibid., 797–98.

30 Ibid., 799, 798.

31 Douglas, *The Montgomery Address,* 551–52.

32 *New York Tribune,* 10 November 1860, in Mitgang, *Lincoln as They Saw Him,* 201, 202.

33 Samuel R. Weed in Wilson, *Intimate Memories of Lincoln,* 323–24.

34 Ibid., 325.

35 Mitgang, *Lincoln as They Saw Him,* 212–13; Nicolay, *An Oral History of Abraham Lincoln,* 106.

36 These moments of worry over New York, changing to exultation, in the telegraph office are from Weed in Wilson, *Intimate Memories of Lincoln,* 326–27.

37 Ibid., 327; Nicolay, *An Oral History of Abraham Lincoln,* 106.

38 Weed in Wilson, *Intimate Memories of Lincoln,* 327–29.

39 Ibid., 328; Pratt, *Concerning Mr. Lincoln,* 27–28.

40 Mitgang, *Lincoln as They Saw Him,* 215.

41 Weed in Wilson, *Intimate Memories of Lincoln,* 329–30.

42 Holzer, *Lincoln at Cooper Union,* 229; Whitney, *Lincoln the Citizen,* 292.

43 Charles S. Morehead in Segal, *Conversations with Lincoln,* 85.

Chapter 29: Firebell in the Night

1 Jefferson, *The Works of Thomas Jefferson,* 12:157–59.

2 Chesnut, *Mary Chesnut's Civil War,* 8.

3 Ibid., 4.

4 Joseph Holt in Nicolay, *An Oral History of Abraham Lincoln,* 72, 76.

5 Lincoln, *Collected Works,* 2:130.

6 Quoted in Fehrenbacher, *Recollected Words of Abraham Lincoln,* 253.

7 Lincoln, *Collected Works,* 4:160.

8 Thomas Webster in Fehrenbacher, *Recollected Words of Abraham Lincoln,* 459.

9   David M. Swarr in ibid., 438.

10 Piatt, *Memories of Men Who Saved the Union,* 33–34.

11 Rankin, *Personal Recollections,* 138–39.

12 Joseph Gillespie in Wilson, *Intimate Memories of Lincoln,* 333.

13 John B. Nicolay in Fehrenbacher, *Recollected Words of Abraham Lincoln,* 343: Lincoln, *Collected Works,* 4:159.

14 Joseph Gillespie in Wilson, *Intimate Memories of Lincoln,* 333–34.

15 For this argument see James Buchanan's last annual message to Congress in Richardson, *A Compilation of the Messages and Papers of the Presidents,* 7:3157–84. See specifically, pp. 3164–67.

16 Baker, *James Buchanan,* 128.

17 Richard C. Parsons in Fehrenbacher, *Recollected Words of Abraham Lincoln,* 353.

18 John G. Nicolay in ibid., 341, 342.

19 Lincoln, *Collected Works,* 4:154

20 Ibid.,142n.

21 Ibid., 160.

22 Douglas, *The Letters of Stephen A. Douglas,* 499–500.

23 John McConnell in Fehrenbacher, *Recollected Words of Abraham Lincoln,* 319.

24 Swett in Wilson and Davis, *Lincoln's Informants,* 163.

25 Angle, *"Here I Have Lived,"* 255; Villard, *Lincoln on the Eve of '61,* p. 62.

26 Herndon and Weik. *Herndon's Life of Lincoln,* 379.

27 Parsons and Alexander Milton Ross, and Carl Schurz in Fehrenbacher, *Recollected Words of Abraham Lincoln,* 352, 386, 391.

28 White in Wilson and Davis, *Herndon's Informants,* 698.

29 *Lexington Globe,* 22 November 1860, quoted in Lincoln, *Collected Works,* 4:144n.

30 Lincoln, *Collected Works,* 4:130n, 129.

31 Hertz, *The Hidden Lincoln,* 102, 103.

32 Herndon and Weik, *Herndon's Life of Lincoln,* 398. See also Fehrenbacher, *Recollected Words of Abraham Lincoln,* 311.

33 Thomas Mather in Wilson and Davis, *Herndon's Informants,* 709.

34 Segal, *Conversations with Lincoln,* 48.

35 Lincoln, *Collected Works,* 4:136.

36 Lincoln's remarks enroute to Chicago are in ibid., 142–44.

37 Herndon and Weik. *Herndon's Life of Lincoln,* 386; Hertz, *The Hidden Lincoln,* 118; Nicolay, *An Oral History of Abraham Lincoln,* 157n.

38 Nicolay, *An Oral History of Abraham Lincoln,* 107–8.

39 Lincoln, *Collected Works,* 4:184.

40 Nicolay, *An Oral History of Abraham Lincoln,* 108.

41 George Julian in Rice, *Reminiscences of Abraham Lincoln,* 49.

42 Nicolay and Hay, *Abraham Lincoln,* 3:347.

43 Lincoln, *Collected Works,* 4:148.

44 Ibid., 149n, 173.

45 Ibid., 168, 168n.
46 Lincoln's conversation with Bunn is in Angle, *Abraham Lincoln by Some Men Who Knew Him*, 114–15. His comment to Ray is in Fehrenbacher, *Recollected Words of Abraham Lincoln*, 375.
47 Edward Bates in Fehrenbacher, *Recollected Words of Abraham Lincoln*, 342–43.
48 Rice, *Reminiscences of Abraham Lincoln*, liii.
49 Lincoln, *Collected Works*, 4:161, 161n.
50 Ibid., 162, 162n.
51 Herndon in Fehrenbacher, *Recollected Words of Abraham Lincoln*, 253; Herndon and Weik, *Herndon's Life of Lincoln*, 386.
52 Fehrenbacher, *Recollected Words of Abraham Lincoln*, 342.
53 Pratt, *Concerning Mr. Lincoln*, 45.
54 James K. Moorhead in Fehrenbacher, *Recollected Words of Abraham Lincoln*, 333.
55 Gustave P. Koerner in ibid., 279–80.
56 Lincoln, *Collected Works*, 4:168, 168.
57 Ibid., 171.
58 In this discussion of Lincoln's angst over Cameron, I also consulted Pratt, "Simon Cameron's Fight for a Place in Lincoln's Cabinet," 3–11.
59 Lincoln, *Collected Works*, 4:62.
60 Wilson and Davis, *Herndon's Informants*, 108.
61 The account of Lincoln's visit to Coles County is from Augustus H. Chapman in ibid., 136–37; and Miers, *Lincoln Day by Day*, 3:8.

Chapter 30: Getting There

1 Weik. *The Real Lincoln*, 4.
2 This last meeting of Lincoln with Herndon is stitched from the account of it in Herndon and Weik, *Herndon's Life of Lincoln*, 389–91. His final words to Herndon on the street were told by Herndon to Edward L. Pierce, quoted in Wilson and Davis, *Herndon's Informants*, 685.
3 Rankin, *Personal Recollections*, 221.
4 These moments before he began to speak from the platform are from an account in the *Illinois State Journal*, 12 February 1861; in Mitgang, *Lincoln as They Saw Him*, 224.
5 Lincoln, *Collected Works*, 4:190.
6 The *Journal's* report is in Mitgang, *Lincoln as They Saw Him*, 225. The young observer recording the moment in his diary was Latham in "A Young Man's View of Lincoln and Douglas in 1861," p. 8.
7 Whitney, *Lincoln the Citizen*, 295.
8 Herndon and Weik, *Herndon's Life of Lincoln*, 393.
9 Mitgang, *Lincoln as They Saw Him*, 227, 225.
10 Nicolay, *An Oral History of Abraham Lincoln*, 110–11, 112.
11 Lincoln, *Collected Works*, 4:187.

12 Stephen Fiske in Wilson, *Lincoln Among His Friends,* 304.

13 Whitney, *Lincoln the Citizen,* 298.

14 Lincoln, *Collected Works,* 4:138, 140.

15 Whitney, *Lincoln the Citizen,* 297.

16 Miers, *Lincoln Day by Day,* 3:11; Lincoln, *Collected Works,* 4:191.

17 Villard, *Lincoln on the Eve of '61,* p. 75; Lincoln, *Collected Works,* 4:192.

18 Lincoln, *Collected Works,* 4:192–93.

19 Ibid., 193–94.

20 Ibid., 195, 196.

21 Nicolay relates the lost carpetbag incident in, *An Oral History of Abraham Lincoln,* 108–10.

22 Lincoln, *Collected Works,* 4:197.

23 Ibid., 197, 198.

24 Ibid., 205, 204.

25 Ibid., 207.

26 Ibid., 209n, 209, 211.

27 Ibid., 215–16.

28 The account of Lincoln's meeting with Grace Bedell is woven from ibid., 219, and Wilson and Davis, *Herndon's Informants,* 517.

29 Lincoln, *Collected Works,* 4:219–20.

30 Ibid., 231.

31 Ibid., 238, 240–41.

32 Ibid., 242.

33 Hertz, *The Hidden Lincoln,* 264; Sandburg, *Abraham Lincoln: The War Years,* 1:48.

34 This account, with the quotes from the newspapers, is in Nicolay, *An Oral History of Abraham Lincoln,* 111, 115–16, 117–18.

35 Fehrenbacher, *Recollected Words of Abraham Lincoln,* 282.

36 The account of Pinkerton's hiring by the railroad and his inadvertent uncovering of the Baltimore plot is from Wilson and Davis, *Herndon's Informants,* 317, 318, 274, 275, 319, 276, 281, 312–13. The brief sketch of his origin and background is from p. 766.

37 Judd's account is in Whitney, *Lincoln the Citizen,* 300–1.

38 Pinkerton in Wilson and Douglas, *Herndon's Informants,* 322.

39 Ibid., 312, 313.

40 Whitney, *Lincoln the Citizen,* 302–3.

41 The description of Lincoln's movements is from Pinkerton's account in Wilson and Davis, *Herndon's Informants,* 323–24.

42 Washburne in Rice, *Reminiscences of Abraham Lincoln,* 37–38.

43 This version of the meeting with Washburne is from Pinkerton in Wilson and Davis, *Herndon's Informants,* 286. Washburne's account of the meeting is far less dramatic. He said he merely stepped out from behind his pillar and said, "How are you, Lincoln?" without the benefit of an elbow from Pinkerton, and

Lincoln said, "This is only Washburne!" See Washburne in Rice, *Reminiscences of Abraham Lincoln*, 38.

44 Washburne in Rice, *Reminiscences of Abraham Lincoln*, 38–39, 36.
45 Ibid., 39.

Chapter 31: The War Comes

1 Nicolay, *Personal Traits of Abraham Lincoln*, 166.
2 Quoted in Donald, *Lincoln*, 279.
3 Adams, *Charles Francis Adams, 1835–1915: An Autobiography*, 75.
4 Wilson, *Intimate Memories of Lincoln*, 336.
5 Fehrenbacher, *Recollected Words of Abraham Lincoln*, 8.
6 Ibid., 253.
7 These warning letters to Trumbull and Washburne are in Lincoln, *Collected Works*, 4:149–50, 151.
8 Ibid., 172.
9 Ibid., 175–76.
10 Ibid., 247.
11 Villard, *Lincoln on the Eve of '61*, p. 41.
12 Noah Brooks in Fehrenbacher, *Recollected Words of Abraham Lincoln*, 55.
13 Pratt, *Concerning Mr. Lincoln*, 65, 67.
14 Charles Francis Adams, Jr. and Charles Aldrich in Wilson, *Intimate Memories of Lincoln*, 368, 365; Herndon and Weik, *Herndon's Life of Lincoln*, 400.
15 *New York Herald*, 4 March 1861 in Mitgang, *Lincoln as They Saw Him*, 236.
16 Charles Aldrich in Wilson, *Intimate Memories of Lincoln*, 362, 365.
17 Herndon and Weik, *Herndon's Life of Lincoln*, 399–400; Leech, *Reveille in Washington*, 43.
18 I owe much in this description of the deployment of the military guard for Lincoln to Leech in *Reveille in Washington*, 41, 43, 42.
19 Ibid., 44.
20 Aldrich in Wilson, *Intimate Memories of Lincoln*, 365.
21 This description of Lincoln's appearance on the platform at the beginning of his address is stitched from accounts varying widely in detail by Henry Watterson in Wilson, *Lincoln Among His Friends*, 286; Herndon and Weik, *Herndon's Life of Lincoln*, 400–1; Charles Aldrich in Wilson, *Intimate Memories of Lincoln*, 365–66; and Poore in Rice, *Reminiscences of Abraham Lincoln*, 225–26.
22 Lincoln's inaugural address is in Lincoln, *Collected Works*, 4:262–71. The specific passages I have drawn from, in order cited, are from pp. 262, 263, 264, 265, 266, 268, 269, 270, and 271.
23 Villard, *Lincoln on the Eve of '61*, p. 4.
24 Herndon and Weik, *Herndon's Life of Lincoln*, 401; Charles Aldrich in Wilson, *Intimate Memories of Lincoln*, 366.

25 Watterson in Wilson, *Lincoln Among His Friends,* 287.

26 John G. Nicolay in Fehrenbacher, *Recollected Words of Abraham Lincoln,* 344.

27 Lincoln's query to Scott and Scott's response are in Lincoln, *Collected Works,* 4:279, 279n.

28 Ibid., 301.

29 Ibid., 302n.

30 Ibid., 321–22.

31 Ibid., 323.

32 John G. Nicolay in Fehrenbacher, *Recollected Words of Abraham Lincoln,* 344.

33 Julian in Rice, *Reminiscences of Abraham Lincoln,* 50.

34 Prince de Joinville in Fehrenbacher, *Recollected Words of Abraham Lincoln,* 269.

35 Nicolay, *An Oral History of Abraham Lincoln,* 62–63, 64.

36 Lincoln, *Collected Works,* 4:317–18n, 317.

37 *New York Tribune,* 17 December 1860, in Wright, *The Oxford Dictionary of Civil War Quotations,* 128.

38 Lincoln, *Collected Works,* 4: 331–32.

39 Lindeman, *The Conflict of Convictions,* 13, 5.

Epilogue: Twilight of the Little Giant

1 George Ashmun in Segal, *Conversations with Lincoln,* 109–11. For the timing and length of the meeting see Fehrenbacher, *Recollected Words of Abraham Lincoln,* 379.

2 All of this, Douglas's last speech to the Illinois legislature and his illness and death, are from Angle, *"Here I Have Lived,"* 265–67; and Douglas, *The Letters of Stephen A. Douglas,* 511, 514. The diary quote is Latham's in "A Young Man's View of Lincoln and Douglas in 1861," p. 9. Also see "Death of a Patriot," 77–81.

3 Nicolay, *An Oral History of Abraham Lincoln,* 54–55.

4 Henry B. Rankin in Wilson, *Lincoln Among His Friends,* 223.

SOURCES CITED

This partial bibliography doesn't include all of the sources consulted in researching this book. It lists only the sources cited in the notes.

Adams, Charles Francis. *Charles Francis Adams, 1835–1915: An Autobiography.* 1916. Reprint. Westport, CT: Greenwood Press, 1973.

Alexander, DeAlva Stanwood. *A Political History of the State of New York.* 4 vols. 1909. Reprint. Port Washington, NY: Ira J. Friedman, 1969.

Angle, Paul M., ed. *Abraham Lincoln by Some Men Who Knew Him.* Chicago: Americana House Publishers, 1950.

———— *"Here I Have Lived": A History of Lincoln's Springfield, 1821–1865.* New Edition. Chicago: Abraham Lincoln Book Shop, 1971.

Arnold, Isaac N. *The Life of Abraham Lincoln.* 1884. Reprint. Lincoln: University of Nebraska Press, 1994.

Baber, Adin. *Nancy Hanks, the Destined Mother of a President.* Kansas, IL: Adin Baber, 1963.

Baker, Jean H. *James Buchanan.* In *The American Presidents.* General Editor Arthur M. Schlesinger, Jr. New York: Times Books/Henry Holt and Co., 2004.

Baker, Richard A. *200 Notable Days: Senate Stories, 1787 to 2002.* Washington, DC: U.S. Government Printing Office, 2006.

Baringer, William E. *Lincoln's Vandalia: A Pioneer Portrait.* New Brunswick, NJ: Rutgers University Press, 1949.

———— "Campaign Technique in Illinois—1860." *Transactions of the Illinois State Historical Society for the Year 1932.* Publication No. 39 (1932): 203–72.

Barton, William E. *The Paternity of Abraham Lincoln: Was He the Son of Thomas Lincoln?* New York: George H. Doran Co., 1920.

Basler, Roy P. ed. "James Quay Howard's Notes on Lincoln." *Abraham Lincoln Quarterly* 4 (December 1947): 386–400.

Bauer, K. Jack. *Zachary Taylor: Soldier, Planter, Statesman of the Old Southwest.* Baton Rouge: Louisiana State University Press, 1985.

Beveridge, Albert J. *Abraham Lincoln, 1890–1858.* 2 vols. Boston: Houghton Mifflin Co., 1928.

Blanchard, Rufus. *History of Illinois, to Accompany an Historical Map of the State.* Chicago: National School Furnishing Co., 1883.

Boggess, Arthur C. *The Settlement of Illinois, 1778–1830.* 1908. Reprint. Freeport, NY: Books for Libraries Press, 1970.

Bonham, Jeriah. *Fifty Years' Recollections, with Observations and Reflections on Historical Events Giving Sketches of Eminent Citizens—Their Lives and Public Services.* Peoria, IL: J. W. Franks & Sons, 1883.

Boston Atlas.

Bray, Robert. "'The Power to Hurt': Lincoln's Early Use of Satire and Invective." *Journal of the Abraham Lincoln Association* 16 (Winter 1995): 39–58.

Capers, Gerald M. *Stephen A. Douglas: Defender of the Union.* Edited by Oscar Handlin. Boston: Little, Brown & Co., 1959.

Carr, Clark E. *Stephen A. Douglas: His Life, Public Services, Speeches and Patriotism.* Chicago: A. C. McClurg & Co., 1909.

Carter, Orrin N. "Lincoln and Douglas as Lawyers." *Proceedings of the Mississippi Valley Historical Association for the Year 1910–1911.* Edited by Benjamin F. Shambaugh. Vol. 4. Cedar Rapids, IA: Torch Press, 1912.

Cartwright, Peter. *Autobiography of Peter Cartwright, the Backwoods Preacher.* Edited by W. P. Strickland. New York: Carlton & Porter, 1857.

Channing, Steven A. *Kentucky: A Bicentennial History.* New York: W. W. Norton & Co., 1977.

Chesnut, Mary. *Mary Chesnut's Civil War.* Edited by C. Vann Woodward. New Haven, CT: Yale University Press, 1981.

Chicago Journal.

Chicago Press & Tribune.

Chicago Times.

Current, Richard N. "Lincoln and the Eighth Circuit." Paper delivered at the Lincoln Colloquium, 11 October, 1987, Springfield, IL.

Davis, Cullom. "Abraham Lincoln, Esq.: the Symbiosis of Law and Politics." In *Abraham Lincoln and the Political Process.* Papers from the Seventh Annual Lincoln Colloquium, 24 October 1992.

Davis, Rodney O. "'I Shall Consider the Whole People of Sangamon My Constituents': Lincoln and the Illinois General Assembly." In *Abraham Lincoln and the Political Process.* Papers from the Seventh Annual Lincoln Colloquium, 24 October 1992.

"Death of a Patriot." *Chicago History* 6 (Spring 1961): 77–81.

Delaware State Journal.

Dickens, Charles. *American Notes and Pictures from Italy.* New York: Oxford University Press, 1957.

Donald, David Herbert. *Lincoln.* New York: Simon & Schuster, 1995.

———. *"We Are Lincoln Men": Abraham Lincoln and His Friends.* New York: Simon & Schuster, 2003.

Douglas, Stephen A. *The Letters of Stephen A. Douglas.* Edited by Robert W. Johannsen. Urbana: University of Illinois Press, 1961.

———. *The Montgomery Address of Stephen A. Douglas.* Edited by David R. Barbee and Milledge L. Bonham, Jr. Reprinted from *The Journal of Southern History* 5 (November 1939): 527–52.

Dyer, Brainard. *Zachary Taylor.* Baton Rouge: Louisiana State University Press, 1946.

Eggleston, George Cary. *The First of the Hoosiers.* Philadelphia: Drexel Biddle, 1903.

Faragher, John Mack. *Sugar Creek: Life on the Illinois Prairie.* New Haven, CT: Yale University Press, 1986.

Fehrenbacher, Don E. *The Dred Scott Case: Its Significance in American Law and Politics.* New York: Oxford University Press, 1978.

———. *Prelude to Greatness: Lincoln in the 1850s.* Stanford, CA: Stanford University Press, 1962.

———. "The Nomination of Lincoln in 1858." *Abraham Lincoln Quarterly* 6 (March 1950–December 1951): 24–36.

———, and Virginia Fehrenbacher, eds. *Recollected Words of Abraham Lincoln.* Stanford, CA: Stanford University Press, 1996.

Ferris, Robert G., ed. *The Presidents from the Inauguration of George Washington to the Inauguration of Jimmy Carter.* Revised Edition. Washington, DC: National Park Service, U.S. Department of the Interior, 1977.

Flint, Henry M. *Life of Stephen A. Douglas . . . with His Most Important Speeches and Reports.* New York: Derby & Jackson, 1860.

Ford, Thomas. *A History of Illinois from Its Commencement as a State in 1818 to 1847.* 2 vols. Edited by Milo Milton Quaife. Chicago: Lakeside Press/R. R. Donnelley & Sons, 1945.

Freidel, Frank. *Our Country's Presidents.* Washington, DC: National Geographic Society, 1979.

French, A. W. "Men and Manners of the Early Days in Illinois." *Transactions of the Illinois State Historical Society for the Year 1903.* Publication No. 8 (1903): 65–74.

Halstead, Murat. *Three Against Lincoln: Murat Halstead Reports the Caucuses of 1860.* Edited by William B. Hesseltine. Baton Rouge: Louisiana State University Press, 1960.

Hamand, Jane E., comp. "Memories of the Rutledge Family of New Salem, Illinois." Decatur, IL: Decatur Lincoln Memorial Collection, 1921.

Hamilton, Holman. *Zachary Taylor: Soldier in the White House.* Indianapolis: Bobbs-Merrill Co., 1951.

Harris, N. Dwight. *The History of Negro Servitude in Illinois and of the Slavery Agitation in That State, 1719–1864.* Chicago: A. C. McClurg & Co., 1904.

Hatfield, Mark O. *Vice Presidents of the United States, 1789–1993.* Washington, DC. Government Printing Office, 1997.

Helm, Katharine. *The True Story of Mary, Wife of Lincoln.* New York: Harper & Row Brothers, 1928.

Herndon, William H., and Jessie W. Weik. *Herndon's Life of Lincoln*. Introduction and Notes by Paul M. Angle. Cleveland: World Publishing Co., 1930.

Hertz, Emanuel, ed. *The Hidden Lincoln: From the Letters and Papers of William H. Herndon*. New York: Viking Press, 1938.

————. *Lincoln Talks: An Oral Biography*. 1939. Reprint. New York: Bramhall House, 1986.

History of Fayette County, Illinois, with Illustrations Descriptive of Its Scenery, and Biographical Sketches of Some of Its Prominent Men and Pioneers. Philadelphia: Brink, McDonough & Co., 1878.

Hitchcock, Caroline Hanks. *Nancy Hanks: The Story of Abraham Lincoln's Mother*. New York: Doubleday & McClure Co., 1899.

Holbrook, Stewart. "Why Did They Go Away?" *American Heritage* 6 (June 1955): 26–35.

Holzer, Harold. *Lincoln at Cooper Union: The Speech that Made Abraham Lincoln President*. New York: Simon & Schuster, 2004.

Horton, James Oliver, and Lois E. Horton. *Slavery and the Making of America*. New York: Oxford University Press, 2005.

Illinois Daily Journal.

Illinois House Journal.

Illinois State Register.

Illinois State Journal.

James, Jennie H., and Wayne C. Temple. *Mrs. Lincoln's Clothing*. Reprinted from *Lincoln Herald* (Summer 1960): 54–65.

Jefferson, Thomas. The Works of Thomas Jefferson. Edited by Paul Leicester Ford. 12 vols. New York: G. P. Putnam's Sons, 1905.

Johannsen, Robert W. *Stephen A. Douglas*. New York: Oxford University Press, 1973.

Johns, Jane Martin. *Personal Recollections of Early Decatur, Abraham Lincoln, Richard J. Oglesby, and the Civil War*. Edited by Howard C. Schaub. Decatur, IL: Decatur Chapter Daughters of the American Revolution, 1912.

Jones, Marty, "The Thirty-One-Day Presidency." *American History* 41 (April 2006): 48–55.

King, Willard L. *Lincoln's Manager: David Davis*. Cambridge, MA: Harvard University Press, 1960.

Kinkaid, Robert L. *The Wilderness Road*. Indianapolis: Bobbs-Merrill Co., 1947.

Kunhardt, Philip B., Jr, and Philip B. Kunhardt III and Peter W. Kunhardt. *The American President*. New York: Riverhead Books/Penguin Putnam, 1999.

Latham, Henry C., "A Young Man's View of Lincoln and Douglas in 1861." *Bulletin of the Abraham Lincoln Association*. No. 52 (June 1938): 7–9.

Leech, Margaret. *Reveille in Washington, 1860–1865*. New York: Harper & Brothers, 1941.

Levering, Julia Henderson. *Historic Indiana*. New York: G. P. Putnam's Sons, 1916.

Lexington (Kentucky) *Globe*.

Lincoln, Abraham. *The Collected Works of Abraham Lincoln.* Edited by Roy P. Basler. 8 vols. New Brunswick, NJ: Rutgers University Press, 1953.

Lindeman, Jack, ed. *The Conflict of Convictions: American Writers Report the Civil War.* Philadelphia: Chilton Book Co., 1968.

Lorant, Stefan. *The Glorious Burden: The History of the Presidency and Presidential Elections from George Washington to James Earl Carter, Jr.* Lenox, MA: Authors Edition, 1976.

Lovejoy, Joseph C., and Owen Lovejoy. *Memoir of the Rev. Elijah P. Lovejoy.* 1838. Reprint. Freeport, NY: Books for Libraries Press, 1970.

Lufkin, Richard Friend. "Mr. Lincoln's Light from under a Bushel—1850." *Lincoln Herald* 52 (December 1950): 2–20.

McConnell, George Murray. "Recollections of Stephen A. Douglas," *Transactions of the Illinois State Historical Society for the Year 1900.* Publication No. 5 (1900): 40–50.

McLaren, William Riley. "Reminiscences of Pioneer Life in Illinois, 1830–1860." Illinois State Historical Library, Springfield, IL.

McPherson, James M., and David Rubel, eds. *"To the Best of My Ability": The American Presidents.* Revised U.S. Edition. New York: DK Publishing, 2004.

Mearns, David C. *The Lincoln Papers.* 2 vols. Garden City, NY: Doubleday & Co., 1948.

Miers, Earl Schenck, ed. *Lincoln Day by Day: A Chronology, 1809–1865.* 3 vols. Washington DC: Lincoln Sesquicentennial Commission, 1960.

Mitgang, Herbert, ed. *Lincoln as They Saw Him.* New York: Rinehart & Co. 1956.

Morgan, James. *Our Presidents: Brief Biographies of Our Chief Magistrates from Washington to Eisenhower, 1789–1958.* 2nd Enlarged Edition. New York: Macmillan Co., 1959.

Morris, Jan. *Lincoln: A Foreigner's Quest.* New York: Simon & Schuster, 2000.

Moses, John. *Illinois, Historical and Statistical.* 2 vols. Chicago: Fergus Printing Co., 1889.

Newton, Joseph Fort. *Lincoln and Herndon.* Cedar Rapids, IA: Torch Press, 1910.

New York Herald.

New York Times.

New York Tribune.

Nichols, Roy Franklin. *The Disruption of American Democracy.* New York: Macmillan Co., 1948.

Nicolay, Helen. *Personal Traits of Abraham Lincoln.* New York: Century Co., 1912.

Nicolay, John G. *An Oral History of Abraham Lincoln: John G. Nicolay's Interviews And Essays.* Edited by Michael Burlingame. Carbondale: Southern Illinois University Press, 1996.

———, and John Hay. *Abraham Lincoln: A History.* 10 vols. New York: Century Co., 1914.

Oliver, William. *Eight Months in Illinois.* 1843. Reprint. Ann Arbor, MI: University Microfilms, 1966.

Pease, Theodore Calvin., ed. *Illinois Election Returns, 1818–1848.* Vol. 18, Statistical Series 1 of *Collections of the Illinois State Historical Library.* Springfield, IL, 1923.

Piatt, Donn. *Memories of the Men Who Saved the Union.* New York: Belford, Clarke & Co., 1887.

Pillsbury, Albert E. *Lincoln and Slavery.* Boston: Houghton Mifflin Co., 1913.

Pond, Fern Nance. *Intellectual New Salem in Lincoln's Day.* An Address Delivered at Lincoln Memorial University, Harrogate, Tennessee, 12 February 1938.

Pratt, Harry E., comp. *Concerning Mr. Lincoln: In Which Abraham Lincoln Is Pictured as He Appeared to Letter Writers of His Time.* Springfield, IL: Abraham Lincoln Association, 1944.

———. *The Personal Finances of Abraham Lincoln.* Springfield, IL: Abraham Lincoln Association, 1943.

———. "Simon Cameron's Fight for a Place in Lincoln's Cabinet." *Bulletin of the Abraham Lincoln Association* 49 (September 1937); 3–11.

———. "Stephen A. Douglas, Lawyer, Legislator, and Judge, 1833–1843." *Lincoln Herald* 51 (December 1949): 11–16; 52 (February 1950): 37–43.

"The Presidential Candidate Attends a Rally." *Abraham Lincoln Quarterly* 4 (September 1946): 123–26.

Putnam, Elizabeth Duncan. "The Life and Services of Joseph Duncan." *Transactions Of the Illinois State Historical Society for 1919.* Publication No. 26 (1919): 107–87.

Rankin, Henry B. *Personal Recollections of Abraham Lincoln.* New York: G. P. Putnam's Sons, 1916.

"Recollections of Lincoln: Three Letters of Intimate Friends." *Bulletin of the Abraham Lincoln Association.* No. 25 (December 1931): 3–9.

Reep. Thomas P. *Lincoln at New Salem.* Petersburg, IL: Old Salem Lincoln League, 1927.

Reynolds, John. *My Own Times: Embracing Also the History of My Life.* 1879. Reprint. Ann Arbor MI: University Microfilms, 1968.

Rice, Allen Thorndike, ed. *Reminiscences of Abraham Lincoln by Distinguished Men of His Time.* 1888. Reprint. New York: Haskell House Publishers, 1971.

Richardson, James D., ed. *A Compilation of the Messages and Papers of the Presidents, 1789–1897.* 10 vols. Washington DC: Government Printing Office, 1896–1899.

Roseboom, Eugene H. *A History of Presidential Elections from George Washington To Richard Nixon.* 3rd Edition. New York: Macmillan Co., 1970.

Ross, Robert W. *Historical Souvenir of Vandalia, Illinois.* Effingham, IL: National Illustrating Co., 1904.

Sandburg, Carl. *Abraham Lincoln: The War Years.* 4 vols. Sangamon Edition. New York: Charles Scribner's Sons, 1943.

Sangamo Journal.

Schlesinger, Arthur M., Jr., ed. *History of American Presidential Elections, 1789–1968.* 4 vols. New York: Chelsea House/McGraw-Hill, 1971.

Schwartz, Thomas F. *Finding the Missing Link: A Promissory Note and the Lost Town of Pappsville.* Historial Bulletin No. 51, Lincoln Fellowship of Wisconsin, 1996.

Scripps, John Locke. *Life of Abraham Lincoln.* Edited by Roy P. Basler and Lloyd A. Dunlap. 1961. Reprint. New York: Greenwood Press, 1968.

Segal, Charles M., ed. *Conversations with Lincoln.* New York: G. P. Putnam's Sons, 1961.

Shakespeare, William. *As You Like It.* In *The Complete Works of Shakespeare.* Edited by David Bevington. 3rd Edition. Glenville, IL: Scott, Foresman & Co., 1980.

———. *Comedy of Errors.* In *The Complete Works of Shakespeare.* Edited by David Bevington. 3rd Edition. Glenville, IL: Scott, Foresman & Co., 1980.

Sheahan, James W. *The Life of Stephen A. Douglas.* New York: Harper & Brothers, 1860.

Simon, Paul. *Freedom's Champion: Elijah Lovejoy.* Carbondale: Southern Illinois University Press, 1994.

Speed, Joshua F. *Reminiscences of Abraham Lincoln and Notes of a Visit to California.* Louisville, KY: John P. Morton & Co., 1884.

Speed, Thomas. *The Wilderness Road.* Filson Club Publications. No. 2. Louisville, KY: John P. Morton & Co., 1886.

"Stephen T. Logan Talks About Lincoln." *Bulletin of the Lincoln Centennial Association* 12 (1 September 1928): 1–5.

Stevens, Frank E. "Life of Stephen A. Douglas." *Journal of the Illinois State Historical Society* 16 (October 1923–January 1924): 247–673.

Stuart, James. *Three Years in North America.* 2 vols. Edinburgh [Scotland]: Robert Cadell & Whittaker & Co., 1833.

Tanner, Henry. *The Martyrdom of Lovejoy: An Account of the Life, Trials and Perils of Rev. Elijah P. Lovejoy ... by an Eyewitness.* 1881. Reprint. New York: Augustus M. Kelley, 1971.

Tarbell, Ida M. *Abraham Lincoln and His Ancestors.* Bison Books Edition. Lincoln: University of Nebraska Press, 1997.

———. *The Early Life of Abraham Lincoln.* New York: S. S. McClure, 1896.

———. *The Life of Abraham Lincoln.* 2 vols. New York: Doubleday, Page & Co., 1909.

Taylor, Troy. *Haunted Alton: History & Hauntings of the Riverbend Region.* Alton, IL: Whitechapel Productions Press, 1999.

Temple, Wayne C., ed. *"The Taste Is in My Mouth a Little ...": Lincoln's Victuals And Potables.* Mohomet, IL: Mayhaven Publishing, 2004.

———, ed. *Mrs. Mary Edwards Brown Tells Story of Lincoln's Wedding.* Harrogate, TN: Lincoln Memorial University Press, 1960.

Thomas, Benjamin P. *Abraham Lincoln: A Biography.* New York: Alfred A. Knopf, 1952.

———. *Lincoln's New Salem.* 1954. Reprint. Carbondale: Southern Illinois University Press, 1988.

———. "Lincoln and the Courts, 1854–1861." *Abraham Lincoln Association Papers* (1934): 47–103.

———. Lincoln's Humor: An Analysis." *Abraham Lincoln Association Papers* (1936): 61–90.

Tillson, Christina Holmes. *A Woman's Story of Pioneer Illinois.* Edited by Milo Milton Quaife. Chicago: Lakeside Press/R. R. Donnelley & Sons, 1919.

Townsend, William H. *Lincoln and His Wife's Home Town.* Indianapolis: Bobbs-Merrill Co., 1929.

U.S. Congress. *Addresses on the Death of the Hon. Stephen A. Douglas, Delivered In the Senate and House of Representatives on Tuesday, July 9, 1861.* Washington, DC: Government Printing Office, 1861.

———. *Report of Senator Douglas, of Illinois, on the Kansas-Lecompton Constitution,* 18 February 1858.

Villard, Henry. *Lincoln on the Eve of '61.* Edited by Harold G. and Oswald Garrison Villard. New York: Alfred A. Knopf, 1941.

———. *Memoirs of Henry Villard, Journalist and Financier, 1835–1900.* 2 vols. Boston: Houghton, Mifflin & Co., 1904.

Warren, Louis A. *Lincoln's Parentage & Childhood.* New York: Century Co., 1926.

———. *Lincoln's Youth: Indiana Years, Seven to Twenty-one, 1816–1830.* New York: Appleon-Century-Croffts, 1959.

———. "Lincoln's $200 Speech." *Lincoln Lore.* No. 1378 (5 September 1855).

Watters, Philip M. *Peter Cartwright.* New York: Easton & Mains; Cincinnati: Jennings & Graham, 1910.

Wead, Hezakiah Morse. Diary, Manuscripts Division. Abraham Lincoln Presidential Library, Springfield, IL.

Weik. Jesse W. *The Real Lincoln: A Portrait.* Boston: Houghton Mifflin Co., 1922.

White, Horace. *Lincoln in 1854.* Address delivered before the Illinois State Historical Society, 1908.

Whitney, Henry C. *Lincoln the Citizen.* Vol 1 of *Life of Lincoln.* New York: Current Literature Publishing Co., 1907.

Wilson, Douglas L. *Honor's Voice: The Transformation of Abraham Lincoln.* New York: Alfred A. Knopf, 1998.

———. *Lincoln Before Washington: New Perspectives on the Illinois Years.* Urbana: University of Illinois Press, 1997.

———, and Rodney O. Davis, eds. *Herndon's Informants: Letters, Interviews, and Statements About Abraham Lincoln.* Urbana: University of Illinois Press, 1998.

Wilson, Rufus Rockwell, ed. *Intimate Memories of Lincoln.* Elmira, NY: Primavera Press, 1945.

———. *Lincoln Among His Friends: A Sheaf of Intimate Memories.* Caldwell, ID: Caxton Printers, 1942.

———. *What Lincoln Read.* Washington, DC: Pioneer Publishing Co. 1932.

Wilson, William E. "'There I Grew Up.'" *American Heritage* 17 (October 1966): 30–31, 98–102.

Winkle, Kenneth J. *The Young Eagle: The Rise of Abraham Lincoln.* Dallas, TX: Taylor Trade Publishing, 2001.

Wright, John D., ed. *The Oxford Dictionary of Civil War Quotations.* New York: Oxford University Press, 2006.

INDEX